Ninth Edition

HARBRACE
COLLEGE
HANDBOOK
1984 Printing

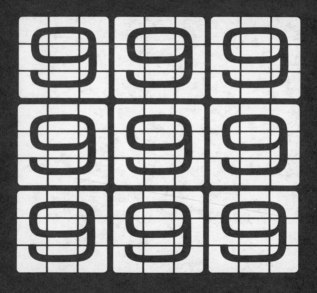

Ninth Edition

HARBRACE COLLEGE HANDBOOK

1984 Printing

With the new MLA documentation style

John C. Hodges
late of the University of Tennessee

and

Mary E. Whitten
North Texas State University

Harcourt Brace Jovanovich, Publishers
*San Diego / New York / Chicago / Washington, D.C. / Atlanta
London / Sydney / Toronto*

ACKNOWLEDGMENTS The author wishes to thank the following for permission to reprint the material listed:

HARCOURT BRACE JOVANOVICH, INC. for the excerpt from *Power of Words* by Stuart Chase and for the photocopied excerpt from *The Collected Essays, Journalism and Letters of George Orwell, Volume 4.*

DEULINDA WEBER HILL for the essay ''Ronnie A. Ward'' by Nicholas J. Weber.

G. & C. MERRIAM COMPANY for the thesaurus entry *empty*. From *Webster's Collegiate Thesaurus;* ©️ 1976 by G. & C. Merriam Co., publishers of the Merriam-Webster Dictionaries.

NATIONAL WILDLIFE FEDERATION for the essay ''Do Animals Really Play?'' by Eugene J. Walter, Jr.; ©️ 1979 by the National Wildlife Federation. Reprinted from the September/October 1979 issue of *International Wildlife Magazine.*

PANTHEON BOOKS, a Division of Random House, Inc., for the essay ''Some Preservation Definitions.'' From *America's Forgotten Architecture* by Tony P. Wrenn and Elizabeth D. Mulloy. Copyright ©️ 1976 by National Trust for Preservation in the United States.

SHAWN REDFIELD for his essay ''Primitives for the Present.''

WILFRID SHEED for his essay ''A Thought a Day Isn't Enough.'' Reprinted by permission of Wilfrid Sheed and International Creative Management. Copyright ©️ 1980 by the New York Times Company.

SIMON & SCHUSTER, INC. for the dictionary entry *empty*. From *Webster's New World Dictionary,* Second College Edition; copyright ©️ 1980 by Simon & Schuster, Inc.

THE H. W. WILSON COMPANY for the excerpts from the *Readers' Guide to Periodical Literature;* copyright ©️ 1980 by the H. W. Wilson Company.

Preface

This 1984 Printing of the Ninth Edition of the *Harbrace College Handbook* updates Section 33, The Research Paper, by closely following the new documentation style of the Modern Language Association. Except for the changes in Section 33, the Ninth Edition remains the same.

The *Harbrace College Handbook* is both a reference guide for the individual writer and a textbook for use in class. A comprehensive yet concise summary of the principles of effective writing, the *Harbrace* provides an easily mastered system for the correction of student papers, and the directness and economy of its rules and examples make it a lasting resource for the writer.

A glance at the front endpapers shows that the organization of the Ninth Edition is very similar to that of the Eighth. Topics are treated in an orderly way, from the smallest elements to the largest. The book begins with a review of the essentials of grammar and ends with a glossary of grammatical terms. The former may be used as needed to introduce the other sections, and the latter may be used as a reference throughout the course. According to the requirements of a particular class, the book may be taught in any order. For example, some instructors may want to begin with Section **32, The Whole Composition**, others with Section **31, The Paragraph**, or with Sections **19-30**, which deal with diction and sentences. In every section, the large number and variety of exercises make it possible for instructors to select activities appropriate to the needs of their class.

The Revision / The Ninth Edition is the result of extensive revision—especially in the larger elements. In response to suggestions from many users and reviewers of the Eighth Edition, the following sections have been substantially revised and expanded: In Section **18**, the list of frequently misspelled words has almost tripled. Section **23** **(Unity and Logical Thinking)** now includes discussions of formal and informal definition, deductive and inductive reasoning, and the most common fallacies. Section **31** includes expanded coverage of the topic sentence and methods of paragraph development, and Section **32** has been completely rewritten in terms of essay writing as a process—from choosing and limiting a topic, gathering ideas and formulating a thesis statement, to revising the second draft. Throughout the section, a single student essay is used to illustrate each step of the process. In this 1984 Printing, Section **33** describes and illustrates the new style of documentation adopted by the Modern Language Association. The sample research paper, accompanied by detailed annotations, adheres to the new MLA style. Also shown in this printing are the American Psychological Association's 1983 changes in reference format. As in previous printings, Section **33** includes material on the computerization of library catalogs, a discussion of formal outlining, and a discussion of plagiarism. Finally, Section **34** includes four sample business letters and two resumés.

Teaching Aids / For the first time, an *Instructor's Guide* (149 pages) is available to users of the *Harbrace College Handbook.* The Guide offers teaching strategies, classroom activities, and answers to exercises for each of the thirty-four sections; a set of criteria for grading papers; and an annotated bibliography of important titles in composition pedagogy and research. Other teaching aids include three forms of the *Harbrace College Workbook* by Sheila Y.

Graham: Form 9A, with sports used as the theme throughout; Form 9B (1983), an alternate version of 9A with a different theme; and Form 9C, with the theme of the world of work. A two-color *Instructor's Edition* is available for each workbook. Also available are a Correction Chart and a new Test Package with both diagnostic and achievement tests, scorable either manually or mechanically.

Acknowledgments / I did not work alone in the

preparation of the Ninth Edition. Eileen B. Evans, Western Michigan University, wrote Section 32 and shared the writing of the *Instructor's Guide*. Peter T. Zoller, Wichita State University, revised most of Section 31 and all of Section 34. These contributors and I worked in close consultation with Natalie Bowen and Paul H. Nockleby, my editors at Harcourt Brace Jovanovich, who guided the scope and nature of change in this edition.

I am indebted to the following instructors and directors of freshman composition, who read all or part of various drafts of the manuscript and made valuable suggestions for its improvement: Percy Adams, University of Tennessee; Lois S. Anderson, Tennessee Technological University; Rance G. Baker, San Antonio College; Barbara J. Cicardo, University of Southwestern Louisiana; Bruce Chadwick, Long Island University; John J. Colaccio, Bergen Community College; William Connelly, Middle Tennessee State University; Richard J. Daigle, University of Bridgeport; Robert V. Dees, Orange Coast College; Kathleen E. Dubs, University of Oregon; Eileen B. Evans, Western Michigan University; Lynn Garrett, Louisiana State University; David Goslee, University of Tennessee; Sheila Y. Graham, University of Tennessee; Rosanna Grassi, Syracuse University; Stanley R. Hauer, University of Southern Mississippi; Dixie Elise Hickman, University of Southern Mississippi; Michael J. Hogan, University of

New Mexico; Robert R. Hoyt, Hillsborough Community College; Marjorie Kirrie, Portland State University; G. Shelby Lee, Broward Community College; Gerald Levin, University of Akron; Donald V. Mehus, Fairleigh Dickinson University; Eleanor Drake Mitchell, Tennessee Technological University; James R. Moore, Mt. San Antonio College; James S. Mullican, Indiana State University; David Perlman; Barbara M. Roberts, James Madison University; Randal F. Robinson, Michigan State University; Martha A. Saunders, West Georgia College; Bain Tate Stewart, University of Tennessee, Knoxville; Ronald Strahl, Indiana University—Purdue University at Indianapolis; Margaret A. Strom, George Washington University; Virginia Thigpen, Volunteer State Community College; John W. Warren, Tennessee Technological University; Charles F. Whitaker, Eastern Kentucky University; David Yerkes, Columbia University; and Peter T. Zoller, Wichita State University.

In addition, I thank others who have contributed to the quality of the Ninth Edition, including Jean T. Davis, Marilyn Marcus, Gail O'Hare, and Elisa Turner, all of Harcourt Brace Jovanovich; Drake Bush; Sarah T. Hogan, North Texas State University; John J. Miniter, Texas Woman's University; and, especially, Audrey Ann Welch.

Very special thanks also go to Joseph Gibaldi of the Modern Language Association for his assistance in reviewing Section 33 of the 1984 Printing to ensure its adherence to the new MLA documentation style.

And I continue to appreciate the work of those editors—particularly Karen H. Kirtley and the late William A. Pullin—who contributed to the success of the *Harbrace College Handbook* in its earlier editions.

Mary E. Whitten

To the Student

Numbers or Symbols / A number or a symbol written in the margin of your paper indicates a need for correction or improvement and calls for revision. If a number is used, turn directly to the corresponding number at the top of the page in the handbook. If a symbol is used, first consult the alphabetical list of symbols inside the back cover to find the number of the section to which you should turn. An appropriate letter after a number or symbol (such as **2c** or **frag/c**) will refer you to a specific part of a section.

References / Your instructor will ordinarily refer you to the number or symbol (**2** or **frag, 9** or **cap, 18** or **sp, 28** or **ref**) appearing at the head of one of the thirty-four sections of the handbook. The rule given in color at the beginning of each section covers the whole section. One of the more specific rules given within the section will usually be needed to guide you in revision. Study the section to which you have been referred—the whole of the section if necessary—and master the specific part of the section that applies to your writing.

Correction and Revision / After you have studied the rules called to your attention, revise your paper carefully, as directed by your instructor. One method of revision is explained and illustrated in Section **8**, page 104.

Contents

GRAMMAR

Contents

PUNCTUATION

Contents

Contents

SPELLING AND DICTION

EFFECTIVE SENTENCES

Contents

LARGER ELEMENTS

32 The Whole Composition

Contents

GRAMMAR

Sentence Sense

1

Master the essentials of the sentence as an aid to clear thinking and effective writing.

A key to good writing is to possess or develop sentence sense. Sentence sense is the awareness of what *makes* a sentence— the ability to recognize its grammatical essentials and to understand the relationships between its parts.

Observing the positions, forms, and meanings of words can help you to understand the relationship between parts of sentences. Notice below how meaning is expressed by the arrangement and the forms of words.

> The hijacked plane has landed safely.

Note the importance of word order. Other arrangements of the same words are possible:

> The hijacked plane has safely landed. [no appreciable differ-
> ence in meaning]
> Has the hijacked plane landed safely? [a change in meaning]

But not every arrangement of words is possible in an English sentence:

> NONSENSICAL Hijacked safely plane has landed the.

Note also that changing the forms of words affects sentence meaning:

> The hijacked planes have landed safely.   [a change in meaning]

Below are five simple sentences. In each, the vertical line separates the two basic grammatical parts of the sentence, the subject and the predicate. The first part functions as the complete subject (the subject and all words associated with it), and the second part functions as the complete predicate (the verb and all words associated with it). Most simple sentences follow this pattern:

Complete subject + complete predicate.

The hijacked **plane** | **has landed** safely.

Sandra | **gave** us three magnolia trees.

These **trees** | **should have been planted** in January.

The **tomato** | **is** a fruit.   **It** | **tastes** good in salads.

In each of these sentences, the subject (or simple subject) and the verb are in boldface. The subject is the part of a sentence about which something is asserted in the predicate. The predicate is the part that asserts something about the subject.

Expanding Sentences

Below are examples of ways that a simple sentence may be expanded.

SENTENCE   The plane has landed.   [subject + predicate]
EXPANSION

The hijacked plane | has landed safely.

The first hijacked plane to arrive at this airport | has landed safely in the south runway.

The first hijacked plane that we have ever seen at this airport | has landed safely in the south runway, which has been closed to traffic for a year.

The base of the expanded sentences may be isolated by striking out those words that have been added.

REDUCTION

The ~~first hijacked~~ plane ~~that we have ever seen at this airport~~ has landed ~~safely in the south runway, which has been closed to traffic for a year~~.

Combining Sentences

Speakers and writers combine sentences and in the process rearrange, add, delete, or substitute words:

The saying is old.   It has a new meaning.

VARIOUS COMBINATIONS

The saying is old, but it has a new meaning.
Although it has a new meaning, the saying is old.
The saying, which is old, has a new meaning.
The old saying has a new meaning.
It is an old saying with a new meaning.

A close study of this section can help you to develop or sharpen your sentence sense. Sentence sense is prerequisite to the intelligent use of this handbook—especially Sections **2** (Sentence Fragment), **3** (Comma Splice), **6** (Agreement), **12** (The Comma), **14** (The Semicolon), **23** (Unity), **24** (Subordination), **25** (Coherence), **26** (Parallelism), **29** (Emphasis), and **30** (Variety). For explanations of any unfamiliar grammatical terms, see the **Glossary of Grammatical Terms** beginning on page 529.

1a

Learn to recognize verbs and their subjects.

You can learn to recognize verbs and the subjects of verbs by observing their meaning, their form, and their position in sentences.

VERBS

Meaning   Verbs are words that express action, occurrence, or existence (a state of being).

> **Play** ball!   The rain **stopped**.
>
> They **exist**.   **Am** I right?

Function   A verb functions as the predicate of a sentence or as an essential part of the predicate.

> **Subject + PREDICATE.**
>
> William   **drives**.
> William   usually **drives** his car to work.

Form   In the present tense, all verbs change form to indicate a singular subject in the third person (I *eat*—he *eats*). When converted from the present to the past tense, nearly all verbs change form (*eat*—*ate*).

PRESENT TENSE		PAST TENSE
I **ski**. Ray **skis**.		I **skied**.
You **win**. She **wins**.		You **won**.
We **quit**. He **quits**.	BUT	He **quit**.

In addition, certain suffixes, such as *-ize* and *-ify*, often indicate that a word is a verb (*legalize, classify*).

Verb phrases   A verb may consist of two or more words (*may see, should have been eaten, will be helping*), a unit called a *verb phrase*. When used with *have, has,* or *had,* most verbs end in *-d* or *-ed* (*have moved, had played*), but some have a special ending (*has been eaten*). Used with a form of *be,* all progressive verbs end in *-ing,* as in *was eating* (see page 80).

> Tom **has moved**.   They **have taken** the tests.
> He **is moving**.   We **had been taking** lessons.

Auxiliary verbs   A verb phrase like *has moved* or *was taking* follows this pattern: **auxiliary verb + main verb**. The following words are commonly used as auxiliaries: *have, has, had, am, is, are, was, were, be, been, do, does, did, will, shall, can, may, must, would, should, could, might.* Word groups like *am going to, is about to, ought to, used to, had better,* and *have to* may function as auxiliary verbs:

> He **had gone** to London.
> We **were enjoying** the game.   They **did** not **enjoy** it.
> Ruth **is going to try**.   [Compare "Ruth *will try*."]

Other words may intervene between the auxiliary and the main verb:

> Television **will** never completely **replace** the radio.   [The auxiliary *will* signals the approach of the verb *replace*.]

The contraction for *not* may be added to many auxiliaries: *haven't, doesn't, aren't, can't.*

Verbs with particles   Many verbs are used with particles like *away, across, in, off, on, down, for, out,* and *up with.* Notice how meaning can be changed by the addition of one of these uninflected words.

SINGLE-WORD VERBS	VERBS WITH PARTICLES
She **called** me.	She **called on** me.
I **put** his picture on my desk.	I **put up with** his picture on my desk.

Other words may intervene between the verb and the particle:

> We **looked** José **up**.   Millie **handed** her report **in**.

SUBJECTS

Meaning   To identify a subject, find the verb; then use the verb in a question beginning with *who* or *what*, as shown in the following examples:

The dog in the cage ate.	The hut was built by Al.
Verb: **ate**	Verb: **was built**
WHO or WHAT ate? **The dog** (not the cage) **ate**.	WHAT was built? **The hut** (not Al) **was built**.
Subject: **dog**	Subject: **hut**

Form   Although other words or word groups may function as subjects, nouns or pronouns are the most frequently used.

Many nouns (words used to name persons, places, things, ideas, animals, and so on) change their form to indicate number (*movement, movements; city, cities; woman, women*) and to indicate the possessive case (*John's* car, the *boys'* dogs, the *women's* vote). Such suffixes as *-ance, -ation, -ence, -ment, -ness,* and *-ship* frequently indicate that a word is a noun (*appearance, determination, reference, atonement, boldness, hardship*). The articles *a, an,* and *the* regularly signal that a noun is to follow (a *chair,* an *activity,* the last *race*).

Form makes it a simple matter to recognize some pronouns. Pronouns such as *I, we, she, he, they,* and *who* function as subjects; when used as objects, these words change to the forms *me, us, her, him, them,* and *whom*. Other pronouns—such as *you, it, mine, ours, yours, hers, his, theirs, that, which*—resemble nouns in that they function as either subjects or objects without a change in form.

Position   Subjects usually come before verbs in sentences.

SUBJECT—verb.
They disappeared.
The youngest **boy** did not smile very often.

Common exceptions to the *subject—verb* pattern occur when subjects are used in questions and after the expletive *there* (which is never the subject).

Was the **statement** true? [verb—subject]
Did these **people survive?** [auxiliary—subject—verb]
There **were** no **objections**. [expletive—verb—subject]

Occasionally, verbs precede their subjects in sentences such as the following:

Over the door **were sprigs** of mistletoe.
Even more important **is** the **waste** of human resources.

Note: Subjects and verbs may be compound.

Cobras and **pythons** lay eggs. [compound subject]
We **sat** by the pool and **waited**. [compound verb]

■ **Exercise 1**   Underline the verbs (including any auxiliaries and particles) and their subjects in the following sentences (selected from *Reader's Digest*).

1. Lasting friendships develop.
2. Secrecy was another problem.
3. Rodgers constantly courts trouble with his boat-rocking comments.
4. The fire gobbled up some of the most expensive real estate on earth.
5. Answers to such questions may never be found.
6. Are vitamins important for sudden bursts of energy?
7. There are now about two million television sets in China.
8. John's simplicity gave his actions the force of parables.
9. Gnats and small flies invade the sheath and pollinate the blossoms.
10. He straightened his glasses, breathed a prayer of thanks, and swung his hoe at a nearby weed.

1b

Learn to recognize objects of verbs, as well as complements of subjects and objects.

You can learn to recognize objects of verbs, subject complements, and object complements by observing their meaning, their form, and their position in sentences.

DIRECT AND INDIRECT OBJECTS OF VERBS

Meaning   To identify a direct object, find the subject and the verb; then use them in a question ending with *whom* or *what* as shown in the following example:

> Karen graciously invited the reporters to lunch.
> Subject and verb: **Karen invited**
> Karen invited WHOM or WHAT? **the reporters**
> Direct object: **reporters**

A verb that has a direct object to complete its meaning is called a *transitive* verb. Notice that a direct object in a sentence like the following is directly affected by the action of the verb:

> High winds leveled a *city* in West Texas.   [The direct object is the receiver of the action.]

Some verbs (such as *give, offer, bring, take, lend, send, buy,* and *sell*) may have both a direct object and an indirect object. An indirect object states *to whom* or *for whom* (or *to what* or *for what*) something is done.

> Richard sent Audrey an invitation.
> Subject, verb, and direct object: **Richard sent invitation**
>
> Richard sent an invitation TO WHOM? **Audrey**
> Indirect object: **Audrey**

Form   Like the subjects of verbs, direct and indirect objects of verbs are generally nouns or pronouns: see **1a**, page 7. See also **1c**, pages 15–16.

Two women robbed the **taxi driver**.   They robbed **him**.
Sam bought **Ann** a new **watch**.   He bought **her that**.

Position   The following sentence patterns and examples
show the usual word order of direct and indirect objects of
verbs.

> **SUBJECT—VERB—OBJECT.**

Mice frighten elephants.
Many **fans were hanging placards** in the stadium.

> **SUBJECT—VERB—INDIRECT OBJECT—DIRECT OBJECT.**

Mary baked Timothy a **cake**.
The **company will** probably **send you** a small **refund**.

But in some sentences—especially questions—the direct object does not take the position indicated by the basic patterns.

What **placards did** the **fans hang** in the stadium?
[direct object—auxiliary—subject—verb]

A test for an object   Knowing how to change an active
verb to the passive voice can also help you to identify an
object, since the object of an active verb can usually be made
the subject of a passive verb:

ACTIVE   The Eagles finally **defeated** the **Lions**.
             [*Lions* is the direct object of *defeated*.]

PASSIVE The **Lions were** finally **defeated** by the Eagles.
             [*Lions* is the subject of *were defeated*.]

Notice above that a form of *be* is added when an active verb
is changed to the passive.

SUBJECT AND OBJECT COMPLEMENTS

Meaning   A subject complement refers to, identifies, or qualifies the subject. Subject complements help to complete the meaning of intransitive linking verbs (*be, am, is, are, was, were, been, seem, become, feel, look, smell, sound, taste,* and so on). See also page 12.

> Diane is my **cousin**.   [*cousin* identifies *Diane,* the subject.]
> Several tourists became **homesick**.   [*Homesick* describes or qualifies *tourists,* the subject.]

In the sentences above, the relationship between the subject and its complement is so close that the words used as subject complements can be placed next to the subject. They can then, in different sentences, serve as an appositive (an added noun explaining or identifying another noun) or as a regular adjective (rather than a predicate adjective).

> Diane, **my cousin**, dropped by.   [appositive]
>
> Several **homesick** tourists did not enjoy the trip.   [adjective]

An object complement refers to, identifies, or qualifies the direct object. Object complements help to complete the meaning of such verbs as *make, name, elect, call, find, consider.*

> We elected Phyllis **president**.
> [Compare: Because of our votes, Phyllis became president.]
>
> The dealer considered it **worthless**.
> [Compare: According to the dealer, it was worthless.]

Form   Nouns, pronouns, and adjectives are used as subject and object complements. See **1a** for a discussion of the forms of nouns and pronouns. Adjectives (which modify or qualify a noun or pronoun) often change form to indicate comparison: *tall, taller, tallest.* In addition to *-er* and *-est,* such suffixes as *-al, -ful, -ish, -like, -ous,* and *-y* often indicate that a word is an adjective: *national, useful, greenish, childlike, famous, lumpy.*

Position   Although word order varies (especially in questions or exclamations), a study of the following basic patterns and examples will help you learn to recognize subject and object complements.

SUBJECT—LINKING VERB—SUBJECT COMPLEMENT.

His **nickname was Skippy**.
The **pie tasted** too **sweet** for me.

SUBJECT—VERB—DIRECT OBJECT—OBJECT COMPLEMENT.

We **called him Skippy**.
I **found** the **pie** too **sweet**.

The ability to recognize objects of verbs and complements of subjects will help you to understand differences in the use of transitive and intransitive verbs. A transitive verb takes an object, and it may be made passive. See also page 10.

TRANSITIVE ACTIVE   These statistics **deceive** many people. [The direct object is *people.*]

TRANSITIVE PASSIVE   Many people **are deceived** by these statistics. [*People* is now the subject of the passive verb *are deceived.*]

Some intransitive verbs take a subject complement; some are complete without a complement.

INTRANSITIVE LINKING   The data **seemed** reliable. [The subject complement is *reliable.*]

INTRANSITIVE COMPLETE   They **did** not **listen**. [No complement is necessary.]

Note: Direct and indirect objects of verbs, subject complements, and object complements may be compound.

She likes **okra** and **spinach**. [compound direct object]

They sent **Elyse** and **Mike** complimentary tickets. [compound indirect object]

The cathedrals are **old** and **famous**. [compound subject complement]

They will name the baby **Jude** or **Judith**. [compound object complement]

■ **Exercise 2**   Underline all direct and indirect objects of verbs and the two subject complements in Exercise 1, page 8.

■ **Exercise 3**   Label all subjects of verbs, subject complements, and object complements in the quotations below. Prepare for a class discussion of the basic sentence patterns (and any variations) and the types of verbs used.

1. The argument bruises old myths. —LANCE MORROW
2. Inventions are the hallmark of mankind. —JAKE PAGE
3. With their world a shambles, people fled. —RONALD SCHILLER
4. In the *Odyssey,* Homer gives us detailed information of wind and stars. —MAURICIO OBREGÓN
5. Sensible people find nothing useless. —LA FONTAINE
6. Neither intelligence nor integrity can be imposed by law.
   —CARL BECKER
7. America has not always been kind to its artists and scholars.
   —LYNDON B. JOHNSON
8. The multitude of books is making us ignorant. —VOLTAIRE
9. There is no little enemy. —BENJAMIN FRANKLIN
10. Only a moral idiot with a suicidal mania would press the button for a nuclear war. —WALTER LIPPMANN

1c

Learn to recognize all the parts of speech.

Two methods of classifying words in a sentence are shown below. The first method classifies words according to their function in a sentence; the second, according to their part of speech.

Waiters usually offer us free coffee at Joe's cafe.

	FUNCTION	PART OF SPEECH
Waiters	subject	noun
usually	modifier	adverb
offer	verb of predicate	verb
us	indirect object	pronoun
free	modifier	adjective
coffee	direct object	noun
at	preposition	preposition
Joe's	modifier	noun
cafe	object of preposition	noun

Notice here that one part of speech—the noun (a naming word with a typical form)—is used as a subject, a direct object, a modifier, and an object of a preposition.

Words are traditionally grouped into eight classes or parts of speech: *verbs, nouns, pronouns, adjectives, adverbs, prepositions, conjunctions,* and *interjections.* Verbs, nouns, adjectives, and adverbs (called vocabulary or content words) make up more than 99 percent of all words listed in the dictionary. But pronouns, prepositions, and conjunctions—although small in number—are important because they are used over and over in our speaking and writing. Prepositions and conjunctions (called function or structure words) connect and relate other parts of speech.

Of the eight word classes, only three—prepositions, conjunctions, and interjections—do not change their form. For a summary of the form changes of the other parts of speech, see **inflection**, page 543.

Carefully study the forms, meanings, and functions of each of the eight parts of speech listed on the following pages. For additional examples or more detailed information, see the corresponding entries in the **Glossary of Grammatical Terms** beginning on page 529.

VERBS   *notify, notifies, is notifying, notified*
             write, writes, is writing, wrote, has written

A verb functions as the predicate of a sentence or as an essential part of the predicate: see **1a**.

> Herman **writes**.
> He **has written** five poems.
> He **is** no longer **writing** those dull stories.

One frequently used verb-forming suffix is *-ize:*

> *terror, idols* (nouns)—*terrorize, idolize* (verbs)

Note: Verb forms classified as participles, gerunds, or infinitives (verbals) cannot function as the predicate of a sentence: see **1d**.

> PARTICIPLES   The man **writing** the note is Bill. [modifier]
>   She gave him **written** instructions. [modifier]
> GERUND   His **writing** all night long disturbed his whole family. [subject]
> INFINITIVES   Herman wants **to write**. [direct object]
>   The urge **to write** left him. [modifier]

NOUNS   *man, men; kindness, kindnesses*
             nation, nations; nation's, nations'
             Carthage, United States, William, NASA
             prudence, the *money,* an *understanding*

Nouns function as subjects, objects, complements, appositives, and modifiers, as well as in direct address and in absolute constructions. Nouns name persons, places, things, ideas, animals, and so on. See also **1a** and **1b** and pages 546–47.

> **Marilyn** drives a **truck** for the **Salvation Army**.

Endings such as *-ation, -ism, -ity, -ment,* and *-ness* are called noun-forming suffixes:

relax, starve (verbs)—*relaxation, starvation* (nouns)
kind, happy (adjectives)—*kindness, happiness* (nouns)

Compound nouns   Words such as *father-in-law, Salvation Army, swimming pool, dropout,* and *breakthrough* are generally classified as compound nouns.

PRONOUNS   *I, me, my, mine, myself; they, you, him, it this, these; who, whose, whom; which, that one, ones, one's; everybody, anyone*

Pronouns serve the function of nouns in sentences:

They bought **it** for **her**.   **Everyone** knows **this**.

ADJECTIVES   *shy, sleepy, attractive, famous three* men, *this* class, *another* one *young, younger, youngest*

The articles *a, an,* and *the* are variously classified as adjectives, determiners, or function words. Adjectives modify or qualify nouns and pronouns (and sometimes gerunds) and are generally placed near the words they modify:

The **beautiful** and **famous** cathedrals no longer interest **homesick** tourists.
Thrifty and **sensible,** he will be promoted soon.

Adjectives may function as complements of the subject or of the object: see **1b**.

The Great Smoky Mountains are most **beautiful** in the fall.
Her tennis serve made Joanne **famous**.

Suffixes such as *-al, -able, -ant, -ative, -ic, -ish, -less, -ous,* and *-y* may be added to certain verbs or nouns to form adjectives:

accept, repent (verbs)—*acceptable, repentant* (adjectives)
angel, effort (nouns)—*angelic, effortless* (adjectives)

ADVERBS   *rarely* saw, call *daily*, *soon* left, left *sooner*
              very short, *too* angry, *never* shy, *not* fearful
              practically never loses, *nearly always* cold

As the examples show, adverbs modify verbs, adjectives, and other adverbs. In addition, an adverb may modify a verbal, a phrase, a clause, or even the rest of the sentence in which it appears:

I noticed a plane **slowly** circling overhead.
Honestly, Ben did catch a big shark.

The *-ly* ending nearly always converts adjectives to adverbs:

rare, honest (adjectives)—*rarely, honestly* (adverbs)

PREPOSITIONS   *on* a shelf, *between* us, *because of* rain
                   to the door, *by* them, *before* class

A preposition always has an object, which is usually a noun or a pronoun. The preposition links and relates its object to some other word in the sentence. The preposition with its object (and any modifiers) is called a *prepositional phrase:*

Byron expressed **with great force** his love **of liberty**.

The preposition may follow rather than precede its object, and it may be placed at the end of the sentence:

What are you selling it **for**?   Faith is what we live **by**.

Words commonly used as prepositions:

about	before	by	in
above	behind	concerning	inside
across	below	despite	into
after	beneath	down	like
against	beside	during	near
along	besides	except	of
among	between	excepting	off
around	beyond	for	on
at	but	from	onto

17

out	round	to	up
outside	since	toward	upon
over	through	under	with
past	throughout	underneath	within
regarding	till	until	without

Phrasal prepositions (two or more words):

according to	by way of	in spite of
along with	due to	instead of
apart from	except for	on account of
as for	in addition to	out of
as regards	in case of	up to
as to	in front of	with regard to
because of	in lieu of	with respect to
by means of	in place of	with reference to
by reason of	in regard to	with the exception of

CONJUNCTIONS   Amy *and* Bill, in *or* out
                      long *but* witty

She acts **as if** she really cares.
I worked, **for** my father needed money.

Conjunctions function as connectors of words, phrases, or clauses: see also **1d** and **1e**.

The coordinating conjunctions (*and, but, or, nor, for, so, yet*) and the correlatives (*both—and, either—or, neither—nor, not only—but also, whether—or*) connect sentence elements of equal grammatical rank.

The subordinating conjunctions (such as *after, as if, because, if, since, till, when, where, while*) connect subordinate clauses with main clauses: see **1d** and the list on page 25.

Conjunctive adverbs   Words like *however, nevertheless, then,* and *therefore* (see the list on page 45) are used as conjunctive adverbs (or adverbial conjunctions):

Don seemed bored in class; **however,** he did listen and learn.

INTERJECTIONS   *Wow!   Oh,* that's a surprise.

Interjections are exclamations, which may be followed by an exclamation point or by a comma: see **12b** and **17c**.

A dictionary labels words according to their part of speech. Some words have only one classification—for example, *notify* (verb), *sleepy* (adjective), *practically* (adverb). Other words have more than one label. The word *living*, for instance, is first treated as a form of the verb *live* and is then listed separately and defined as an adjective and as a noun. The actual classification depends on the use of the word in a given sentence:

> They were **living** wretchedly.   [verb]
> She is a **living** example of patience.   [adjective]
> He barely makes a **living**.   [noun]

Another example is the word *up:*

> Look **up**!   [adverb]
> They dragged the sled **up** the hill.   [preposition]
> The **up** escalator is jerking again.   [adjective]
> He follows the **ups** and downs of the market.   [noun]
> "They will **up** the rent again," he complained.   [verb]

■ **Exercise 4**   Using your dictionary as an aid if you wish, classify each word in the following sentences according to its part of speech.

1. He struts with the gravity of a frozen penguin.   —TIME
2. Men are often taken, like rabbits, by the ears. And though the tongue has no bones, it can sometimes break millions of them.   —F. L. LUCAS
3. Awesome is the tyranny of the fixed idea.   —ERIC LARABEE
4. Of all persons, adolescents are the most intensely personal; their intensity is often uncomfortable to adults.
   —EDGAR Z. FRIEDENBERG
5. They pick a President and then for four years they pick on him.   —ADLAI STEVENSON

1d

Learn to recognize phrases and subordinate clauses.

The sentences below consist only of the basic grammatical parts along with the articles *the* and *a:* see the sentence patterns in **1a** and **1b**.

> We explored the beach. We used metal detectors.
> We found a doubloon. It was battered.

Most sentences, however, contain groups of words used as single parts of speech. Such word groups are either phrases or subordinate clauses.

> SENTENCES COMBINED
>
> **Exploring the beach with metal detectors**, we found **a battered doubloon**. [phrases]
>
> **When we were exploring the beach with metal detectors**, we found a battered doubloon. [subordinate clause preceding a main clause—see **1e**]

PHRASES

A phrase is often defined as a group of related words without a subject and a predicate. Phrases are generally classified as follows:

> VERB PHRASES The rose **has wilted**. **Did** you **see** it?
> Mr. Kelly **may run up** the bill. The roof **used to leak**.
>
> NOUN PHRASES **The severe drought** struck **many Midwestern States**. I introduced Greer, **a very interesting speaker**.
>
> PREPOSITIONAL PHRASES The oldest car **on campus** is mine.
> We were exploring the beach **with metal detectors**.
>
> PARTICIPIAL PHRASES **Exploring the beach**, we found many sand dollars. The beach, **covered with seaweed**, looked uninviting.

GERUND PHRASES **Exploring the beach** is fun. They enjoyed **feeding the seagulls**.

INFINITIVE PHRASES We wanted **to explore the beach**. That is the problem **to be solved now**. Vernon and I went to Boston **to visit relatives**.

ABSOLUTE PHRASES **The van loaded**, we headed for the mountains. The Nobel Prize winner left the room, **reporters clustering around him**. [See also page 529].

Notice in the examples above that *exploring*—a verb form ending in *-ing*—is used as an adjective and also as a noun. The grammatical classification is not based on form but on use in the sentence: the participle functions as an adjective and the gerund functions as a noun.

Participles, gerunds, and infinitives are derived from verbs. (See also the note on page 15 and **verbal** on page 556.) They are much like verbs in that they have different tenses, can take subjects and objects, and can be modified by adverbs. But they cannot serve as the only verb form in the predicate of a sentence. Participial, gerund, and infinitive phrases function as adjectives, nouns, or adverbs and are therefore only parts of sentences, as the following sentence combinations illustrate.

SENTENCES

Dr. Ford explained the process. He drew simple illustrations.

PHRASES IN SENTENCES

Explaining the process, Dr. Ford drew simple illustrations.

OR

Simple illustrations **drawn by Dr. Ford** explained the process. [participial phrases]

Dr. Ford explained the process by **drawing simple illustrations**. [gerund phrase]

Dr. Ford drew simple illustrations **to explain the process**. [infinitive phrase]

(1) Phrases used as nouns

Gerund phrases are always used as nouns. Infinitive phrases are often used as nouns (although they may also function as modifiers). Occasionally a prepositional phrase functions as a noun (as in "*After supper* is too late!").

NOUNS	PHRASES USED AS NOUNS
The **decision** is important.	**Choosing a major** is important. [gerund phrase—subject]
She likes the **job**.	She likes **to do the work**. [infinitive phrase—direct object]
His **action** prompted the **change**.	**His leaving the farm** prompted **her to seek a job in town**. [gerund phrase—subject; infinitive phrase—direct object]
He uses my room for **storage**.	He uses my room for **storing all his auto parts**. [gerund phrase—object of a preposition]
He wants two things: **money** and **power**.	He wants two things: **to make money** and **to gain power**. [infinitive phrases—a compound appositive]

■ **Exercise 5**   Underline the gerund phrases and the infinitive phrases used as nouns in the following sentences (selected from *Time*). Be sure to underline any prepositional phrases modifying words in the gerund or the infinitive phrases.

1. Successfully merchandising a product is creative.
2. Americans have always needed to know the point of it all.
3. They have also been getting tougher by enforcing strict new anti-litter laws.
4. Taking criticism from others is painful but useful.
5. Merely to argue for the preservation of park land is not enough.

6. Angry and proud, Claire resolved to fight back.
7. After giving birth, most women lapse into some sort of melancholy.
8. Workers managed to pipe the gas through a purifying plant and into a pipeline.
9. All human acts—even saving a stranger from drowning or donating a million dollars to the poor—may be ultimately selfish.
10. This method of growing plants without soil has long been known to scientists but has only recently begun to attract amateurs' attention.

(2) Phrases used as modifiers

Prepositional phrases nearly always function as adjectives or adverbs. Infinitive phrases are also used as adjectives or adverbs. Participial phrases are used as adjectives. Absolute phrases are used as adverbs.

ADJECTIVES

It is a **significant** idea.

Appropriate language is best.

Destructive storms lashed the Midwest.

The **icy** bridge was narrow.

PHRASES USED AS ADJECTIVES

It is an idea **of significance**. [prepositional phrase]

Language **to suit the occasion** is best. [infinitive phrase]

Destroying many crops of corn and oats, storms lashed the Midwest. [participial phrase containing a prepositional phrase]

The bridge **covered with ice** was narrow. [participial phrase containing a prepositional phrase]

ADVERBS

Drive **carefully**.

I nodded **respectfully**.

PHRASES USED AS ADVERBS

Drive **with care on wet streets**. [prepositional phrases]

I nodded **to show respect**. [infinitive phrase]

23

ADVERBS	PHRASES USED AS ADVERBS
Consequently, we could hardly see the road.	**The rain coming down in torrents**, we could hardly see the road. [absolute phrase—see page 529]

The preceding examples demonstrate how phrases function in the same way as single-word modifiers. Remember, however, that phrases are not merely substitutes for single words. Many times phrases express more than can be packed into a single word:

> The gas gauge fluttered **from empty to full**.
> He telephoned his wife **to tell her of his arrival**.
> The firefighters **hosing down the adjacent buildings** had very little standing room.

■ **Exercise 6**   Underline each phrase used as a modifier in the following sentences. Then state whether the phrase functions as an adjective or as an adverb.

1. A moment like that one should last forever.
2. The fans blinded by the sun missed the best plays.
3. Crawling through the thicket, I suddenly remembered the box of shells left on top of the truck.
4. The people to watch closely are the ones ruling behind the political scene.
5. A motorcycle racing along the beach zoomed over our big sand castle.
6. The number on that ticket indicates a seat in the balcony.
7. I came to college to get a liberal education and to learn a trade.
8. They worked fast, one man sawing logs and the other loading the truck.
9. Not wanting to appear in court, Marilyn decided to pay the fine.
10. All told, fame is fickle.

SUBORDINATE CLAUSES

A clause is often defined as a group of related words that contains both a subject and a predicate. Like a phrase, a subordinate (or dependent) clause is not a sentence. The subordinate clause functions as a single part of speech—as a noun, an adjective, or an adverb. Notice the relationship of the sentences below to the clauses that follow.

SENTENCES   **That fact I must admit.**
            Ralph was my first and only blind date.
            I married him.

SUBORDINATE CLAUSES IN SENTENCES

I must admit **that Ralph was my first and only blind date.** [noun clause—direct object]

The first and only blind date **that I ever had** was Ralph. [adjective clause]

Ralph was my first and only blind date **because I married him.** [adverb clause]

In the examples above, *that* and *because* are used as *subordinators:* they subordinate the clauses they introduce, making these clauses dependent. The following words are commonly used to mark subordinate clauses.

RELATIVE PRONOUNS   *that, what, which, who whoever, whom, whomever, whose*

SUBORDINATING CONJUNCTIONS   *after, although, as, because, before, if, once, since, that, though, till, unless, until, when, whenever, where, wherever, while*

Subordinators may consist of more than one word:

as if, as soon as, as though, even though, in order that, in that, no matter how, so that

No matter how hard I try, I cannot float with my toes out of the water.

We bought three dozen doughnuts **so that everyone would be sure to have enough.**

(3) Subordinate clauses used as nouns

NOUNS	NOUN CLAUSES
The **news** may be false.	**What the newspapers say** may be false. [subject]
I do not know his **address**.	I do not know **where he lives**. [direct object]
Give the tools to **Rita**.	Give the tools to **whoever can use them best**. [object of a preposition]
That fact—Karen's **protest**—amazed me.	The fact **that Karen protested** amazed me. [appositive]

The conjunction *that* before a noun clause may be omitted in some sentences:

> I know **she is right**. [Compare ''I know *that she is right*.'']

(4) Subordinate clauses used as modifiers

Two types of subordinate clauses, the adjective clause and the adverb clause, are used as modifiers.

Adjective clauses   Any clause that modifies a noun or a pronoun is an adjective clause. Adjective clauses, which nearly always follow the words modified, are most frequently introduced by a relative pronoun but may begin with such words as *when, where,* or *why.*

ADJECTIVES	ADJECTIVE CLAUSES
Everyone needs **loyal** friends.	Everyone needs friends **who are loyal**.
The **golden** window reflects the sun.	The window, **which shines like gold**, reflects the sun.
Peaceful countrysides no longer exist.	Countrysides **where one can find peace of mind** no longer exist.

If it is not used as a subject, the relative pronoun in an adjective clause may sometimes be omitted:

He is a man **I admire**.
[Compare "He is a man *whom I admire.*"]

Adverb clauses   An adverb clause usually modifies a verb but may modify an adjective, an adverb, or even the rest of the sentence in which it appears. Many adverb clauses can take various positions in a sentence: see **12b** and **12d**. Adverb clauses are ordinarily introduced by subordinating conjunctions.

ADVERBS	ADVERB CLAUSES
Soon the lights went out.	**When the windstorm hit**, the lights went out.
No alcoholic beverages are sold **locally**.	No alcoholic beverages are sold **where I live**.
The price is **too** high for me.	The price is higher **than I can afford**.
Speak **very** distinctly.	Speak as distinctly **as you can**.

Some adverb clauses may be elliptical. See also **25b**.

If I can save enough money, I'll go to Alaska next summer. **If not,** I'll take a trip to St. Louis.   [Omitted words are clearly implied.]

■ **Exercise 7**   Find each subordinate clause in the following sentences (selected from the *New York Times Magazine*) and label it as a noun clause, an adjective clause, or an adverb clause.

1. Food manufacturers contend that modern processing often robs food of its natural color.
2. What my son wants to wear or be or try to be is now almost entirely his business.
3. Grocers today must deal with shoppers whose basic attitudes are drastically changed.

4. As I talked to my neighbors, I found that all of them did depend on a world that stretched far beyond their property lines.

5. As it declines in value, money becomes more of an obsession.

6. If a pitcher who throws only a fastball and a curveball is in a tight situation, the batter can reasonably expect the fastball.

7. Bloodhounds do not follow tracks as people often believe. . . . Because a trail so often hangs several inches or sometimes feet above the ground, hounds can follow a person even if he wades through water.

8. At present, computers are rapidly moving into offices around the world to take over secretarial chores that involve processing words.

9. We are a plugged-in society—plugged in to the tube, which all but assumes the role of parent, or teacher, or lover.

10. The language is what it is, and not what you want it to be.

1e

Learn to recognize main clauses and the various types of sentences.

A main clause can stand alone as a sentence, a grammatically independent unit of expression, although it may require other sentences to complete its meaning. Coordinating conjunctions (*and, but, or, nor, for, so, yet*) often connect and relate main clauses.

MAIN CLAUSES IN SENTENCES

I had lost my passport, but **I did not worry about it**.
[A coordinating conjunction links the two main clauses.]

Although I had lost my passport, **I did not worry about it**.
[A subordinate clause precedes the main clause.]

MAIN CLAUSES CONVERTED TO SENTENCES

I had lost my passport.
I did not worry about it. OR **But I did not worry about it.**

Unlike main clauses, subordinate clauses become fragments if isolated and written as sentences: see **2b**.

Sentences may be classified according to their structure as *simple, compound, complex,* or *compound-complex.*

1. A simple sentence has only one subject and one predicate (either or both of which may be compound):

   Dick started a coin collection. [**SUBJECT—VERB—OBJECT.** See also the various patterns of the simple sentence in **1a** and **1b**.]

2. A compound sentence consists of at least two main clauses:

   Dick started a coin collection, and his wife bought an album of rare stamps. [**MAIN CLAUSE, and MAIN CLAUSE.** See **12a**.]

3. A complex sentence has one main clause and at least one subordinate clause:

   As soon as Dick started a coin collection, his wife bought an album of rare stamps. [**ADVERB CLAUSE, MAIN CLAUSE.** See **12b**.]

4. A compound-complex sentence consists of at least two main clauses and at least one subordinate clause:

   As soon as Dick started a coin collection, his wife bought an album of rare stamps; on Christmas morning they exchanged coins and stamps. [**ADVERB CLAUSE, MAIN CLAUSE; MAIN CLAUSE.** See **14a**.]

Sentences may also be classified according to their purpose as *statements, commands* or *requests, questions,* or *exclamations* and are punctuated accordingly:

   STATEMENT He refused the offer.

   COMMAND OR REQUEST Refuse the offer.

   QUESTIONS Did he refuse the offer? He refused, didn't he? He refused it?

   EXCLAMATIONS What an offer! He refused it! Refuse it!

■ **Exercise 8**   Underline the main clauses in the following sentences (selected from *Natural History*). Put subordinate clauses in brackets: see **1d**. (Noun clauses may be an integral part of the basic pattern of a main clause, as in the second sentence.)

1. Practice never really makes perfect, and a great deal of frustration invariably accompanies juggling.
2. Nature is his passion in life, and colleagues say he is a skilled naturalist and outdoorsman.
3. The two clouds have a common envelope of atomic hydrogen gas, which ties them firmly together.
4. Transportation comes to a halt as the steadily falling snow, accumulating faster than snowplows can clear it away, is blown into deep drifts along the highways.
5. Agriculture is the world's most basic industry; its success depends in large part on an adequate supply of water.
6. Probably because their whirling sails were new and strange to Cervantes, windmills outraged the gallant Don Quixote.
7. There have been several attempts to explain this rhythm, but when each hypothesis was experimentally explored, it had to be discarded.
8. Allegiance to a group may be confirmed or denied by the use or disuse of a particular handshake, as Carl's experience indicates.
9. Some black stem rust of wheat has been controlled by elimination of barberry, a plant that harbored the rust.
10. We know that innocent victims have been executed; fortunately, others condemned to death have been found innocent prior to execution.

■ **Exercise 9**   Classify the sentences in Exercise 8 as *compound* (there are two), *complex* (five), or *compound-complex* (three).

■ **Exercise 10**   First identify the main and subordinate clauses in the sentences in the following paragraph; then classify each sentence according to structure.

¹ Jim angrily called himself a fool, as he had been doing all the way to the swamp. ² Why had he listened to Fred's mad idea? ³ What did ghosts and family legends mean to him, in this age of

computers and solar-energy converters?   [4] He had enough mysteries of his own, of a highly complex sort, which involved an intricate search for values.   [5] But now he was chasing down ghosts, and this chase in the middle of the night was absurd.   [6] It was lunacy!   [7] The legends that surrounded the ghosts had horrified him as a child, and they were a horror still.   [8] As he approached the dark trail that would lead him to the old mansion, he felt almost sick.   [9] The safe, sure things of every day had become distant fantasies.   [10] Only this grotesque night—and whatever ghosts might be lurking in the shadows—seemed hideously real.

■ **Exercise 11**   Observing differences in emphasis, convert each pair of sentences below to (a) a simple sentence, (b) a compound sentence consisting of two main clauses, and (c) a complex sentence with one main clause and one subordinate clause.

EXAMPLE

Male sperm whales occasionally attack ships. These whales jealously guard their territory.

a. *Jealously guarding their territory, male sperm whales occasionally attack ships.*
b. *Male sperm whales occasionally attack ships; these whales jealously guard their territory.*
c. *Since male sperm whales jealously guard their territory, they occasionally attack ships.*

1. The men smuggled marijuana into Spain. They were sentenced to six years in prison.
2. The council first condemned the property. Then it ordered the owner's eviction.
3. Uncle Oliver applied for a patent on his invention. He learned of three hundred such devices already on the market.
4. The border guards delayed every tourist. They carefully examined passports and luggage.

Sentence Fragments

2

As a rule, do not write sentence fragments.

A fragment is a nonsentence. It is a part of a sentence—such as a phrase or subordinate clause—written as if it were a sentence.

FRAGMENTS	SENTENCES
My father always planting a spring garden.	My father always plants a spring garden.
Because he likes to eat vegetables.	He likes to eat vegetables.
That help the body to combat infection.	He eats foods that help the body to combat infection—
For example, yellow and green vegetables.	for example, yellow and green vegetables.

Recognizing intonation patterns may help you avoid some types of fragments in your writing. Read the following sentences aloud, and note how your voice indicates the end of each complete statement.

We saw that.   We saw that movie.
We saw that movie on TV last summer.

The best way to avoid fragments, however, is to recognize the structural differences between sentences and non-sentences. Remember that a complete statement is an independent unit containing at least one subject and predicate. Study Section **1**, especially **1d** and **1e**.

Not all fragments are to be avoided. Some types of fragments are standard. Exclamations, as well as questions and their answers, are often single words, phrases, or subordinate clauses written as sentences:

> **Why? Because governments cannot establish heaven on earth.**
> Where does Peg begin a mystery story? **On the last page. Always!**

Written dialogue that mirrors speech habits often contains grammatically incomplete sentences or elliptical expressions within the quotation marks: see **9e**. Occasionally, professional writers deliberately use fragments for rhetorical effect:

> The American grain calls for plain talk, for the unvarnished truth. **Better to err a little in the cause of bluntness than soften the mind with congenial drivel. Better a challenging half-truth than a discredited cliché.** —WRIGHT MORRIS [The reader can readily supply omitted words in the two bold-faced fragments. Note the effective repetition and the parallel structure.]

Despite their suitability for some purposes, sentence fragments are comparatively rare in formal expository writing. In formal papers, sentence fragments are to be used—if at all—sparingly and with care. College students are often advised to learn the fundamentals of English composition before permitting themselves to take liberties with the accepted patterns of the complete sentence.

Test for Sentence Completeness

Before handing in a composition, proofread each word group written as a sentence. Test each one for completeness.

First, be sure that it has at least one subject and one predicate.

FRAGMENTS MISSING EITHER A SUBJECT OR A PREDICATE

And for days tried to change my mind. [no subject]
Water sparkling in the moonlight. [no predicate]

Next, be sure that the word group is not a dependent clause beginning with a subordinating conjunction or a relative pronoun (see page 25).

FRAGMENTS WITH SUBJECT AND PREDICATE

When he tried for days to change my mind. [subject and verb: *he tried;* subordinating conjunction: *When*]
Which sparkles in the moonlight. [subject and verb: *Which sparkles;* relative pronoun: *Which*]

Revision of a Sentence Fragment

Since a fragment is often an isolated, mispunctuated part of an adjacent sentence, one way to revise a fragment is to make it a part of the complete sentence. Another way to revise a fragment is to make it into a sentence. Revisions need not alter the meaning.

FRAGMENT   Henry smiled self-consciously. **Like a politician before a camera**. [an isolated phrase]
REVISED   Henry smiled self-consciously, like a politician before a camera. [phrase included in sentence]
OR
Henry smiled self-consciously—like a politician before a camera. [The use of the dash instead of the comma tends to emphasize the material that follows.]
OR
Henry smiled self-consciously. He looked like a politician before a camera. [fragment made into a sentence]

Caution: When revising fragments, do not misuse the semicolon between parts of unequal grammatical rank: see **14c**.

2a

Do not carelessly capitalize and punctuate a phrase as you would a sentence.

FRAGMENT   Soon I began to work for the company. **First in the rock pit and later on the highway.** [prepositional phrases]

REVISED   Soon I began to work for the company, first in the rock pit and later on the highway. [fragment included in the preceding sentence]

FRAGMENT   He will have a chance to go home next weekend. **And to meet his new stepfather.** [infinitive phrase]

REVISED   He will have a chance to go home next weekend and to meet his new stepfather. [fragment included in the preceding sentence]

FRAGMENT   Astronauts venturing deep into space may not come back to earth for fifty years. **Returning only to discover an uninhabitable planet.** [participial phrase]

REVISED   Astronauts venturing deep into space may not come back to earth for fifty years. They may return only to discover an uninhabitable planet. [fragment made into a sentence]

FRAGMENT   The children finally arrived at camp. **Many dancing for joy, and some crying for their parents.** [absolute phrases]

REVISED   The children finally arrived at camp. Many were dancing for joy, and some were crying for their parents. [fragment made into a sentence]

■ **Exercise 1**   Eliminate each fragment below by including it in the adjacent sentence or by making it into a sentence.

1. They enjoy reading a few types of novels. Such as science fiction.
2. The pampered Dennis finally left home. Earnestly seeking to become an individual in his own right.

3. It is wise to ignore her sarcasm. Or to make a quick exit.
4. She did not recognize Gary. His beard gone and hair cut.
5. Louise likes to pretend that she is very old. And to speak of the "days of her youth."
6. They will visit our campus soon. Maybe next month.
7. These commercials have a hypnotic effect. Not only on children but on adults too.
8. A few minutes later. A news bulletin interrupted the show.
9. Eric just stood there speechless. His face turning redder by the minute.
10. He killed six flies with one swat. Against the law of averages but possible.

2b

Do not carelessly capitalize and punctuate a subordinate clause as you would a sentence.

FRAGMENT   Thousands of young people became active workers in the community. **After this social gospel had changed their apathy to concern.** [subordinate clause]

REVISED   Thousands of young people became active workers in the community after this social gospel had changed their apathy to concern. [fragment included in the preceding sentence]

FRAGMENT   I didn't know where he came from. **Or who he was.** [subordinate clause]

REVISED   I didn't know where he came from or who he was. [fragment included in the preceding sentence]

FRAGMENT   I was trying to read the directions. **Which were confusing and absurd**. [subordinate clause]

REVISED   I was trying to read the directions, which were confusing and absurd. [fragment included in the preceding sentence]

OR

I was trying to read the directions. They were confusing and absurd. [fragment made into a sentence]

OR

I was trying to read the confusing, absurd directions. [fragment reduced to adjectivals that are included in the preceding sentence]

■ **Exercise 2** Eliminate each fragment below by including it in the preceding sentence or by making it into a sentence.

1. I decided to give skiing a try. After I had grown tired of watching other people fall.
2. Pat believes that everyone should go to college. And that all tests for admission should be abolished.
3. Many students were obviously victims of spring fever. Which affected class attendance.
4. Paul faints whenever he sees blood. And whenever he climbs into a dentist's chair.
5. I am making a study of cigarette advertisements. That use such slogans as "less tar, more taste" and "the lowest in tar and nicotine."

2c

Do not carelessly capitalize and punctuate any other fragment (such as an appositive or a part of a compound predicate) as you would a sentence.

FRAGMENT   The new lawyer needed a secretary. **A secretary with intelligence and experience**.

REVISED   The new lawyer needed a secretary—a secretary with intelligence and experience.

OR

The new lawyer needed a secretary with intelligence and experience.

FRAGMENT   He lost the gold watch. **The one which had belonged to his grandfather**.

REVISED   He lost the gold watch, the one which had belonged to his grandfather. [fragment included in the preceding sentence]

OR

He lost the gold watch which had belonged to his grandfather.

FRAGMENT   Sarah was elected president of her class. **And was made a member of the National Honor Society.** [detached part of a compound predicate]

REVISED   Sarah was elected president of her class and was made a member of the National Honor Society.

■ **Exercise 3**   Eliminate each fragment below by including it in the preceding sentence or by making it into a sentence.

1. My roommate keeps all her shoes, scuba gear, books, and clothes in one closet. The worst disaster area on campus.
2. According to Macaulay, half-knowledge is bad. Even worse than ignorance.
3. The group met during the summer and made plans. And decided on the dates for action in the fall.
4. The hydraulic lift raises the plows out of the ground. And lowers them again.
5. I had a feeling that some sinister spirit brooded over the place. A feeling that I could not analyze.

■ **Exercise 4**   Find the nine fragments in the following paragraph. Revise each fragment by attaching it logically to an adjacent sentence or by rewriting the fragment so that it stands by itself as a sentence.

[1] The little paperback almanac I found at the newsstand has given me some fascinating information. [2] Not just about the weather and changes in the moon. [3] There are also intriguing statistics. [4] A tub bath, for example, requires more water than a shower. [5] In all probability, ten or twelve gallons more, depending on how dirty the bather is. [6] And one of the Montezumas

downed fifty jars of cocoa every day.   [7] Which seems a bit exaggerated to me.   [8] To say the least.   [9] I also learned that an average beard has thirteen thousand whiskers.   [10] That, in the course of a lifetime, a man could shave off more than nine yards of whiskers, over twenty-seven feet.   [11] If my math is correct.   [12] Some other interesting facts in the almanac.   [13] Suppose a person was born on Sunday, February 29, 1976.   [14] Another birthday not celebrated on Sunday until the year 2004.   [15] Because February 29 falls on weekdays till then—twenty-eight birthdays later.   [16] As I laid the almanac aside, I remembered that line in *Slaughterhouse-Five:* "And so it goes."

Comma Splice
and Fused Sentence

3

Do not carelessly link two sentences with only a comma (comma splice) or run two sentences together without any punctuation (fused sentence).

Carefully observe how three sentences have been linked to make the one long sentence below.

SENTENCES SEPARATED   These are mysteries performed in broad daylight before our very eyes. We can see every detail. And yet they are still mysteries.

SENTENCES LINKED   These are mysteries performed in broad daylight before our very eyes; we can see every detail, and yet they are still mysteries. —ANNIE DILLARD

[MAIN CLAUSE; MAIN CLAUSE, *and* MAIN CLAUSE.]

When you connect the end of one sentence to the beginning of another, be especially careful about punctuation.

NOT   The current was swift, he could not swim to shore. [comma splice—sentences are linked with only a comma]

40

NOT   The current was swift he could not swim to shore.
[fused sentence—sentences are run together with no
punctuation]

VARIOUS METHODS OF REVISION

Because the current was swift, he could not swim to shore.
[first main clause subordinated: see **12b**]

The current was so swift that he could not swim to shore.
[second main clause subordinated]

Because of the swift current he could not swim to shore.
[first clause reduced to an introductory phrase]

The current was swift. He could not swim to shore.   [each
main clause converted to a sentence]

The current was swift; he could not swim to shore.   [main
clauses separated by a semicolon: see **14a**]

The current was swift, so he could not swim to shore.
[comma preceding the connective *so:* see **12a**]

He could not swim to shore, for the current was swift.
[comma preceding the coordinating conjunction *for*]

When you revise carelessly connected sentences, choose a
method that achieves the emphasis you want.

If you cannot always recognize a main clause and distinguish it from a phrase or from a subordinate clause, study **1d**
and **1e**.

3a

**Use a comma between main clauses *only* when they
are linked by the coordinating conjunctions *and, but,
or, for, nor, so,* or *yet*.** See also **12a**.

COMMA SPLICE   Our country observed its Bicentennial in
1976, my hometown celebrated its fiftieth anniversary
the same year.

REVISED   Our country observed its Bicentennial in 1976**, and** my hometown celebrated its fiftieth anniversary the same year. [the coordinating conjunction *and* added after the comma]
OR
Our country observed its Bicentennial in 1976**;** my hometown celebrated its fiftieth anniversary the same year. [A semicolon separates the main clauses. See **14a**.]

COMMA SPLICE   Her first novel was not a best seller, it was not a complete failure either.

REVISED   Her first novel was not a best seller**, nor** was it a complete failure. [Note the shift in the word order of subject and verb after the coordinating conjunction *nor.*]
OR
Her first novel was **neither** a best seller **nor** a complete failure. [a simple sentence with a compound complement]

COMMA SPLICE   The old tree stumps grated against the bottom of our boat, they did not damage the propeller.

REVISED   The old tree stumps grated against the bottom of our boat**, but** they did not damage the propeller. [the coordinating conjunction *but* added after the comma]
OR
Although the old tree stumps grated against the bottom of our boat**,** they did not damage the propeller. [Addition of *although* makes the first clause subordinate: see **12b**.]

Caution: Do not omit punctuation between main clauses not linked by *and, but, or, for, nor, so,* and *yet.*

FUSED SENTENCE   She wrote him a love letter he answered it in person.

REVISED   She wrote him a love letter**.** He answered it in person. [each main clause written as a sentence]

OR

She wrote him a love letter; he answered it in person.
[main clauses separated by a semicolon: see **14a**]

Note 1: Either a comma or a semicolon may be used between short main clauses not linked by *and, but, or, for, nor, so,* or *yet* when the clauses are parallel in form and unified in thought:

> School bores them, preaching bores them, even television bores them.   —ARTHUR MILLER
>
> One is the reality; the other is the symbol.   —NANCY HALE

Note 2: The comma is used to separate a statement from a tag question:

> He votes, doesn't he? [affirmative statement, negative question]
>
> You can't change it, can you? [negative statement, affirmative question]

■ **Exercise 1**   Connect each pair of sentences below in two ways, first with a semicolon and then with one of these coordinating conjunctions: *and, but, for, or, nor, so,* or *yet.*

EXAMPLE

I could have walked up the steep trail. I preferred to rent a horse.

  a. *I could have walked up the steep trail; I preferred to rent a horse.*

  b. *I could have walked up the steep trail, but I preferred to rent a horse.*

1. Dexter goes hunting. He carries his Leica instead of his Winchester.
2. The stakes were high in the political game. She played to win.
3. The belt was too small for him. She had to exchange it.
4. At the drive-in, they watched the musical comedy on one screen. We enjoyed the horror movie on the other.

■ **Exercise 2**   Use a subordinating conjunction (see the list on page 25) to combine each of the four pairs of sentences in Exercise 1. For the use of the comma, refer to **12b**.

EXAMPLE
Although I could have walked up the steep trail, I preferred to rent a horse.

■ **Exercise 3**   Proofread the following sentences (selected and adapted from *National Geographic*). Place a checkmark after a sentence with a comma splice and an X after a fused sentence. Do not mark correctly punctuated sentences.

1. The second-home craze has hit hard, everyone wants a piece of the wilderness.
2. The orchid needs particular soil microbes those microbes vanished when the virgin prairie was plowed.
3. Ty fought back the urge to push hard on the accelerator, which might have wrecked or disabled the van on the rough road.
4. Attempts to extinguish such fires have often failed some have been burning for decades.
5. Some of them had never seen an automobile, the war had bred familiarity with aircraft.
6. When the mining machines rumbled away, the ruined mountain was left barren and ugly.
7. The winds lashed our tents all night, by morning we had to dig ourselves out from under a snowdrift.
8. South Pass country is still short on roads and people, and so I was delighted to discover an experienced guide in Charley Wilson, son of Pony Express rider Nick Wilson.
9. The song that awakened me carried an incredible sense of mournfulness, it seemed to be the prolonged cry of a lone animal calling in the night.
10. I had thought that the illegal aliens headed mostly to farms, a sub-rosa international work force consigned to the meanest stoop labor, some do, but many bring blue-collar skills to the cities.

■ **Exercise 4**   Use various methods of revision (see page 41) as you correct the comma splices or fused sentences in Exercise 3.

3b

Be sure to use a semicolon before a conjunctive adverb or transitional phrase placed between main clauses. See also 14a.

COMMA SPLICE   TV weather maps have various symbols, for example, a big apostrophe means drizzle.

REVISED   TV weather maps have various symbols; for example, a big apostrophe means drizzle.   **[MAIN CLAUSE;** *transitional expression,* **MAIN CLAUSE.]**

FUSED SENTENCE   The tiny storms cannot be identified as hurricanes therefore they are called neutercanes.

REVISED   The tiny storms cannot be identified as hurricanes; therefore they are called neutercanes.
[MAIN CLAUSE; *conjunctive adverb* **MAIN CLAUSE.]**

Below is a list of frequently used conjunctive adverbs and transitional phrases; they function as both an adverb and a conjunctive:

CONJUNCTIVE ADVERBS

also	incidentally	nonetheless
anyway	indeed	otherwise
besides	instead	still
consequently	likewise	then
finally	meanwhile	therefore
furthermore	moreover	thus
hence	nevertheless	
however	next	

TRANSITIONAL PHRASES

after all	even so	in the second place
as a result	for example	on the contrary
at any rate	in addition	on the other hand
at the same time	in fact	
by the way	in other words	

Expressions such as *that is* and *what is more* also function as adverbials connecting main clauses:

> The new members have paid their dues; **what is more**, they are all eager to work hard for our organization.

Conjunctive adverbs and transitional phrases are not grammatically equivalent to coordinating conjunctions. A coordinating conjunction has a fixed position between the main clauses it links, but many conjunctive adverbs and transitional phrases may either begin the second main clause or take another position in it:

> She doubted the value of daily meditation, **but** she decided to try it. [The coordinating conjunction has a fixed position.]
>
> She doubted the value of daily meditation; **however,** she decided to try it. [The conjunctive adverb begins the second main clause.]
>
> She doubted the value of daily meditation; she decided, **however,** to try it. [The conjunctive adverb appears later in the clause.]

Caution: Do not let a divided quotation trick you into making a comma splice.

COMMA SPLICE	"Marry her," Martin said, "after all, she's very rich."
REVISED	"Marry her," Martin said. "After all, she's very rich."
COMMA SPLICE	"Who won?" Elizabeth asked, "what was the score?"
REVISED	"Who won?" Elizabeth asked. "What was the score?"

Compare:

CORRECT	"The Rams led at the half," she said, "by twenty-one points." [See **12d(3)**.]
CORRECT	"The Rams led at the half," she said. "By twenty-one points." [See **9e**.]

■ **Exercise 5**   Connect each pair of sentences below, following the pattern of the example.

EXAMPLE

At first the slogan shocked. After a year or two, however, it became a platitude.

At first the slogan shocked; however, after a year or two it became a platitude.

1. The art company sent a sample collection of famous American paintings. The work of Norman Rockwell, however, was carelessly omitted.
2. The loud arguments sounded convincing. The majority, therefore, voted for the motion.
3. I don't mind lending him money. He is, after all, my favorite cousin.
4. India is not poor. It has, as a matter of fact, a huge amount of coal and iron reserves.

■ **Exercise 6**   Divide the following quotations without creating a comma splice, as shown in the example below.

EXAMPLE

Eric Sevareid has said, "Let those who wish compare America with Rome. Rome lasted a thousand years."

"Let those who wish compare America with Rome," Eric Sevareid has said. "Rome lasted a thousand years."

1. "I never saw her again. In fact, no one ever saw her again," wrote Kenneth Bernard.
2. W. C. Fields once said, "I am free of all prejudice. I hate everyone equally."
3. "I am saddest when I sing. So are those who hear me," Artemus Ward commented.
4. Gene Marine asked ironically, "What good is a salt marsh? Who needs a swamp?"
5. Pablo Picasso stated, "There is no abstract art. You must always start with something. Afterward you can remove all traces of reality."

■ **Exercise 7**   Correct the comma splices and fused sentences in the following paragraph. Do not revise a correctly punctuated sentence.

[1] "Age is just a frame of mind," Nellie often says, "you're as old or as young as you think you are." [2] Does she really believe this, or is she just making conversation? [3] Well, when she was sixteen, her father said, "Baby Nell, you're not old enough to marry Johnny, besides he's a Democrat." [4] So Nellie ran away from her Missouri home in Oklahoma she found another Democrat, Frank, and married him. [5] When Nellie was thirty-nine, Frank died. [6] A year later she shocked everyone by marrying a Texan named William, he was a seventy-year-old veteran of the Spanish-American War. [7] "Billy thinks young," Nellie explained, "and he's just as young as he thinks he is." [8] Maybe she was right that happy marriage lasted eighteen years. [9] Nellie celebrated her seventieth birthday by going to Illinois, there she married Tom, who in her opinion was a youngster in his late sixties. [10] But her third marriage didn't last long, because Tom soon got hardening of the arteries and died of a heart attack, however, Nellie's arteries were fine. [11] In 1975, when Nellie was eighty-three, she found and finally married her old Missouri sweetheart, then eighty-seven-year-old Johnny whisked her away to his soybean farm in Arkansas. [12] Nellie's fourth wedding made front-page news, and then the whole town echoed Nellie's words: "Life doesn't begin at sixteen or at forty. It begins when you want it to, age is just a frame of mind."

■ **Exercise 8**   First review Section **2** and study Section **3**. Then proofread the following for sentence fragments, comma splices, and fused sentences. Make appropriate revisions. Put a checkmark after each sentence that needs no revision.

1. Juan first enrolled for morning classes only, then he went job-hunting.
2. The cabin was originally built to house four people a family of ten lives in it now. Not to mention all the dogs and cats.
3. Becky signed up for the swimming relay, however, she is not really interested in competitive sports.

cs/fs **3b**

4. The Optimists Club sponsors a flea market every year, it is not, however, an easy way to make money.
5. Edgar Allan Poe attended West Point, where he was not a success.
6. Mr. Jordan requires us clerks to be on time for work. The reason being that bargain hunters start shopping early, almost before the doors open.
7. Our choir will go to Holland in May, when the tulip gardens are especially beautiful.
8. A long article in the magazine describes botulism, this is just another name for food poisoning.
9. That is absurd. It's nonsense. An argument that is riddled with stupid assumptions.
10. After class, I often drop by the college bookstore. Usually buying best-selling paperbacks, then never getting around to reading any of them.

Adjectives and Adverbs

4

Distinguish between adjectives and adverbs and use the appropriate forms.

Adjectives and adverbs function as modifiers; that is, they qualify or restrict the meaning of other words. Adjectives modify nouns and pronouns. Adverbs modify verbs (or verbals), adjectives, and other adverbs.

ADJECTIVES	ADVERBS
the **sudden** change	changed **suddenly**
a **probable** cause	**probably** caused
an **unusual, large** one	an **unusually** large one

The -*ly* ending can be an adjective-forming suffix as well as an adverb-forming one.

NOUNS TO ADJECTIVES   earth—earthly, ghost—ghostly
ADJECTIVES TO ADVERBS   rapid—rapidly, lucky—luckily

A number of words ending in -*ly* (such as *deadly, cowardly*), as well as many not ending in -*ly* (such as *far, fast, little, well*), may function either as adjectives or as adverbs. Some adverbs have two forms (such as *loud, loudly; quick, quickly; slow, slowly*).

When in doubt about the correct form of a given modifier—such as *slow* or *slowly*—consult your dictionary. Look for the labels *adj.* and *adv.* and for examples of usage. Read any usage notes.

> I drove through the water **slowly.** Fry it **slowly.**
> Drive **slow.** Fry it **slow.** [limited usage]

Also consult your dictionary when in doubt about the forms of comparison and their spellings.

Present and past participles function as adjectives: "a *startling* comment," "the *startled* coach." Do not carelessly omit the *-d* or *-ed* of a past participle: "injured players," "a prejudiced person," "the experienced driver."

Caution: Do not use the double negative: see also page 541.

> NONSTANDARD   They don't have no home.
> STANDARD   They don't have any home.
>   OR   They have no home.

4a

Use adverbs to modify verbs, adjectives, and other adverbs.

> His clothes fit him **perfectly.**   [The adverb modifies the verb *fit.*]
> We have a **reasonably** secure future.   [The adverb modifies the adjective *secure.*]
> Jean eats **exceptionally** fast.   [The adverb *exceptionally* modifies the adverb *fast.*]

Most dictionaries still label the following as informal usage: *sure* for *surely, real* for *really,* and *good* for the adverb *well.*

> INFORMAL   I played **good.**
> GENERAL   I played **well.**   [appropriate in both formal and informal usage]

■ **Exercise 1** In the phrases below, convert adjectives into adverbs, following the pattern of the examples.

> EXAMPLE
> abrupt reply   *replied abruptly* [OR *abruptly replied*]

1. vague answer   3. fierce fight   5. hearty welcome
2. safe travel   4. quick refusal   6. blind conformity

> EXAMPLE
> complete happiness   *completely happy*

7. clear possibility   9. sudden popularity
8. unusual anger   10. strange sadness

■ **Exercise 2** In the following sentences, convert any non-standard or informal modifier into an adverb form. Put a checkmark after each sentence that needs no revision.

1. A pocket calculator sure does help.
2. He took the joke serious.
3. Our team played well but did not win.
4. He was lucky to escape as easy as he did.
5. I do not practice as regular as I should.
6. It all happened very sudden.
7. The price will probable come down eventually.
8. Last night Venus seemed exceptional bright.
9. He talks very loudly when he is not sure of himself.
10. My notes are hard to read when I have to write that rapid.

4b

Use adjectives (not adverbs) for complements modifying the subject or the object. See 1b.

As subject complements (predicate adjectives), adjectives always modify the subject. Subject complements are used with such verbs as *feel, look, smell, sound,* and *taste,* which are called *linking verbs* when they connect a subject with its predicate adjective.

The soup tastes **different** with these herbs in it.
The speech sounded **bold**.

As object complements, adjectives always modify the object.

These herbs make the soup **different**.
He considered the speech **bold**.

Note: Both *bad* and *badly* are now standard when used with *feel* as a subject complement, but writers generally prefer *bad: They felt bad.*

Compare the meaning of the adjectives and adverbs below.

Jo looked **angry** to me.   [adjective—subject complement]
Jo looked **angrily** at me.   [adverb modifying *looked*]
He considered Jane **happy**.   [adjective—object complement]
He considered Jane **happily**.   [adverb modifying *considered*]

■ **Exercise 3**   Using adjectives as complements, write two sentences that illustrate each of the following patterns.

    Subject—linking verb—subject complement.

    Subject—verb—direct object—object complement.

4c

Use the appropriate forms for the comparative and the superlative.

In general, the shorter adjectives (and a few adverbs) form the comparative degree by adding *-er* and the superlative by adding *-est.* The longer adjectives and most adverbs form the comparative by the use of *more* (*less*) and the superlative by the use of *most* (*least*). A few modifiers have irregular comparatives and superlatives.

POSITIVE	COMPARATIVE	SUPERLATIVE
warm	warmer	warmest
warmly	more warmly	most warmly
helpful	less helpful	least helpful
good, well	better	best
bad, badly	worse	worst

Many writers prefer to use the comparative degree for two persons or things and the superlative for three or more:

COMPARATIVE   Was Monday or Tuesday **warmer**?
James was the **taller** of the two.

SUPERLATIVE   Today is the **warmest** day of the year.
William was the **tallest** of the three.

Caution: Do not use a double comparative or superlative: NOT more busier BUT busier; NOT least busiest BUT least busy.

Note: Current usage, however illogical it may seem, accepts comparisons of many adjectives or adverbs with absolute meanings, such as "a *more perfect* society," "the *deadest* campus," and "*less completely* exhausted." But many writers make an exception of *unique*—using "*more nearly* unique" rather than "more unique." They consider *unique* an absolute adjective—one without degrees of comparison.

Be sure to make your comparisons complete: see **22c**.

4d

Avoid awkward or ambiguous use of a noun form as an adjective.

Many noun forms are used effectively to modify other nouns (as in *boat* race, *show* business, *college* student and so on), especially when appropriate adjectives are not available. But

such forms should be avoided when they are either awkward
or confusing.

AWKWARD   Many candidates entered the president race.
BETTER   Many candidates entered the presidential race.
CONFUSING The Representative Landor recess maneuvers led
           to victory.
BETTER   Representative Landor's maneuvers during the
           recess led to victory.

■ **Exercise 4**   Correct all errors in the use of adjectives or adverbs. Also eliminate any awkward use of nouns as adjectives.
Put a checkmark after any sentence that needs no revision.

1. The repair estimates mechanic was out to lunch.
2. She was even more livelier than her daughter.
3. The class enjoyed writing autobiography compositions.
4. The magazine has been published continuous since 1951,
   but it does not sell good now.
5. Baseball is more easy followed than football.
6. The older of the two is doing well in school.
7. Maribeth lives in a reasonable exclusive Kansas City resi-
   dent area.
8. That food, I thought, can't taste as bad as it looks.
9. That is the worse grade I have ever received.
10. The recession and inflation kept getting worser.

Case

5

Choose the case form that shows the function of pronouns or nouns in sentences.

Case refers to the form of a word that indicates its use in a sentence as the subject of a verb, the object of a preposition, and so on. The English language has three cases: subjective, possessive, objective. Most nouns, many indefinite pronouns, and the personal pronouns *it* and *you* have a distinctive case form only for the possessive: *Rebecca's* coat, *someone's* dog, *its* color, *your* hands: see **15a**. But six common pronouns—*I, we, he, she, they, who*—have distinctive forms in all three cases:

Case forms

SUBJECTIVE	I	we	he, she	they	who
POSSESSIVE	my	our	his, her	their	whose
	(mine)	(ours)	(hers)	(theirs)	
OBJECTIVE	me	us	him, her	them	whom

SUBJECTIVE CASE   *I, we, he, she, they, who*

Frank and **I** met in Paris.   [subject of verb]
The only ones on stage were Lola and **she**.   [subject complement]

Morris met the man **who** invented it. [subject in clause—
see **5b**]

These people—**he** and **they**—remained silent. [appositives
identifying the subject—see **5a**]

Subjects of verbs (but not of infinitives) are put in the subjective case.

POSSESSIVE CASE *my, our, his, her, their, whose, its,*
your, mine, ours, hers, theirs, yours

Their dog finally learned to obey **its** master. [before a noun]

Theirs is better than **ours** is. [in the noun position]

Whose car did Terry drive? [before a noun]

His telling the story was a good idea. [before a gerund—
see **5d**]

Note: The possessive forms *his* and *their* are nonstandard
when made a part of a *-self* pronoun. Use *himself, themselves.* (See also *myself:* **19i**, page 238.)

OBJECTIVE CASE *me, us, him, her, them, whom*

Fran likes Glenda and **me**. [direct object]

Weston sends **them** a package now and then. [indirect
object]

The man did check the tires for **us**. [object of preposition]

Potter, for **whom** the party was given, did not want to make a
speech. [object of preposition in clause—see **5c**]

The officer ticketed us both, Rita and **me**. [appositive identifying the object of the verb, the pronoun *us*—see **5a**]

Our guests expected **us** to entertain **them**. [subject and object of the verbal *to entertain,* an infinitive—see **5e**]

Ignoring Hank and **me**, the twins talked about old times.
[object of the verbal *ignoring,* a participle]

Note: Use *who, whose,* or *whom* [NOT *which*] to refer to people: see page 245.

CASE IN COMBINED SENTENCES

Observe that the case (subjective or objective) of the italicized pronouns does not change when the following pairs of sentences are combined.

> **We** need this.   We are students.
> **We** students need this.

> Don told **us** that.
> Don told **us** students that.

> [The insertion of a plural noun after the boldface pronoun does not affect the form of the pronoun.]

> My wife saw it.   **I** saw it.
> My wife and **I** saw it.

> He wrote to Al.   He wrote to **me**.
> He wrote to Al and **me**.

> [See also **5a**. Formal English does not accept *myself* as a substitute for *me* or *I:* see **19i**, page 238.]

> **I** eat fast.   She eats faster.
> She eats faster than **I**.

> I met Ed.   I think **he** is shy.
> I met Ed, **who** I think is shy.

> [See also **5b**.]

> Then I called on Warren.   I can always depend on **him**.
> Then I called on Warren, **whom** I can always depend on.   [OR on whom I can always depend]

> [See also **5c**.]

Observe the change in the case of the boldface pronouns in these sentences:

> **I** grew up fast.   New responsibilities caused this.
> New responsibilities caused **me** to grow up fast.
> [*I* is subject of *grew up* (verb with particle); *me* is subject of *to grow up* (an infinitive). See **5e**.]

He smokes a smelly pipe.   She complains about it.
She complains about **his** smoking a smelly pipe.
[*He* is subject of *smokes* (a verb). *His* (the possessive case) is
    used before *smoking* (a gerund). See **5d** and page 542.]

In sentences such as the following, subjects and subject complements are interchangeable.

You and I are the losers.   The losers are **you and I**.
[See also **5f**.]

5a

**Take special care with pronouns in compound con-
structions (including compound appositives).**

She and her brother played golf.   [subject]
Clara may ask **you or me** about it.   [object of verb]
They sat in front of **her and me**.   [object of preposition]
My best friends are **Bob and he**.   [subject complement—see
    5f]

Notice below that the form of the pronoun used as an appositive depends on the function of the noun that the appositive
explains or identifies.

Two members of the cast, **he and I**, assist the director.
[Compare "*He and I,* members of the cast, assist the
    director."]

The director often calls on her assistants: **him and me**.
[Compare "The director often calls on *him and me,* her
    assistants."]

In general usage, *me* is the appropriate form in the expression *Let's you and me* (although *Let's you and I* is used informally). Compare "Let *us*—just you and *me*." Be sure to use
objective pronouns as objects of prepositions:

between you and **me**	like you and **me**
for you and **her**	to her brother and **her**
except Elmer and **him**	with Carla and **him**

■ **Exercise 1**   Choose the correct pronoun within the parentheses in each sentence below.

1. (He, Him) and (I, me) wrote and directed three one-act plays.
2. Joe and (I, me, myself) arrived an hour early.
3. It was Oliver and (they, them) who volunteered to address the envelopes.
4. (He, Him) and his brother are looking for part-time jobs.
5. Between Charlotte and (she, her) there is a friendly rivalry.
6. Mr. Rodriguez will hire a new engineer, either Williams or (he, him).
7. Leaving James and (he, him) at home, they went to the airport to meet the actor and (she, her).
8. My family and (I, me, myself) expected Frank and (she, her) to support (theirselves, themselves).
9. Two players on our team, Tom and (he, him), talked with the coach after the game.
10. After the game the coach talked with two players on our team, Tom and (he, him).

5b

Determine the case of each pronoun by its use in its own clause.

(1) *Who* or *whoever* as the subject of a clause

The subject of a verb in a subordinate clause takes the subjective case, even when the whole clause is used as an object:

> I forgot **who** won the Superbowl in 1980.   [In its own clause, *who* is the subject of the verb *won*. The complete clause *who won the Superbowl in 1980* is the object of the verb *forgot.*]
> He has respect for **whoever** is in power.   [*Whoever* is the subject of *is*. The complete clause *whoever is in power* is the object of the preposition *for.*]

(2) *Who* or *whom* before *I think, he says,* and so on

Such expressions as *I think, he says, she believes,* and *we know* may follow either *who* or *whom.* The choice depends on the use of *who* or *whom* in its own clause:

> Gene is a man **whom** we know well. [*Whom* is the direct object of *know.* Compare "We know him well."]
> Gene is a man **who** we know is honest. [*Who* is the subject of the second *is.* Compare "We know that Gene is a man *who* is honest."]

(3) Pronoun after *than* or *as*

In sentences such as the following, which have implied (rather than stated) elements, the choice of the pronoun form is important to meaning:

> She admires Kurt more than **I**. [meaning "more than I do"]
> She admires Kurt more than **me**. [meaning "more than she admires me"]
>
> He talks about food as much as **she**. [meaning "as much as she does"]
> He talks about food as much as **her**. [meaning "as much as he talks about her"]

Formal usage still requires the use of the subjective case of pronouns in sentences such as the following:

> Mr. Ames is older than **I**. [Compare "older than I am."]
> Aristotle is not so often quoted as **they**. [Compare "as they are."]

■ **Exercise 2** In sentences 1, 2, and 3 below, insert *I think* after each *who;* then read each sentence aloud. Notice that *who,* not *whom,* is still the correct case form. In sentences 4 and 5, complete each comparison by using first *they* and then *them.* Prepare to explain the differences in meaning.

1. George Eliot, who was a woman, wrote *Adam Bede.*
2. It was Elizabeth Holland who served as the eighth president of the university.
3. Maugham, who was an Englishman, died in 1965.
4. My roommate likes you as much as _____ .
5. The director praised her more than _____ .

5c

In formal writing use *whom* for all objects. See also **5b.**

In sentences:

> **Whom** do they recommend?   [object of the verb *do recommend*]
>
> For **whom** did the board of directors vote?   [object of the preposition *for*]
>
> Danny told Chet **whom** to call. Danny told Chet to call **whom**?   [object of the infinitive *to call*—see also **5e**]

In subordinate clauses:

> The artist **whom** she loved has gone away.   [object of the verb *loved* in the adjective clause]
>
> This is a friend **whom** I write to once a year.   [object of the preposition *to* in the adjective clause]

Formal and informal English accept the omission of *whom* in sentences such as the following:

> The artist she loved has gone away.
>
> This is a friend I write to once a year.

Note: Informal English accepts *who* rather than *whom*, except after a preposition:

> Who do they recommend?   She told me who to call.

■ **Exercise 3**   Using the case form in parentheses, convert each pair of sentences below into a single sentence.

EXAMPLES

I understand the daredevil. He motorcycled across the Grand Canyon.   (*who*)

I understand the daredevil who motorcycled across the Grand Canyon.

Evelyn consulted an astrologer. She had met him in San Francisco.   (*whom*)

Evelyn consulted an astrologer whom she had met in San Francisco.

1. Hercule Poirot is a famous detective. Agatha Christie finally kills him off in *Curtain.*   (*whom*)
2. Some parents make an introvert out of an only child. They think they are protecting their offspring.   (*who*)
3. Does anyone remember the name of the Frenchman? He built a helicopter in 1784.   (*who*)
4. One of the officials called for a severe penalty. The players had quarreled with the officials earlier.   (*whom*)

■ **Exercise 4**   Formalize usage by changing *who* to *whom* when the pronoun functions as an object. Put a checkmark after sentences containing *who* correctly used as the subject of a verb or as a subject complement.

1. Who do they suspect?
2. Who could doubt that?
3. He knows who they will promote.
4. He knows who will be promoted.
5. The witness who the lawyer questioned next could remember nothing.
6. Guess who I ran into at the airport.
7. No one cares who they are or what they stand for.
8. In a crowded emergency room she knows exactly who to help first.
9. To find out who deceived who, be sure to tune in for the next episode.
10. During registration whoever I asked for directions gave me a map of the campus.

5d

As a rule, use the possessive case immediately before a gerund.

> I resented **his** criticizing our every move. [Compare "I resented his criticism, not him."]
>
> **Harry's** refusing the offer was a surprise. [Compare "Harry's refusal was a surprise."]

The *-ing* form of a verb can be used as a noun (gerund) or as an adjective (participle). The possessive case is not used before participles:

> **Caroline's** radioing the Coast Guard solved our problem. [*Radioing* is a gerund. Compare "*Her action* solved our problem."]
>
> The **man** sitting at the desk solved our problem. [*Sitting* is a participle. Compare "*He* solved our problem."]

Note: Do not use an awkward possessive before a gerund.

> AWKWARD The board approved of something's being sent to the poor overseas.
>
> BETTER The board approved of sending something to the poor overseas.

5e

Use the objective case for the subject or the object of an infinitive.

> They expected Nancy and **me** to do the scriptwriting. [subject of the infinitive *to do*]
>
> I did not want to challenge Victor or **him**. [object of the infinitive *to challenge*]

5f

Use the subjective case for the complement of the verb *be*.

It was **she** who called. [Compare "She was the one who called."]

The man who will get all the credit is no doubt Blevins or **he**. [Compare "Blevins or he is no doubt the man who will get all the credit."]

It's me (him, her, us, and *them)* is standard in informal speech or writing:

If there had to be just one saved, I'm glad it was him.
—JAMES HERRIOT

But many writers avoid this structure.

■ **Exercise 5**   Find and revise in the sentences below all case forms that would be inappropriate in formal writing. Put a checkmark after each sentence that needs no revision.

1. I soon became acquainted with Ruth and her, whom I thought were agitators.
2. It was Doris and she who I blamed for me not making that sale.
3. Jack's racing the motor did not hurry Tom or me.
4. Between you and I, I prefer woodblock prints.
5. Who do you suppose will ever change Earth to Eden?
6. Since Joan eats less than I, I weigh more than she.
7. Let's you and I plan the curriculum of an ideal university.
8. The attorney who I interviewed yesterday is going to make public the records of three men who she believes are guilty of tax evasion.
9. We players always cooperate with our assistant coach, who we respect and who respects us.
10. The librarian wanted us—Kurt Jacobs and I—to choose Schlesinger's *The Bitter Heritage.*

Agreement

6

Make a verb agree in number with its subject; make a pronoun agree in number with its antecedent.

Verb and subject

In sentences such as those below, the forms of the verb and the subject (a noun or a noun substitute) agree grammatically:

SINGULAR   The **list** of items **was** long.
PLURAL   The **lists** of items **were** long.

Singular subjects take singular verbs (*list was*), and plural subjects take plural verbs (*lists were*).

The *-s* (or *-es*) suffix

Remember that *-s* (or *-es*) is (1) a plural-forming suffix for most nouns and (2) a singular-forming suffix for verbs—those present-tense verbs taking third-person singular subjects.

THIRD-PERSON SUBJECTS WITH PRESENT-TENSE VERBS

SINGULAR	PLURAL
The bell rings.	The bells ring.
The rope stretches.	The ropes stretch.

SINGULAR	PLURAL
The church remains.	The churches remain.
A hero doesn't.	Heroes don't.

All present-tense verbs change form to agree with third-person singular subjects: *I remain, he remains; I do, it does; I have, she has.* (See also **person**, page 550.) The verb *be* is the most irregular verb in the language: *I am, you are, she is* (present); *I was, you were, he was* (past). (See also **conjugation**, pages 535–36.)

Probably the best way for you to eliminate errors in subject-verb agreement in your writing is to proofread carefully. But if you find it difficult to distinguish verbs and relate them to their subjects, review **1a**.

Pronoun and antecedent

As a rule, a pronoun and its antecedent (the word the pronoun refers to) also agree in number:

SINGULAR   Even an **animal** has **its** own territory.
PLURAL   Even **animals** have **their** own territory.

Singular antecedents are referred to by singular pronouns (*animal* ← *its*); plural antecedents, by plural pronouns (*animals* ← *their*). See also Section **28**.

Note: A pronoun also agrees with its antecedent in person and in gender. Lack of agreement in person causes a shift in point of view: see **27b**.

NOT   **One** reads for pleasure during **our** spare time. [shift from third person to first person]

BUT   **We** read for pleasure during **our** spare time. [first person]

OR   **You** read for pleasure during **your** spare time. [second person]

OR   **People** read for pleasure during **their** spare time. [third person]

Agreement in gender is usually easy and natural: "the *boy* and *his* dog," "the *girl* and *her* dog." The masculine pronoun may be used to refer to common gender:

> **One** reads for pleasure if **he** has the time.

Two pronouns may refer to paired antecedents of different genders: "Every father and mother makes *his* or *her* mistakes." See also page 74.

6a
Make a verb agree in number with its subject.

(1) Do not be misled by nouns or pronouns intervening between the subject and the verb or by subjects and verbs with endings difficult to pronounce.

> The **repetition** of the drumbeats **helps** to stir emotions.
> Every **one** of you **is invited** to the panel discussion.
>
> **Scientists** sift the facts.
> The **scientist asks** several pertinent questions.

As a rule, the grammatical number of the subject is not changed by the addition of expressions beginning with such words as *accompanied by, along with, as well as, in addition to, including, no less than, not to mention, together with*.

> **Unemployment** as well as taxes **influences** votes.
> **Taxes**, not to mention unemployment, **influence** votes.

(2) Subjects joined by *and* are usually plural.

> My **parents** and my **uncle do** not **understand** this.
> The **band** and the **team were leading** the parade.
> **Building a good marriage** and **building a good log fire are** similar in many ways. —JOSEPHINE LOWMAN [gerund phrases—Compare "Two actions are similar."]

Exceptions: Occasionally, such a compound subject takes a singular verb because the subject denotes one person or a single unit.

> Its **inventor** and chief **practitioner is** a native son of Boston, Robert Coles. —MARTHA BAYLES
>
> **Pushing** and **shoving** in public places **is** characteristic of Middle Eastern culture. —EDWARD T. HALL

Every or *each* preceding singular subjects joined by *and* calls for a singular verb:

> Every silver knife, fork, and spoon **has** to be counted.
> Each cat and each dog **has** its own toy.

Placed after a plural subject, *each* does not affect the verb form. Some writers use a singular verb when *each* follows a compound subject:

> The cat and the dog each **have** their own toys.
> [Or, sometimes, "The cat and the dog each *has* its own toy."]

(3) Singular subjects joined by *or, either . . . or,* or *neither . . . nor* usually take a singular verb.

> Paula or her secretary **answers** the phone on Saturday.
> Either the mayor or the governor **is** the keynote speaker.
> Neither criticism nor praise **affects** them. [Informal "Neither criticism nor praise affect them."]

If one subject is singular and one is plural, the verb usually agrees with the nearer subject:

> Neither the quality nor the prices **have** changed.
> Neither the prices nor the quality **has** changed.
> [Compare "The prices *and* the quality *have not* changed."]

The verb also agrees with the nearer subject in person in sentences like those below. (See also pages 67 and 550.)

Doesn't **he** or I deserve it?   Pat or **you were** supposed to call.

Don't **I** or he deserve it?   You or **Pat was** supposed to call.

(4) Do not let inverted word order (VERB + SUBJECT) or the structure *there* + VERB + SUBJECT cause you to make a mistake in agreement.

VERB + SUBJECT

Hardest hit by the high temperatures and the drought **were** American **farmers.** —TIME

Among our grandest and longest-lived illusions **is** the **notion** of the noble savage. —JOHN PFEIFFER

Neither **do vegetarians** eat only vegetables.
—CONSUMER REPORTS
[Here *neither* is a conjunction meaning *nor yet*. See **6a(6)**.]

There + VERB + SUBJECT

There **were** Vietnam War **protests,** draft-card **burnings,** and civil rights **marches.** —LOUISE LEVATHES

There **were anger** and **hatred** in that voice. —JOHN CIARDI

[Compare "Why *are* there fewer *quasars* now than there *were* in the past?" —ADRIAN WEBSTER (verb + *there* + subject . . . *there* + verb)]

(5) A relative pronoun (*who, which, that*) used as subject has the same number as its antecedent.

It is the **pharmacist who** often **suggests** a new brand.
Tonsillitis is among those **diseases that are** curable.
This is the only **one** of the local papers **that prints** a daily horoscope. [*That* refers to *one* because only one paper prints a daily horoscope; the other papers do not.]

It is not better things but better **people that make** better living. —CARLL TUCKER [Compare "Better people (not better things) make better living."]

(6) When used as subjects, such words as *each, either, neither, one, everybody,* and *anyone* regularly take singular verbs.

Neither likes the friends of the other.
Each of them **does have** political ambitions.
Everybody in the office **has** tickets.

Subjects such as *all, any, half, most, none,* and *some* may take a singular or a plural verb; the context generally determines the choice of the verb form.

Evelyn collects stamps; **some are** worth a lot. [Compare "Some of them are worth a lot."]

The honey was marked down because **some was** sugary. [Compare "Some of it was sugary."]

(7) Collective nouns (and phrases denoting a fixed quantity) take a singular verb when they refer to the group as a unit and take a plural verb when they refer to individuals or parts of the group.

Singular (regarded as a unit)

My **family has** its traditions.
The number is very small.
A **billion dollars is** a lot of money.
The **majority** of it **was** wasted.
Two-thirds of this **has** been finished.

Plural (regarded as individuals or parts)

A number were absent.
The **majority** of us **are** for it.
Two-thirds of these **have** been finished.

OPTIONS

Ten gallons of gas is/are expensive.
A thousand bushels of grain was/were crated.
The data is/are being studied.

(8) A linking verb agrees with its subject, not with its complement (predicate noun).

His **problem is** frequent headaches.
Frequent **headaches are** his problem.

Note: Because the number of the pronoun *what* depends on the number of the word (or word group) referred to, the verb does agree with its complement in sentences like these:

Of course, what you see in the final commercial **are** pretty pictures—the bear in a canoe, the bear in a Jeep, the bear padding behind the man. —JONATHAN PRICE
[Compare "Pretty pictures are what you see."]

What I do, at these times, **is** to change the way the system works. —LEWIS THOMAS
[Compare "That is what I do."]

(9) Nouns plural in form but singular in meaning usually take singular verbs. In all doubtful cases, consult a good dictionary.

Nouns that are regularly treated as singular include *economics, electronics, measles, mumps, news, physics,* and *tactics.*

News **is traveling** faster than ever before.
Physics **has fascinated** my roommate for months.

Some nouns ending in *-ics* (such as *athletics, politics,* and *statistics*) are considered singular when referring to an organized body of knowledge and plural when referring to activities, qualities, or individual facts:

Athletics **is required** of every student. [Compare "Participation in games *is required* of every student."]
Athletics **provide** good recreation. [Compare "Various games *provide* good recreation."]

(10) The title of a single work or a word spoken of as a word, even when plural in form, takes a singular verb.

Romeo and Juliet never **grows** old. [The play, not the characters, never grows old.]
"Autumn Leaves" **is** a beautiful song.
Children certainly **does** have an interesting history.

■ **Exercise 1**   The following sentences are all correct. Read them aloud, stressing the italicized words. If any sentence sounds wrong to you, read it aloud two or three more times so that you will gain practice in saying and hearing the correct forms.

1. The *timing* of these strikes *was* poorly planned.
2. There *are* a few *cookies* and *pickles* left.
3. A *wrench* and a *hubcap were* missing.
4. *Every one* of my cousins, including Larry, *has* brown eyes.
5. Sandy was the *only one* of the singers *who was* off-key.
6. *Doesn't it* make sense?
7. *Each* of the episodes *is* exciting.
8. Every *one* of you *is* invited.
9. *A number* in this group *are* affected.
10. There *were* several *reasons* for this.

■ **Exercise 2**   Choose the correct form of the verb within parentheses in each sentence below. Make sure that the verb agrees with its subject according to the rules of formal English.

1. Neither Anita nor Leon (feels, feel) that the evidence is circumstantial.
2. Tastes in reading, of course, (differs, differ).
3. Every one of the figures (was, were) checked at least twice.
4. A fountain and a hanging basket (adorns, adorn) the entrance.

5. Neither of them ever (asks, ask) for a second helping.
6. There (comes, come) to my mind now the names of the two or three people who were most influential in my life.
7. The booby prize (was, were) green apples.
8. A rustic lodge, as well as a game refuge and fishing waters, (is, are) close by.
9. Hidden cameras, which (invades, invade) the privacy of the unwary few, (provides, provide) entertainment for thousands.
10. The study of words (is, are) facilitated by breaking them down into prefixes, suffixes, and roots.

6b

Make a pronoun agree in number with its antecedent.

A singular antecedent (one that would take a singular verb) is referred to by a singular pronoun; a plural antecedent (one that would take a plural verb) is referred to by a plural pronoun:

SINGULAR   An **actor** during early rehearsals often **forgets his** lines.

PLURAL   **Actors** during early rehearsals often **forget their** lines.

(1) As a rule, use a singular pronoun to refer to such antecedents as *each, either, neither, one, anyone, everybody, a person.*

Each of these companies had **its** books audited.   [NOT *their*]
One has to live with **oneself**.   [NOT *themselves*]

Usage varies regarding the choice of pronoun referring to such antecedents as *everyone* or *a person* when the meaning includes both sexes or either sex (common gender):

A **person** needs to see **his** dentist twice a year.   [OR *his or her*]

Every man and woman shows his/her essence by reaction to the soil.   —ROBERT S. De ROPP

So everybody gets married—unmarried—and married, but they're all married to somebody most of the time.

———MARGARET MEAD

In fact, the fear of growing old is so great that every aged person is an insult and a threat to the society. They remind us of our own death. . . . ———SHARON CURTIN

(2) Two or more antecedents joined by *and* are referred to by a plural pronoun; two or more singular antecedents joined by *or* or *nor* are referred to by a singular pronoun.

Andrew and Roger lost **their** self-confidence.
Did **Andrew or Roger** lose **his** self-confidence?

If one of two antecedents joined by *or* or *nor* is singular and one is plural, the pronoun usually agrees with the nearer antecedent:

Neither the **package nor** the **letters** had reached **their** destination. [*Their* is closer to the plural antecedent *letters*.]
Stray **kittens or** even an abandoned grown **cat** has **its** problems finding enough food to survive long. [*Its* is closer to the singular antecedent *cat*.]

(3) Collective nouns are referred to by singular or plural pronouns, depending on whether the collective noun is used in a singular or plural sense. See also **6a(7)**.

Special care should be taken to avoid treating a collective noun as both singular and plural within the same sentence.

INCONSISTENT	The choir **is** writing **their** own music. [singular verb, plural pronoun]
CONSISTENT	The choir **is** writing **its** own music. [both singular]
CONSISTENT	The group of students **do** not agree on methods, but **they** unite on basic aims. [both plural]

■ **Exercise 3**   Choose the correct pronoun or verb form within parentheses in each sentence below; follow the rules of formal English usage.

1. A number of people, such as Kate Swift and Warren Farrell, (has, have) offered (his, her and his, their) suggestions for a "human" singular pronoun, like *te* for *he or she* to refer to the antecedent *a person*.
2. If any one of the sisters (needs, need) a ride to church, (she, they) can call Trudy.
3. Neither the pilot nor the flight attendants mentioned the incident when (he, they) talked to reporters.
4. The Washington team (was, were) opportunistic; (it, they) took advantage of every break.
5. If the board of directors (controls, control) the company, (it, they) may vote (itself, themselves) bonuses.

■ **Exercise 4**   All the following sentences are correct. Change them as directed in parentheses, revising other parts of the sentence to secure agreement of subject and verb, pronoun and antecedent.

1. Everyone in our Latin class thoroughly enjoys the full hour. (Change *Everyone* to *The students.*)
2. Every activity in that class seems not only instructive but amusing. (Change *Every activity* to *The activities.*)
3. Since the students eat their lunch just before the class, the Latin professor keeps coffee on hand to revive any sluggish thinkers. (Change *the students* to *nearly every student.*)
4. Yesterday one of the students was called on to translate some Latin sentences. (Change *one* to *two.*)
5. We were busily following the oral translation in our textbooks. (Change *We* to *Everyone else.*)
6. One or perhaps two in the class were not paying attention when the student, Jim Melton, said, "Who do you see?" (Use *Two or perhaps only one* instead of *One or perhaps two.*)
7. The Latin professor ordered, "Look at those inflections that indicate case! *Whom! Whom* do you see! Not *who!*" (Change *those inflections* to *the inflection.*)

8. Nobody in the room was inattentive as Jim translated the sentence again: *"Whom* do *youm* see?" (Change *Nobody* to *Few.*)

9. The students, who understood Jim's problem with inflections, were smiling as the professor exclaimed, *"Youm!* Whoever heard of *youm!"* (Change *The students* to *Everyone.*)

10. A student who sometimes poses questions that provoke thought about the nature of language, Jim politely replied, "But, sir, whoever heard of *whom?"* (Change *questions* to *a question.*)

Verb Forms

7

Use the appropriate form of the verb. (See also **6a**.)

Verb forms indicate tense, number and person, voice, and mood.

Tense

Tense refers to the form of the verb that indicates time:

> We often **ask** questions.   [present tense]
> After the lecture we **asked** questions.   [past tense]
>
> I **see** the point now.   [present tense]
> I finally **saw** the point.   [past tense]

The suffix *-ed* or *-d* marks the past tense of regular verbs: *asked, hoped.* Irregular verbs do not form their past tense by the addition of *-ed* or *-d: saw, went, gave, flew.*

Various auxiliary verbs indicate time in verb phrases:

will see	**had** asked	**do** hope	**were** going
can see	**have** asked	**did** hope	**has been** going

There are six tenses. Single-word verbs are used for two of these (the simple present and the simple past), and auxiliary verbs are used for the other four:

SIMPLE TENSES

present:	ask (asks)	see (sees)
past:	asked	saw
future:	will (shall) ask	will (shall) see

PERFECT TENSES

present:	have (has) asked	have (has) seen
past:	had asked	had seen
future:	will (shall) have asked	will (shall) have seen

The six tenses are based on primary forms called principal parts (*see, saw, seen*). See **7a**.

Number and Person

Verb forms also indicate the number of their subjects:

SINGULAR Only one question **was** asked.
PLURAL Many questions **were** asked.

In the present tense, all verbs change form to agree grammatically with third-person singular subjects: *I see, he sees.* See Section **6**, pages 66–67.

Voice

Voice is the form of a transitive verb that indicates whether or not the subject named performs the action denoted by the verb. There are two voices, active and passive. Only transitive verbs have voice. Transitive active verbs take direct objects (see **1b**).

ACTIVE Burglars often **steal** jewelry. [The subject acts. The object is *jewelry.*]

The object of a transitive active verb can usually be converted into the subject of a transitive passive verb. When an active verb is made passive, a form of *be* is used.

PASSIVE Jewelry **is** often **stolen** by burglars. [The prepositional phrase *by burglars* could be omitted.]

Compare the active and the passive forms of the verb *see* in the conjugation on pages 535–36. See also **29d**.

Note: Intransitive verbs do not take objects: see page 12.

> The rookies **did** not **go**.
> Carol **became** an engineer.   [a linking verb with subject complement]

Mood

Verbs change form to indicate mood, or the way an assertion is conceived. There are three moods: indicative, imperative, and subjunctive.

> INDICATIVE   She usually **rents** a car.   [a factual statement]
>   **Does** she usually **rent** a car?   [a question]
>
> IMPERATIVE   **Rent** a car.   [a command or request]
>
> SUBJUNCTIVE   If I **were** she, I **would rent** a car.   [a condition contrary to fact]
>   I suggested that she **rent** a car.   [a recommendation]

See **7c** and **7d**.

Progressive Forms

The English language also has progressive verb forms, which are verb phrases consisting of a form of *be* plus an *-ing* verb (the present participle). These phrases denote an action in progress.

PRESENT	am (is, are) seeing
PAST	was (were) seeing
FUTURE	will be seeing
PRESENT PERFECT	have (has) been seeing
PAST PERFECT	had been seeing
FUTURE PERFECT	will have been seeing

Passive progressive forms include *am (is, are) being seen, was (were) being seen,* and so on.

Note: Infinitives, participles, and gerunds (verbals) also have progressive forms, as well as tense—but not all six tenses.

	Infinitives
PRESENT	to see, to be seen, to be seeing
PRESENT PERFECT	to have seen, to have been seen, to have been seeing

	Participles
PRESENT	seeing, being seen
PAST	seen
PRESENT PERFECT	having seen, having been seen

	Gerunds
PRESENT	seeing, being seen
PRESENT PERFECT	having seen, having been seen

Forms of *be*

Be is the most irregular verb in the English language. This verb has eight forms: *am, are, is, was, were, be, been, being.*

They *are* happy.   That **may be** true.
We **will be leaving** soon.   He *was being* difficult.
His shoulder **had** *been* **injured** before.

Below is a list of forms of *be* used with various subjects in the simple tenses.

PRESENT	I am	you are	he/she/it is	[singular]
	we are	you are	they are	[plural]
PAST	I was	you were	he/she/it was	[singular]
	we were	you were	they were	[plural]
FUTURE	will be OR shall be [all subjects, singular or plural]			

The perfect-tense forms are *have (has) been, had been,* and *will (shall) have been.*

7a

Avoid misusing the principal parts of verbs and confusing similar verbs.

(1) Avoid misusing the principal parts of verbs.

The principal parts of a verb include the *present* form (which is also the stem of the infinitive), the *past* form, and the *past participle*.

PRESENT STEM (INFINITIVE)	PAST TENSE	PAST PARTICIPLE
ask	asked	asked
begin	began	begun

Note: The *present participle* (the present form plus -*ing: asking, beginning*) is sometimes considered as a fourth principal part.

The *present* form may function as a single-word verb or may be preceded by words such as *will, do, may, could, have to, ought to,* or *used to.*

> I **ask**, he **does ask**, we **begin**, it **used to begin**

The *past* form functions as a single-word verb.

> He **asked** questions.
> The show **began** at eight.

The *past participle*, when used as a part of a verb phrase, always has at least one auxiliary.

> they **have asked**, she **was asked**, he **has been asked**
> it **has begun**, the work **will be begun**, we **have begun**

Caution: Do not omit a needed -*d* or -*ed* because of the pronunciation. For example, although it is easy to remember a clearly pronounced -*d* or -*ed* (*faded, repeated*), it is sometimes difficult to remember to add a needed *-d* or *-ed* in such expressions as *hoped to* or *opened the*. Observe the use of the *-ed* or *-d* ending in these sentences:

Yesterday I ask**ed** David.   Then I talk**ed** to her.
Perhaps we had price**d** our vegetables too high.
It had happen**ed** before.   She was not experienc**ed**.
He use**d** to smoke.   I am not suppose**d** to do it.
A judge may be prejudice**d**.   [Compare "a prejudice**d** judge."]

When in doubt about the forms of a verb, consult a good dictionary. (If forms are not listed after an entry, the verb is generally a regular one, taking the *-d* or *-ed* ending.)

The following list gives the principal parts of a number of verbs that are sometimes misused. Give special attention to any forms unfamiliar to you.

Principal Parts of Verbs

PRESENT STEM (INFINITIVE)	PAST TENSE	PAST PARTICIPLE
become	became	become
begin	began	begun
blow	blew	blown
break	broke	broken
bring	brought	brought
burst	burst	burst
catch	caught	caught
choose	chose	chosen
cling	clung	clung
come	came	come
dive	dived OR dove	dived
do	did	done
draw	drew	drawn
drink	drank	drunk
drive	drove	driven
eat	ate	eaten
fall	fell	fallen

PRESENT STEM (INFINITIVE)	PAST TENSE	PAST PARTICIPLE
fly	flew	flown
forgive	forgave	forgiven
freeze	froze	frozen
give	gave	given
go	went	gone
grow	grew	grown
know	knew	known
ride	rode	ridden
ring	rang	rung
rise	rose	risen
run	ran	run
see	saw	seen
shake	shook	shaken
sing	sang OR sung	sung
sink	sank OR sunk	sunk
speak	spoke	spoken
spin	spun	spun
steal	stole	stolen
swear	swore	sworn
swim	swam	swum
swing	swung	swung
take	took	taken
tear	tore	torn
throw	threw	thrown
wear	wore	worn
write	wrote	written

Note: Mistakes with verbs sometimes involve spelling errors. Use care when you write troublesome verb forms such as the following:

PRESENT STEM (INFINITIVE)	PAST TENSE	PAST PARTICIPLE	PRESENT PARTICIPLE
lead	led	led	leading
loosen	loosened	loosened	loosening
lose	lost	lost	losing
pay	paid	paid	paying
study	studied	studied	studying

■ **Exercise 1**   Respond to the questions in the past tense with a past tense verb; respond to the questions in the future tense with a present perfect verb (*have* or *has* + a past participle). Follow the pattern of the examples.

EXAMPLES   Did she criticize Don?   *Yes, she criticized Don.*
Will they take it?   *They have already taken it.*

1. Did he give it away?
2. Will you run a mile?
3. Did the man drown?
4. Will they begin that?
5. Did the wind blow?
6. Will she choose it?
7. Did it really happen?
8. Will the river rise?
9. Did you do that?
10. Will they steal it?
11. Did you spin your wheels?
12. Will they freeze it?
13. Did he cling to that belief?
14. Will they go to the police?
15. Did she know them?
16. Will the fire alarm ring?
17. Did the sack burst?
18. Will he eat it?
19. Did you grow these?
20. Will Bert speak out?

(2) Do not confuse *set* with *sit* or *lay* with *lie*.

Sit means "be seated," and *lie down* means "rest in or get into a horizontal position." To *set* or *lay* something down is to place it or put it somewhere.

Learn the distinctions between the forms of *sit* and *set* and those of *lie* and *lay*.

PRESENT STEM (INFINITIVE)	PAST TENSE	PAST PARTICIPLE	PRESENT PARTICIPLE
(to) sit	sat	sat	sitting
(to) set	set	set	setting
(to) lie	lay	lain	lying
(to) lay	laid	laid	laying

As a rule, the verbs (or verbals) *set* and *lay* take objects; *sit* and *lie* do not.

She had **laid** the book aside.   [*Book* is the object.]
I wanted to **lie** in the sun.   [*To lie* has no object.]
After asking me to **sit** down, she seemed to forget I was there.   [*To sit* has no object.]

Study the examples below, noting the absence of objects.

I did not sit down.	You should lie down.
Al sat up straight.	He lay down awhile.
She had sat too long.	It has lain here a week.
It was sitting here.	The coat was lying there.

Note: Because they take objects, the verbs *set* and *lay* may be passive as well as active.

Somebody **had set** the pup in the cart.   [active]
The pup **had been set** in the cart.   [passive]

We **ought to lay** our prejudices aside.   [active]
Our prejudices **ought to be laid** aside.   [passive]

■ **Exercise 2**   Substitute the correct forms of *sit* and *lie* for the italicized word in each sentence. Follow the pattern of the example. Do not change the tense of the verb.

> EXAMPLE   I *remained* in that position for twenty minutes.
>
> *I **sat** in that position for twenty minutes.*
> *I **lay** in that position for twenty minutes.*

1. Jack doesn't ever want to *get* down.
2. The dog *stayed* near the luggage.
3. The toy soldier has been *rusting* in the yard.
4. He often *sleeps* on a park bench.
5. Has it *been* there all along?

■ **Exercise 3**   Choose the correct verb form within the parentheses.

1. After lunch I wanted to (lie, lay) down for a few minutes.
2. Yesterday we (lay, laid) the rest of the tiles ourselves.
3. The garden hose has (lain, laid) there for weeks.
4. The money for the tickets was still (lying, laying) on my desk.
5. He had just (lain, laid) the child down.
6. Alice and Dawn were (sitting, setting) up watching a late movie.
7. Alice and Dawn were (sitting, setting) up chairs for the concert.

8. They came in and (sat, set) down for a chat.
9. How long had the visitors (sat, set) there?
10. Sometimes I just (sit, set) there and watch the tide come in.

7b

Learn the meaning of tense forms. Use logical tense forms in sequence.

The six tenses are based on the three principal parts of verbs: the *present* (stem of the infinitive—to *see,* to *use*); the *past* (*saw, used*); and the *past participle* (*seen, used*). See **7a**.

(1) Learn the meaning of the six tense forms.

Although tense indicates time (see pages 78–79), the tense forms of verbs do not always agree with divisions of actual time. The present tense, for example, is by no means limited to the present time.

PRESENT TENSE

I **see** what you meant by that remark. [now, present time]
He **uses** common sense. [habitual action]
Human beings **make** mistakes. [a timeless truth]
In the fall of 1939 Hitler **attacks** Poland. [historical present]
Officially winter **begins** next week. [present form (used with the adverbial *next week*) indicating future time]

Note: Auxiliaries indicate present tense in the following verb phrases.

He *does* **use** common sense. [emphatic present]
I *am* **learning** from my mistakes. [a progressive form indicating past, present, and (probably) future time]
Mistakes *are* often **made**. [passive form, habitual action]

PAST TENSE—past time, not extending to the present
I **saw** the accident. [at a definite time before now]
We **used** makeshift tools. [action completed in the past]

Note: Auxiliaries also indicate past tense:

> I *did* see the accident.   [emphatic]
> We *were* using makeshift tools.   [progressive]
> The accident *was* seen by three people.   [passive]
> Talk shows *used to* be worse than they are now.   [Compare "*were* worse then."]

> FUTURE TENSE—at a future time, sometime after now
> He **will see** his lawyer.
> We **will use** a different strategy.

The auxiliary *will* also indicates future time in progressive and passive forms of the verb:

> He **will be seeing** his lawyer.   [progressive]
> A different strategy **will be used**.   [passive]

> PRESENT PERFECT TENSE—sometime before now, up to now
> I **have seen** the movie.   [sometime before now]
> He **has used** his savings wisely.   [up to now]

> PAST PERFECT TENSE—before an indicated time in the past
> She **had seen** me before the game started.
> When he **had used** his savings, he applied for a loan.

Note: Sometimes the simple past is used for the past perfect: "She *saw* me before the game started."

> FUTURE PERFECT TENSE—after now and before an indicated time in the future
> They **will have seen** the report by next week.

Speakers and writers often substitute the simple future for the future perfect:

> They **will see** the report by next week.

Examples of progressive and passive forms in the present perfect tense follow.

> Kevin **has been using** the money wisely.
> The Crawfords **have been seeing** deer in the woods.

The money **has been used** wisely.

Deer **have been seen** in the woods.

Again, the simple future usually replaces the future perfect:

By 1990 they **will have been seeing** their dreams in action. [USUAL: "they *will be seeing*"]

By 1990 their dreams **will have been seen** in action. [USUAL: "their dreams *will be seen* in action"]

■ **Exercise 4**   Be prepared to explain the differences in the meaning of tense forms separated by slashes in the following sentences.

1. It *has rained* / *had rained* for days.
2. Mary *waxed* / *did wax* / *was waxing* the car.
3. Walter *teaches* / *is teaching* Spanish.
4. I *spoke* / *have spoken* to him about this.
5. The Bowens *had sold* / *will have sold* their house by then.
6. Time *passes* / *does pass* / *has passed* / *had been passing* rapidly.
7. In 1840 Thomas Carlyle *calls* / *called* time a great mystery, a miracle.

(2) Use logical tense forms in sequence.

Verbs

Notice in the examples below the relationship of each verb form to actual time:

When the speaker **entered**, the audience **rose**. [Both actions took place at the same definite time in the past.]

I **have ceased** worrying because I **have heard** no more rumors. [Both verb forms indicate action at some time before now.]

When I **had been** at camp four weeks, I **received** word that my application **had been accepted**. [The *had* before *been* indicates a time prior to that of *received*.]

Infinitives

Use the present infinitive to express action occurring at the same time as, or later than, that of the main verb; use the present perfect infinitive for action prior to that of the main verb:

> I would have liked **to live** (NOT *to have lived*) in Shakespeare's time. [present infinitive—for the same time as that of the main verb]
>
> She wanted **to win**. She wants **to win**. [present infinitives—for time later than *wanted* or *wants*]
>
> I would like **to have won** that prize. [present perfect infinitive—for time prior to that of the main verb. Compare "I wish I *had won*."]

Participles

Use the present form of participles to express action occurring at the same time as that of the main verb; use the present perfect form for action prior to that of the main verb:

> **Walking** along the streets, he met many old friends. [The walking and the meeting were simultaneous.]
>
> **Having climbed** that mountain they felt a real sense of achievement. [The climbing took place first; then came their sense of achievement.]

■ **Exercise 5**   Choose the verb form inside parentheses that is the logical tense form in sequence.

1. When the fire sale (ended, had ended), the store closed.
2. Fans cheered as the goal (had been made, was made).
3. The team plans (to celebrate, to have celebrated) tomorrow.
4. We should have planned (to have gone, to go) by bus.
5. (Having finished, Finishing) the test, Leslie left the room.
6. (Having bought, Buying) the tickets, Mr. Selby took the children to the circus.
7. The president had left the meeting before it (had adjourned, adjourned).
8. It is customary for ranchers (to brand, to have branded) their cattle.

9. Marilyn had not expected (to see, to have seen) her cousin at the rally.
10. The pond has begun freezing because the temperature (dropped, has dropped).

7c

Use the subjunctive mood in the few types of expressions in which it is still appropriate.

Distinctive forms for the subjunctive occur only in the present and past tenses of *be* and in the present tense of other verbs used with third-person singular subjects.

INDICATIVE	I **am**, you **are**, he **is**, others **are** [present]
	I **was**, you **were**, he **was**, others **were** [past]
SUBJUNCTIVE	(with all subjects) **be** [present], **were** [past]
INDICATIVE	he **sees**, others **see** [present]
SUBJUNCTIVE	(that) he **see**, (that) others **see** [present]

The subjunctive has been largely displaced by the indicative. Compare the following optional usages:

Suppose he **were** to die.	Suppose he dies.
I will ask that he **do** this.	I will ask him to do this.
It is necessary that she **be** there on time.	She must be there on time.

Especially in formal English, however, the subjunctive is still used to express a contrary-to-fact condition.

> Drive as if every other car on the road **were** out to kill you.
> —ESQUIRE

The subjunctive is required (1) in *that* clauses of motion, resolution, recommendation, command, or demand and (2) in a few idiomatic expressions.

> I move that the report **be** approved.
> Resolved, that dues for the coming year **be** doubled.
> I recommend (order, demand) that the prisoner **see** his lawyer.

I demand (request, insist) that the messenger **go** alone.
If need **be** . . . **Suffice** it to say . . . **Come** what may
   . . . [fixed subjunctive in idiomatic expressions]

■ **Exercise 6**   Prepare for a class discussion of the use of the
subjunctive and of the indicative used informally in the following
sentences.

1. If Linda was here, she would explain everything.
2. We insist that he be punished.
3. I wish that peace were possible.
4. Americans now speak of Spain as though it were just across
   the river.
5. Present-day problems demand that we be ready for any
   emergency.
6. If there was time, I could finish my report.
7. Come what may, we will never choose anarchy.
8. I demand that he make amends.
9. If I were you, I would apply tomorrow.
10. The man acts as though he were the owner.

■ **Exercise 7**   Compose five sentences in which the subjunctive is required.

7d

Avoid needless shifts in tense or mood. See also **27a**.

INCONSISTENT   He **walked** up to me in the cafeteria and **tries**
to start a fight. [Tense shifts from past to present.]

BETTER   He **walked** up to me in the cafeteria and **tried** to start
a fight.

INCONSISTENT   It is necessary to restrain an occasional foolhardy park visitor. If a female bear **were** to mistake his
friendly intentions and **supposes** him a menace to her cubs, he
would be in trouble. [Mood shifts from subjunctive to
indicative.]   But females with cubs **were** only one of the dangers. [a correct sentence if standing alone, but here inconsistent with present tense of preceding sentence and there-

fore misleading]   One **has** to remember that all bears **were** wild animals and not domesticated pets.   [Tense shifts from present to past.]   Though a bear **may seem** altogether peaceable and harmless, he **might** not **remain** peaceable, and he is never harmless.   [Tense shifts from present to past.]   It **is** therefore an important part of the park ranger's duty **to watch** the tourists and above all **don't** let anyone try to feed the bears.   [Mood shifts from indicative to imperative.]

BETTER   It is necessary to restrain an occasional foolhardy park visitor. If a female bear **were** to mistake his friendly intentions and **suppose** him a menace to her cubs, he would be in trouble. But females with cubs **are** only one of the dangers. One **has** to remember that all bears **are** wild animals and not domesticated pets. Though a bear **may seem** altogether peaceable and harmless, he **may** not **remain** peaceable, and he is never harmless. It **is** therefore an important part of the park ranger's duty **to watch** the tourists and above all not **to let** anyone try to feed the bears.

■ **Exercise 8**   In the following passage correct all errors and inconsistencies in tense and mood as well as any other errors in verb usage. Put a checkmark after any sentence that is satisfactory as it stands.

¹ Charles Dickens creates many memorable characters in *David Copperfield.*   ² He give many of his characters names that suggest their personalities.   ³ Mr. Murdstone is unfeeling, Little Emily is shy, and Dr. Strong is virtuous.   ⁴ Dickens also tags his characters with recurring peculiarities of speech; these may even be call their trademarks.   ⁵ For example, Barkis continues to have proposed marriage with these words: "Barkis is willin'."   ⁶ The proud Uriah Heep, a hypocrite, keeps calling himself a humble man.   ⁷ Over and over Mr. Micawber rambled on and then concludes, "In short—"   ⁸ When he owed debts, this character shrugs off what he terms his "pecuniary difficulties."   ⁹ With cheerful certainty, he repeats his favorite prophecy: "Something is bound to turn up."   ¹⁰ Set down and read *David Copperfield* through to become acquainted with these interesting people.

7e

Observe such distinctions as exist between *should* and *would*.

(1) Use *should* to express a mild obligation or a condition.

> I (You, He, We, They) **should** help the needy.
> If I (you, he, we, they) **should** resign, the program would not be continued.

(2) Use *would* to express a customary action.

> I (You, He, We, They) **would** spend hours lying on the beach every summer.

Caution: Do not use *would have* as a substitute for *had*.

> If you **had** (NOT *would have*) arrived earlier, you would have seen the president.

■ **Exercise 9**   Revise any incorrect verb forms in the sentences below. Put a checkmark after any sentence that needs no revision. Prepare to explain the reason for each change you make.

1. If he would have registered later, he would have had night classes.
2. If Leslie enrolled in the class at the beginning, she could have made good grades.
3. A stone lying in one position for a long time may gather moss.
4. The members recommended that all delinquents be fined.
5. It was reported that there use to be very few delinquents.
6. After Douglas entered the room, he sat down at the desk and begins to write rapidly.
7. Until I received that letter, I was hoping to have had a visit from Marty.
8. Follow the main road for a mile; then you need to take the next road on the left.
9. The two suspects could not deny that they had stole the tapes.
10. I would have liked to have been with the team on the trip to New Orleans.

MECHANICS

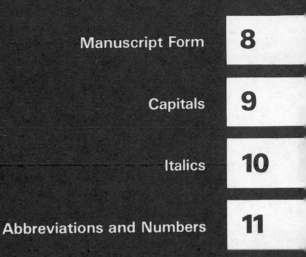

Manuscript Form

8

Put your manuscript in acceptable form. Divide words at the ends of lines according to standard practices. Revise and proofread with care.

8a
Use the proper materials.

Unless you are given other instructions, follow these general practices.

(1) Handwritten papers Use regular notebook paper, size $8\frac{1}{2} \times 11$ inches, with widely spaced lines. (Narrow spaces between lines do not allow sufficient room for corrections.) Use black or blue ink. Write on only one side of the paper.

(2) Typewritten papers Use regular white typing paper (not sheets torn from a spiral notebook), size $8\frac{1}{2} \times 11$ inches. Or use a good grade of bond paper (not onionskin). Use a black ribbon. Double-space between lines. Type on only one side of the paper.

8b

Arrange your writing in clear and orderly fashion on the page.

(1) **Margins** Leave sufficient margins—about an inch and a half at the left and top, an inch at the right and at the bottom—to prevent a crowded appearance. The ruled vertical line on notebook paper marks the left margin.

(2) **Indention** Indent the first lines of paragraphs uniformly, about an inch in handwritten copy and five spaces in typewritten copy.

(3) **Paging** Use Arabic numerals—without parentheses or periods—in the upper right-hand corner to mark all pages after the first.

(4) **Title** *Do not put quotation marks around the title or underline it* (unless it is a quotation or the title of a book), and use no period after the title. Capitalize the first and last words of the title and all other words except articles, short conjunctions, and short prepositions. See also **9c**.

When you do not use a title page, center the title on the page about an inch and a half from the top or on the first ruled line. Leave the next line blank and begin the first paragraph on the third line. In this way the title will stand off from the text. When you do use a title page, attractively space the following information on the separate sheet of paper: the title of your paper, your name, the course title and number, the instructor's name, and the date. See the example on page 473.

(5) **Quoted lines** When you quote over four lines of another's writing to explain or support your ideas, set the quotation off by indention: see **16a(1)** and **(2)** and Section **33**. Acknowledge the source of quotations: see Section **33**, pages 459–67.

(6) Punctuation   Never begin a line with a comma, a colon, a semicolon, or a terminal mark of punctuation; never end a line with the first of a set of brackets, parentheses, or quotation marks.

(7) Identification   Usually papers carry the name of the student, the course title and number, the instructor's name, and the date. Often the number of the assignment is given.

8c

Write or type your manuscript so that it can be read easily and accurately.

(1) Legible handwriting   Form each letter clearly; distinguish between each *o* and *a*, *i* and *e*, *t* and *l*, *b* and *f*. Be sure that capital letters differ from lower-case letters. Use firm dots, not circles, for periods. Make each word a distinct unit. Avoid flourishes.

(2) Legible typing   Before typing your final draft, check the quality of the ribbon and the cleanness of the type. Do not forget to double-space between lines. Do not strike over an incorrect letter; make neat corrections. Leave one space after a comma or a semicolon, one or two after a colon, two after a period, a question mark, or an exclamation point. To indicate a dash, use two hyphens without spacing before, between, or after. Use a pen to insert marks that are not on your typewriter, such as accent marks, mathematical symbols, or brackets.

8d

Whenever possible avoid the division of a word at the end of a line. When a division is necessary, make the break only between syllables and according to standard practices.

You will seldom need to divide words if you leave a reasonably wide right margin. Remember that the reader expects a somewhat uneven right margin but may be distracted or slowed down by a series of word divisions at the ends of consecutive lines.

When you do need to divide a word at the end of a line, use a hyphen to mark the separation of syllables. In college dictionaries, dots usually divide the syllables of words:

   re · al · ly   pre · fer   pref · er · ence

   sell · ing   set · ting

But not every division between syllables is an appropriate place for dividing a word at the end of a line. The following principles are useful guidelines:

(1) One-letter syllables   Do not put the first or last letter of a word at the end or beginning of a line. Do not divide:

   o · mit   a · ble   spunk · y   bo · a

(2) Two-letter endings   Do not put the last two letters of a word at the beginning of a line. Do not divide:

   dat · ed   does · n't   safe · ly   grav · el   tax · is

(3) Misleading divisions   Do not make divisions that may cause a misreading. Do not divide:

   sour · ces   on · ions   an · gel   colo · nel

The red vertical line in the examples of the next three guidelines marks an appropriate end-of-the-line division.

(4) Hyphenated words   Divide hyphenated words only at the hyphen.

> mass-| produced
> father-| in-law   OR   father-in-| law

(5) *-ing* words   Divide words ending in *-ing* between those consonants that you double when adding *-ing*.

> set-| ting   jam-| ming   plan-| ning
> [Compare sell-| ing.]

(6) Consonants between vowels   Divide words between two consonants that come between vowels—except when the division does not reflect pronunciation.

> pic-| nic   dis-| cuss   thun-| der

(7) Abbreviations and acronyms   Do not divide abbreviations, initials, or capitalized acronyms like

> B. A. [degree],   U.S.A.F.,   CBS,   UCLA,   UNESCO.

(8) Caution: Do not divide one-syllable words, such as *twelfth, through,* or *grabbed.*

■ **Exercise 1**   First put a checkmark after the words below that should not be divided at the end of a line; then, with the aid of your dictionary, write out the other words by syllables and insert hyphens followed by a vertical line to indicate appropriate end-of-the-line divisions.

1. cross-reference
2. economic
3. fifteenth
4. NATO
5. gripped
6. gripping
7. guessing
8. against
9. present (gift)
10. present (give)

11. seacoast
12. eventual
13. recline
14. C.P.A.
15. magical

16. WFAA-FM
17. matches
18. dissolve
19. cobwebs
20. cobras

8e

Revise and proofread your manuscript with care.

(1) Revise and proofread your paper before submitting it to the instructor.

When doing in-class papers, use the last few minutes for proofreading and making corrections. When doing out-of-class papers, write a first draft, put the paper aside for a few hours or a day, and then revise it. You will be able to see more objectively what parts need to be expanded or changed.

As you revise, focus your attention on content and style. Use the Reviser's Checklist in Section **32**, page 414. As you proofread, focus your attention on manuscript form—on mechanics, punctuation, spelling. Use the Proofreader's Checklist on the next page.

If only a few changes are needed, the paper may be handed in—after clear, legible corrections have been made—without rewriting. Changes may be made as follows:

(a) Deletion of words

> Billboards ~~along the highway~~
> can save travelers time.

(b) Addition of words

> These samples ^often^ last for weeks.
> They save ^the consumer^ money.

(c) Correction of misspellings, substitution of words

> Those ~~Thoes~~ who ~~dam~~ damn advertising ~~talk~~ stress
> ~~about~~ its disadvantages.

(d) Changes in capitalization and in punctuation

> ᶜgonsumers should appreciate
> advertising, ᵐ₦ot condemn it.

Proofreader's Checklist

1. **Title**   Is there any unnecessary punctuation in the title? Is it centered on the line? Are key words capitalized? See **8b(4)**.

2. **Indention**   Is the first line of each paragraph indented? Is any lengthy quoted passage set off from the text? See · **8b(2)** and **16a(1)–(2)**.

3. **Sentences**   Does each sentence begin with a capital and end with the appropriate end mark? Are there any fragments, comma splices, or fused sentences? See **9e**, **17a–c**, and Sections **2–3**.

4. **Spelling, mechanics**   Are there any misspellings or mistakes in typing or handwriting? Are capitals and underlining (italics) used correctly? Should any abbreviations or numbers be spelled out? See **8c** and Sections **9–11** and **18**.

5. **Punctuation**   Have any end marks been omitted? Are apostrophes correctly placed? Are there any superfluous commas? See Sections **12–17**.

Caution: Do not put words to be deleted in parentheses or make unsightly erasures. Do not forget to use a caret (∧) at the point in the line where an addition is made:

and ∧present for m∧atha.

If extensive changes are necessary, make a full, clean copy to submit to the instructor.

(2) Revise your paper after the instructor has marked it.

One of the best ways to learn how to write is to revise returned papers carefully. Give special attention to any comment on content or style, and become familiar with the numbers or abbreviations used by your instructor to indicate specific errors or suggested changes.

Unless directed otherwise, follow this procedure as you revise a marked paper:

(a) Find in this handbook the exact principle that deals with each error or recommended change.

(b) After the instructor's mark in the margin, write the letter designating the appropriate principle, such as **a** or **c**.

(c) Rather than rewrite the composition, make the corrections on the marked paper. To make the corrections stand out distinctly from the original, use ink of a different color or a no. 2 pencil.

The purpose of this method of revision is to help you not only to understand why a change is desirable but to avoid repetition of the same mistakes.

On the following page are examples of a paragraph marked by an instructor and the same paragraph corrected by a student.

A Paragraph Marked by an Instructor

Those who damn advertising stress its

3   disadvantages, however, it saves consumers time,

labor, and money. Billboards can save travelers

12   time for many billboards tell where to find a meal

18   or a bed. TV commercials announce new labor-saveing

2   products. Such as a spray or a cleaner. In

addition, some advertisers give away free samples

19   of shampoo, toothpaste, soap flakes, and etc.

24   These samples often last for weeks. They save the

consumer money. Consumers should appreciate

advertising, not condemn it.

The Same Paragraph Corrected by a Student

Those who damn advertising stress its

3 b   disadvantages*;* however, it saves consumers time,

labor, and money. Billboards can save travelers

12 a   time*,*for many billboards tell where to find a meal

18 c   or a bed. TV commercials announce new labor-~~saveing~~ *saving*

2 c   products*,* ~~Such~~ *such* as a spray or a cleaner. In

addition, some advertisers give away free samples

19 i   of shampoo, toothpaste, soap flakes, ~~and~~ etc.

24 a   These samples *which* often last for weeks*,* ~~They~~ save the

consumer money. Consumers should appreciate

advertising, not condemn it.

The method of revision shown opposite works equally well if your instructor uses abbreviations or other symbols instead of numbers. In that case, instead of putting **c** after **18**, for example, you would put **c** or **18c** after **sp**.

Individual Record of Errors

You may find that keeping a record of your errors will help you to check the improvement in your writing. A clear record of the symbols on your revised papers will show your progress at a glance. As you write each paper, keep your record in mind; avoid mistakes that have already been pointed out and corrected.

One way to record your errors is to write them down as they occur in each paper, grouping them in columns according to the seven major divisions of the handbook, as illustrated below. In the spaces for paper no. 1 are the numbers and letters from the margin of the revised paragraph on the opposite page. In the spelling column is the correctly spelled word rather than **18c**. You may wish to add on your record sheet other columns for date, grade, and instructor's comments.

RECORD OF ERRORS

Paper No.	Grammar 1–7	Mechanics 8–11	Punctuation 12–17	Words Misspelled 18	Diction 19–22	Effective- ness 23–30	Larger Elements 31–34
1	3b 2c		12a	saving	19i	24a	

■ **Exercise 2**   Proofread the following composition; circle mis-takes. Prepare to discuss in class the changes that you would make.

Programmed People.

A lot of people in the workaday world is a machine—an insensitive, unhearing, unseeing, unthinking, unfeeling mechanism. They act like they are programmed, all their movements or responses triggered by clocks. Take, for example my brother. At 7:30 A.M. he automatically shuts off the alarm, then for the next hour he grumbles and sputter around like the cold, sluggish motor that he is.

On the way to work he did not see the glorious sky or notice ambulance at his neighbor's house. At 8:20 he unlocks his store and starts selling auto parts; however, all mourning long he never once really sees a customers' face. While eating lunch at Joe's cafe, the same music he spent a half dollar for yesterday is playing again. he does not hear it. At one o'clock my brother is back working with invoices and punching at a calculator; The clock and him ticks on and on.

When the hour hand hits five, it pushes the "move" button of my brother: lock store, take bus, pet dog at front door, kiss wife and baby, eat supper, read paper, watch TV, and during the 10-o'clock news he starts his nodding. His wife interrupts his light snoring to say that thier neighbor had a mild heart attach while mowing the lawn. My brother jerks and snorts. Then he mumbles, "Tell me tomorrow. I'm to tired now."

Capitals

9

Capitalize words according to standard conventions. Avoid unnecessary capitals.

A study of the principles in this section should help you use capitals correctly. When special problems arise with individual words or phrases, consult a good recent college dictionary. Dictionary entries of words that are regularly capitalized begin with capitals:

Satanism	Milky Way	Statue of Liberty
Halloween	Library of Congress	Buckeye State

Dictionaries also list capitalized abbreviations, along with options if usage is divided:

Dr., Mrs.	Ph.D.	A.M., a.m., AM
AMA, A.M.A.	M.A.	uhf, UHF

A recent dictionary is an especially useful guide when a trademark (such as *Band-Aid, Frisbee,* or *Kleenex*) begins to function as a common noun (*bandaid, frisbee, kleenex*), and when a generally uncapitalized word is capitalized because of a specific meaning in a given sentence:

These are **mosaic** pictures.   [having a certain design]
These are **Mosaic** laws.   [of or pertaining to Moses]

Most capitalized words fall into three main categories: proper names, key words in titles, and the first words of sentences.

9a

Capitalize proper names, words used as an essential part of proper names, and, usually, derivatives and abbreviations of proper names.

Proper names begin with capitals, but names of classes of persons, places, or things do not:

T. H. Brady, Jr.	on Main Street	the Constitution
a sophomore	a main street	any constitution

(1) Proper names

Capitalize the names of specific persons, places, and things; peoples and their languages; religions and their adherents; members of national, political, racial, social, civic, and athletic groups; geographical names and regions; organizations and institutions; historical documents, periods, and events; calendar designations; trademarks; holy books and words denoting the Supreme Being.

> Tom Evans, Europe, the Olympics, Jews, English
> Christianity, a Christian, Americans, Southern Democrat
> a Methodist, the Jaycees, Detroit Lions, Los Angeles
> Arctic Ocean, the Midwest, the Red Cross, Newman Club
> the U.S. Senate, Indiana University, the Fifth Amendment
> the Middle Ages, the Haymarket Riot, Monday, September
> Labor Day, Masonite, the Bible, Koran, God, Allah, Yahweh

Note 1: Some writers still capitalize pronouns (except *who, whom, whose*) referring to the Deity. Many writers capitalize such pronouns only when the capital is needed to prevent ambiguity, as in the following sentence:

> The Lord commanded the prophet to warn **His** people.

Note 2: Capitalize names of objects, animals, or ideas when they are personified. See also **20a(4)**.

> I could feel **Old Man Time** breathing down the back of my neck.　　　　　　　　　　　　—PATRICK McMANUS

(2) Words used as an essential part of proper names

Words like *college, river, park, memorial, street,* and *company* are capitalized only when they are part of proper names:

Yale University	Cape Cod Bay	Grand Canyon
Long Island City	Madison Avenue	A&M Feed Store

[Compare Norwegian elkhounds, a Honda hatchback, Parkinson's disease, Quaker guns.]

Note: In instances such as the following, capitalization depends on word placement:

> on the Erie and Huron lakes　　　on Lakes Erie and Huron

(3) Derivatives

Words derived from proper names are usually capitalized:

> Americanize　　Israelite　　Stalinism　　Arabic　　Orwellian

(4) Abbreviations

As a rule, capitalize abbreviations of (or acronyms formed from) capitalized words. See also **17a(2)**.

> D.C.　　G. B. Shaw　　NBC　　USMC　　NATO　　MIRV

Note 1: Both *no.* and *No.* are correct abbreviations for *number,* as in *No. 444* or *no. 444*.

Note 2: When proper names and their derivatives become names of a general class, they are no longer capitalized.

> malapropism　[derived from *Mrs. Malaprop*]
> chauvinistic　[derived from *Nicholas Chauvin*]

9b

In ordinary writing, capitalize titles that precede a proper name, but not those that follow it.

> Governor Paul Smith, Captain Palmer, Aunt Edith
> Paul Smith, our governor; Palmer, the captain; Edith, my aunt

Note: Usage is divided regarding the capitalization of titles indicating high rank or distinction when not followed by a proper name, or of words denoting family relationship when used as substitutes for proper names.

> Who was the President (OR president) of the United States?
> "Oh, Dad (OR dad)!" I said. "Tell Mother (OR mother)."

9c

In titles of books, plays, student papers, and so on, capitalize the first and last words and all other words except articles (*a, an, the*), short conjunctions, and short prepositions.

> *Crime and Punishment, Midnight on the Desert*
> "A Code to Live By," "Journalists Who Influence Elections"

Note 1: In titles a conjunction or a preposition of five or more letters is usually capitalized.

> *The Man Without a Country, Coming Through the Rye*

Note 2: In a title capitalize the first word of a hyphenated compound. As a rule, capitalize the word following the hyphen if it is a noun or a proper adjective or if it is equal in importance to the first word.

> *A Substitute for the H-Bomb*   [noun]
> *The Arab-Israeli Dilemma*   [proper adjective]
> "Hit-and-Run Accidents"   [parallel words]

Usage varies with respect to the capitalization of words following such prefixes as *anti-, ex-, re-,* and *self-:*

The Anti-Poverty Program, "Re-covering Old Sofas"

9d

Capitalize the pronoun *I* and the interjection *O* (but not *oh,* except when it begins a sentence).

David sings, "Out of the depths I cry to thee, O Lord."

9e

Capitalize the first word of every sentence and the first word of directly quoted speech.

She asked me what time it was.

The reply is always "Not today."

"Wow, college is great," I said. "Especially on weekends." [The first word of a fragment in dialogue is capitalized.] COMPARE "Wow, college is great," I said, "especially on weekends." [See also **12d(3)**.]

In the lobby we had a chance to get reacquainted. (It was a fifteen-minute intermission.) We talked about how much fun we had in high school. [a parenthetical sentence between sentences] COMPARE In the lobby we had a chance to get reacquainted (it was a fifteen-minute intermission), and we talked about how much fun we had in high school. [a parenthetical main clause within a sentence]

Option:

One thing is certain: we are still a free people. [regular usage]

One thing is certain: We are still a free people. [used for emphasis] [See also **17d**.]

Note: For the treatment of directly quoted written material, see Section **33**, pages 454–55.

9f

Avoid unnecessary capitals.

If you have a tendency to overuse capitals, review **9a** through **9e**. Also keep in mind this rule: common nouns may be preceded by the indefinite articles (*a, an*) and by such limiting modifiers as *every* or *several*.

a speech course in radio and television writing
COMPARE   Speech 245: Radio and Television Writing

every university, **several** schools of medicine
COMPARE   the University of Colorado School of Medicine

When preceded by *a, an,* or modifiers like *every* or *several,* capitalized nouns name one or many of the members of a class: *a St. Bernard,* *an Iowan,* **several** *Catholics.*
   Study the following style sheet:

Style Sheet for Capitalization

CAPITALS	NO CAPITALS
Dr. Freda E. Watts	every doctor, my doctor
the War of 1812	a space war in 1999
English, Spanish, French	the language requirement
Harvard University	a university like Harvard
the U.S. Navy	a strong navy
December, Christmas	winter, holiday
the West, Westerners	to fly west, western regions
the Student Association	an association for students
Parkinson's disease	flu, asthma, leukemia
a Chihuahua, Ford trucks	a beagle, pickup trucks
two Democratic candidates	democratic procedures
our Bill of Rights	a kind of bill of rights

■ **Exercise 1**   Write brief sentences correctly using each of the following words.

(1) professor (2) Professor (3) college (4) College (5) south (6) South (7) avenue (8) Avenue (9) theater (10) Theater

■ **Exercise 2**   Supply capitals wherever needed below.

1. Trying to raise my grade average in both english and history, i spent my thanksgiving holidays reading articles on recently proposed amendments to the u.s. constitution.
2. The west offers grand sights for tourists: the carlsbad caverns, yellowstone national park, the painted desert, the rockies, the pacific ocean.
3. At the end of his sermon on god's social justice as set forth in the bible, he said, ''we democrats really ought to reelect senator attebury.''
4. The full title of robert sherrill's book is *the saturday night special and other guns with which americans won the west, protected bootleg franchises, slew wildlife, robbed countless banks, shot husbands purposely and by mistake, and killed presidents—together with the debate over continuing same.*

Italics

10

To indicate italics, underline words and phrases (along with the punctuation) in accordance with customary practices. Use italics sparingly for emphasis.

In handwritten or typewritten papers, italics are indicated by underlining. Printers set underlined words in italic type.

TYPEWRITTEN	PRINTED
It was on <u>60 Minutes</u>.	It was on *60 Minutes*.

10a

Titles of separate publications (books, magazines, newspapers, pamphlets, long musical works) and titles of plays, films, radio and television programs, and long poems are underlined (italicized).

Kaplan's *O My America!* is a funny novel.   [The italicized punctuation is a part of the title.]

Tickets to *The Homecoming* were easy to find.   [An initial *a, an,* or *the* is italicized and capitalized in a title.]

I had never before heard Beethoven's *Moonlight Sonata.* [Note that the composer's name is not italicized.]

He pored over *Time,* the *Atlantic Monthly,* and the *New York Times* (OR the New York *Times*). [An initial *the* in titles of periodicals is usually not italicized; the name of the city in titles of newspapers is sometimes not italicized.]

Occasionally quotation marks are used for titles of separate publications and of radio and television programs. The usual practice, however, is to reserve quotation marks for titles of the individual parts of longer works (such as short stories, essays, songs, short poems) and for titles of episodes of a radio or television series. See **16b**.

"Human Character as a Vital Lie" is one of the best chapters in *The Denial of Death.*

I switched the channel to *M*A*S*H* and watched a rerun of an episode called "Dreams."

Exceptions

Neither italics nor quotation marks are used in references to the Bible and its parts or to legal documents.

The Bible begins with the Book of Genesis.
How many Americans have actually read the Bill of Rights?

10b

Foreign words and phrases are usually underlined (italicized) in the context of an English sentence.

It is an open-and-shut case of *caveat emptor,* and the FTC ought to stay out of it.   —BARRY FARRELL

The rice water weevil (*Lissorhoptrus oryzophilus*) is a potential threat to the California rice crop.   —SCIENTIFIC AMERICAN

Countless words borrowed from other languages are a part of the English vocabulary and are therefore not italicized:

amigo (Spanish)	dilemma (Greek)	karate (Japanese)
alumni (Latin)	disco (French)	pizza (Italian)

Dictionaries that label certain words and phrases as foreign are fairly dependable guides to the writer in doubt about the use of italics. The labels, however, are not always up-to-date, and writers must depend on their own judgment after considering current practices.

10c

Names of ships, airplanes, and trains and titles of works of art are underlined (italicized).

> The U.S.S. *Enterprise* was the first aircraft carrier of its kind. The artist named the portrait *Innocence*.

Note: Names of spacecraft like the *Eagle* or *Columbia* are generally italicized. Practice varies, however, with names like Apollo 14 and Skylab 3.

> Skylab's fall during the week of the Voyager 3 flyby was a serious event. —SMITHSONIAN
>
> *Voyagers 1* and 2 carried antennae more than four times the diameter of *Mariner 4*'s. —SCIENCE 80

10d

Words, letters, or figures spoken of as such or used as illustrations are usually underlined (italicized).

> In no other language could a foreigner be tricked into pronouncing *manslaughter* as *man's laughter*. —MARIO PEI
>
> The letters *qu* replaced *cw* in such words as *queen, quoth,* and *quick*. —CHARLES C. FRIES
>
> The first *3* and the final *0* of the serial number are barely legible.

10e

Use underlining (italics) sparingly for emphasis. Do not underline the title of your own paper.

Writers occasionally use italics to show stress, especially in dialogue:

> Out comes the jeer-gun again: "Whose side are *you* on?"
> —GEORGE P. ELLIOTT

Sometimes italics are used to emphasize the meaning of a word, especially when the exact meaning might be missed without the italics.

> To *do* justice means to treat all men with respect and human dignity—Negroes, whites, cops, and all of creation.
> —DICK GREGORY

But overuse of italics for emphasis (like overuse of the exclamation point) defeats its own purpose. If you overuse italics to stress ideas, study Section **29**. Also try substituting more specific or more forceful words for those you are tempted to underline.

A title is not italicized when it stands at the head of a book or article. Accordingly, the title at the head of your paper (unless the title happens to be also that of a book) should not be underlined. See also **8b(4)**.

■ **Exercise**   Underline all words in the following sentences that should be italicized.

1. While waiting for the dentist, I thumbed through an old issue of U.S. News & World Report and scanned an article on "Changes in Grading Policies."
2. On the Queen Mary from New York to London, Eleanor said she was so bored that she read all three books of Dante's The Divine Comedy!

3. Spelling errors involving the substitution of d for t in such words as partner and pretty reflect a tendency in pronunciation.

4. In Paris my young cousin attended a performance of Mozart's opera The Magic Flute, which she characterized in her letter as très magnifique.

5. Michelangelo's Battle of the Centaurs and his Madonna of the Steps are among the world's finest sculptures.

Abbreviations and Numbers

11

In ordinary writing use abbreviations only when appropriate, and spell out numbers that can be expressed simply.

Abbreviations and figures are desirable in tables, footnotes, and bibliographies (see the list on pages 441–43) and in some kinds of special or technical writing. In ordinary writing, however, only certain abbreviations are appropriate, and numbers that can be expressed in one word or two (like *forty-two* or *five hundred*) are usually spelled out.

All the principles in this section apply to ordinary writing, which of course includes the kind of writing often required in college.

Abbreviations

11a

In ordinary writing use the abbreviations *Mr., Mrs., Ms., Dr.,* and *St.* (for *Saint*). Spell out *doctor* and *saint* when not followed by proper names.

Mr. W. W. Kirtley, Mrs. Kay Gibbs, Dr. Bell, St. Francis
the young doctor, the early life of the saint

Note 1: The period is sometimes omitted after *Ms* (a short-ened, combined form of *Miss* and *Mrs.*).

Caution: Do not use redundant titles: NOT Dr. E. T. Fulton, M.D. BUT Dr. E. T. Fulton OR E. T. Fulton, M.D. See also page 122.

Note 2: Such abbreviations as *Prof., Sen., Rep., Gen.,* and *Capt.* may be used before full names or before initials and last names, but not before last names alone.

Sen. John Sherman Cooper   Senator Cooper
Capt. P. T. Gaines   Captain Gaines

11b

In ordinary writing spell out names of states, countries, continents, months, days of the week, and units of measurement.

On Sunday, October 10, we spent the night in Tulsa, Oklahoma; the next day we flew to South America.
Only four feet tall, Susan weighs ninety-one pounds.
An acre is 4,047 square meters.

11c

In ordinary writing spell out *Street, Avenue, Road, Park, Mount, River, Company,* and similar words used as an essential part of proper names.

Fifth Avenue is east of Central Park.
The Ford Motor Company does not expect a strike soon.

Note: Avoid the use of & (for *and*) and such abbreviations as *Bros.* or *Inc.*, except in copying official titles.

    AT&T   Gold Bros.   Lord & Taylor   G. Bell & Sons, Ltd.

11d

In ordinary writing spell out the words *volume, chapter,* and *page* and the names of courses of study.

    The chart is on page 46 of chapter 9.
    I registered for physical education and for child psychology.

Permissible Abbreviations

In addition to the abbreviations listed in **11a**, the following abbreviations and symbols are permissible and usually desirable.

1. *Titles and degrees after proper names:*

    E. R. Ames, Sr.   Alice Johnson, D.V.M.   Sam Jones, C.P.A.

2. *Certain words used with dates or figures:*

    in 586 B.C., in A.D. 70 $14.25, £349   25.5 mpg
    at 8:00 A.M. [OR a.m.]   No. 13 [OR no. 13]
    8:30 EST   [OR E.S.T. OR e.s.t.]

3. *The District of Columbia and the United States used adjectivally:*

    Washington, D.C.   the U.S. Navy   U.S.-French relations

4. *The names of organizations, agencies, countries, persons, or things usually referred to by their capitalized initials:*

    NAACP   NBC   IBM   OAS   IRS   USMC   CIA
    FDA   JFK   U.S.S.R.   TV   CB   DNA   GNP

5. *Certain common Latin expressions* (although the English term is usually spelled out in formal writing, as indicated in brackets below):

cf.   [compare]

e.g.   [for example]

et al.   [and others]

etc.   [and so forth]

i.e.   [that is]

vs. OR v. [versus]

For a list of abbreviations used in bibliographies, see pages 441–43.

Note: Periods are not used with clipped forms (such as *math* or *prep school*) or acronyms (such as CORE or UNICEF). Before using an acronym, writers often spell out the phrase the acronym stands for to make the meaning of the acronym clear.

> Then there is the anti-satellite intercepter (ASAT). Consider ASAT's cost and value.

■ **Exercise 1** Strike out any form below that is not appropriate in formal writing. (In a few items two forms are appropriate.)

1. Ms. Janet Hogan; a dr. but not a saint
2. in the U.S. Senate; in the United States; in the U.S.
3. 21 mpg; on TV; in Calif. and Ill.
4. on Magnolia St.; on Magnolia Street
5. Washington, D.C.; Charleston, S.C.
6. FBI; Federal Bureau of Investigation
7. on Aug. 15; on August 15
8. for Jr.; for John Evans, Jr.
9. e.g.; for example
10. before 6 A.M.; before six in the A.M.

Numbers

11e

Although usage varies, writers tend to spell out numbers that can be expressed in one word or two; they regularly use figures for other numbers.

after twenty-two years	after 124 years
only thirty dollars	only $29.99
five thousand voters	5,261 voters
ten million bushels	10,402,317 bushels
over three liters	3.785 liters

Special Usage Regarding Numbers

1. *Specific time of day*

   2 A.M. OR 2:00 A.M. OR two o'clock in the morning
   4:30 P.M. OR half-past four in the afternoon

2. *Dates*

   May 7, 1977 OR 7 May 1977 [NOT May 7th, 1977]
   May sixth OR the sixth of May OR May 6 OR May 6th
   the eighties OR the 1980's OR the 1980s
   the twentieth century
   in 1900 in 1981–1982 OR in 1981–82
   from 1980 to 1985 OR 1980–1985 OR 1980–85
     [NOT from 1980–1985, from 1980–85]

3. *Addresses*

   Apartment 3C, 8 Redwood Drive, Prescott, Arizona 86301
     [OR Apt. 3c, 8 Redwood Dr., Prescott, AZ 86301]

16 Tenth Street
350 West 114 Street   OR   350 West 114th Street

4. *Identification numbers*

Channel 13   Interstate 35   Henry VIII   Room 10

5. *Pages and divisions of books and plays*

page 30   chapter 6   part 4
    in act 3, scene 2   OR   in Act III, Scene ii

6. *Decimals and percentages*

a 2.5 average   12½ percent   0.907 metric ton

7. *Numbers in series and statistics*

two cows, five pigs, and forty-two chickens
125 feet long, 50 feet wide, and 12 feet deep
scores of 17 to 13 and 42 to 3   OR   scores of 17–13 and 42–3
The members voted 99 to 23 against it.

8. *Large round numbers*

four billion dollars   OR $4 billion   OR $4,000,000,000
    [Figures are used for emphasis only.]
12,500,000   OR   12.5 million

9. *Numbers beginning sentences*

Six percent of the students voted.   [NOT 6 percent of the students voted.]

10. *Repeated numbers (in legal or commercial writing)*

The agent's fee will not exceed one hundred (100) dollars.
OR
The agent's fee will not exceed one hundred dollars ($100).

■ **Exercise 2**   All items below are appropriate in formal writing. Using desirable abbreviations and figures, change each item to an acceptable shortened form.

EXAMPLES
Jude, the saint   *St. Jude*
at two o'clock that afternoon   *at 2* P.M.

1. on the fifteenth of June
2. Ernest Threadgill, a doctor
3. thirty million dollars
4. Janine Keith, a certified public accountant
5. the United Nations
6. one o'clock in the afternoon
7. by the first of December, 1985
8. at the bottom of the fifteenth page
9. the Navy of the United States
10. four hundred years before Christ
11. in the second scene of the first act
12. a five-year plan (from 1985 to 1990)

PUNCTUATION

The Comma

12

Use the comma (which ordinarily indicates a pause and a variation in voice pitch) where it is required by the structure of the sentence.

Just as pauses and variations in voice pitch help to convey the meaning of spoken sentences, commas help to clarify the meaning of written sentences.

> When the lightning struck, James Harvey fainted.
> When the lightning struck James, Harvey fainted.

The sound of a sentence can serve as a guide in using commas.

But many times sound is not a dependable guide. The use of the comma is primarily determined by the structure of the sentence. If you understand this structure (see Section **1**), you can learn to apply the basic principles governing comma usage. The following rules cover the usual practices of the best modern writers:

Commas—

a   precede the coordinating conjunctions *and, but, or, nor, for* and the connectives *so* and *yet* between main clauses;

b   follow certain introductory elements;

c separate items in a series (including coordinate adjectives);

d set off nonrestrictive, parenthetical, and miscellaneous elements.

Between Main Clauses

12a

Use a comma before *and, but, or, nor, for, so,* **and** *yet* **when they link main clauses.** See also **1e**.

Study the sentence structure of the examples that follow the pattern below.

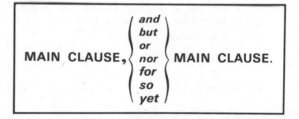

We are here on the planet only once, and we might as well get a feel for the place. —ANNIE DILLARD

Serious automation remains largely a myth here, but in Japan it is quickly becoming reality. —JOHN HILTON

Justice stands upon Power, or there is no justice.

—WILLIAM S. WHITE

The peoples of the Sahara have never been united, nor have they even considered uniting in any common cause.

—JAMES R. NEWMAN

[Note the word order: *nor + auxiliary + subject.*]

No one watches the performance, for everybody is taking part. —JAN KOTT

They are hopeless and humble, so he loves them.

—E. M. FORSTER

> Here is a great mass of people, yet it takes an effort of intellect and will even to see them.   —MICHAEL HARRINGTON

The pattern and examples illustrate the punctuation of a compound sentence. The rule also applies to coordinating conjunctions that link the main clauses of a compound-complex sentence (that is, a sentence with at least two main clauses and one subordinate clause):

> Men who are engaged in a daily struggle for survival do not think of old age, for they do not expect to see it.
> —JOHN KENNETH GALBRAITH

Exceptions to 12a

1. *Omission of the comma*

   The comma may be omitted when there is no possibility of confusing the reader or when the comma is not needed to make reading easier.

   > The next night the wind shifted and the thaw began.
   > —RACHEL CARSON

   > Either the answer was true or it was false.

2. *Substitution of the semicolon*

   Occasionally, especially when the main clauses are long or when the second main clause reveals a striking contrast, a semicolon is used instead of the usual comma.

   > Unfortunately, society says that winning is everything ; but I would be foolish to believe that.   —WILLIAM FULLER RUSSELL

A semicolon is often preferred when one of the main clauses contains commas. Sharply dividing the main clauses contributes to readability. See also **14a**.

> Everyone there made allowances, of course; but being young is no excuse.
> Readings must be taken while the strip is in place; so, if you're taking your own temperature, you'll have to use a mirror. —CONSUMER REPORTS

Note: When linking main clauses with coordinating conjunctions, be aware of the various meanings of these connectives as you relate the clauses:

> **and**—in addition, also, moreover, besides
>
> **but** OR **yet**—nevertheless, however, still
>
> **for**—because, seeing that, since
>
> **or**—as an alternative, otherwise
>
> **nor**—and not, or not, not either   [used after a negative]
>
> **so**—therefore, as a result

When in doubt about the meaning of any connective, consult the dictionary. See also **3b** and **31c(4)**.

■ **Exercise 1** Following the punctuation pattern of **12a**, link the sentences in the items below with an appropriate *and, but, or, nor, for, so,* or *yet.*

EXAMPLE
We cannot win the battle. We cannot afford to lose it.
We cannot win the battle, nor can we afford to lose it.

1. A crisis strikes. Another presidential fact-finding committee is born.
2. The new leash law did not put all dogs behind bars. It did not make the streets safe for cats.
3. Motorists may admit their guilt and pay a fine immediately. They may choose to appear in court within thirty days and plead not guilty.
4. They decided not to take a vacation. They needed the money to remodel their kitchen.
5. The band leader can sing and dance and whistle. She cannot play the trombone.

■ **Exercise 2** Follow rule **12a** as you insert commas before connectives linking main clauses in the sentences below. (Remember that not all coordinating conjunctions link main clauses and that *but, for, so,* and *yet* do not always function as coordinating conjunctions.)

1. The students had finished taking the various tests and answering the long questionnaires and they had gone to lunch.
2. There are now special shoes for someone to fill for Bob has resigned and is going to business school.
3. I decided to withdraw from that eight-o'clock class so that I could sleep later but I plan to enroll again for the same class in January.
4. We had seen the stage play and the movie and the College Players' performance was the best of all.
5. Everyone in our group was invited to the party but Gary and Irene decided to go to the hockey game.

After Introductory Elements

12b

Use a comma after introductory elements such as adverb clauses, long phrases, transitional expressions, interjections, and an introductory *yes* or *no*.

(1) Introductory adverb clauses

Introductory adverb clauses begin with such subordinators as *after, although, as, as far as, as long as, as soon as, because, before, if, inasmuch as, insofar as, lest, no matter how, now that, once, provided, since, supposing, though, unless, until, when, whenever, where, wherever, whether or not, while.*

ADVERB CLAUSE, MAIN CLAUSE.

When Americans are not happy, they feel guilty.
—JOHN LEONARD

Once these sea floors are thrust up by the natural forces that create mountains, the sculpting process begins.
—ROY A. GALLANT

Note 1: Rule **12b** also applies to elliptical adverb clauses and to introductory adverbial phrases that are parenthetical. See also **12d(3)**.

> While writing his last novel, James recognized and faced his solitude. —LEON EDEL [Compare "While he was writing. . . ." See also **25b(3)**.]
>
> These differences aside, the resemblance between 1972 and 1980 is very striking. —NORMAN PODHORETZ [Compare "Even when these differences are put aside. . . ." See also page 529.]

A writer may omit the comma after an introductory adverb clause, especially when the clause is short, if the omission does not make for difficult reading.

> When we talk to people we always mean something quite different from what we say. —ANTHONY BURGESS

Note 2: When the adverb clause *follows* the main clause, there is usually no pause and no need for a comma.

> She moved as if she owned the earth and conferred grace upon it. —JAMES A. MICHENER

Adverb clauses in this position, however, may be preceded by a comma if they are loosely connected with the rest of the sentence, especially if the subordinating conjunction seems equivalent to a coordinating conjunction.

> Marine life is concentrated in about 4 percent of the ocean's total body of water, whereas roughly 96 percent is just about as poor in life as is a desert ashore. —THOR HEYERDAHL

(2) Long introductory phrases

> Within this iron regime of dollars and ratings, a few ghettos of do-goodism exist. —DOUGLASS CATER
>
> In a country with a frontier tradition and a deep-rooted enthusiasm for hunting and target shooting, firearms have long been part of the national scene. —TREVOR ARMBRISTER

Sometimes commas are omitted after long introductory phrases when no misreading would result:

> After months of listening for some meager clue he suddenly began to talk in torrents. —ARTHUR L. KOPIT

Introductory phrases containing a gerund, a participle, or an infinitive, even though short, must often be followed by a comma to prevent misreading.

> Before leaving, the soldiers demolished the fort.
>
> Because of his effort to escape, his punishment was increased.

Short introductory prepositional phrases, except when they are distinctly parenthetical expressions (such as *in fact* or *for example*), are usually not followed by a comma.

> Through the Middle Ages the Church was not an agent of oppression. —RICHARD N. GOODWIN

(3) Introductory transitional expressions, interjections, and an introductory *yes* or *no*.

Interjections, transitional expressions (such as *for example, in fact, on the other hand, in the second place*), and an introductory *yes* or *no* are generally considered parenthetical: see **12d(3)**. When used as introductory elements, they are ordinarily followed by commas:

> Intelligent she was not. In fact, she veered in the opposite direction. —MAX SHULMAN
>
> "Well, move the ball or move the body." —ALLEN JACKSON
>
> Yes, every vote counts. No, it is not illegal.

■ **Exercise 3** In sentences 1–4 and 7–8 below, find the main clause and identify the preceding element as an adverb clause or as a phrase. Then determine whether or not to use a comma after the introductory element.

¹ If you walk into any bookstore these days you will notice a relatively new category of books prominently displayed. ² For example you will see titles like *Looking Out for Number One, How to Increase Your Personal Effectiveness, How to Deal with Almost Anything.* ³ In my opinion their message is the same: "Read me, enjoy me, and improve yourself." ⁴ With about as much subtlety as a sledgehammer these titles imply that there are short cuts to nearly anything your heart desires. ⁵ Do you lack confidence? ⁶ Do you crave success, riches, recognition? ⁷ If you do buy this book—or that book—and read it. ⁸ In a matter of hours you will be on your way. ⁹ The life you change will be your own.

Between Items in a Series

12c

Use commas to separate items in a series (including coordinate adjectives).

The punctuation of a series depends on its form:

> The air was *raw, dank, gray.*   [*a, b, c*]
> The air was *raw, dank,* and *gray.*   [*a, b,* and *c*]
> The air was *raw* and *dank* and *gray.*   [*a* and *b* and *c*]

(1) Words, phrases, and clauses in a series

> A miner's life is a long series of wanderings, searchings, booms, and blow-outs.   —DAVID JOHN THOMAS

> He's as steady as a weather vane—liberal today, conservative tomorrow, reactionary next week.   —WALTER F. MURPHY
> [Note the parallel structure of the phrases: see also **26a(1)**.]

> Go to your favorite drugstore tomorrow, buy yourself a bottle of the American Dream in the new economy size, shake well before using, and live luxuriously ever afterward.
> —DAVID L. COHN

The comma before the conjunction may be omitted in the series *a, b, and c* if there is no danger of misreading:

> Women still account for a very small percentage of the nation's lawyers, physicians and clergy.
> —U.S. NEWS & WORLD REPORT

(2) Coordinate adjectives

Adjectives are coordinate when they modify the same word or word group. Use a comma between coordinate adjectives not linked by a coordinating conjunction:

> It is a waiting, silent, limp room. —EUDORA WELTY
> [*Waiting, silent,* and *limp* all modify *room.* Compare "It is a silent, limp waiting room."]

> They are young, alert social workers.
> [*Young* and *alert* modify the word group *social workers.* Compare "They are young, social, alert workers."]

> She was a frowsy, middle-aged woman with wispy, drab-brown hair. She sat behind a long wooden table on a high platform overlooking her disciples with her narrow, piercing eyes. —EVELYN KOSSOFF

Exception to 12c

If the items in a series contain internal punctuation, semicolons are used instead of commas for clarity: see **14b**.

■ **Exercise 4** Using commas as needed, supply coordinate adjectives to modify any six of the following twelve word groups.

> EXAMPLE
> metric system   *the familiar, sensible metric system*

1. apple pie
2. social climbers
3. electronic music
4. pop art
5. minimum wage
6. traveler's checks
7. Baltimore oriole
8. rhetorical question
9. apartment buildings
10. major oil companies
11. blue cheese
12. secondary school

With Parenthetical and Miscellaneous Elements

12d

Use commas to set off nonrestrictive clauses and phrases and other parenthetical and miscellaneous elements, such as transitional expressions, items in dates, words used in direct address, and so on. Restrictive clauses and phrases are not set off by commas.

To set off a word or a word group with commas, use two commas unless the element is placed at the beginning of the sentence or at the end:

> Darwin's *Origin of Species*, as Robert Ardrey points out, explains everything except the origin of species.
> —F. W. HOLIDAY

> Socially, death is as taboo as Victorian sex.
> —OSBORN SEGERBERGER, JR.

> Just take a look around El Barrio, the section where so many Puerto Ricans live.   —OSCAR LEWIS

Caution: When two commas are needed to set off an element, do not forget one of the commas.

CONFUSING	An experienced driver generally speaking, does not fear the open road.
CLEAR	An experienced driver, generally speaking, does not fear the open road.

(1) Nonrestrictive clauses and phrases are set off by commas. Restrictive clauses and phrases are not set off.

Adjective clauses and phrases are classified as nonrestrictive (parenthetical) or restrictive (not parenthetical).

137

NONRESTRICTIVE CLAUSES AND PHRASES

Nonrestrictive clauses and phrases are not essential to the meaning of the main clause and may be omitted. Such modifiers are parenthetical and are set off by commas.

> There are many Pygmalion-style directors, **who like to discover new people (even amateurs) and mold them into actors.** —ABE BURROWS
> [The *who-* clause does not restrict or limit the meaning of directors (already identified) but does provide a parenthetical explanation of what is meant by *Pygmalion-style.*]

> Solar energy, **which is safe, renewable, environmentally benign,** has serious disadvantages, too. —STEPHEN CHAPMAN
> [The *which*-clause is informative but nonessential.]

> Huge cranes, **delicate as a dinosaur's head,** moved over the street. —BELVA PLAIN
> [Compare "Huge cranes, *which looked as* delicate as a dinosaur's head, moved over the street."]

> He tossed the letter aside and pulled his apple pie, **topped with a melting scoop of vanilla ice cream,** toward him.
> —TRUMAN CAPOTE
> [The parenthetical phrase describes but does not identify the pie.]

> Claud got up, **groaning and growling,** and limped off.
> —FLANNERY O'CONNOR
> [Compare "Claud got up (*he was* groaning and growling) and limped off."]

RESTRICTIVE CLAUSES AND PHRASES

Restrictive clauses and phrases follow and limit the words they modify. They are essential to the meaning of the main clause and are not set off by commas.

> We punish those **who hurt us** by making them feel guilty.
> —WILLARD GAYLIN
> [The adjective clause identifies the kind of people we punish. Contrast "He punishes his only daughter, who hurts him, by making her feel guilty."]

138

Couponing is merely the latest way **Americans have found to beat the system**. —WILL STANTON
[This is a contact clause (with the connective *that* or *which* omitted—see page 537). Contact clauses used as adjectives are restrictive.]

The poor live on a diet **heavy in bread**. —NOEL GRAVE
[The phrase identifies the kind of diet.]

The two things **most universally desired** are power and admiration. —BERTRAND RUSSELL
[The essential phrase can be expanded to a restrictive clause: "*that* (OR *which*) *are* most universally desired."]

Note: Although some writers prefer to use the connective *that* at the beginning of restrictive clauses, *which* is also acceptable.

Sometimes a clause or phrase may be either nonrestrictive or restrictive. The writer signifies the meaning by using or by omitting commas.

NONRESTRICTIVE   He spent hours nursing the Indian guides**, who were sick with malaria**.   [He cared for all the Indian guides. They were all sick with malaria.]

RESTRICTIVE   He spent hours nursing the Indian guides **who were sick with malaria**.   [Some of the Indian guides were sick with malaria. He cared only for the sick ones.]

■ **Exercise 5**   Use commas to set off nonrestrictive clauses and phrases in the following sentences. Put a checkmark after any sentence that needs no further punctuation.

1. Red snapper fried in butter is better than baked red snapper.
2. The smoke that filled the room is now gone.
3. My hometown which no one around here has ever heard of is a little place called Crossroads.
4. All players who broke the rules will sit on the bench next Saturday.
5. Martha Thompson sitting near the window smiled knowingly.
6. The coach chewing gum and clapping his hands is Teddy.

7. Venice which he visited next was torn by rival factions.
8. Venice is a city he likes to visit.
9. I will interview Mary Smith who manages the bank.
10. I will interview the Mary Smith who manages the bank.

(2) Use commas to set off nonrestrictive appositives, contrasted elements, geographical names, and most items in dates and addresses.

NONRESTRICTIVE APPOSITIVES

Fun, **a rare jewel,** is hard to find.   —SUZANNE BRITT JORDAN

The most visible victims of pollution, fish are only a link in a chain from microscopic life to man.   —GEORGE GOODMAN
[The appositive precedes rather than follows *fish.*]

The peaks float in the sky, **fantastic pyramids of flame.**
—ARTHUR C. CLARKE   [Notice that the appositive could be shifted to the beginning of the sentence.]

Was the letter from Frances Evans, **Ph.D.,** or from F. H. Evans, **M.D.**?   [Abbreviations after names are treated like nonrestrictive appositives.]

Note: Commas do not set off restrictive appositives.

His son *James* is sick.   [*James,* not his son William]
The word *malapropism* is derived from Sheridan's *The Rivals.*
Do you refer to Samuel Butler *the poet* or to Samuel Butler *the novelist?*

CONTRASTED ELEMENTS

Racing is supposed to be a test of skill, **not a dice game with death**.   —SONNY KLEINFIELD

His phrases dribbled off, **but not his memories**.
—JAMES A. MICHENER

The goal was achievement, **not adjustment**; the young were taught to work, **not to socialize**.   —ALLEN WHEELIS   [Only one comma sets off an element before a semicolon.]

140

Note: Usage is divided regarding the placement of a comma before *but* in such structures as the following:

> Other citizens who disagree with me base their disagreement, not on facts different from the ones I know, but on a different set of values. —RENÉ DUBOS

> Today the Black Hills are being invaded again, not for gold but for uranium. —PETER MATTHIESSEN

GEOGRAPHICAL NAMES, ITEMS IN DATES AND ADDRESSES

> Pasadena, California, is the site of the Rose Bowl.

> The letter was addressed to Mr. J. L. Karnes, Clayton, Delaware 19938. [The zip code is not separated by a comma from the name of the state.]

> Leslie applied for the job in October, 1981, and accepted it on Friday, March 5, 1982. OR

> Leslie applied for the job in October 1981 and accepted it on Friday, 5 March 1982.
> [Note that commas may be omitted when the day of the month is not given or when the day of the month precedes rather than follows the month.]

■ **Exercise 6**   Combine each pair of sentences by reducing the second sentence to an appositive or to a contrasted element set off by commas. Insert commas where needed to set off items in dates or addresses.

EXAMPLES
Michael Roger was born on January 7 1982 in Alabama. He is my only son.
Michael Roger, my only son, was born on January 7, 1982, in Alabama.

Carla's social security number is 452-25-7648. It is not 152-25-7648.
Carla's social security number is 452-25-7648, not 152-25-7648.

1. The General Sherman Tree is about 270 feet tall. It is a giant sequoia in California.
2. Those are pill bugs. They are not insects.
3. On April 1 1980 his divorced wife married his lawyer. His lawyer was Bill Wynne.
4. The publisher's address is 757 Third Avenue New York New York 10017. It is not 757 Madison Avenue.
5. We moved to Taos New Mexico on 30 September 1978. New Mexico is one of the popular sun states.

(3) Use commas to set off parenthetical elements.

The term *parenthetical* is correctly applied to all nonrestrictive elements discussed under **12d**. But it may also be applied to such transitional expressions as *however, first of all, in fact, to summarize,* or *that is* and to such expressions as *I believe* or *experts argue* (often called interrupters). Expressions that come at the beginning of a sentence are treated by both **12b** and **12d**.

PARENTHETICAL ELEMENTS

Finally, banks devise means of protecting the money.
—MALCOLM BRADBURY

Language**, then,** sets the tone of our society.
—EDWIN NEWMAN

Many farmers**, for example,** would like direct access to the detailed forecast maps. —SCIENCE 80

Well, global peace may be a dream. [mild interjection]

Animal lovers, write letters of protest. [direct address]

Science**, at its best,** is unifying. —STEPHEN JAY GOULD [parenthetical phrase]

No, the "characters" are vanishing in Velva**, just as they are vanishing in our cities**. —ERIC SEVAREID [introductory *no* and a parenthetical clause]

The Age of Television has dawned in China**, a generation later than in the West**. —LINDA MATHEWS [appended element]

He was thumping at a book, his voice growing louder and louder. —JOYCE CAROL OATES [absolute phrase]

Note 1: Expressions such as *also, too, of course, perhaps, at least, therefore,* and *likewise,* when they cause little or no pause in reading, are frequently not set off by commas.

The times **also** have changed in ways that soften the rhetoric.
  —HENRY FAIRLIE

Study circles are **therefore** the most pervasive method of bringing education to Swedes of all ages and walks of life. —WILLIAM L. ABBOTT

Note 2: With direct quotations, such expressions as *he said, she asked, I replied,* and *we shouted* are set off by commas. See also **16a(4)**.

He said, "My opinion is really different."
"My opinion," he said, "is really different."
"My opinion is really different," he said.

12e

Occasionally a comma, although not called for by any of the major principles already discussed, may be needed to prevent misreading.

Use **12e** sparingly to justify your commas. In a general sense, nearly all commas are used to prevent misreading or to make reading easier. Your mastery of the comma will come through application of the more specific major principles (**a**, **b**, **c**, **d**) to the structure of your sentences.

CONFUSING	A few weeks before I had seen him in an off-Broadway play.
BETTER	A few weeks before, I had seen him in an off-Broadway play. [The comma clearly indicates intonation.]

CONFUSING	Those who can pay and forego consumption of other essential goods.
BETTER	Those who can, pay and forego consumption of other essential goods. —ERIK P. ECKHOLM

■ **Exercise 7** All commas in the following paragraphs are correctly used. Explain the reason for each comma by referring to one of the principles discussed in this section (**12a**, **12b**, **12c**, or **12d**).

[1] Conflicts would not be restricted to conventional warfare. [2] True, we do have a treaty forbidding the use of "weapons of mass destruction" in outer space. [3] However, the treaty does not define "weapons of mass destruction," and although it does require inspection of all installations on celestial bodies, it says nothing about stations or space colonies in orbit. [4] In any case, the moral force of this treaty, all by itself, is hardly likely to deter the greedy ones, the bullies, the maniacs, the suicidal types, or the various champions of human "progress," "liberation," or "rejuvenation."

[5] Every colony, as well as the Earth itself, would be in danger from outer space at all times. [6] No matter how many problems we may have today, we can still look at the stars with fair assurance that they constitute no immediate threat to us. [7] But with millions of space colonies roaming the solar system, life could degenerate into a series of preparations for and recoveries from attacks—an updated version of the life-style of centuries past when raids of the Normans, Berbers and other seafaring people depopulated Europe's coastline—except that this time the weaponry would be a great deal more destructive.

—PAUL L. CSONKA, *"Space Colonization: An Invitation to Disaster?"*

■ **Exercise 8** Insert commas where needed in the following sentences (selected and adapted from the works of modern writers). Be prepared to explain the reason for each comma used. Also be prepared to point out where optional commas might be placed as a matter of stylistic preference.

1. Police action in arresting drunks will never prevent drunkenness nor can it cure an alcoholic. ——RAMSEY CLARK

2. Fifty years ago *Hazel Beverly Marian Frances* and *Shirley* were all perfectly acceptable boys' names.
——ALLEEN PACE NILSEN

3. Thus the ocean floors far from being the oldest features on earth were relatively young. ——ALLISON R. PALMER

4. When language does change the alteration first occurs in the spoken not the written form. ——ROBERT BURCHFIELD

5. Hooper said ''Look Chief you can't go off half-cocked looking for vengeance against a fish. That shark isn't evil.''
——PETER BENCHLEY

6. Incidentally supporting the tobacco habit is very expensive some adults having been known to sacrifice much-needed family grocery money for a carton of cigarettes.
——DAVID TATELMAN

7. The crowd's answer was polite almost dainty applause the kind that has a lot of coughing at the end instead of a release of spirit. ——ANTHONY TUTTLE

8. Hard as it is for many of us to believe women are not really superior to men in intelligence or humanity——they are only equal. ——ANNE ROIPHE

9. The earth breathes in a certain sense. ——LEWIS THOMAS

10. December is the most violent month the time of murder robbery assault suicide and Christmas. ——EARL SHORRIS

11. They can stand just so much eh Doctor? ——E. B. WHITE

12. As if to celebrate the arrival of the Antarctic spring a brilliant flash of light illuminated the date of September 22 1979 in the southern hemisphere. ——S. T. COHEN

13. In Detroit weather weighs heavily upon everyone.
——JOYCE CAROL OATES

14. The temptation in describing a film like this one is to string together several adjectives——witless ugly brutal insensate stupid. ——TIME

15. As almost everyone outside Texas understands Alaska is a very big place. ——JOHN G. MITCHELL

16. I stand in the moonlight the hot desert at my back.
——MARK KRAMER

17. He disliked being categorized no matter what the category. ——IRWIN SHAW

18. "I had to see where J.R. lived" said Mick Pattemore his accent revealing not Sweetwater Texas but Somerset England.   —JANE HALL
19. If there was ever an American boy who was saved by sports it was I.   —JAMES A. MICHENER
20. Theirs has been described as a love/hate relationship smooth and pliable when they are of a mind and roof-shaking when they are not.   —JOY G. SPIEGEL

■ **Exercise 9**   For humorous effect, the writer of the following paragraph deliberately omits commas that can be justified by rules **12a**, **b**, or **d**. Be prepared for a discussion of the paragraph. Where could commas be inserted to contribute to ease in reading?

> The commas are the most useful and usable of all the stops. It is highly important to put them in place as you go along. If you try to come back after doing a paragraph and stick them in the various spots that tempt you you will discover that they tend to swarm like minnows into all sorts of crevices whose existence you hadn't realized and before you know it the whole long sentence becomes immobilized and lashed up squirming in commas. Better to use them sparingly, and with affection, precisely when the need for each one arises, nicely, by itself.   —LEWIS THOMAS, *The Medusa and the Snail*

Superfluous Commas

13

Do not use superfluous commas.

Unnecessary or misplaced commas are false or awkward signals that may confuse the reader. If you tend to use too many commas, remember that although the comma ordinarily signals a pause, not every pause calls for a comma. As you read each sentence in the following paragraph aloud, you may pause naturally at places other than those marked by a period, but no commas are necessary.

> Springboard divers routinely execute maneuvers in which their body rotates in space. The basic maneuvers are the somersault and the twist. In the somersault the body rotates head over heels as if the athlete were rotating about an axis extending from his left side to his right side through his waist. In the twist the body spins or pirouettes in midair as if the athlete were rotating about an axis extending from his head to his toes.
>
> —CLIFF FROHLICH, *"The Physics of Somersaulting and Twisting"*

To avoid using unnecessary commas, first review Section **12** and then study and observe the following rules.

13a
Do not use a comma to separate the subject from its verb or the verb from its object.

147

The commas circled below should be omitted.

> Even people with unlisted telephone numbers⊙ receive
> crank calls.
> [needless separation of subject and verb]

> The man said⊙ that the old tires were guaranteed.
> [needless separation of verb and object (a noun clause)]

13b

Do not misuse a comma before or after a coordinating conjunction. See **12a**.

The commas circled below should be omitted.

> The facts were selected⊙ and organized with care.
> The USAF debunked UFO sightings, but⊙ millions of Americans didn't listen.

13c

Do not use. commas to set off words and short phrases (especially introductory ones) that are not parenthetical or that are very slightly so.

The commas circled below should be omitted.

> Art Tatum was born⊙ in Toledo⊙ in 1910
> Maybe⊙ the battery cables needed cleaning.

13d

Do not use commas to set off restrictive (necessary) clauses, restrictive phrases, and restrictive appositives.

The commas circled below should be omitted.

> Everyone⊙ who smokes cigarettes⊙ risks losing about ten
> years of life.   [restrictive clause: see **12d(1)**]

For years she has not eaten anything⊙ seasoned with onions or garlic.   [restrictive phrase: see **12d(1)**]

The word⊙ *nope*⊙ is an interesting substitute for *no*.
   [restrictive appositive: see **12d(2)**]

13e

Do not use a comma before the first item or after the last item of a series (including a series of coordinate adjectives).

The commas circled below should be omitted.

Field trips were required in a few courses, such as⊙ botany, geology, and sociology.

The company hires talented, smart, ambitious⊙ women.

■ **Exercise 1**   Study the structure of the sentence below; then answer the question that follows by giving a specific rule number (such as **13a**, **13d**) for each item. Be prepared to explain your answers in class.

Now when you say "newly rich" you picture a middle-aged and corpulent man who has a tendency to remove his collar at formal dinners and is in perpetual hot water with his ambitious wife and her titled friends.   —F. SCOTT FITZGERALD

Why is there no comma after (1) *Now,* (2) *say,* (3) *middle-aged,* (4) *man,* (5) *collar,* (6) *dinners,* or (7) *wife?*

■ **Exercise 2**   Change the structure and the punctuation of the following sentences according to the pattern of the examples.

EXAMPLE
A motorcyclist saw our flashing lights**,** and he stopped to offer aid.   [an appropriate comma: see **12a**]
A motorcyclist saw our flashing lights and stopped to offer aid. [second main clause reduced to a part of compound predicate—comma no longer needed]

1. The hail stripped leaves from trees, and it pounded early gardens.
2. Some science fiction presents newly discovered facts, and it predicts the future accurately.
3. Rob likes the work, and he may make a career of it.

EXAMPLE

If any students destroyed public property, they were expelled.   [an appropriate comma: see **12b**]
Any students who destroyed public property were expelled.
[introductory adverb clause converted to restrictive clause—comma no longer needed]

4. When people lead rather than demand, they often get good results.
5. If a boy is willing to work, he can get a job here.

■ **Exercise 3**   In the following paragraph some of the commas are needed and some are superfluous. Circle all unnecessary commas. Be prepared to explain (see Section **12**) each comma that you allow to stand.

[1] There are, at least, three kinds of fishermen.   [2] First, is the boat owner.   [3] He usually gets up at 4 a.m., grabs a thermos of coffee, picks up his favorite, fishing buddy, and goes to the exact spot, where the trout or bass are striking.   [4] Fishing for a certain kind of fish, is his specialty, and he, generally, gets exactly the kind he goes after.   [5] Next is the person, who fishes with friends on a crowded pier, jetty, or barge.   [6] He expects the fish to come to him, and is happy to catch anything, fit to eat, such as, perch or carp.   [7] The third type is the loner, the one who fishes in some out-of-the-way place on the bank, by himself.   [8] After he anchors one, great big, wad of bait on his hook, he throws his line out, and props up his pole, so that he doesn't have to hold it.   [9] Then, he leans back, watches the cloud formations, or lazily examines a leaf or flower.   [10] He, sometimes, dozes.   [11] Also, he daydreams.   [12] Lounging there with a kind of half smile on his face, he enjoys his solitude.   [13] His fishing pole is merely an excuse for being there.   [14] He forgets to watch his line, and, to rebait his hook.

The Semicolon

14

Use the semicolon (a) between main clauses not linked by *and, but, or, nor, for, so,* or *yet* and (b) between coordinate elements containing commas. Do not use the semicolon between parts of unequal grammatical rank.

Read aloud the following sentences; notice the way your voice reflects the differences in punctuation.

> The letters did not arrive until Thursday, although I had mailed them early Monday morning.
> The letters did not arrive until Thursday; however, I had mailed them early Monday morning.

A stronger mark of punctuation than the comma, the semicolon is sometimes called a weak period.

If you can distinguish between main and subordinate clauses and between phrases and clauses (see **1d** and **1e**), you should have little trouble using the semicolon. As you study the rules in this section, notice that the semicolon is used *only* between closely related coordinate elements.

14a

Use the semicolon between two main clauses not linked by *and, but, or, nor, for, so, yet*. See also 12a.

MAIN CLAUSES LINKED WITHOUT A CONNECTIVE

> MAIN CLAUSE**;** MAIN CLAUSE**.**

The dark is not mysterious**;** it is merely dark.
—ARCHIBALD MacLEISH

No person is born arrogant**;** arrogance must be taught.
—CLARA M. DOBAY

She will say something**;** he will disagree**;** she will nod and let him have the last word. —ROBERT COLES

Observe that each main clause above could be written as a separate sentence: see also **1d**, page 28.

Rule **14a** also applies in compound-complex sentences:

A close friend of mine lived on a farm**;** I assumed he would always be there. —WILLIAM MUELLER [two main clauses and one subordinate clause]

Curing is a process in which harvested tobacco is slowly dried**;** it removes excess starch and permits other chemical reactions, which lead to a milder smoke. —WILLIAM BENNETT [two main clauses and two subordinate clauses]

MAIN CLAUSES LINKED BY ADVERBIALS See also 3b.

Be sure to use a semicolon before conjunctive adverbs (*however, therefore, then,* and so on) and transitional phrases (*for example, on the contrary,* and so on) when these adverbial connectives are placed between main clauses. See the lists on page 45.

> MAIN CLAUSE; { conjunctive adverb <br> or <br> transitional phrase } (,) MAIN CLAUSE.

In the pattern the comma (in parentheses) is generally omitted after an adverbial connective when the connective is not considered parenthetical or when the comma is not needed to prevent misreading or to mark intonation. See also **12d(3)**.

New Orleans is unique among American cities; indeed in many ways it is scarcely American.   —PHELPS GAY

Many farms do not require a labor input every day; hence commuting could be lessened.   —MARION CLAWSON

We no longer confide in each other; in fact, there are many things I could not mention to her.   —SAUL BELLOW

They have not yet been molded by experience; therefore, the immediate moment makes a great impression on them because that is all they know.   —WILLIAM J. HARRIS

Caution: Do not overwork the semicolon. Often it is better to revise compound sentences according to the principles of subordination: see Section **24** and also **14c**.

Exceptions to 14a:

1. A semicolon (instead of the usual comma) may precede *and, but, or, nor, for, so,* and *yet* when a main clause has internal commas or when the writer wishes to make a sharp division of the two main clauses. See also **12a**, page 130.

I was, if anything, disintegrated; and I was puzzled.
—WILLIAM GOLDING

Food is obviously necessary for survival; so you might pay more for it than you would for almost anything else.
—HARRY BROWNE

2. Sometimes a comma (instead of the usual semicolon) separates short main clauses like those below: see also **3a**, page 43.

> He isn't funny, he isn't romantic, he is neither urbane nor fancy free. ——PHILIP TERIGAN

3. A colon (instead of the usual semicolon) appears between main clauses when the second main clause explains or amplifies the first. See also **17d**, page 178.

> This type of construction is like building a house of cards or of children's blocks: slabs of stone are set upright (orthostats) and other slabs are laid across the uprights as capstones.
> ——GLYN DANIEL

■ **Exercise 1** Change each of the following items to conform to pattern **14a**, as shown in the examples below.

EXAMPLES

An engagement is not a marriage. Nor is a family quarrel a broken home.

An engagement is not a marriage; a family quarrel is not a broken home.

All members of my family save things they will never use. My sister, for example, saves old calendars and bent or rusty nails.

All members of my family save things they will never use; for example, my sister saves old calendars and bent or rusty nails.

1. The scientists did not accept this theory. Nor did they ridicule it.
2. Popular TV comedy series occasionally have spinoffs. From *The Mary Tyler Moore Show,* for instance, there came *Rhoda, Lou Grant,* and *Too Close for Comfort.*
3. He took a course in the art of self-defense. But later, during a class demonstration, he broke his wrist.
4. Tony himself cut and polished the turquoise. And it is a beauty.
5. The team kept on losing. And, as a result, the morale of the whole school was low.

14b

Use the semicolon to separate a series of items which themselves contain commas.

This use of the semicolon instead of the comma in a series is for clarity. The semicolon sharply separates the items so that the reader can distinguish the main divisions of the series at a glance.

> A board is elected or appointed from each of three general categories of citizens: for example, a judge or lawyer of good repute; a professor of art, literature, or one of the humanities; and a social worker, psychologist, or clergyman.
> —GEORGE P. ELLIOTT

Note: Occasionally, for emphasis, semicolons may divide a series of items that do not contain internal punctuation— especially a series of main clauses.

> Among scholars there are discoverers; there are critics; and there are teachers. —GILBERT HIGHET

■ **Exercise 2** Combine the following sentences by deleting words and using a series of items separated by semicolons. Use the colon to introduce each series, as in the example.

EXAMPLE

On stage all set to fight were three debaters. One was Eric Dunn, a zero-population-growth advocate. Another was Susan Miles, a theologian. And the third was K. C. Osborn, president of the freshman class.

On stage all set to fight were three debaters: Eric Dunn, a zero-population-growth advocate; Susan Miles, a theologian; and K. C. Osborn, president of the freshman class.

1. On the talk show were three guests. One was T. J. Ott, a psychic. Another was Charles Shelton, a local ufologist. And the third was Abbish Ludah, a guru.
2. We sold everything at our benefit flea market. We sold many dishes and vases, old and cracked. We also sold fishing gear, garden tools, and half-used tubes of lipstick.

14c

Do not use a semicolon between parts of unequal grammatical rank, such as a clause and a phrase or a main clause and a subordinate clause.

NOT   Along came Harvey; the dormitory clown.

BUT   Along came Harvey, the dormitory clown. [a parenthetical appositive phrase—see **12d(2)**]

NOT   We took a detour; the reason being that the bridge was under construction.

BUT   We took a detour, the reason being that the bridge was under construction. [a parenthetical phrase, an absolute—see **12d(3)**]

NOT   Lucy has three topics of conversation; her courses, her career, and her travels.

BUT   Lucy has three topics of conversation: her courses, her career, and her travels. [series—see **17d(1)**]

NOT   If this report is true; then we should act now.

BUT   If this report is true, then we should act now. [introductory adverb clause—see **12b**]

NOT   We heard about the final decision; which really surprised us.

BUT   We heard about the final decision, which really surprised us. [nonrestrictive clause—see **12d(1)**]

NOT   The truck needed a valve job; although it would still run.

BUT   The truck needed a valve job, although it would still run. [parenthetical clause—see note 2 on page 133 and **12d(3)**]

■ **Exercise 3**   Find the semicolons used between parts of unequal rank and substitute a correct mark of punctuation. Do not change properly placed semicolons.

1. Don went jogging one afternoon; never returning; then he was numbered among the tens of thousands who disappear every year.

2. Although the educational TV channel is sometimes a bore; at least tedious ads do not interrupt the programs.

3. I have two main pet peeves; jokes that are pointless and animals that get on furniture.
4. Before the derby she will take the motor apart and overhaul it; her supervisor will be an ace mechanic; her sister Alicia.
5. The tormented bull lowered his head in readiness for another charge; the one-sided contest not being over yet.

■ `Exercise 4` Compose four sentences to illustrate various uses of the semicolon.

General Exercise on the Comma and the Semicolon

■ **Exercise 5** First, review Sections **12** and **14**. Then, using the following examples as guides, punctuate sentences 1–10 appropriately.

12a Pat poured gasoline into the hot tank, for he had not read the warning in his tractor manual.

12b Since Pat had not read the warning in his tractor manual, he poured gasoline into the hot tank.
In very large print in the tractor manual, the warning is conspicuous.

12c Pat did not read the tractor manual, observe the warning, or wait for the tank to cool.
Pat was a rash, impatient young mechanic.

12d Pat did not read his tractor manual, which warned against pouring gasoline into a hot tank.
Pat, a careless young man, poured gasoline into the hot tank of his tractor.
First, warnings should be read.

12e A week before, he had glanced at the manual.

14a Pat ignored the warning in the tractor manual; he poured gasoline into the hot tank.
Pat poured gasoline into the hot tank; thus he caused the explosion.

14b At the hospital Pat said that he had not read the warning; that he had, of course, been careless; and that he would never again, under any circumstances, pour gasoline into a hot tank.

1. Many students were unhappy in the early 1980s for draft registration threatened their future plans.
2. Dr. Felipe a visiting professor from Kenya says that often it is not fun to learn but that it is always fun to know.
3. The stalls of the open market along the wharf were filled with tray after tray of glassy-eyed fish slender stalks of pink rhubarb mounds of home-grown tomatoes and jars of bronze honey.
4. Two or three scrawny mangy-looking hounds lay sprawled in the shade of the cabin.
5. While Diana was unpacking the cooking gear and Grace was chopping firewood I began to put up our shelter.
6. Slamming the door of his four-wheel drive to cut short the argument with his wife Jerry grabbed the grocery list from her and stalked into the supermarket.
7. Still in high school we had to memorize dates and facts such as 1066 the Battle of Hastings 1914–1918 World War I 1939–1945 World War II and 1969 the first moon landing.
8. The dream home that they often talk about is a retreat in the Rockies to tell the truth however they seem perfectly happy in their mobile home on the outskirts of Kansas City.
9. The criminal was asking for mercy his victim was pleading for justice.
10. Chris and I felt that our blustery argument would never end however my weather-watching roommate reminded us that thunderstorms are usually of short duration.

The Apostrophe

15

**Use the apostrophe to indicate the posses-
sive case (except for personal pronouns), to
mark omissions in contracted words or numerals, and to form certain plurals.**

15a
**Use the apostrophe to indicate the possessive case of
nouns and indefinite pronouns.**

The possessive (or genitive) case shows ownership or a com-
parable relationship: *Donald's* car, two *weeks'* pay. The
possessive case of nouns and of indefinite pronouns may be
indicated by the use of *'s* (or by the apostrophe alone) or by
an *of*-phrase.

>   everybody's friend   OR   the friend of everybody
>   the students' laughter   OR   the laughter of students

Occasionally, the possessive is indicated by the use of both
an *of*-phrase and *'s:*

>   that pie **of** Al's   [a double possessive]
>   COMPARE   this description of Al   [Al is described.]
>   this description of Al's   [Al did the describing.]

A possessive noun or pronoun may be related to a word (or word group) that precedes it or that is clearly implied.

Is that old broken-down dune buggy **Frank's** or **Jane's**?

(1) For singular nouns and indefinite pronouns, add the apostrophe and s.

Laura's idea	a week's work	a dime's worth
anyone's guess	somebody's coat	one's choices

Option: If a singular noun ends in *s*, add the apostrophe and *s* or only the apostrophe.

Keats's poetry	OR	Keats' poetry
a waitress's tips	OR	a waitress' tips

When a singular word ends in *s*, many writers use the apostrophe and *s* to reflect pronunciation, but they prefer to use only the apostrophe when the word following begins with an *s* or a *z* sound.

Chris's enthusiasm	BUT	Chris' zeal
the hostess's idea	BUT	for the hostess' sake

(2) For plural nouns ending in s, add only the apostrophe. For plurals not ending in s, add the apostrophe and s.

boys' shoes (shoes for *boys*)	two dollars' worth
babies' toes (toes of *babies*)	the Joneses' reunion

BUT	men's clothing	women's job	children's rights

(3) For compounds or word groups, add the apostrophe and s only to the last word.

my sister-in-law's shop	someone else's turn
the Secretary of Labor's idea	George Heming, Jr.'s reply

(4) To indicate individual ownership, add the apostrophe and s to each name.

Al's and Sue's cars   [Note that *cars* is plural.]
the doctor's and the dentist's offices

Note: To indicate joint ownership, add the apostrophe and *s* only to the last name or to each name.

Al and Sue's car   OR   Al's and Sue's car

Variation to 15a

The use of the apostrophe or the possessive form varies with proper names (organizations, geographical designations, and so on).

Devil's Island   Devils Tower   Devil Mountain

■ **Exercise 1**   Change the modifier after the noun to a possessive form before the noun, following the pattern of the examples.

EXAMPLES

the laughter of the crowd   *the crowd's laughter*
suggestions made by James   *James's suggestions*
                                   OR *James' suggestions*

1. the tape decks belonging to Johnny
2. the boat bought by the Weinsteins
3. the voices of Bess and Mary
4. the efforts of the editor-in-chief
5. the strategy that Doris uses
6. worth a quarter
7. ideas of somebody else
8. stories by Dickens
9. shoes for women
10. a song written by Henry and Ross

15b

Use an apostrophe to mark omissions in contracted words or numerals.

didn't   he'll   they're   there's   class of '85
o'clock   [reduction of "of the clock"]

Note: Contractions in writing mirror speech. As a rule, they are avoided in formal writing: see **19d**. But they are common (and often preferable) both in informal writing and in dialogue.

INFORMAL

With all the books he reads, how come the guy is so illiterate? And why do people just naturally assume that you'll know what they're talking about? No, I don't know, and nobody knows. The planets don't, the stars don't, infinite space doesn't. ——SAUL BELLOW

DIALOGUE

"Well, Curley's pretty handy," the swamper said skeptically. "Never did seem right to me. S'pose Curley jumps a big guy an' licks him. Ever'body says what a game guy Curley is." ——JOHN STEINBECK

15c

Use the apostrophe and *s* to form the plural of lowercase letters and of abbreviations followed by periods. When needed to prevent confusion, use the apostrophe and *s* to form the plural of capital letters, of symbols, of abbreviations not followed by periods, and of words referred to as words.

His *a*'s look like *o*'s.   [The '*s* is not italicized (underlined). See also **10d**.]

Over half of the Ph.D.'s were still looking for jobs.

Her *I*'s are illegible, and her *miss*'s appear to be *mess*'s.

Either '*s* or *s* may be used to form such plurals as the following:

the 1900's	OR the 1900s	his 7's	OR his 7s
two *B*'s	OR two *B*s	the &'s	OR the &s
her *and*'s	OR her *and*s	the VFW's	OR the VFWs

15d

Do not use the apostrophe with the pronouns *his*, *hers*, *its*, *ours*, *yours*, *theirs*, or *whose* or with plural nouns not in the possessive case.

> **His** parents sent money; **ours** sent food.
> A friend of **theirs** knows a cousin of **yours**.
> The **sisters** design **clothes** for **babies**.

Caution: Do not confuse *its* with *it's* or *whose* with *who's*:

> **Its** motor is small.   [the motor *of it*]
> **It's** a small motor.   [*It is* a small motor.]
> **Whose** is that?   [*Who owns* that?]
> **Who's** that?   [*Who is* that?]

■ **Exercise 2**   Insert apostrophes where needed in the following sentences. Put a checkmark after any sentence that needs no change in punctuation.

1. Many students attitudes changed completely in the mid-1970s.
2. Some students dropped these courses because of the stiff requirements.
3. Those newsstands sell Marian Rosss homemade candy.
4. Theyre not interested in hockey; its roughness repels them.
5. Snapshots of everyone in the class of 84 cover Jerrys bulletin board.
6. "Its just one C.P.A.s opinion, isnt it?" Otis commented.
7. Is that dog yours or theirs?
8. There are two *e*s and two *d*s in Hildegardes name, but not any *u*s.
9. The computer confused my account with somebody elses.
10. Marnie often quotes her Granddads favorite expression: "Everybodys useful, but nobodys indispensable!"
11. Its an expensive book, but its cover came unglued.
12. Theres nothing wrong with her attitude or idea, but theirs is not like hers.

Quotation Marks

16

Use quotation marks to set off all direct quotations, some titles, and words used in a special sense. Place other marks of punctuation in proper relation to quotation marks.

Quotations usually consist of passages borrowed from the written work of others or the direct speech of individuals, especially dialogue (conversation).

> QUOTED WRITING Thomas Griffith has written: **"**We have become a no-fault society, and it is adolescent to look for villains.**"** [The words and punctuation within quotation marks are exactly as they appear in ''Party of One: Bigger than Politics,'' *The Atlantic* (Jan. 1980), p. 22.]

> QUOTED SPEECH **"**Sure enough, I'd like to own a slave,**"** Donna explained. **"**A compact, push-button robot!**"** [Within quotation marks are the exactly recorded words of the speaker; the punctuation is supplied by the writer.]

Notice that quotation marks are used in pairs: the first one marks the beginning of the quotation, and the second marks the end. Be careful not to omit or misplace the second one.

Remember that the speaker and the verb of saying (such as *Donna explained*) should be outside the quotation marks.

16a

Use double quotation marks to enclose direct (but not indirect) quotations; use single marks to enclose a quotation within a quotation.

Double quotation marks:

> Making fun of Cooper, Mark Twain said, "He saw nearly all things as through a glass eye, darkly." [a directly quoted sentence]
>
> According to Mark Twain, Cooper "saw nearly all things as through a glass eye, darkly." [part of a sentence quoted directly]
>
> Mark Twain said that Cooper saw nearly everything darkly, as if he were looking through a glass eye. [indirect quotation—no quotation marks]

Single quotation marks within double:

> She said, "Earl keeps calling my idea 'an impossible dream.'" [a quotation within a quotation]

Note: The double quotation marks enclosing a minor title (see **16b**) are reduced to single marks when the title appears within a direct quotation:

> "Edgar Allan Poe's 'A Predicament' is one of the funniest short stories I've ever read!" Chet exclaimed. [a title within a quotation]

(1) Long prose quotations (not dialogue) In printed matter, quoted material of ten or more lines is usually set off from the rest of the text by the use of smaller type, indention, or both. Quotation marks are used only if they appear in the original. In typewritten papers, lengthy quoted passages (more than four lines) are either single-spaced and indented from the left margin five spaces (as shown below) or double-spaced and indented ten spaces (see Section **33**). The first line is indented an additional three spaces when it marks the beginning of a paragraph.

```
Most people say that spring or summer is their

favorite season.  As an art major, I like all the

seasons because as Emerson (in his essay

"Nature") observed,

        To the attentive eye, each moment of the year
        has its own beauty, and in the same field, it
        beholds, every hour, a picture which was
        never seen before, and which shall never be
        seen again. The heavens change every moment,
        and reflect their glory or gloom on the
        plains beneath.

I read and marked these lines last summer, when I

had time to read a book given to me months before.
```

For the proper documentation of sources in a research paper, see Section **33**.

(2) **Poetry** In both printed matter and typewritten papers, except for very special emphasis, a single line of poetry or less is handled like other short quotations—run in with the text and enclosed in quotation marks. A two-line quotation may be run in with the text, with a slash marking the end of the first line. Or it may be set off from the text like longer quotations and quoted line by line exactly as it appears in the original:

```
The poet asks, "If there were dreams to

sell, / What would you buy?"
```

OR

The poet asks,

```
    If there were dreams to sell,
      What would you buy?
```

In printed matter, longer passages (sometimes italicized) are usually set off by smaller type. In typewritten papers, they are single-spaced and indented from the left five spaces. (The numbers in parentheses indicate the line numbers of the poem.)

```
        Persons who angered the czar were

   sent to Siberia.  James Mangan describes

   in "Siberia" the land and its effect on

   the exiled:
            In Siberia's wastes
              Are sands and rocks.
            Nothing blooms of green or soft,
            But the snowpeaks rise aloft
              And the gaunt ice-blocks.

            And the exile there
              Is one with those;
            They are part, and he is part,
            For the sands are in his heart,
              And the killing snows.  (21-30)
```

(3) Dialogue (conversation)   Written dialogue represents the directly quoted speech of two or more persons talking together. Standard practice is to write each person's speech, no matter how short, as a separate paragraph. Verbs of saying, as well as closely related bits of narrative, are included in the paragraph along with the speech:

Through an interpreter, I spoke with a Bedouin man tending nearby olive trees.

"Do you own this land?" I asked him.

He shook his head. "The land belongs to Allah," he said.

"What about the trees?" I asked. He had just harvested a basket of green olives, and I assumed that at least the trees were his.

"The trees, too, are Allah's," he replied.

I marveled at this man who seemed unencumbered by material considerations . . . or so I was thinking when, as if in afterthought, he said, "Of course, I own the *olives!*"

—HARVEY ARDEN, "In Search of Moses"

(4) Punctuation of dialogue   Commas are used to set off expressions such as *he said* and *she asked* in quoted dialogue: see **12d(3)**.

He said, "Pro football is like nuclear warfare."
"Pro football," he said, "is like nuclear warfare."
"Pro football is like nuclear warfare," he said.

When the quoted speech is a question or an exclamation, the question mark or exclamation point replaces the usual comma.

"Pro football?" she asked. "Like nuclear warfare!" she added.

When an expression such as *he said* introduces a quotation of two or more sentences, it is often followed by a colon: see **17d(1)**.

It is as Frank Gifford said: "Pro football is like nuclear warfare. There are no winners, only survivors."

■ **Exercise 1**   In the following sentences, change each indirect quotation to a direct quotation and each direct quotation to an indirect one.

1. Doris said that she had a theory about me.
2. Allen announced that he had read "The Sunless Sea."

3. A Weight Watcher, Eileen explained that she could eat as much as she wanted—of vegetables like spinach, eggplant, and zucchini.
4. Clyde asked, "Will you go to the opera with me?"
5. Last night Pruett said that he thought that Amanda's favorite quotation was "Tomorrow belongs to me."

16b

Use quotation marks for minor titles (short stories, essays, short poems, songs, episodes of a radio or television series, articles in periodicals) and subdivisions of books.

"She Loves Me" was part of the BBC *Great Performances* series.

Gregg Easterbrook's "The Spruce Goose of Outer Space," in the April 1980 issue of *The Washington Monthly*, is about an expensive but grounded flying machine.

Max Shulman's *Guided Tour of Campus Humor* contains numerous poems and short stories, including "Tears from One Who Didn't Realize How Good He Had It" and "Love Is a Fallacy."

Note: Quotation marks are sometimes used to enclose titles of books, periodicals, and newspapers, but italics are generally preferred: see **10a**.

16c

Words used in a special sense are sometimes enclosed in quotation marks.

Such "prophecy" is intelligent guessing.
His "castle" was in reality a cozy little rattrap.

Note: Either quotation marks or italics may be used in definitions such as the following. See also **10d**.

> "Puritanical" means "marked by stern morality."
> *Puritanical* means "marked by stern morality."
> *Puritanical* means *marked by stern morality.*

16d
Do not overuse quotation marks.

Do not use quotation marks to enclose the title of your composition: see **8b(4)**. In general, do not enclose in quotation marks common nicknames, bits of humor, technical terms, or trite or well-known expressions. Instead of using slang and colloquialisms within quotation marks, use more formal English. Do not use quotation marks for emphasis.

> NEEDLESS PUNCTUATION   "Kitty" will not "cop out."
> BETTER   Kitty will not quit.

■ **Exercise 2**   Add correctly placed quotation marks below.

1. In a poem entitled 2001, scientists turn one Einstein into three Einsteins.
2. Here, stoked means fantastically happy on a surfboard.
3. David enjoyed reading the short story A Circle in the Fire.
4. *Learning to Live Without Cigarettes* opens with a chapter entitled Sighting the Target.
5. Bernice replied, Thomas Jefferson once said, Never spend your money before you have it.

16e
When using various marks of punctuation with quoted words, phrases, or sentences, follow the conventions of American printers.

(1) Place the period and the comma within the quotation marks.

"Jenny," he said, "let's have lunch."
She replied, "OK, but first I want to finish 'The Machine Stops.'"

Exception:

The author states: "Time alone reveals the just" (p. 471). [The period follows the reference to the source of the direct quotation.]

(2) Place the colon and the semicolon outside the quotation marks.

She spoke of "the protagonists"; yet I remembered only one in "The Tell-Tale Heart": the mad murderer.

(3) Place the dash, the question mark, and the exclamation point within the quotation marks when they apply only to the quoted matter; place them outside when they apply to the whole sentence.

Pilate asked, "What is truth?" [The question mark applies only to the quoted matter.]

What is the meaning of the term "half truth"? [The question mark applies to the whole sentence.]

Why did he ask, "What is truth?" [Both the quoted matter and the sentence as a whole are questions, but a second question mark does not follow the quotation marks.]

Gordon answered, "No way!" [The exclamation point applies only to the quoted matter.]

Stop whistling "All I Do Is Dream of You"! [The whole sentence, not the song title, is an exclamation.]

■ **Exercise 3**   Insert quotation marks where they are needed in the following sentences.

1. At the beginning of *All in the Family,* Archie and Edith always sang Those Were the Days.
2. Get aholt, instead of get ahold, is still heard occasionally in that region.
3. No, Peg said, I didn't agree to do that for her. I may be a softie, but I haven't gone bananas yet!
4. It was then that I discovered Housman's poem Loveliest of Trees.
5. Why cry over spilled milk? my grandmother used to ask. Be glad that you had the milk to spill.
6. As for me, Socrates said, all I know is that I know nothing.
7. Wasn't it on the *Phil Donahue in Denver* show that Shirley MacLaine asked Isn't travel the best form of self-search?
8. The Old Folks is one of the funniest of Carol Burnett's regular skits.
9. Who wrote The Star-Spangled Banner?
10. Catherine said, Do the townspeople ever say to me You're a born leader? Yes, lots of times, and when they do, I just tell them my motto is Lead, follow, or get the heck out of the way!

The Period and Other Marks

17

Use the period, the question mark, the exclamation point, the colon, the dash, parentheses, brackets, the slash, and the ellipsis mark according to standard practices. (For the use of the hyphen, see 18f.)

Read the following sentences aloud. Observe how the punctuation in color signals intonation (pitch, stress, stops) and helps to reveal sentence meaning:

> "Why are you so depressed?" they want to know. "The universe is expanding!" he explains. —ALBERT ROSENFELD

> In *Lady Windermere's Fan* (1892) is this famous line: "I [Lord Darlington] can resist everything except temptation."

> No day / night cycle exists there. The inhabitants have no way of measuring time—even years—by our standards.
> —JOHN A. KEEL

> The pilot had "abnormally low blood sugar. The effects . . . include subtle mental confusion . . . and decrease of psychomotor ability." —SATURDAY REVIEW

This section covers the main principles of usage of these punctuation marks in ordinary (rather than technical or special) writing.

The Period

17a
Use the period after declarative and mildly imperative sentences, after indirect questions, and after most abbreviations.

(1) Use the period to mark the end of a declarative sentence, a mildly imperative sentence, and an indirect question.

Everyone should drive defensively. [declarative]

Learn how to drive defensively. [mild imperative]

She asks how drivers can cross the city without driving offensively. [indirect question]

"What is that?" she asked. [declarative containing a direct question]

"Get with it!" he hollered. [declarative containing an exclamation]

(2) Use periods after most abbreviations.

Mrs.   an M.D.   R.S.V.P.   No. 444   etc.
1:10 p.m.

In current usage the period is frequently omitted after many abbreviations: see also Section **11**, page 122.

IRS   RR   USAF   APO   ASCAP   mpg   mph

Do not use periods after shortened or clipped forms:

2nd   10th   math   premed   gym   lab   psych

When in doubt about the punctuation of an abbreviation, consult a good college dictionary. Dictionaries often list a range of choices (for example, *A.W.O.L., a.w.o.l., AWOL, awol*).

Caution: When an abbreviation ending in a period appears last in the sentence, do not add a second period:

Someday I hope to be an R.N.

The Question Mark

17b

Use the question mark after direct (but not indirect) questions.

Who started the rumor?
Did he ask **who started the rumor?** [The sentence as a whole is a direct question despite the indirect question at the end.]
Did you hear her ask, "Are you accusing me of starting the rumor?" [double direct question followed by a single question mark]

Declarative sentences may contain direct questions:

"Who started the rumor?" he asked. [No comma follows the question mark.]
He asked, "Who started the rumor?" [No period follows the question mark.]
She told me—did I hear her correctly?—who started the rumor. [interpolated question]

A declarative or an imperative sentence may be converted into a question:

He drove to Boston?
Drive to Boston?

Question marks may be used between the parts of a series:

Did he rent the house? buy the house? buy the adjoining land? [Question marks cause full stops and emphasize each part. Compare "Did he rent the house, buy the house, and buy the adjoining land?"]

175

Note: A question mark within parentheses is used to express the writer's uncertainty as to the correctness of the preceding word, figure, or date:

> Chaucer was born in 1340 (?) and died in 1400.

Caution: Do not use a comma or a period after a question mark.

> "Are *gobbledygook* and *Jabberwocky* synonyms?" he asked.
> He asked, "Are *gobbledygook* and *Jabberwocky* synonyms?"

The Exclamation Point

17c

Use the exclamation point after an emphatic interjection and after a phrase, clause, or sentence to express a high degree of surprise, incredulity, or other strong emotion.

> Wow! What a desperation pass!
> "Man! We've been conned!" he said.
> Act now! Get involved!

Caution 1: Avoid overuse of the exclamation point. Use a comma after mild interjections, and end mildly exclamatory sentences and mild imperatives with a period. See also **17a(1)**.

> Oh, don't get involved.
> How quiet the lake was.

Caution 2: Do not use a comma or a period after an exclamation point.

> "Get off the road!" he yelled.
> He yelled, "Get off the road!"

■ **Exercise 1**   Illustrate the chief uses of the period, the question mark, and the exclamation point by composing and correctly punctuating brief sentences of the types specified.

EXAMPLE
a declarative sentence containing a quoted direct question
"What does fennel taste like?" she asked.

1. a direct question
2. a mild imperative
3. a declarative sentence containing a quoted exclamation
4. a declarative sentence containing an indirect question
5. a declarative sentence containing an interpolated question

The Colon

17d

Use the colon as a formal introducer to call attention to what follows and as a mark of separation in scriptural and time references and in certain titles.

(1) The colon may direct attention to an explanation or summary, an appositive, a series, or a quotation.

One thing only was equivalent in value to a man: another man.   —HERBERT GOLD

Three times he drags me over to the bulletin board to show me his team's enviable record: five straight league titles.
    —HAROLD BRODKEY

Theories which try to explain the secret of fire walking fall into three categories: physical, psychological, and religious.
    —LEONARD FEINBERG

The sense of unity with nature is vividly shown in Zen Buddhist paintings and poetry: "An old pine tree preaches wisdom. And a wild bird is crying out truth."
    —ANNE MORROW LINDBERGH

The colon may separate two main clauses or sentences when the second explains or amplifies the first:

> The sorrow was laced with violence: In the first week of demolition, vandals struck every night.   —SMITHSONIAN

> The American conceives of fishing as more than a sport: it is his personal contest against nature.   —JOHN STEINBECK

Note: After the colon, quoted sentences regularly begin with a capital, but other sentences (as the preceding examples show) may begin with either a capital letter or a lower-case letter, although the latter is generally preferred.

(2) Use the colon between figures in scriptural and time references and between titles and subtitles.

> The text of the sermon was Matthew 6:10.
> At 2:15 A.M. the phone rang.
> I had just read *On Being Funny: Woody Allen and Comedy* by Eric Lax.

Note: The colon is also used after the salutation of a business letter and in bibliographical data: see **33b(4)** and **34a(3)**.

(3) Do not use superfluous colons.

As a rule, superfluous or unnecessary colons interrupt the sentence base. Sometimes they follow *such as.*

> SUPERFLUOUS   These handicapped people can repair almost anything, such as: old lawnmowers, broken clocks, frayed wires, cracked vases.
>
> REVISED   These handicapped people can repair almost anything, such as old lawnmowers, broken clocks, frayed wires, cracked vases.   [colon omitted]
>
> OR   These handicapped people can repair almost anything: old lawnmowers, broken clocks, frayed wires, cracked vases.   [*such as* omitted]

SUPERFLUOUS   The six survivors were: one man, two women, and three children.

REVISED   The six survivors were one man, two women, and three children.

OR   There were six survivors **:** one man, two women, and three children.

OR   The six survivors were as follows **:** one man, two women, and three children.   [Although *survivors* is plural, *as follows* (not *as follow*) is standard usage.]

■ **Exercise 2**   Punctuate the following sentences by adding colons. Put a checkmark after any sentence that needs no change.

1. At 1230 A.M. he was still repeating his favorite quotation ''TV is the opiate of the people.''
2. The downtown streets are narrow, rough, and junky.
3. Even people in rural areas were not safe many criminals had left the cities and the suburbs.
4. During our tour of the library, our guide recommended that we find one of the following periodicals *Intellect, Smithsonian, Commentary,* or *The Chronicle of Higher Education.*
5. All their thoughts were centered on equal pay for equal work.

■ **Exercise 3**   Decide whether to use a colon or a semicolon between the main clauses of the following sentences. See also **14a**.

1. These laws all have the same purpose they protect us from ourselves.
2. Some of these laws have an obvious purpose others seem senseless.
3. Few things in life are certain perhaps we could name them all on one hand.
4. One thing is certain the future looks bright.

The Dash

17e

Use the dash to mark a sudden break in thought; to set off (for emphasis or clarity) an added explanation, or illustration, or parenthetical element; and to mark the end of an introductory series.

On the typewriter, the dash is indicated by two hyphens without spacing before, between, or after. In handwriting, the dash is an unbroken line about the length of two or three hyphens.

(1) Use the dash to mark a sudden break in thought, an abrupt change in tone, or faltering speech.

A hypocrite is a person who—but who isn't?
—DON MARQUIS

When I was six I made my mother a little hat—out of her new blouse.   —LILLY DACHÉ

In most food products—not many, *most*—two to four corporations already have seized control of the market.
—DANIEL ZWERDLING

Quickly regaining speech, but still in a state of disbelief, I stammered: "No. Uh, yes. Uh—it's all right."
—DOROTHY K. DUFFEY

(2) Use the dash to set off (for emphasis or clarity) an added explanation or illustration.

Lightning is an electrical discharge—an enormous spark.
—RICHARD E. ORVILLE

Some do not succeed in shedding their old problems—such as an ailing marriage, for instance—when they get to Columbia.   —VANCE PACKARD

The other course— to give trust, in the hope of being trusted— carries the promise of mutual benefit and survival. —SIDNEY LENS

She did not have a particularly light touch with flavors and textures— her roasts were dredged with flour, her seasonings heavily dependent on cayenne, parsley, and tomato.

—LAURA SHAPIRO

[A colon, which might be used here instead of the dash, would be more formal.]

(3) Use the dash to set off a parenthetical element for emphasis or (if it contains commas) for clarity.

Maybe a third of the thefts from libraries are— and always have been— inside jobs. —DAVID LAMPE

All change— I hesitate to call it progress— is bought at a price. —PAUL A. SAMUELSON

A true book is a report upon the mystery of existence; it tells what has been seen in a man's life in the world— touched there, thought of, tasted. —ARCHIBALD MacLEISH

Sentiments that human shyness will not always allow one to convey in conversation— sentiments of gratitude, of apology, of love— can often be more easily conveyed in a letter.

—ARISTIDES

(4) Use the dash between an introductory series and the main part of the sentence that explains or amplifies the series.

Items in an introductory series are often referents of *all, everything, none, such,* or *these* in the main part of the sentence.

Patience, diligence, painstaking attention to detail— these are the requirements. —MARK TWAIN

Keen, calculating, perspicacious, acute and astute— I was all of these. —MAX SHULMAN

Marble-topped tables, two Singer sewing machines, a big vase of pampas grass— everything was rich and grand.
— CARSON McCULLERS

Caution: Use the dash carefully in formal writing. Do not use dashes as awkward substitutes for commas, semicolons, or end marks.

Parentheses

17f

Use parentheses to set off parenthetical, supplementary, or illustrative matter and to enclose figures or letters when used for enumeration within a sentence.

I can still tell a ripsaw from a crosscut saw by what was taught me (by a lady carpentry teacher, Miss Sprague) in the fourth grade. — THEODORE H. WHITE

Some states (New York, for instance) outlaw the use of *any* electronic eavesdropping device by private individuals.
— MYRON BRENTON

When confronted with ambiguities, we are not certain as to how we should interpret (1) single words or phrases, (2) the sense of a sentence, (3) the emphases or accents desired by the writer or speaker, or (4) the significance of a statement.
— LIONEL RUBY

Each entry will be judged on the basis of (*a*) its artistic value, (*b*) its technical competence, and (*c*) its originality.

Note: In sentences such as the following, the commas and periods are placed after the closing parenthesis, not before the opening parenthesis.

Cuban schools, especially on the Isle of Youth (formerly the Isle of Pines), bear names of prominent African figures (Agostinho Neto, Eduardo Mondlane). — MARY LOU SUHOR

If a whole sentence beginning with a capital is in parentheses, the period or other end mark is placed just before the closing parenthesis. See also **9e**.

> Whatever else may be happening, Madame Colette is never *really* unaware, never *really* confused, never *really* afraid. (She can get mighty irritated sometimes.) —STEPHEN KOCH

Punctuation of Parenthetical Matter

Dashes, parentheses, commas—all are used to set off parenthetical matter. Dashes set off parenthetical elements sharply and usually emphasize them:

> Man's mind is indeed—as Luther said—a factory busy with making idols. —HARVEY COX [See **17e(3)**.]

Parentheses generally minimize the importance of the elements they enclose:

> Man's mind is indeed (as Luther said) a factory busy with making idols. [See **17f**.]

Commas are the most commonly used separators:

> Man's mind is indeed, as Luther said, a factory busy with making idols. [See **12d**.]

Brackets

17g

Use brackets to set off interpolations in quoted matter and to replace parentheses within parentheses.

> The *Home Herald* printed the beginning of the mayor's speech: "My dear fiends [sic] and fellow citizens." [A bracketed *sic*—meaning "thus"—tells the reader that the error appears in the original.]

There is a pair of sentences that anyone over thirty heard with guaranteed regularity during his childhood. With only slight variations the pattern was: "Why aren't you eating your spinach? Think of the poor starving children of Armenia [China, Turkey, India]!" —RUTH GAY

She recommended several source books (for example, Jules H. Guilder's *Computer Programs in Science and Engineering* [Rochelle Park, N.J.: Hayden, 1980]).

The Slash

17h

Use the slash between terms to indicate that either term is applicable and to mark the end of a line of quoted poetry. See also 16a(2).

Note that the slash is used unspaced between terms, but with a space before and after it between lines of poetry.

Today visions of the checkless /cashless society are not quite as popular as they used to be. —KATHRYN H. HUMES

Equally rare is a first-rate adventure story designed for those who enjoy a smartly told tale that isn't steeped in blood and /or sex. —JUDITH CRIST

When in "Mr. Flood's Party" the hero sets down his jug at his feet, "as a mother lays her sleeping child / Down tenderly, fearing it may awake," one feels Robinson's heart to be quite simply on his sleeve. —WILLIAM H. PITCHARD

■ **Exercise 4**   Correctly punctuate each of the following sentences by supplying commas, dashes, parentheses, brackets, or the slash. Be prepared to explain the reason for all marks you add, especially those you choose for setting off parenthetical matter.

1. Gordon Gibbs or is it his twin brother? plays the drums.
2. Joseph who is Gordon's brother is a lifeguard at the Beachfront Hotel.

3. "I admit that I" he began, but his voice broke; he could say no more.
4. This organization needs more of everything more money, brains, initiative.
5. Some of my courses for example, French and biology demand a great deal of work outside the classroom.
6. In the TV version of *The Lone Ranger,* Jay Silverheels 1918–1980 played the role of Tonto.
7. This ridiculous sentence appeared in the school paper: "Because of a personal fool sic the Cougars failed to cross the goal line during the last seconds of the game."
8. The word *zipper* once a trademark like Polaroid is now a common noun.
9. Gently rolling hills, rich valleys, beautiful lakes these things impress the tourist in Connecticut.
10. Some innovations for example the pass fail system did not contribute to grade inflation.

The Ellipsis Mark

17i

Use three spaced periods (the ellipsis mark) to indicate an omission within a quoted passage and to mark a reflective pause or hesitation.

It is generally considered unnecessary to use the ellipsis mark at the beginning or the end of a quoted passage.

OMISSION WITHIN A QUOTED PASSAGE

Clinton Rossiter writes: "My own answer to the question 'What is liberty?' is essentially this: Liberty **. . .** cannot be defined but can be understood." [Note the use of single quotation marks: see **16a**.]

Compare the quoted passage above with the original:

> My own answer to the question "What is liberty?" is essentially this: Liberty, like truth and justice and all the other great abstractions, cannot be defined but can be understood, and the first step toward understanding is to identify the most important uses of the word.   —CLINTON ROSSITER

If a complete sentence in the quotation precedes the omission, use a period before the ellipsis mark:

> "Nevertheless, inflation really is a horror," Martin Mayer contends, "because it demeans work. In a developed economy, people necessarily work for money. . . . If the money they receive in return for their labors is continually diminishing in value, they feel an insult to themselves and to their function in society, even if as installment debtors they benefit by it."   [Note that no space precedes the period before the ellipsis mark.]

Compare the quotation with the original:

> Nevertheless, inflation really is a horror, because it demeans work. In a developed economy, people necessarily work for money. Obviously, they want money to buy something, but at the time of work, and of thinking about work, they do not normally have in their heads the idea of what they are going to buy with the proceeds. If the money they receive in return for their labors is continually diminishing in value, they feel an insult to themselves and to their function in society, even if as installment debtors they benefit by it.   —MARTIN MAYER

The ellipsis mark indicates that a part of a sentence, one or more sentences, or (sometimes) a full paragraph or more has been left out. Spaced periods covering a whole line mark the omission of at least one paragraph in prose or a full line in poetry.

> All I can say is—I saw it!
> . . . .
> Impossible! Only—I saw it!   —ROBERT BROWNING

A REFLECTIVE PAUSE OR HESITATION

The ellipsis mark is also used to indicate a pensive or thought-filled pause, deliberate hesitation, or an intentionally unfinished statement (not an interruption).

> Love, like other emotions, has causes . . . and consequences. —LAWRENCE CASLER

> It's a bird . . . it's a plane . . . well, it's the Gossamer Penguin, a 68-pound flying machine fueled only by the sun.
> —CATHLEEN McGUIGAN

> "It's well for you . . ." began Lucille. She bit the remark off. —ELIZABETH BOWEN
> [a deliberately unfinished statement]

The ellipsis mark may come after a period marking the end of a sentence:

> All channels are open. The meditation is about to begin. . . . —TOM ROBBINS

■ **Exercise 5** Beginning with *According to John Donne,* or with *As John Donne has written,* quote the following passage, omitting the words placed in brackets. Use three or four periods as needed to indicate omissions.

> No man is an island [entire of itself;] every man is a piece of the continent, a part of the main. [If a clod be washed away by the sea, Europe is the less, as well as if a promontory were, as well as if a manor of thy friend's or of thine own were]. Any man's death diminishes me because I am involved in mankind [and therefore never send to know for whom the bell tolls; it tolls for thee]. —JOHN DONNE

■ **Exercise 6** First, observing differences in meaning and emphasis, use an ellipsis mark in place of the dash, commas, and the italicized words below. Then write two sentences of your own to illustrate the use of the ellipsis mark to indicate a pause or hesitation.

1. My father was dying—*and, I wondered,* what would happen to us?
2. Our lives would have been different if *he had lived.*

■ **Exercise 7**   Punctuate the following sentences (selected and adapted from *The Atlantic*) by supplying appropriate end marks, commas, colons, dashes, and parentheses. Do not use unnecessary punctuation. Be prepared to explain the reason for each mark you add, especially when you have a choice of correct marks (for example, commas, dashes, or parentheses).

1. Freeways in America are all the same aluminum guardrails green signs white lettering
2. "Is it is it the green light then" was all I managed to say
3. I tell you again What is alive and young and throbbing with historic current in America is musical theater
4. Things aren't helped by the following typo "The second study involved 177,106 of the approximately 130,000 refugees"
5. "Judy" she exploded "Judy that's an awful thing to say" She raised an arm to slap her daughter but it wouldn't reach
6. Emily formerly Mrs. Goyette caught McAndless' sleeve where no one could see and tugged it briefly but urgently
7. At last she had become what she had always wished to be a professional dancer
8. My own guess is that sociobiology will offer no comfort to thinkers conservatives or liberals who favor tidy ideas about what it means to be human
9. As one man put it "Rose Bowl Sugar Bowl and Orange Bowl all are gravy bowls"
10. "Good and" can mean "very" "I am good and mad" and "a hot cup of coffee" means that the coffee not the cup is hot

SPELLING AND DICTION

Spelling and Hyphenation

18

Spell every word according to established usage as shown by your dictionary. Hyphenate words in accordance with current usage.

Spelling

Spelling is a highly individual problem. You can improve your spelling by following these six suggestions:

1. Proofread to detect misspellings. Many misspellings are a result of mistakes in typing or in handwriting. Below are samples of a proofreader's corrections of typical misspellings:

   alot   dosen't   durring   therefore

   what ever   wordly

2. Make good use of your dictionary. When you consult the dictionary for a correct spelling, give attention to syllabication, pronunciation, and (when helpful) etymology. Check meaning to be sure that you have found the exact word you have in mind.

Look for any labels that may restrict the use of a given spelling—like *British* or *chiefly British*.

BRITISH	AMERICAN
connexion	connection
humour	humor
jeweller	jeweler
offence	offense
realise	realize

Check for labels like *obsolete* or *archaic* (*compleat* for *complete*), *regional* or *dialectal* (*heighth* for *height*), or *slang* (*weirdy, weirdo*).

If your dictionary lists unlabeled optional spellings—such as *likable/likeable, theater/theatre,* or *tornados/tornadoes*—either form is correct.

3. Study in context pairs of spellings (like *device, devise*) that you confuse. Visualize the words as you pronounce them. Practice writing them in phrases that bring out their denotations.

4. Spell by rule. Take time to analyze the structure of a word. Learn regular patterns of spellings (as well as exceptions) to avoid repetition of similar errors.

5. Study word lists. The lists in this section consist of hundreds of frequently misspelled words. Single out for special study those words that you find troublesome.

6. Keep an individual spelling list. List for study those words that you have misspelled or tend to misspell. Be sure that each word on your list is correctly written.

18a

Do not allow pronunciation (whether incorrect or correct) to cause you to misspell words by omitting, adding, or transposing letters.

Mispronunciation often leads to the misspelling of such words as those listed below. To avoid difficulties resulting from mispronunciation, pronounce problem words aloud several times, clearly and distinctly, in accordance with the pronunciation shown by a dictionary. Be careful not to omit, add, or transpose any letter or syllable.

athlete	drowned	modern	quantity
barbarous	escape	pertain	recognize
candidate	everything	prescribe	represent
disastrous	gratitude	probable	umbrella

A word that is difficult to spell may have two correct pronunciations. Of these, one may be a better guide to spelling. For example, the person who correctly leaves out the first /n/ when saying *government* or the first /r/ when saying *surprise* may be more likely to omit the *n* or *r* when writing these words than one who, again correctly, pronounces these sounds.

Each word in the following list has more than one correct pronunciation. If you tend to misspell any of these words because of the way you say them, then depend on your vision and memory to learn their correct spellings.

arctic	hundred	sophomore
boundary	interest	temperature
February	literature	veteran
generally	perhaps	where

As you check pronunciations in the dictionary, give special attention to /ə/, the symbol for a neutral vowel sound in unaccented syllables, usually an indistinct *uh* sound (as in *confidence*). Be especially careful not to omit letters representing /ə/. (The term *schwa* is used to refer to the vowel sound or to its phonetic symbol.)

Caution: Do not misspell words like *and*, *have*, or *than* because they are not stressed in context.

We had ham and [NOT *an*] eggs.
I should have [NOT *of*] won.
The movie is even more exciting than [NOT *then*] the book.

18b

Distinguish between words of similar sound and spelling; use the spelling required by the meaning.

Words such as *forth* and *fourth* or *sole* and *soul* sound alike but have vastly different meanings. Always be sure to choose the right word for your context.

A number of frequently confused spellings may be studied in groups:

Contractions and possessive pronouns:

It's best to wait.	The team did **its** best.
You're required to attend.	**Your** attendance is required.
There's a change in plans.	**Theirs** have changed.

Single words and two-word phrases:

It's an **everyday** event.	It happens nearly **every day.**
Maybe that is true.	That **may be** true.
I ran **into** trouble.	I ran **in to** get it.
Nobody cared.	The ghost had **no body.**

*Singular nouns ending in **nce** and plural nouns ending in **nts**:*

not much **assistance**	too many **assistants**
for **instance**	just **instants** ago
even less **patience** with	several **patients**

As you study the list of words below, use your dictionary to check the meaning of words not thoroughly familiar to you. You may find it helpful to devise examples of usage such as these:

breath—a deep breath	**breathe**—to breathe deeply
passed—had passed	**past**—in the past

Words Frequently Confused

accept, except	descent, dissent
access, excess	dam, damn
advice, advise	desert, dessert
affect, effect	device, devise
aisle, isle	dominant, dominate
alley, ally	dyeing, dying
allude, elude	envelop, envelope
already, all ready	fair, fare
altar, alter	formerly, formally
10 altogether, all together	40 forth, fourth
always, all ways	gorilla, guerrilla
angel, angle	hear, here
ascent, assent	heard, herd
assistance, assistants	hole, whole
bare, bear	holy, wholly
birth, berth	human, humane
board, bored	its, it's
born, borne	later, latter
breath, breathe	lead, led
20 canvas, canvass	50 lesson, lessen
Calvary, cavalry	lightning, lightening
capital, capitol	lose, loose
censor, censure	maybe, may be
choose, chose	minor, miner
cite, sight, site	moral, morale
clothes, cloths	of, off
coarse, course	passed, past
complement, compliment	patience, patients
conscience, conscious	peace, piece
30 council, counsel	60 personal, personnel

plain, plane
precede, proceed
presence, presents
principle, principal
prophecy, prophesy
purpose, propose
quiet, quite, quit
respectfully, respectively
reverend, reverent
70 right, rite, -wright, write
sense, since
stationary, stationery

statue, stature, statute
straight, strait
taut, taunt
than, then
their, there, they're
through, thorough
to, too, two
80 tract, track
weather, whether
were, where
who's, whose
your, you're

18c

Apply the rules for spelling when adding prefixes and suffixes to the root.

The root is the base to which the prefix or the suffix is added.

PREFIXES

(1) Add the prefix to the root without doubling or dropping letters.

Do not double the last letter of the prefix when it is different from the first letter of the root (as in *disappear*). Do not drop the last letter of the prefix when the root begins with the same letter (as in *immortal*).

dis + agree = disagree	dis + satisfied = dissatisfied
un + usual = unusual	un + noted = unnoted
mis + used = misused	mis + spent = misspent
re + do = redo	re + elect = reelect [OR re-elect]

SUFFIXES

(2) Drop an unpronounced final *e* before a suffix beginning with a vowel but not before a suffix beginning with a consonant.

like → liking BUT likely, likeness, likelihood
use → usage, using BUT useful, useless

Dropped -e before vowel:		*Retained -e before consonant:*	
age	aging	care	careful
combine	combination	entire	entirely
desire	desirable	manage	management
fame	famous	rude	rudeness
scarce	scarcity	safe	safety

Caution: To keep the sound /s/ of *-ce* or /j/ of *-ge,* do not drop the final *e* before *-able* or *-ous:*

noticing BUT noticeable
changing BUT changeable
raging BUT outrageous
engaging BUT courageous

Similarly, keep the *e* before *-ance,* as in *vengeance.*

Other exceptions:

acreage hoeing lineage mileage [-e kept before vowel]
argument ninth truly wholly [-e dropped before consonant]

■ **Exercise 1** Practice adding suffixes to words ending in an unpronounced *e.*

EXAMPLES

-ing: rise, lose, guide   *rising, losing, guiding*
-ly, -er, -ness: late   *lately, later, lateness*

1. -ly: like, safe, sure
2. -able, -ing, -ment: excite
3. -ful: care, hope, use
4. -ing, -ment, -able: argue

5. -ing: come, notice, hope
6. -ing, -less: use
7. -ous: continue, courage
8. -ly, -ing: complete
9. -able: desire, notice
10. -ing, -ment: manage

(3) Double a final single consonant before a suffix beginning with a vowel (*a*) if the consonant ends a stressed syllable or a word of one syllable and (*b*) if the consonant is preceded by a single vowel. Otherwise, do not double the consonant.

One-syllable words:		*Words stressed on last syllable:*	
drag	dragged	abhor	abhorrent
hid	hidden	begin	beginning
shop	shoppers	occur	occurrence
stun	stunning	regret	regrettable
wet	wettest	unwrap	unwrapped

Compare: benefited, reference   [stressed on first syllable]

■ **Exercise 2**   Write the present participle (-*ing* form) and the past tense of each verb: *rob*—robbing, robbed.

admit	conceal	hope	plan	stop
brag	grip	jog	rebel	audit

(4) As a rule, change final *y* to *i* before adding a suffix, but keep the *y* before -*ing*.

apply → applies, applied, appliance   BUT   applying
study → studies, studied   BUT   studying
happy → happily, happiness, happier, happiest

Exceptions: Verbs ending in *y* preceded by a vowel do not change the *y* before -*s* or -*ed*: *stay, stays, stayed.* Following the same pattern of spelling, nouns like *joys* or *days* have *y* before *s*. The following irregularities in spelling are especially troublesome:

lays, laid   pays, paid   [*Compare:* says, said.]

(5) Do not drop a final *l* when you add *-ly.*

formal	formally	usual	usually
real	really	wool	woolly

■ **Exercise 3**   Add the designated suffixes to the following words.

1. -able: vary, ply
2. -er: funny, carry
3. -ous: vary, luxury
4. -ly: easy, final
5. -ed: supply, stay

6. -ing: study, worry
7. -d: pay, lay
8. -hood: lively, likely
9. -ness: friendly, lonely
10. -ly: usual, cool

18d

Apply the rules for spelling to avoid confusion of *ei* and *ie.*

When the sound is /ē/ (*ee*), write *ie* (except after *c*, in which case write *ei*).

				(after *c*)	
chief	grief	pierce	wield	ceiling	deceive
field	niece	relief	yield	conceit	perceive

When the sound is other than /ē/ (*ee*), usually write *ei*.

counterfeit	foreign	heifer	heir	sleigh	vein
forfeit	freight	height	neighbor	stein	weigh

Exceptions: friend, mischief, seize, sheik

■ **Exercise 4**   Fill in the blanks with the appropriate letters: *ei* or *ie.*

1. p____ce
2. ach____ve
3. rec____ve
4. n____gh
5. fr____ght

6. ap____ce
7. bel____f
8. conc____ve
9. th____r
10. dec____t

11. n____ce
12. sh____ld
13. w____rd
14. shr____k
15. pr____st

18e

As a rule, form the plural of nouns by adding s or es to the singular.

(1) Form the plural of most nouns by adding s to the singular:

| two boys | many nations | a few scientists |
| several safes | three cupfuls | all the radios |

both sisters-in-law   [chief word pluralized]
the Dudleys and the Berrys   [proper names]

Note: To form the plural of some nouns ending in *f* or *fe*, change the ending to *ve* before adding the *s: a thief, two thieves; one life, our lives.*

(2) Add *es* to singular nouns ending in s, ch, sh, or x.

| many losses | these mailboxes | the Rogerses |
| two approaches | a lot of ashes | two Dorises |

[Note that each plural above makes an extra syllable.]

(3) Add *es* to singular nouns ending in *y* preceded by a consonant, after changing the *y* to *i*.

eighty—eighties
strawberry—strawberries
company—companies
industry—industries

Note: Although *es* is often added to a singular noun ending in *o* preceded by a consonant, usage varies:

echoes	heroes	potatoes	vetoes	[-*es* only]
autos	memos	pimentos	pros	[-*s* only]
nos/noes	mottos/mottoes	zeros/zeroes		[-*s* or -*es*]

Exceptions: Irregular plurals (including retained foreign spellings) are not formed by adding *s* or *es*.

SINGULAR	woman	goose	analysis	alga	species
PLURAL	women	geese	analyses	algae	species

■ **Exercise 5** Supply plural forms (including any optional spelling) for the following words, applying rule **18e**. (If a word is not covered by the rule, use your dictionary.)

1. belief	6. bath	11. radius	16. phenomenon
2. theory	7. hero	12. scarf	17. halo
3. church	8. story	13. wife	18. child
4. genius	9. wish	14. speech	19. handful
5. Kelly	10. forty	15. tomato	20. rodeo

A List of Words Frequently Misspelled

Like the words discussed in Section **18b**, the following list may be studied in groups of ten or twenty at a time. Blank spaces are provided at the end of the list for the addition of other words which you may wish to master (possibly those from your special field of interest) or which your instructor may recommend.

	absence		achievement		advised
	acceptable		acquainted		affected
	accessible		acquire		affectionately
	accidentally		acreage		aggravate
	accommodate		across		aggression
	accompanied		actually		aisles
	accomplish		address		alcohol
	accordion		admission		all right
	accuracy		adolescent		a lot of
10	accustomed	20	advice	30	always

amateur	barbarous	chief
among	bargain	children
analysis	basically	chocolate
ancestry	beautiful	chosen
angel	beginning	Christianity
annihilate	belief	coarsely
announcement	believed	commercial
anywhere	beneficial	commitment
apiece	benefited	committee
40 apology	70 biggest	100 competent

apparent	birthday	competition
appearance	boundary	completely
appoint	breath	conceited
appreciate	breathe	conceive
appropriate	bulletin	concentrate
approximately	bureaucracy	condemn
arguing	business	confident
argument	cafeteria	conscience
arrest	calculator	conscientious
50 article	80 calendar	110 consensus

aspirin	carrying	consistent
assassination	category	continuous
associate	cemetery	contradict
atheist	census	controlled
athletics	certain	controversial
attached	challenge	convenient
attacked	changeable	coolly
attendance	changing	courses
authentic	channel	courteous
60 average	90 characteristic	120 criticism

201

	criticize		disturb		experiment
	crowd		divide		explanation
	cruelty		divine		extremely
	curiosity		doctor		familiar
	curious		dormitory		family
	dealt		easily		fascinate
	deceive		ecstasy		favorite
	decision		effect		February
	decorate		efficient		finally
130	definitely	160	eighth	190	financially

	delicate		elaborately		fluorine
	descend		embarrass		foreign
	description		empty		foresee
	desirable		enemy		foretell
	despair		entirely		forty
	desperate		environment		forward
	despicable		equipment		friend
	destroy		equipped		fulfill
	develop		escape		gauge
140	different	170	especially	200	generally

	disagree		everything		government
	disappear		evidently		governor
	disappoint		exaggerate		grammar
	disapprove		excellent		group
	disastrous		except		gruesome
	discipline		exercise		guaranteed
	discussion		exhaust		guard
	disease		existence		guerrilla
	dispel		expense		guidance
150	distinct	180	experience	210	happened

happily	indispensable	likelihood
harass	individually	listening
heard	influential	liveliest
height	initiative	lose
here	innocuous	luxury
heroes	instead	lying
hindrance	insurance	magazine
holiday	intelligent	magnificent
hoping	interest	maintenance
220 human	**250** interference	**280** manageable
humane	integrate	management
humorous	interrupt	maneuver
hundred	introduce	manual
hungry	involve	marriage
hurriedly	irrelevant	material
hypocrisy	irresistible	mathematics
hypocrite	irritated	meanness
ideally	jealousy	meant
idiosyncrasy	jewelry	medicine
230 ignorant	**260** knowledge	**290** mere
illogical	laboratory	miniature
imaginary	laid	minor
imagine	led	minutes
imitate	leisure	mirror
immediately	length	mischievous
immensely	lenient	missile
incalculable	liable	morale
incidentally	library	morals
incredible	license	mortgage
240 independent	**270** lightning	**300** morning

muscle
mysterious
narrative
naturally
necessary
nevertheless
nickel
niece
nineteen
310 ninety

opposite
oppression
optimism
ordinarily
originally
paid
pamphlet
parallel
paralleled
340 parole

poison
politician
pollute
possession
possibly
practical
practically
precede
predominant
370 preferred

ninth
noticeable
noticing
nowadays
nuclear
nuisance
numerous
occasion
occasionally
320 occurred

particle
particularly
past
pastime
peaceable
peculiar
penetrate
perceive
performance
350 perhaps

prejudice
prepare
preparation
pretty
prevail
prevalent
principle
prisoner
privilege
380 probably

occurrence
occurring
off
official
omission
omit
omitted
omitting
opponent
330 opportunity

permanent
permissible
persuade
pertain
phase
physical
pigeon
pitiful
planned
360 pleasant

procedure
proceed
processes
professor
prominent
pronunciation
propaganda
prophecy
prophesy
390 psychology

publicly
pumpkin
purpose
pursue
pursuing
pursuit
quandary
quantity
questionnaire
400 quiet

remember
remembrance
reminisce
repetition
representative
reproduce
resemblance
resistance
resources
430 restaurant

several
sheriff
shining
shoulder
shrubbery
significant
similar
simply
since
460 sincerely

quite
quizzes
rarity
reality
realize
really
rebel
receipt
receive
410 recession

review
rhythm
ridiculous
roommate
sacrifice
safety
sandwich
satellite
Saturday
440 saxophone

ski
skiing
sophomore
source
souvenir
speak
speeches
specimen
sponsor
470 statistics

recipe
recognize
recommend
referring
regular
regulate
rehearsal
relief
relieve
420 religious

scarcity
scenery
schedule
secede
secretary
seize
senseless
sentence
separate
450 sergeant

stayed
stepped
stopped
straight
strategy
strength
strenuous
stretch
strict
480 stubbornness

studies	thorough	view
studying	though	villain
suburban	thought	violence
succeed	through	visible
succession	till	vitamins
sufficient	tobacco	warrant
suicide	together	warring
summary	tomorrow	weather
superintendent	too	Wednesday
490 supersede	520 tragedy	550 weird

suppose	transferred	where
suppress	tremendous	wherever
surely	trouble	whether
surprise	truly	whichever
surround	twelfth	wholly
suspicious	typical	whose
susceptible	tyranny	without
swimming	unanimous	woman
symbol	unconscious	women
500 technical	530 undoubtedly	560 writing

technique	until	written
temperature	usage	yield
temporary	using	_____
tendency	usually	_____
than	vacuum	_____
their	valuable	_____
theirs	various	_____
themselves	vegetable	_____
then	vengeance	_____
510 therefore	540 vice	_____

Hyphenation

18f

Hyphenate words chiefly to express the idea of a unit and to avoid ambiguity. For the division of words at the end of a line, see **8d**.

Words forming a compound may be written separately, written as one word, or connected by hyphens. For example, three modern dictionaries all have the same listings of these compounds:

>   hair stylist   hairsplitter   hair-raiser

Another modern dictionary, however, lists *hairstylist,* not *hair stylist.* Compounding is in such a state of flux that authorities do not always agree.

(1) Use the hyphen to join two or more words serving as a single adjective before a noun.

>   the bluish-green sea   chocolate-covered peanuts
>   peace-loving natives   his know-it-all glance
>   the twenty-two-year-old laboratory technician
>   [Note the singular form of the noun *year* after the numeral
>   in the hyphenated modifier.]

Notice that in the examples below the modifiers after the noun are not hyphenated:

>   The sea was bluish green.
>   The peanuts, which were chocolate covered, tasted stale.
>   The laboratory technician was twenty-two years old.
>   [Numbers like *twenty-two* are hyphenated wherever they
>   appear in a sentence.]

More than one hyphenated adjectival, of course, may precede the noun modified:

>   "I reject get-it-done, make-it-happen thinking," he says.
>   —THE ATLANTIC

"Suspension" hyphens are used in such series as the following:

> two-, three-, and four-hour classes

Note: The hyphen is generally omitted after an adverb ending in -*ly* in such phrases as the following:

> a hopelessly lost cause   a frequently used example

■ **Exercise 6** Convert the following word groups according to the pattern of the examples.

> EXAMPLES
> an initiation lasting two months   *a two-month initiation*
> ideas that shake the world   *world-shaking ideas*

1. an apartment with six rooms
2. examinations that exhaust the mind
3. fingers stained with ink
4. a voter who is eighteen years old
5. shoppers who are budget minded
6. tents costing a hundred dollars
7. peace talks that last all night
8. a program that trains teachers
9. a hitchhiker who was waving a flag
10. ponds covered with lilies

(2) Use the hyphen with compound numbers from twenty-one to ninety-nine (or twenty-first to ninety-ninth).

> forty-six, fifty-eighth BUT three hundred twenty

Note: Usage varies regarding the hyphenation of fractions. The hyphen is required, however, only when the fraction functions as a compound modifier. See also **18f(1)**.

> almost one-half full BUT eating only one half of it
> a two-thirds vote BUT two thirds of the voters

(3) Use the hyphen to avoid ambiguity or an awkward combination of letters or syllables between prefix and root or suffix and root.

a dirty movie-theater   [Compare "a dirty-movie theater."]
to re-sign a petition   [Compare "to resign a position."]
semi-independent, shell-like   BUT   semifluid, childlike

(4) Use the hyphen with the prefixes *ex-* ("former"), *self-, all-;* with the suffix *-elect;* and between a prefix and a capitalized word.

ex-wife   self-help   all-inclusive   mayor-elect
mid-September   non-Biblical   anti-American

Note: The hyphen is also used with figures or letters such as *mid-1980s* or *T-shirt*.

■ **Exercise 7**   Refer to **18f** and to your dictionary as you convert each phrase (or words within each phrase) to a compound or to a word with a prefix. Use hyphens when needed.

EXAMPLES
glasses used for water   *water glasses* OR *waterglasses*
not Communistic   *non-Communistic*
a man who makes   *a $75,000-a-year man*
   $75,000 a year

1. respect for oneself
2. persons keeping the score
3. bacon cured with sugar
4. a plan for sharing the profit
5. a latch used at night
6. four and twenty
7. a cleaner for all purposes
8. a woman who is ninety-two years old
9. in the shape of a V
10. fences that are covered with snow
11. the flight from Montreal to Portland
12. a sale lasting two or three days

Good Usage and Glossary

19

Use a good dictionary to help you select the words that express your ideas exactly.

You can find valuable information about words by referring to a good college dictionary, such as one of the following:

> *Funk & Wagnalls Standard College Dictionary*
> *The American Heritage Dictionary*
> *The Random House Dictionary*
> *Webster's New Collegiate Dictionary*
> *Webster's New World Dictionary*

Occasionally you may need to refer to an unabridged dictionary or to a special dictionary: see the two lists on pages 428–29.

19a
Use a good dictionary intelligently.

Intelligent use of a dictionary requires some understanding of its plan and of the special abbreviations given in the introductory matter. Knowing how the dictionary arranges and presents material will enable you to interpret much of the information provided in its entries.

Below is a sample dictionary entry. First, note the various definitions of *empty* as an adjective, as a transitive verb, as an intransitive verb, as a noun, and as part of an idiomatic phrase (with *of*). Next, observe the examples of usage. Finally, note the various other kinds of information (labeled in color) that the dictionary provides.

Pronunciation

Syllabication

Adjective forms

Spelling ——

Etymology

emp·ty (emp′tē) *adj.* **-ti·er, -ti·est** [ME. *emti* & (with intrusive -*p*-) *empti* < OE. *æmettig*, unoccupied, lit., at leisure < *æmetta*, leisure (< *æ-*, without + base of *motan*, to have to: see MUST¹) + -*ig*, -Y²] **1.** containing nothing; having nothing in it **2.** having no one in it; unoccupied; vacant *[an empty house]* **3.** carrying or bearing nothing; bare **4.** having no worth or purpose; useless or unsatisfying *[empty pleasure]* **5.** without meaning or force; insincere; vain *[empty promises]* **6.** [Colloq.] hungry —*vt.* **-tied, -ty·ing 1.** to make empty **2.** *a)* to pour out or remove (the contents) of something *b)* to transfer (the contents) *into, onto,* or *on* something else **3.** to unburden or discharge (oneself or itself) —*vi.* **1.** to become empty **2.** to pour out; discharge *[the river empties into the sea]* —*n., pl.* **-ties** an empty freight car, truck, bottle, etc. —**empty of** lacking; without; devoid of —**emp′ti·ly** *adv.* —**emp′ti·ness** *n.*
SYN.—**empty** means having nothing in it *[an empty box, street, stomach, etc.]*; **vacant** means lacking that which appropriately or customarily occupies or fills it *[a vacant apartment, position, etc.]*; **void,** as discriminated here, specifically stresses complete or vast emptiness *[void of judgment]*; **vacuous,** now rare in its physical sense, suggests the emptiness of a vacuum See also VAIN —**ANT. full**

Special usage (*Colloquial*)

Verb forms

Synonyms with definitions and distinctions

Other forms (noun plural, idiom, adverb, derived word)

Antonym

(1) Spelling, syllabication, and pronunciation As a writer, use your dictionary not only to check spelling but also to find where words may be divided at the end of a line: see **8d.** As a speaker, check the pronunciation of unfamiliar words in your dictionary. Keys to the sound symbols are at the bottom of each two-page spread as well as in the introductory matter at the front of the dictionary. A primary stress mark (′) normally follows the syllable that is most heavily accented. Secondary stress marks follow lightly accented syllables.

■ **Exercise 1** With the aid of your dictionary, write out the following words using sound symbols and stress marks to indicate the correct pronunciation (or a correct one if options are given).

1. harass
2. incongruous
3. performance
4. Mozart
5. pica
6. interest
7. egalitarian
8. advertisement
9. pogonip
10. oceanography

(2) Parts of speech and inflected forms Your dictionary provides labels indicating the possible uses of words in sentences—for instance, *adj.* (adjective), *adv.* (adverb), *v.t.* (verb, transitive). It also lists ways that nouns, verbs, and modifiers change form to indicate number, tense, or comparison or to serve as another part of speech (for example, under *repress*, *v.t.*, may appear *repressible*, *adj.*).

■ **Exercise 2** With the aid of your dictionary, classify each of the following words as a verb (transitive or intransitive), a noun, an adjective, an adverb, a preposition, or a conjunction. Give the principal parts of each verb, the plural (or plurals) of each noun, and the comparative and superlative of each adjective and adverb. (Note that some words are used as two or more parts of speech.)

1. permit
2. lonely
3. sweet-talk
4. tattoo
5. subtle
6. for
7. late
8. bring
9. crisis
10. fine

(3) Definitions and examples of usage Observe how your dictionary arranges the definitions of a word: whether the most common meaning is given first or whether the definitions are listed in historical order. Notice also that an illustration of the usage of a word often clarifies a definition.

■ **Exercise 3** Study the definitions of any five of the following pairs of words, paying special attention to any examples of usage in your dictionary; then write sentences to illustrate the shades of difference in meaning.

1. rot—putrefy
2. sensual—sensuous
3. viable—practicable
4. yukking—guffawing
5. mercy—clemency
6. charisma—charm
7. burgoo—gumbo
8. free—liberate
9. jaded—a jade
10. draw—draft

(4) Synonyms and antonyms Lists and discussions of synonyms in dictionaries often help to clarify the meaning of closely related words. By studying the denotations and connotations of words with similar meanings, you will find that you are able to choose your words more exactly and to convey more subtle shades of meaning. Lists of antonyms can help you to find a word that is the direct opposite of another in meaning.

Note: For more complete lists of synonyms, antonyms, related and contrasted words, refer to a special dictionary or thesaurus. Below is a sample thesaurus entry.

empty *adj* **1** lacking contents that could or should be present <an *empty* apartment> <the whole book is *empty* of meaning>

Synonyms —— *syn* bare, clear, stark, vacant, vacuous, void

Related words —— *rel* barren, blank; abandoned, deserted, emptied, forsaken, godforsaken, unfilled, unfurnished uninhabited, untenanted, vacated; destitute, devoid; depleted, drained, exhausted

Contrasted words —— *con* complete, replete; filled, occupied, packed, teeming

Antonym —— *ant* full

2 *syn* VAIN 1, hollow, idle, nugatory, otiose
rel paltry, petty, trifling, trivial; banal, flat, inane, ineffectual, insipid, jejune, vapid; dumb, fatuous, foolish, ignorant, silly, simple
con meaningful, pregnant, significant; authentic, bona fide, genuine, veritable

3 *syn* EXPRESSIONLESS, blank, deadpan, inexpressive, unexpressive, vacant

4 *syn* DEVOID, innocent, void

213

Before choosing a synonym or closely related word from such a list, look it up in the dictionary to make sure that it expresses your meaning exactly. Although *stark, idle,* and *inexpressive* are all listed above as synonyms of *empty,* they have vastly different connotations.

■ **Exercise 4**   With the aid of your dictionary or thesaurus, list two synonyms and one antonym for each of the following words. (1) hatred   (2) pleasure   (3) false   (4) oppose   (5) stingy

(5) Origin: development of the language   In college dictionaries the origin of the word—also called its *derivation* or *etymology*—is shown in square brackets. For example, after *expel* might be this information: "[< L *expellere* < *ex-* out + *pellere* to drive, thrust]." This means that *expel* is derived from (<) the Latin (L) word *expellere,* which is made up of *ex-,* meaning "out," and *pellere,* meaning "to drive or thrust." Breaking up a word, when possible, into *prefix—root—suffix* will often help to get at the basic meaning of a word.

	prefix		root		suffix
dependent	**de-** down	+	**pend** to hang	+	**-ent** one who
interruption	**inter-** between	+	**rupt** to break	+	**-ion** act of
preference	**pre-** before	+	**fer** to carry	+	**-ence** state of

The bracketed information given by a good dictionary is especially rich in meaning when considered in relation to the historical development of our language. English is one of the Indo-European (IE) languages, a group of languages apparently derived from a common source.* Within this group of

---

*The parenthetical abbreviations for languages here and on the next few pages are those commonly used in bracketed derivations in dictionaries.

languages, many of the more familiar words are remarkably alike. Our word *mother*, for example, is *mater* in Latin (L), *meter* in Greek (Gk.), and *matar* in ancient Persian and in the Sanskrit (Skt.) of India. Words in different languages that apparently descend from a common parent language are called *cognates*. The large number of cognates and the many correspondences in sound and structure in most of the languages of Europe and some languages of Asia indicate that they are derived from the common language that linguists call Indo-European, which it is believed was spoken in parts of Europe about six thousand years ago. By the opening of the Christian era the speakers of this language had spread over most of Europe and as far east as India, and the original Indo-European had developed into eight or nine language families. Of these, the chief ones that influenced English were the Hellenic (Greek) group on the eastern Mediterranean, the Italic (Latin) on the central and western Mediterranean, and the Germanic in northwestern Europe. English is descended from the Germanic.

Two thousand years ago the Hellenic, the Italic, and the Germanic branches of Indo-European each comprised a more or less unified language group. After the fall of the Roman Empire in the fifth century, the several Latin-speaking divisions developed independently into the modern Romance languages, chief of which are Italian, French, and Spanish. Long before the fall of Rome the Germanic group was breaking up into three families: (1) East Germanic, represented by the Goths, who were to play a large part in the history of the last century of the Roman Empire before losing themselves in its ruins; (2) North Germanic, or Old Norse (ON), from which modern Danish (Dan.), Swedish (Sw.), Norwegian (Norw.), and Icelandic (Icel.) derive; and (3) West Germanic, the direct ancestor of English, Dutch (Du.), and German (Ger.).

The English language may be said to have begun about the middle of the fifth century, when the West Germanic Angles, Saxons, and Jutes began the conquest of what is now England

and either absorbed or drove out the Celtic-speaking inhabitants. (Celtic—from which Scots Gaelic, Irish Gaelic, Welsh, and other languages later developed—is another member of the Indo-European family.) The next six or seven hundred years are known as the Old English (OE) or Anglo-Saxon (AS) period of the English language. The fifty or sixty thousand words then in the language were chiefly Anglo-Saxon, with a small mixture of Old Norse words as a result of the Danish (Viking) conquests of England beginning in the eighth century. But the Old Norse words were so much like the Anglo-Saxon that they cannot always be distinguished.

The transitional period from Old English to Modern English—about 1100 to 1500—is known as Middle English (ME). The Norman Conquest began in 1066. The Normans, or "Northmen," had settled in northern France during the Viking invasions and had adopted Old French (OF) in place of their native Old Norse. Then, crossing over to England by the thousands, they made French the language of the king's court in London and of the ruling classes—both French and English—throughout the land, while the masses continued to speak English. Only toward the end of the fifteenth century did English become once more the common language of all classes. But the language that emerged at that time had lost most of its Anglo-Saxon inflections and had taken on thousands of French words (derived originally from Latin). Nonetheless, it was still basically English, not French, in its structure.

The marked and steady development of the English language (until it was partly stabilized by printing, introduced in London in 1476) is suggested by the following passages, two from Old English and two from Middle English.

Hē ǣrest scēop	eorðan bearnum
He first created	*for earth's children*
heofon tō hrōfe,	hālig Scyppend.
heaven as a roof,	*holy creator.*

From the "Hymn of Cædmon"
(middle of the Old English period)

Ēalā, hū lēas and hū unwrest is þysses middan-eardes wēla.
Alas! how false and how unstable is this midworld's weal!

Sē þe wæs ǣrur rīce cyng and maniges landes hlāford,
He that was before powerful king and of many lands lord,

hē næfde þā ealles landes būton seofon fōt mæl.
he had not then of all land but seven foot space.

From the *Anglo-Saxon Chronicle,* A.D 1087
(end of the Old English period)

A knight ther was, and that a worthy man,
That fro the tyme that he first bigan
To ryden out, he loved chivalrye,
Trouthe and honour, fredom and curteisye.

From Chaucer's Prologue to the
Canterbury Tales, about 1385

Thenne within two yeres king Uther felle seke of a grete
maladye. And in the meane whyle hys enemyes usurpped
upon hym, and dyd a grete bataylle upon his men, and slewe
many of his peple.

From Sir Thomas Malory's *Morte d'Arthur,*
printed 1485

A striking feature of Modern English (that is, English since
1500) is its immense vocabulary. As already noted, Old English used some fifty or sixty thousand words, very largely
native Anglo-Saxon; Middle English used perhaps a hundred
thousand words, many taken through the French from Latin
and others taken directly from Latin; and unabridged dictionaries today list over four times as many. To make up this
tremendous word hoard, we have borrowed most heavily
from Latin, but we have drawn some words from almost
every known language. English writers of the sixteenth century were especially eager to interlace their works with
words from Latin authors. And, as the English pushed out to
colonize and to trade in many parts of the globe, they
brought home new words as well as goods. Modern science

and technology have drawn heavily from the Greek. As a result of all this borrowing, English has become one of the richest and most cosmopolitan of languages.

In the process of enlarging our vocabulary we have lost most of our original Anglo-Saxon words. But those that are left make up the most familiar, most useful part of our vocabulary. Practically all our simple verbs, our articles, conjunctions, prepositions, and pronouns are native Anglo-Saxon; and so are many of our familiar nouns, adjectives, and adverbs. Every speaker and writer uses these native words over and over, much more frequently than the borrowed words. Indeed, if every word is counted every time it is used, the percentage of native words runs very high—usually between 70 and 90 percent. Milton's percentage was 81, Tennyson's 88, Shakespeare's about 90, and that of the King James Bible about 94. English has been enriched by its extensive borrowings without losing its individuality; it is still fundamentally the *English* language.

■ **Exercise 5**   With the aid of your dictionary, give the etymology of each of the following words:

1. aspirin
2. ecology
3. gardenia
4. geriatrics
5. guerrilla
6. helicopter
7. laser
8. OK
9. polyester
10. Teflon

(6) Special usage labels   Dictionaries ordinarily carry no usage labels for the bulk of English words. Unlabeled, or general, words range from the learned words appropriate in the most formal situations to the words used every day in both formal and informal situations.

Most dictionaries, however, provide a variety of special usage labels for words or for particular definitions of words. These labels indicate varieties of usage that differ from the general. Here is a sampling of labeled definitions, each of them found in two or more college dictionaries:

unalienable	*Archaic, Obsolete*	inalienable
lift	*Informal, Colloquial*	plagiarize
nowheres	*Nonstandard, Dialect, Colloquial*	not anywhere, nowhere
stink	*Slang*	to be of low quality

As the examples above indicate, the classification of words is often difficult and controversial because our language is constantly changing. Good writers try to choose the words, whatever their labels, that exactly fit the audience and the occasion, informal or formal.

■ **Exercise 6**   Classify the following words and phrases according to the usage labels in your dictionary. If a word has no special usage label, classify it as *General.* If a given definition of a word has a usage label, give the meaning after the label.

> EXAMPLES
> tote bag—general
> aholt—dialectal
> nutty—informal for *silly,* slang for *insane*

1. doll
2. dude
3. funky
4. holler
5. irregardless
6. junk
7. macho
8. rube
9. snigger
10. unto

19b

Avoid informal words in formal writing.

Words or expressions labeled *Informal* or *Colloquial* in college dictionaries are standard English and are used by speakers and writers every day. These words are thus appropriate in informal writing, especially in dialogue. But informal words or expressions are usually inappropriate in formal expository compositions. In formal writing, use instead the general English vocabulary, the unlabeled words in your dictionary.

> INFORMAL   In class the teacher gave a definition of *polyunsaturated,* but I didn't **get it**.
>
> FORMAL   In class the teacher gave a definition of *polyunsaturated,* but I did not **understand it**.

Contractions are common in informal English, especially in dialogue: see the examples on page 162. But contracted forms (like *won't* or *there's*) are usually written out (*will not, there is*) in a formal composition—which is not as casual or spontaneous as conversational English is.

■ **Exercise 7**   Make a list of ten words that you would consider informal in your writing. Then check your dictionary to see how (or if) each definition you have in mind is labeled.

19c

Use slang and jargon only when appropriate to the audience.

Slang words, including certain coinages and figures of speech, are variously considered as breezy, racy, extremely informal, nonstandard, facetious, taboo, offbeat, or vigorous. On occasion, slang can be used effectively, even in formal writing. Below is an example of the effective use of the word *spiel,* still labeled by dictionaries as *Slang:*

> Here comes election year. Here come the hopefuls, the conventions, the candidates, the spiels, the postures, the press releases, and the TV performances. Here comes the year of the hoopla.   —JOHN CIARDI

A few years ago the word *hoopla* was also generally considered as slang, but now dictionaries disagree: one classifies this word *Standard* (unlabeled); another, *Colloquial* (*Infor-*

mal); still another, *Slang*. Like *hoopla*, words such as *spiel, uptight, paddy wagon, raunchy, schlep,* and *party pooper* have a particularly vivid quality; they soon may join former slang words such as *sham* and *mob* as part of the general English vocabulary.

But much slang is trite, tasteless, and inexact. For instance, when used to describe almost anything disapproved of, *gross* becomes inexact, flat.

Caution: As you avoid the use of ineffective slang in your writing, remember that many of the most vivid short words in our language are general, standard words. Certain long words can be as inexact and as drab as trite slang. For examples of the ineffective use of big words, see Exercise 9, page 223.

■ **Exercise 8** Replace the italicized words in the following sentences with more exact words or specific phrases.

1. After dress rehearsal the whole cast *goofed off.*
2. Lately the weather has been *lousy* on weekends.
3. Jean's new haircut is *dynamite.*
4. That *wisecrack ticked* him *off.*

19d

Use regional words only when appropriate to the audience.

Regional, or *dialectal*, words (also called *localisms* or *provincialisms*) should normally be avoided in speaking and writing outside the region where they are current. Speakers and writers may, however, safely use regional words known to the audience they are addressing.

REGIONAL   Monty was **fixing to** feed his steak to the **critter**.
GENERAL   Monty was **about to** feed his steak to the **dog**.
           [OR *animal* OR *creature*]

19e

Avoid nonstandard words and usages.

Words and expressions labeled by dictionaries as *Nonstandard* or *Illiterate* should be avoided in most writing and speaking. Many common illiteracies are not listed in college dictionaries.

NONSTANDARD   **They's** no use asking them.
STANDARD   **There's** no use asking them.

19f

Avoid archaic and obsolete words.

All dictionaries list words (and meanings for words) that have long since passed out of general use. Such words as *ort* (fragment of food) and *yestreen* (last evening) are still found in dictionaries because these words, once the standard vocabulary of great authors, occur in our older literature and must be defined for the modern reader.

A number of obsolete or archaic words—such as *worser* (for *worse*) or *holp* (for *helped*)—are still in use but are now nonstandard.

19g

Use technical words only when appropriate to the audience.

When you are writing for the general reader, avoid all unnecessary technical language. Since the ideal of good writing is to make one's thought clear to as many people as possible, the careful writer will not describe an apple tree as a *Malus pumila* or a high fever as *hyperpyrexia*. (Of course, technical language, with its greater precision, is highly desirable when one is addressing an audience that can understand it, as when a physician addresses a group of physicians.)

19h

Avoid overwriting, an ornate or flowery style. Do not needlessly combine distracting sounds.

Overwriting, as well as the combination of distracting sounds, calls attention to words rather than to ideas. Such writing is generally fuzzy and repetitious, or carelessly indifferent to the importance of sound and its relationship to meaning.

ORNATE	Since the halcyon days of my early youth I have always anticipated with eagerness and pleasure the exciting vistas of distant climes and mysterious horizons.
BETTER	Since childhood I have looked forward to seeing the world.
DISTRACTING	The use of catalytic converters is just one contribution to the solution of the problem of air pollution.
BETTER	The use of catalytic converters is just one way to help solve the problem of air pollution.

Equally unpleasing to the average reader is the overuse of alliteration (repetition of the same consonant sound), as in "Some people *sh*un the *seash*ore."

■ **Exercise 9** Using simple, formal, straightforward English, rewrite the following sentences (from Stuart Chase's *Power of Words*).

1. It is obvious from the difference in elevation with relation to the short depth of the property that the contour is such as to preclude any reasonable developmental potential for active recreation.

2. Verbal contact with Mr. Blank regarding the attached notification of promotion has elicited the attached representation intimating that he prefers to decline the assignment.

3. Voucherable expenditures necessary to provide adequate dental treatment required as adjunct to medical treatment

being rendered a pay patient in in-patient status may be incurred as required at the expense of the Public Health Service.

4. I hereby give and convey to you, all and singular, my estate and interests, right, title, claim and advantages of and in said orange, together with all rind, juice, pulp and pits, and all rights and advantages therein.

5. I prefer an abbreviated phraseology, distinguished for its lucidity.

6. Realization has grown that the curriculum or the experiences of learners change and improve only as those who are most directly involved examine their goals, improve their understandings and increase their skill in performing the tasks necessary to reach newly defined goals.

Glossary of Usage

19i

Consult the following glossary to determine the standing of a word or phrase and its appropriateness to your purpose.

The entries in the following glossary are authoritative only to the extent that they describe current usage. The usage labels included do not duplicate the descriptions in any one dictionary, but justification for each can usually be found in at least two of the leading dictionaries.

For a discussion of the special usage labels used in dictionaries, see **19a(6)**. The following labels appear most frequently in this glossary:

General   Words in the standard English vocabulary, listed in dictionaries without special usage labels and appropriate in both formal and informal writing and speaking.

Informal   Words or expressions labeled *Informal* or *Colloquial* in dictionaries—words widely used by educated as well as uneducated writers and speakers but not appropriate in a formal context. See also **19b**.

Standard   All general and informal words or expressions.

Nonstandard   Words or expressions labeled in dictionaries as *Archaic, Illiterate, Nonstandard, Obsolete, Slang,* or *Substandard*—words not considered a part of the standard English vocabulary. See also **19c**, **e**, and **f**.

Of course, the following glossary can include only a few of the words likely to cause difficulty. If the word you are looking for is not included, or if you need more information about any word in the list, consult a good college dictionary.

a, an Use *a* before a consonant sound, *an* before a vowel sound.

| a history | a union | a one-dollar bill | a new dress | a C |
| an hour | an uncle | an only child | an NBA game | an F |

accept See **except, accept.**

accidentally, incidentally When using these adverbs, remember that *-ly* is added to the adjective forms *accidental* and *incidental,* not to the noun forms *accident* and *incident.*

> NONSTANDARD   Mr. Kent **accidently** overheard the report.
> STANDARD   Mr. Kent **accidentally** overheard the report.

adapt, adopt Do not confuse. To *adapt* is to adjust or make suitable. To *adopt* is to select as one's own or to choose to use or follow.

> We **adapted** the guidelines to our needs. [made them fit]
> The company **adopted** new guidelines. [chose to use]

advice, advise Pronounced and spelled differently, *advice* is a noun, *advise* a verb.

> Patients should follow their doctors' **advice.**
> Patients should do what their doctors **advise.**

affect, effect Do not confuse the verb *affect* with the noun *effect.* To *affect* is to rouse the emotions or to influence, change. An *effect* is a result, an outcome. (When used as a verb, *effect* means "bring about" or "accomplish": "The medicine *effected* a complete cure.")

His tears **affected** her deeply.   The **effect** surprised me.
The drug **affects** one's appetite.   The drug has side **effects**.

aggravate   Informally *aggravate* means "to annoy or to irritate." In general usage it means "to make worse" or "to intensify."

INFORMAL   Undisciplined children **aggravate** baby sitters.
GENERAL   Lack of water **aggravated** the suffering.

a half a   Informal for *half a* or *a half.*

ain't   A nonstandard contraction generally avoided in writing, unless used in dialogue or for humorous effect.

all the farther, all the faster   Regional, or dialectal, for *as far as, as fast as.*

NONSTANDARD   A mile is all the farther Mae can jog.
STANDARD   A mile is **as far as** Mae can jog.

allude, elude   See **elude, allude.**

allusion, illusion   Do not confuse. An *allusion* is a casual or indirect reference. An *illusion* is a false idea or an unreal image.

The author's **allusion** to a heaven on earth amused me.
The author's concept of a heaven on earth is an **illusion**.

almost, most   See **most.**

a lot   Sometimes misspelled as *alot.*

already, all ready   *Already* means "before or by the time specified." *All ready* means "completely prepared."

The theater was **already** full by seven o'clock.
The cast was **all ready** for the curtain call.

alright   Not yet a generally accepted spelling of *all right.*

altogether, all together   *Altogether* means "wholly, thoroughly." *All together* means "in a group."

That law is **altogether** unnecessary.
They were **all together** in the lobby.

A.M., P.M. (OR **a.m., p.m.**)   Use only with figures.

> NOT   The wedding begins at ten thirty in the **a.m.**
>
> BUT   The wedding begins at 10:30 A.M. [OR at ten thirty in the morning]

among, between   Prepositions with plural objects (including collective nouns). As a rule, use *among* with objects denoting three or more (a group), and use *between* with those denoting only two (or twos).

> walked **among** the crowd, quarreling **among** themselves
> a choice **between** war and peace, reading **between** the lines

amount of, number of   *Amount of* is followed by singular nouns; *number of,* by plural nouns.

> an **amount of** money, light, work, or postage   [singular]
> a **number of** coins, lights, jobs, or stamps   [plural]

See also **a number, the number.**

an   See **a, an.**

and etc.   Omit the redundant *and. Etc.* is an abbreviation of *et* ("and") *cetera* ("other things"). See also **etc.**

ante-, anti-   Do not confuse these prefixes. *Ante-* means "before, in front of." The more frequently used *anti-* means "against, opposite to" or "hostile to."

> antedate, anteroom, antenatal, antebellum, antecedent
> antiwar, anticlimax, antichrist, anti-Semitic, antidote, antibiotic

a number, the number   As subjects, *a number* is generally plural and *the number* is singular. Make sure that the verb agrees with the subject.

> **A number** of options **are** available.
> **The number** of options **is** limited.

anyone, any one   *Anyone* means "any person at all." *Any one* refers to a specific person or thing in a group. Similar forms are *everyone, every one; someone, some one.*

> **Anyone** can wax a floor.
> **Any one** of those men can wax a floor.

anyways, anywheres Dialectal or colloquial for *anyway, anywhere.*

as (1) Do not use *as* in place of the preposition *like* in making a comparison.

NOT Natalie, as her mother, stands tall.
BUT Natalie, **like** her mother, stands tall.

See also **like**.

(2) In your formal writing, do not use *as* in place of *whether, if,* or *that* after such verbs as *feel, know, say,* or *see.*

INFORMAL I do not know as the President's adviser is right.
GENERAL I do not know **whether** the President's adviser is right.

(3) If there is even a slight chance of ambiguity, many writers prefer not to use *as* for *because, since,* or *while.*

GENERAL As it was raining, we watched TV. [probably clear in context but possibly not]
PREFERRED **While** it was raining, we watched TV.
OR **Because** it was raining, we watched TV.

at Redundant after *where.* See **where at, where to**.

awful An overworked word for *ugly, shocking, very bad.* Informal as a substitute for *very,* as in "awful pretty" or "awful important."

awhile, a while Distinguish between the adverb *awhile* and the article and noun *a while* (ordinarily used as an object of a preposition).

After our long swim, we rested **awhile**.
After our long swim, we rested for **a while**.

bad, badly The adverb *badly* is preferred after most verbs. But either *bad* or *badly* is now standard in the sense of "ill" or "sorry," and writers now usually prefer *bad* after such verbs as *feel* or *look.*

The organist plays **badly**.
Charles feels **bad**.

be sure and Write *be sure to* in such sentences as "*Be sure to* consult a lawyer."

because See **reason . . . because.**

being as, being that Nonstandard for *since, because.*

beside, besides Always a preposition, *beside* usually means "next to," sometimes "apart from." As a preposition meaning "in addition to" or "other than," *besides* is now more common in writing than *beside.* When used adverbially, *besides* means "also" or "moreover."

> Marvin was sitting **beside** Bunny.
> **Besides** countless toys, these children have their own TV set.
> The burglars stole our silver—and my stereo **besides.**

better, had better In the sense of an emphatic "ought to," *better* is an informal shortening of *had better.*

> INFORMAL He better watch out!
> GENERAL He **had** better watch out! [OR He'**d** better watch out!]

between See **among, between.**

boys See **girls, boys.**

broke Archaic for *broken.*

> STANDARD Only my little finger was **broken** [NOT broke].

bug Slang if used as a verb. As a noun, *bug* is slang in the sense of "fan, enthusiast."

> SLANG Loud noises bug her.   I am a tennis bug.
> STANDARD Loud noises bother her.   I love tennis.

bunch Informal if used to refer to people.

bust, busted, bursted The principal parts of *burst* are *burst, burst, burst. Bursted* is archaic. *Bust* and *busted* are still considered slang. When *burst* does not fit the context, use a different verb, such as a form of *break* (NOT "busted the record" BUT "*broke* the record").

but what Informal after *no* or *not* following such expressions as "no doubt" or "did not know."

> INFORMAL There was no doubt but what they would win.
> GENERAL There was no doubt **that** they would win.

can, may Formal English still distinguishes between *can* referring to ability and *may* referring to permission.

> **Can** student nurses give injections? [Are they able to?]
> **May** student nurses give injections? [Are they permitted to?]

can't hardly, can't scarcely Double negatives in implication. Use *can hardly, can scarcely*. See also **hardly, scarcely**.

case, line Often used in wordy expressions.

> WORDY   In the case of Jones there were good intentions.
> CONCISE   Jones had good intentions.
> WORDY   Buy something in the line of fruit.
> CONCISE   Buy some fruit.

cause of . . . on account of, due to Redundant. Omit the *on account of* or *due to;* or recast to avoid wordiness.

> WORDY   One cause of misunderstandings is on account of lack of communication.
> BETTER   One cause of misunderstandings is lack of communication.
> CONCISE   Lack of communication causes misunderstandings.

compare to, compare with Formal English prefers *compare to* for the meaning "regard as similar" and *compare with* for the meaning "examine to discover similarities or differences."

> The speaker **compared** the earth **to** a lopsided baseball.
> Putting one under the other, the expert **compared** the forged signature **with** the authentic one.

complementary, complimentary Do not confuse. *Complementary* means "completing" or "supplying needs." *Complimentary* means "expressing praise" or "given free."

> His talents and hers are **complementary.**
> Admiring the performance, he made several **complimentary** remarks.

conscious, conscience Do not confuse. An adjective, *conscious* means "aware, able to feel and think." A noun, *conscience* means "the sense of right and wrong."

> After the accident, when I became **conscious** of my guilt, my
> **conscience** started bothering me.

could of Nonstandard for *could have*. See **of**.

couple, couple of Informal for *two* or for *several* in such phrases
as "a couple aspirin," "a couple more gallons of paint," or "in just
a couple of seconds."

data, criteria, phenomena The plurals of *datum* (rarely used),
criterion, and *phenomenon*. *Criterion* and *phenomenon* have alternate plurals: *criterions, phenomenons*. The plural *data* is often con-
strued as a collective noun: "This *data has* been verified."

different from In the United States the preferred preposition
after *different* is *from*. But the less formal *different than* is accepted by many writers if the expression is followed by a clause.

> The Stoic philosophy is **different from** the Epicurean.
> The outcome was **different from** what I expected   OR   The
> outcome was **different than** I had expected.

differ from, differ with *Differ from* means "to stand apart because of unlikeness." *Differ with* means "to disagree."

disinterested, uninterested Often used interchangeably. Some
authorities, however, do not accept *disinterested* ("impartial") as a
substitute for *uninterested* ("indifferent").

done Standard as an adjective and as the past participle of the
verb *do*. Nonstandard as an adverb and as a substitute for *did*.

NONSTANDARD	The bread is done sold.
STANDARD	The bread is **already** sold. The bread is **done**.
NONSTANDARD	Do the police know who done it?
STANDARD	Do they know who **did** it? Who **has done** it?

don't A contraction of *do not* rather than of *does not*.

NONSTANDARD	He don't smoke. (He do not smoke.)
STANDARD	He **doesn't** smoke. (He *does not* smoke.)
STANDARD	They **don't** smoke. (They *do not* smoke.)

each and every Redundant.

effect See **affect, effect**.

elicit, illicit A verb, *elicit* means "bring out or evoke," as in "to *elicit* information." An adjective, *illicit* means "illegal or improper," as in "an *illicit* sale."

elude, allude To *elude* is to escape the notice of. To *allude* is to refer to casually or indirectly. The corresponding adjectives are *elusive* and *allusive*.

> Exact dates often **elude** me.
> Carol likes to **allude** to the ghost of Hamlet's father.

See also **allusion, illusion.**

emigrate from, immigrate to The prefix *e-* (a variant of *ex-*) means "out of"; *im-* (a variant of *in-*) means "into." To *emigrate* is to go out of one's own country to settle in another. To *immigrate* is to come into a different country to settle there. The corresponding adjective or noun forms are *emigrant* and *immigrant.* (Compare: *export, import.*)

> Many workers **emigrated from** Mexico. The number of **emigrants** increased during the 1970s.
> Many Mexicans **immigrated to** the United States. These **immigrant** workers contributed to the growth of our economy.

eminent, imminent *Eminent* means "distinguished." *Imminent* means "about to happen, threatening."

> Charlotte is an **eminent** scientist.
> Bankruptcy seemed **imminent.**

enthuse, enthused *Enthuse* is informal as a verb meaning "to show enthusiasm." *Enthused* is informal as a synonym for *enthusiastic.*

> INFORMAL We were all **enthused** about the new club.
> GENERAL We were all **enthusiastic** about the new club.

etc. Appropriate informally but used sparingly in formal writing. Many writers prefer to substitute *and so on* or *and so forth.* (Since *etc.* means "and other things," *and etc.* is redundant.)

> NEEDLESS Ordinary games like Monopoly, backgammon, etc., did not interest these electronics hobbyists.

REVISED Ordinary games like Monopoly and backgammon did not interest these electronics hobbyists.

ever so often, every so often Do not confuse. *Ever so often* means "very often, frequently." *Every so often* means "every now and then, occasionally."

everyone, every one See **anyone, any one.**

except, accept Do not confuse. To *except* is to exclude or make an exception of. To *accept* is to approve of or receive.

These laws **except** juveniles.	Present company **excepted!**
These schools **accept** juveniles.	I **accepted** their apologies.

explicit, implicit *Explicit* means "expressed directly or precisely." *Implicit* means "implied or expressed indirectly."

The advertisement was **explicit**: "All sales final."
Reading between the lines, I understood the **implicit** message.

farther, further Used interchangeably. Some writers, however, prefer *farther* in references to geographic distance (as in "six miles *farther*"). *Further* is used as a synonym for *additional* in more abstract references (such as "without *further* delay," "*further* proof").

fewer, less Informally used interchangeably in the sense of "not many." Formally, *fewer* refers to numbers (how many), and *less* refers to amount, extent, or collective quantity (how much).

fewer seeds	fewer hours	fewer than twenty students
less seed	less time	less than $7,500 a year

fine Informal for *very well,* as in "did fine on that test." Use sparingly as a vague word of approval.

fixing to Regional or dialectal for "about to" or "getting ready to."

REGIONAL Congress is fixing to adjourn.
GENERAL Congress is about to adjourn.

folks Informal for *parents, relatives.*

former   Refers to the first named of two. If three or more items are named, use *first* and *last* instead of *former* or *latter*.

> The Folger and the Huntington are two famous libraries; the **former** is in Washington, D.C., and the latter is in San Marino, California.

fun   Informal if used adjectivally, as in "a fun person," "a fun car."

further   See **farther, further**.

get   Useful in numerous idioms but not appropriate formally in such expressions as "get with the times," "always gets in with his instructors," and "a stubborn attitude that gets me."

girls, boys   Informal if used to refer to grown people of any age.

good   Informal if used adverbially.

> INFORMAL   Watson plays good under pressure.
> GENERAL   Watson plays **well** under pressure.

great   Overworked informally for *skillful, good, clever, enthusiastic,* or *very well,* as in "really great at guessing the answers" or "with everything going great for us."

guy(s)   Informal for *any person(s)*.

had of, had have   Nonstandard for *had*.

> NONSTANDARD   I wish I had of [OR had have] said that.
> STANDARD   I wish I **had** said that.

had ought, hadn't ought   Nonstandard for *ought, ought not* or *oughtn't*.

hang   Useful in numerous idioms but slang in such expressions as "his hang-up about marriage" and "to hang out in discos."

hanged, hung   Informally interchangeable in the sense of "put to death by hanging." Formally, it is *hanged* (often used figuratively nowadays) that refers to such an act.

> Whenever my parents supplied enough rope, I usually **hanged** myself—but not always.

hardly, scarcely Words with negative force, usually considered nonstandard if used with an unnecessary negative like *not, nothing,* or *without.*

NOT I couldn't hardly quit then.
BUT I **could hardly** quit then.

NOT Hardly nothing was in order.
BUT **Hardly anything** was in order.

NOT The motion passed without scarcely a protest.
BUT The motion passed **with scarcely** a protest.

hisself Nonstandard for *himself.*

hooked on Slang for *addicted to* or *obsessed with.*

hopefully Still questionable for *it is hoped.*

how come Informally used as a substitute for *why.*

INFORMAL I do not know how come they did that.
GENERAL I do not know **why** they did that.

illusion See **allusion, illusion.**

immigrate See **emigrate from, immigrate to.**

imply, infer Used interchangeably as synonyms for *hint at, intimate, suggest.* Most writers, however, carefully distinguish between *infer* (meaning "draw a conclusion based on evidence") and *imply* ("suggest without actually stating").

His attitude **implies** that money is no problem.
I **infer** from his attitude that money is no problem.

incredible, incredulous *Incredible* means "unbelievable, improbable." *Incredulous* means "skeptical, doubting."

The witness's story was **incredible.**
The judge gave the witness an **incredulous** look.

inferior than Use *inferior to* or *worse than.*

ingenious, ingenuous *Ingenious* means "clever, resourceful"; *ingenuous* means "open, frank," "artless."

This electric can opener is an **ingenious** device.
Don's **ingenuous** smile disarms the critics.

in regards to   Nonstandard for *in regard to* or *as regards*.

irregardless   Nonstandard for *regardless*.

is when, is where   Do not use *when* or *where* after *is* in giving definitions.

> NOT   Begging the question is when [OR is where] a person argues by taking the conclusion for granted.
> BUT   Begging the question is taking the conclusion for granted in an argument.
> OR   A person begs the question by taking the conclusion for granted in an argument.

its, it's   *Its* is a possessive pronoun ("for *its* beauty"). *It's* is a contraction of *it is* (*It's* beautiful!") or of *it has* ("*It's* been a beautiful day!").

kick   Slang or very informal in such expressions as "to kick in my share," "on another kick," "just for kicks," "always kicking about grades," "gets kicked out of class," "just kicking around town."

kind, sort   Singular forms, which may be modified by *this* or *that*. The use of *these* or *those* is increasingly common but is still questionable.

> QUESTIONABLE   These kind of arguments are deceptive.
> PREFERRED   **These kinds** of arguments are deceptive.
> OR   **This kind** of argument is deceptive.

kind of, sort of   Informal when used adverbially in the sense of "to a degree, somewhat, a bit" or "in a way" (as in "kind of silly," "sort of hesitated," or "kind of enjoying it").

kind of a, sort of a   Omit the *a* in your formal writing: NOT "this kind of a tour"   BUT   "this *kind of* tour."

later, latter   Comparative forms of *late* often confused in writing. In modern English, *later* (like *sooner*) refers to time; *latter* (like *former*) refers to one of two—to the second one (but not to the last of several).

> We set a **later** date.   They arrived **later** than usual.
> She wrote a song and a play. The **latter** won a prize.

See also **former**.

lay (laying, laid) Nonstandard for *lie* (*lying, lay, lain*) meaning "to rest or recline." See also **7a(2)**.

NONSTANDARD	I did lay down awhile. Had he laid down? The truck was laying on its side.
STANDARD	I did **lie** down awhile. Had he **lain** down? The truck was **lying** on its side.
NONSTANDARD	After lunch, I laid down awhile.
STANDARD	After lunch, I **lay** down awhile. [past of *lie*]

learn Nonstandard for *teach, instruct, inform*.

NOT	That'll learn him!
BUT	That'll **teach** him!

leave Nonstandard for *let* except when followed by an object and *alone*, as in "*Leave* [OR Let] them alone."

NONSTANDARD	He won't leave me go now.
STANDARD	He won't **let** me go now. [OR let me leave]
NONSTANDARD	Leave us not protest too much.
STANDARD	**Let** us not protest too much.

less See **fewer, less.**

let's us Redundant. Use *let's* or *let us*.

liable to Informally used in place of *likely to* in reference to mere probability. Formally, *liable to* not only denotes likelihood or possibility but also suggests the idea of harm or danger.

INFORMAL	It's liable to be cooler soon. [mere likelihood]
GENERAL	The roof is **liable** to collapse. [likelihood + danger]

lie (lying, lay, lain) Nonstandard for *lay* (*laying, laid*) in the sense of "put, place." See also **7a(2)**.

NONSTANDARD	Onion slices are then lain on the fillets.
STANDARD	Onion slices are then **laid** on the fillets.
NONSTANDARD	Last night I lay my homework aside.
STANDARD	Last night I **laid** my homework aside.

like Widely used as a conjunction (in place of *as, as if*, or *as though*) in conversation and in public speaking. Formal English, however, still rejects the use of *like* as a conjunction.

FORMAL   He drives **as** [NOT like] I did before my accident.
      OR   He drives **the way** I did before my accident.
FORMAL   They acted **as though** [NOT like] they owned the town.

line See **case, line**.

lose, loose Do not confuse. *Lose* is a verb: *to lose, did lose, will lose. Loose* is chiefly an adjective: "a *loose* sentence," "to become *loose*," "at *loose* ends."

lousy Slang, overworked informally, for *mean, bad, painful, inferior, nasty, messy.*

may be, maybe Do not confuse the verb phrase *may be,* with the adverb *maybe.*

The story **may be** [OR might be] true.
Maybe [OR Perhaps] the story is true.

me and Nonstandard as part of a compound subject. See also **5a**.

NONSTANDARD   Me and Drake took an early flight.
STANDARD   Drake and I took an early flight.

mighty Informal for *very* or *extremely* (as in "mighty fine" or "mighty big").

morale, moral Do not confuse. *Morale* (a noun) refers to mood or spirit. *Moral* (chiefly an adjective) refers to right conduct or ethical character.

the **morale** of our team, affecting **morale**, low **morale**
a **moral** person, **moral** judgments, an im**moral** act

most Informal if used in place of *almost.*

INFORMAL   Most everyone needs to take a daily walk.
GENERAL   **Almost** everyone needs to take a daily walk.

myself Standard as an intensive or a reflexive pronoun: "I *myself* saw a UFO" (intensive). "Momentarily I hated *myself*" (reflexive). Not acceptable formally and still questionable informally as a replacement for the subjective form *I* or the objective *me.*

My sister and **I** [NOT myself] prefer soccer.
He confided in Hayden as well as **me** [NOT myself].

neither Nonstandard for *either* in double negatives such as "I don't like spinach neither." See **not . . . no/none/nothing**.

no-account, no-count, no-good Informal for *worthless, good-for-nothing*.

nohow Nonstandard for *not at all, in no way, anyway*.

no such a Omit the *a*: NOT "no such a place" BUT "no such place."

not . . . no/none/nothing A nonstandard construction when the two negatives have a negative meaning.

NONSTANDARD	He did not keep no records. [double negative]
STANDARD	He did not keep any records. [one negative: *not*]
	OR He kept no records. [one negative: *no*]
NONSTANDARD	We needed gas but couldn't buy none.
STANDARD	We needed gas but couldn't buy any.
	OR We needed gas but could buy none.
NONSTANDARD	I cannot do nothing about it.
STANDARD	I cannot do anything about it.
	OR I can do nothing about it.

nowheres Nonstandard or regional for *nowhere*.

number See **amount of, number of; a number, the number**.

of Do not write *of* for an unstressed *have*.

COMPARE	I could have it done. [stressed]
	I could have done it. [unstressed]
NONSTANDARD	I might of [may of, could of, would of, must of, should of, ought to of] said that.
STANDARD	I might **have** [may *have*, could *have*, would *have*, must *have*, should *have*, ought to *have*] said that.

See also **had of**.

off of In formal writing, omit the *of* after *off* in such phrases as "fell off of the ladder."

OK, O.K., okay   All three are accepted as standard forms expressing general approval. However, a more specific word usually replaces *OK* in a formal context.

per   Used especially in commercial writing. Many authors prefer to use *per* only in Latinisms ("per capita," "per se," or "per cent/percent").

COMMERCIAL	over $1.50 per gallon	as per regulations
PREFERRED	over $1.50 **a** gallon	**according to** regulations

phenomena   See **data**.

plenty   Informal when used adverbially to mean *quite* or *sufficiently* (as in "plenty good enough") or adjectivally for *plenty of* ("in plenty time").

plus   Informal if used as a substitute for *and* between main clauses or if used as a conjunctive adverb (for *moreover, besides, in addition*) between main clauses or sentences. See also **12a** and **14a**.

INFORMAL	Barbara is taking five courses, plus she has to work three hours a day.
GENERAL	Barbara is taking five courses, **and** she has to work three hours a day.
INFORMAL	Barbara is taking five courses; plus, she has to work three hours a day. [OR . . . courses. Plus, she has to work. . . .]
GENERAL	Barbara is taking five courses; **moreover,** she has to work three hours a day. [OR . . . courses. *Moreover,* she has to work. . . .]

P.M., A.M.   See **A.M., P.M.**

practical, practicable   *Practical* means "useful, sensible" or "not theoretical." *Practicable* means "feasible, capable of being put into practice."

The sponsors are **practical** people. These plans are **practicable**.

principal, principle   Distinguish between *principal,* an adjective or noun meaning "chief" or "chief official," and the noun *principle,* meaning "fundamental truth."

A **principal** factor in his decision was his belief in the **principle** that men are born equal.

quote   Still considered chiefly informal for *quotation* (as in "a quote from Chaucer").

raise, rise   Do not confuse. *Raise* (*raised, raising*) means "to lift or cause to move upward, to bring up or increase." *Rise* (*rose, risen, rising*) means "to get up, to move or extend upward, ascend." *Raise* (a transitive verb) takes an object; *rise* (an intransitive verb) does not.

Retailers **raised** prices.   Retail prices **rose** sharply.

rap   Informal for *chat, discuss,* or *talk.* Slang in such expressions as "to beat a murder rap" or "took the rap for cheating."

rarely ever   In formal writing, either omit the *ever,* or use *hardly* instead of *rarely.*

NOT   He rarely ever mentioned money.
BUT   He **rarely** mentioned money.
OR   He **hardly ever** mentioned money.

real   Informal when used as an adverb meaning "very, extremely."

INFORMAL   The victorious team was **real** tired.
GENERAL   The victorious team was **extremely** tired.

reason . . . because   Informal redundancy. Use *that* instead of *because* or recast the sentence.

INFORMAL   The reason why he missed his class was because he overslept.
GENERAL   The **reason** why he missed his class was **that** he overslept.
OR   He missed his class **because** he overslept.

reckon   Informal for *guess, think.*

respectively, respectfully   Do not confuse. *Respectively* means "in the order given." *Respectfully* means "in a courteous manner."

I considered becoming a farmer, a landscape artist, and a florist, **respectively.**
I considered the rabbi's suggestion **respectfully.**

right   Archaic or dialectal for *very* (as in "a right nice apartment").

rise   See **raise, rise**.

said   Except in legal writing, questionable as an adjectival meaning "already specified or mentioned before." Substitute a demonstrative like *this* or *these* for *the said*.

> LEGAL   The said machines were defective.
> GENERAL   **These** machines were defective.

same   Used as a pronoun without *the* chiefly in commercial or legal writing. General usage prefers *it, this,* or *that*.

> COMMERCIAL   I had a service policy but did not renew same.
> GENERAL   I had a service policy but did not renew **it**.

says   Avoid the use of *says* for *said* after a past-tense verb: NOT "stood up and says" BUT "stood up and *said*." See also **27a**.

scarcely   See **hardly, scarcely**.

seldom ever   Omit the *ever* in your formal writing.

set, setting   Nonstandard for *sit* or *sat, sitting*. It is the verb *sit* (NOT *set*) that means "be seated or be situated." See also **7a(2)**.

> NONSTANDARD   I didn't even set down. He yawned and set up.
>   Some cabins were setting in two feet of water.
> STANDARD   I didn't even **sit** down. He yawned and **sat** up.
>   Some cabins were **sitting** in two feet of water.

show up   Informal for *arrive* or *come* and for *outdo* (as in "might show up at the party" and "trying to show me up").

sit   Occasionally misused for *set* (*put, place*): NOT "to sit something" BUT "to *set* something." See also **7a(2)**.

so   Often overworked as an intensive (as in "so very pleased") and as a connective between main clauses (see **24b**).

some   Informal for *remarkable, extraordinary* and for *somewhat, a little* (as in "was some dog," "is some better," and "was talking some").

someone, some one   See **anyone, any one**.

somewheres   Nonstandard for *somewhere*.

sort   See **kind, sort**.

sort of a   Omit the *a* in your formal writing.

stationary, stationery   *Stationary* means "in a fixed position"; *stationery* means "writing paper and envelopes."

superior than   Nonstandard. Use *superior to* or *better than*.

suppose to   Be sure to add the *-d*.

> Who is **supposed to** be in charge?
> You were **supposed to** read this chapter.

sure   Informal for *surely* or *certainly*.

> INFORMAL   The sunrise **sure** was beautiful.
> GENERAL   The sunrise **certainly** was beautiful.

sure and   See **be sure and**.

their, there, they're   Do not confuse. *Their* is the possessive form of *they; there* is ordinarily an adverb or an expletive; *they're* is a contraction of *they are*.

> **There** is no explanation for **their** refusal.
> **They're** installing a traffic light **there**.

theirself, theirselves   Nonstandard for *themselves*.

them   Nonstandard when used adjectivally: NOT them apples BUT *those* [OR *these*] apples.

then   Sometimes incorrectly used for *than*. See also pages 192–93. Unlike *then, than* does not relate to time.

> Last summer, we paid more **than** that.   [Compare "We paid more *then*."]
> Other **than** a social-security check, they had no income.

these kind, these sort, those kind, those sort   See **kind, sort**.

thing   Often used in wordy constructions.

> WORDY   One thing that we need is a map.
> CONCISE   We need a map.

this here, that there, these here, them there   Nonstandard expressions. Use *this, that, these, those*.

thusly   Grammatically redundant. Write *thus* (already an adverb without the *-ly*).

to, too, two   Distinguish the preposition *to* from the adverb *too* and the numeral *two*.

If it isn't **too** cold, I will take my **two** poodles **to** the park.

try and   Informal for *try to*.

type   Informal for *type of* (as in "that type program").

use to, used to   Be sure to àdd the *-d* to *use* unless the auxiliary is accompanied by *did* in questions or in negative constructions.

NOT   Our coins use to contain silver.
BUT   Our coins **used to** contain silver.

NOT   Did he used to smoke?   He didn't used to smoke.
BUT   Did he **use to** smoke?   He didn't **use to** smoke.

used to could   Nonstandard for *used to be able*.

very   Omit when superfluous (as in "very unique" or "very terrified"). If you tend to overuse *very* as an intensifier, try using more exact words; in place of "very strange," for example, try *outlandish, grotesque*, or *bizarre*.

wait on   Informal for *wait for*.

INFORMAL   The taxi was waiting on him.
GENERAL   The taxi was **waiting for** him.

want for   Omit the nonstandard *for* in such sentences as "I want for you to quit."

want in, out, down, up, off, through   Informal or regional for *want to get in, out, down, up, off, through*.

want that   Nonstandard when a *that* clause is the object of *want*.

NONSTANDARD   I want that he should have a chance.
STANDARD   I **want** him to have a chance.

ways Informal for *way* when referring to distance.

> INFORMAL It's a long ways to Chicago.
> GENERAL It's a long **way** to Chicago.

what Nonstandard for *who* or *that*.

> NOT The man what did it got away.
> BUT The man **who** did it got away.

where Informal for *that.*

> INFORMAL I saw in the newspaper where the strike had been settled.
> GENERAL I saw in the newspaper **that** the strike had been settled.

where . . . at, where . . . to Omit the superfluous *at, to.*

> NOT Where is she at? Where is she going to?
> BUT Where is she? Where is she going?

which, who Use *who* or *that* instead of *which* to refer to persons.

while Do not overuse as a substitute for *and* or *but.* The conjunction *while* usually refers to time.

would of Nonstandard for *would have.* See *of.*

Xmas Standard for *Christmas* but used chiefly in commercial or informal writing.

you was Nonstandard for *you were.*

your, you're Do not confuse. *You're* is a contraction: "You're [You are] always right!" *Your* is the possessive form of *you:* "Your idea is a good one."

Exactness

20

Select words that are exact, idiomatic, and fresh.

Note: Sections **20** and **21** of this handbook deal with diction, the term used to refer to a writer's or speaker's choice of words.

Especially when writing, you should strive to choose words which express your ideas and feelings exactly. The choice of a right word will depend on your purpose, your point of view, and your reader.

If you can make effective use of the words you already know, you need not have a huge vocabulary. In fact, as shown by the following example, good writing often consists of short, familiar words.

> The ball was loose, rolling free near the line of scrimmage. I raced for the fumble, bent over, scooped up the ball on the dead run, and turned downfield. With a sudden burst of speed, I bolted past the line and past the linebackers. Only two defensive backs stood between me and the goal line. One came up fast, and I gave him a hip feint, stuck out my left arm in a classic straight-arm, caught him on the helmet, and shoved him to the ground. The final defender moved toward me, and I cut to the sidelines, swung sharply back to the middle for three steps, braked again, and reversed my direc-

tion once more. The defender tripped over his own feet in confusion. I trotted into the end zone, having covered seventy-eight yards on my touchdown run, happily flipped the football into the stands, turned and loped casually toward the sidelines. Then I woke up.

—JERRY KRAMER, *Farewell to Football*

Of course, as you gain experience in writing, you will become increasingly aware of the need to add to your vocabulary. When you discover a valuable new word, make it your own by mastering its spelling, meaning, and exact use.

20a
Select the exact word needed to express your idea.

(1) Select the word that precisely denotes what you have in mind.

WRONG	A loud radio does not detract me when I am reading a good novel. [*Detract* means "to subtract a part of" or "to remove something desirable."]
RIGHT	A loud radio does not **distract** me when I am reading a good novel. [*Distract* means "to draw the attention away."]
INEXACT	Arnold was willing to pay the bill, and his billfold was empty. [*And* adds or continues.]
EXACT	Arnold was willing to pay the bill, **but** his billfold was empty. [*But* contrasts.]
WRONG	What they did was unjustful.
RIGHT	What they did was **unjust**.
WRONG	He never reverts to himself as an expert.
RIGHT	He never **refers** to himself as an expert.
	OR He never **reminds** anyone that he is an expert.

■ **Exercise 1**   The italicized words in the following sentences are wrong or inexact. Correct the errors in diction and replace inexact words with exact ones.

1. Every gardener should have a *compote* bin.
2. Bo was interested in photography, *and* I bought her a new camera.
3. They did not do anything about this *disjustice*.
4. The lyrics are perfectly *adopted* to the music.
5. Strangers on campus are *awfully nice.*
6. Perhaps she just missed getting that job by some *misfortunate* chance.
7. I frequently consult the classified ads, *and* I can seldom find what I want.
8. She didn't say it but she *intimidated* it.
9. Hurricanes are *seasonable.*
10. Liquor *effects* the brain and nervous system.

■ **Exercise 2**   With the aid of your dictionary, give the exact meaning of each italicized word in the quotations below. (Italics have been added.)

1. Ignorance of *history* is dangerous.   ——JEFFREY RECORD

    Those who cannot remember *the past* are condemned to repeat it.   ——GEORGE SANTAYANA

2. The capacity for rage, spite and aggression is part of our endowment as *human beings.*   ——KENNETH KENISTON

    Man, all down his history, has defended his uniqueness like a point of honor.   ——RUTH BENEDICT

3. Travel is no cure for melancholia; space-ships and time machines are no *escape* from the human condition.

          ——ARTHUR KOESTLER

    Well, Columbus was probably regarded as an *escapist* when he set forth for the New World.   ——ARTHUR C. CLARKE

4. Once, a full high school education was the best achievement of a minority; today, it is the *barest minimum* for decent employment or self-respect.   ——ERIC SEVAREID

    Study and planning are an *absolute prerequisite* for any kind of intelligent action.   ——EDWARD BROOKE

5. We had a *permissive* father. He *permitted* us to work.

          ——SAM LEVENSON

■ **Exercise 3** Prepare for a class discussion of diction. After the first quotation below are several series of words that the author might have used but did not select. Note the differences in meaning when an italicized word is substituted for the related word at the head of each series. Be prepared to supply your own alternatives for each of the words that follow the other four quotations.

1. Creeping gloom hits us all. The symptoms are usually the same: not wanting to get out of bed to start the day, failing to smile at ironies, failing to laugh at oneself.
   —CHRISTOPHER BUCKLEY
   a. gloom: *sadness, depression, dismals* (hit), *melancholy*
   b. hits: *strikes, assaults, infects, zaps*
   c. usually: *often, frequently, consistently, as a rule*
   d. failing: *too blue, unable, neglecting, too far gone*

2. Our plane rocked in a rain squall, bobbed about, then slipped into a patch of sun. —THEODORE H. WHITE
   a. rocked   b. bobbed   c. slipped   d. patch

3. A raw fall wind swirled leaves and dust in small tornadoes and sent pedestrians scurrying for indoor warmth.
   —ARTHUR HAILEY
   a. raw   b. swirled   c. small   d. scurrying

4. The most wonderful thing about the Moon is that it is there. —ISAAC ASIMOV
   a. wonderful   b. there

5. No emotion is so corrosive of the system and the soul as acute envy. —HARRY STEIN
   a. corrosive   b. system   c. soul   d. acute   e. envy

(2) Select the word with the connotation, as well as the denotation, appropriate to the idea you wish to express.

The denotation of a word is what the word actually signifies. According to the dictionary, the word *hair* denotes "one of the fine, threadlike structures that grow from the skin of most mammals." The connotation of a word is what the word suggests or implies. *Hair*, for instance, may connote beauty, fertility, nudity, strength, uncleanliness, temptation, rebellion, or primitivism.

The connotation of a word includes the emotions or associations that surround it. For instance, *taxi, tin lizzie, limousine, dune buggy, station wagon, dump truck, hot rod*—all denote much the same thing. But to various readers, and in various contexts, each word may have a special connotation. *Taxi* may suggest a city rush hour; *tin lizzie*, a historical museum; *limousine*, an airport; *dune buggy*, a seaside vacation; *station wagon*, children and dogs; *dump truck*, highway construction; *hot rod*, noise and racing. Similarly, *hatchback, bus, clunker, bookmobile, moving van, ambulance, squad car*—all denote a means of transportation, but each word carries a variety of connotations.

A word may be right in one situation, wrong in another. *Female parent*, for instance, is a proper expression in a biology laboratory, but it would be very inappropriate to say "John wept because of the death of his female human parent." *Female human parent* used in this sense is literally correct, but the connotation is wrong. The more appropriate word, *mother*, conveys not only the meaning denoted by *female human parent* but also the reason why John wept. The first expression simply implies a biological relationship; the second includes emotional suggestions.

■ **Exercise 4**   Give one denotation and one connotation for each of the following words.

1. blue
2. mountain
3. astrology
4. Miami
5. conservative
6. law
7. dog
8. tennis shoes
9. technology
10. Saudi Arabia

(3) Select the specific and concrete word rather than the general and abstract.

A *general* word is all-inclusive, indefinite, sweeping in scope.
A *specific* word is precise, definite, limited in scope.

GENERAL	SPECIFIC	MORE SPECIFIC / CONCRETE
food	dessert	apple pie
prose	fiction	short stories
people	Americans	the Smiths

An *abstract* word deals with concepts, with ideas, with
what cannot be touched, heard, or seen. A *concrete* word has
to do with particular objects, with the practical, with what
can be touched, heard, or seen.

ABSTRACT WORDS   democracy, loyal, evil, hate, charity
CONCRETE WORDS   mosquito, spotted, crunch, wedding

All writers must sometimes use abstract words and must
occasionally resort to generalizations, as in the following
sentence:

> I still believe that a liberal education, even if it will not solve
> the problems of individuals or the world, will help us to un-
> derstand those problems.   —CONRAD A. BALLIET

In a case like this, abstractions and generalizations are vital
to the communication of ideas and theories. To be effective,
however, the use of these words must be based upon clearly
understood and well-thought-out ideas.

Experienced writers may have little difficulty handling
general and abstract words. Many inexperienced writers,
however, tend to use too many such words, leaving their
writing drab and lifeless due to the lack of specific, concrete
words. As you select words to fit your context, be as specific
as you can. For example, instead of the word *bad*, consider
using a more precise adjective (or adjectival) in phrases such
as the following:

bad planks: rotten, warped, scorched, knotty, termite-eaten
bad children: rowdy, rude, ungrateful, selfish, perverse
bad meat: tough, tainted, overcooked, contaminated

To test whether or not a word is specific, ask one or more of these questions about what you want to say: Exactly who? Exactly what? Exactly when? Exactly where? Exactly how? As you study the examples below, notice what a difference specific, concrete words can make in the expression of an idea. Notice, too, how specific details can be used to expand or develop ideas.

VAGUE   I always think of a good museum as one that is very big.

SPECIFIC   I always think of a good museum as one I get lost in.   ——EDWARD PARKS

VAGUE   After a tolerably long practice as a mechanic, I firmly believe that a lot of auto parts that are sold are not needed.

SPECIFIC   After a tolerably long practice as a mechanic, I firmly believe that at least two-thirds of the batteries, starters, alternators, ignition coils, carburetors, and water pumps that are sold are not needed.   ——DON SHARP

VAGUE   I remember my pleasure at discovering new things about language.

SPECIFIC   I remember my real joy at discovering for the first time how language worked, at discovering, for example, that the central line of Joseph Conrad's *Heart of Darkness* was in parentheses.

——JOAN DIDION

Notice in the second sentence below how specific details can be used to develop an idea.

Much of a Cuban's day is spent waiting. People wait for taxis, for buses, for newspapers, for ice cream, for cakes, for restaurants, for movies, for picture postcards.   ——STANLEY MEISLER

■ **Exercise 5**   Replace the general words and phrases in italics with specific ones.

1. I always think of a pawn shop as *very small.*
2. *A lot of people* are threatened by *pollution.*
3. The *movie* was *great.*

4. Every Monday he has *the same thing* in his lunch box.
5. Our history professor suggested that we subscribe to *some magazines*.
6. Backpacking has *numerous advantages*.
7. The *dog walked* over to his *food*.
8. My father looked at my grade in science and said *what I least expected to hear*.
9. *Various aspects of the television show* were criticized *in the newspaper*.
10. *Cities* have their *problems*.

(4) Use appropriate figurative language to create an imaginative or emotional impression.

A figure of speech is a word or words used in an imaginative rather than in a literal sense. The two chief figures of speech are the *simile* and the *metaphor*. A *simile* is an explicit comparison between two things of a different kind or quality, usually introduced by *like* or *as*. A *metaphor* is an implied comparison of dissimilar things. In a metaphor, words of comparison, such as *like* or *as*, are not used.

SIMILES

The first thing people remember about failing at math is that it felt like sudden death. —SHEILA TOBIAS

She shot me a glance that would have made a laser beam seem like a birthday candle. —LARRY SERVAIS

The bowie knife is as American as a half-ton pickup truck. —GEOFFREY NORMAN

The two men passed through the crowd as easily as the Israelites through the Red Sea. —WILLIAM X. KIENZLE

You should learn to scan a menu (especially the big ostentatious ones) the way you examine a medical insurance policy. —JAMES VILLAS [*The way* is used in place of *as* or *like* (informal): see **19i**, pages 237–38.]

METAPHORS

Dress is language. —LANCE MORROW

Successful living is a journey toward simplicity and a triumph over confusion. —MARTIN E. MARTY

Wolf pups make a frothy ribbon of sound like fat bubbling. —EDWARD HOAGLAND [a metaphor and a simile]

Single words are often used metaphorically:

These roses must be **planted** in good soil. [literal]

A man's feet must be **planted** in his country, but his eyes should survey the world. —GEORGE SANTAYANA [metaphorical]

Similes and metaphors are especially valuable when they are concrete and tend to point up essential relationships that cannot otherwise be communicated. (For faulty metaphors, see **23c**.) Sometimes writers extend a metaphor beyond a sentence:

Some women have managed to shape up and ship out into the mainstream of life, handling the currents and the rapids and the quiet pools with a gracious, confident ease. Others are trapped in one eddy after another, going nowhere at all, hung up in swirling pockets of confusion. Everyone gets sidetracked once in a while, and requires a rescue operation. That's the way life is. But some have been caught in an eddy or a piece of dead wood for so long that they have forgotten that life was meant to be lived in the mainstream.
—GLADYS HUNT, *Ms. Means Myself*

Two other frequently used figures of speech are *hyperbole* and *personification*. *Hyperbole* is deliberate overstatement or fanciful exaggeration. *Personification* is the attribution to the nonhuman (objects, animals, ideas) of characteristics possessed only by the human.

HYPERBOLE
I, for one, don't expect till I die to be so good a man as I am at this minute, for just now I'm fifty thousand feet high—a tower with all the trumpets shouting. —G. K. CHESTERTON

PERSONIFICATION
Time talks. It speaks more plainly than words. . . . It can shout the truth where words lie. —EDWARD T. HALL

■ **Exercise 6** Complete each of the following sentences by using a simile, a metaphor, hyperbole, or personification. Use vivid and effective figures of speech.

EXAMPLES

The grass rolls out to the bleachers like *a freshly brushed billiard table*. —JAY WRIGHT

As dam builders, Americans are a nation of *beavers*.
—THOMAS Y. CANBY

1. Sightseers flocked around the TV crew like _____.
2. Viewed from outer space, the earth is _____.
3. The mosquitoes in those weeds _____.
4. The third hurricane of the season slashed through Louisiana swamps _____.
5. Death in a hovel or in a penthouse is _____.
6. Like _____, the class sat speechless.
7. The lecture was as _____.
8. Her eyes looked like _____.
9. Surging forward, the crowd _____.
10. Constant bickering is as _____.
11. She was as self-confident as _____.
12. The alarm sounded like _____.

20b

Select words that are idiomatic.

An idiomatic expression—such as *many a man, Sunday week,* or *hang fire*—means something beyond the simple combination of the definitions of its individual words. An idiom may be metaphorical: *He gets under my skin.* Such expressions cannot be meaningfully translated word for word into another language. Used every day, they are at the very heart of the English language.

Be careful to use idiomatic English, not unidiomatic approximations. *Many a man* is idiomatic; *many the man* is not. Ordinarily, native speakers use idiomatic English naturally and effectively, but once in a while they may have difficulty choosing idiomatic prepositions. When you are in doubt about what preposition to use after a given word, look up that word in the dictionary. For instance, *agree* may be followed by *about, on, to,* or *with.* The choice depends on the context. Below is a list of troublesome idioms for study.

FAULTY	IDIOMATIC
according with	according to
accuse with	accuse of
adverse against	adverse to
comply to	comply with
conform in	conform to/with
desirous to	desirous of
die with	die of
in accordance to	in accordance with
independent from	independent of
inferior than	inferior to
jealous for	jealous of
prior than	prior to
superior than	superior to

■ **Exercise 7** Using your dictionary, classify the following expressions as idiomatic or unidiomatic. Revise any expressions that are unidiomatic. Classify idiomatic expressions according to the usage labels in your dictionary, using *General* as the classification for unlabeled expressions.

EXAMPLES
similar with   *Unidiomatic—similar to*
to let on   *Idiomatic, Informal*

1. oblivious about
2. to go at
3. to dress down
4. capable to
5. in search for
6. to compare against
7. to break with
8. prior than
9. to drop in
10. plan on going

256

20c

Select fresh expressions instead of trite, worn-out ones.

Such trite expressions as *to the bitter end, get it all together,* and *clean as a hound's tooth* were once striking and effective. Excessive use, however, has drained them of their original force and made them clichés. Some euphemisms (pleasant-sounding substitutions for more explicit but possibly offensive words) are not only trite but wordy—for example, *laid to rest* for *buried* or *sanitary engineer* for *janitor.* Many political slogans and the catchy phraseology of advertisements soon become hackneyed. Faddish or trendy words—like *impacted on, viable, upbeat,* or *be into* (as in "I am into dieting")—are so overused (or misused) that they quickly become trite and lose their force.

Nearly every writer uses clichés from time to time because they are so much a part of the language, especially of spoken English, and do contribute to the clear expression of ideas in written English.

> We feel free when we escape—even if it be but **from the frying pan into the fire**.   —ERIC HOFFER

It is not unusual for a professional writer to give a new twist to an old saying or a well-known literary passage.

> If a thing is worth doing, it is worth doing badly.
> —G. K. CHESTERTON

> Into each life a little sun must fall.   —L. E. SISSMAN

> Washington is Thunder City—full of the sound and fury signifying power.   —TOM BETHELL [Compare Shakespeare's "full of sound and fury,/Signifying nothing."   —*Macbeth*]

Many writers use familiar lines from literature or the Bible and quote proverbs.

Our lives are empty of belief. They are **lives of quiet desperation**. —ARTHUR M. SCHLESINGER, JR. [Compare Thoreau's *Walden:* "The mass of men lead lives of quiet desperation."]

Slowly but steadily, in the following years, a new vision began gradually to replace the dream of political power—a powerful movement, the rise of another ideal to guide the unguided, another **pillar of fire by night** after a clouded day. —W. E. B. DU BOIS [Compare Exodus 13:21: "And the Lord went before them . . . by night in a pillar of fire, to give them light."]

Good writers, however, do not rely heavily on the phraseology of others; they choose their own words to communicate their own ideas.

■ **Exercise 8**   Below is a list of trite expressions—only a sampling of the many in current use. Select ten that you often use or hear, and rewrite them in carefully chosen words.

EXAMPLES
a bolt from the blue   *a shock*
beyond the shadow of a doubt   *undoubtedly*

1. a brilliant performance
2. a chip off the old block
3. a crying shame
4. a good Samaritan
5. abreast of the times
6. after all is said and done
7. as cold as ice
8. as happy as a lark
9. at a complete loss for words
10. at the crack of dawn
11. at one fell swoop
12. beating around/about the bush
13. bite the bullet
14. bored to tears/death
15. few and far between
16. follow in the footsteps of
17. hightailed/hotfooted it out of there
18. hoping against hope
19. in the last analysis
20. in this day and age
21. it goes without saying
22. like a bull in a china shop/hog on ice
23. like water off a duck's back
24. little bundle of joy
25. makes my blood boil
26. nipped in the bud
27. no thinking man

28. over and done with
29. selling like hot cakes
30. slept like a top/log
31. stick to your guns
32. straight from the shoulder/hip
33. the depths of despair
34. the powers that be
35. the spitting image of
36. the very picture of health
37. water under the bridge/ over the dam
38. went in one ear and out the other
39. working like a Trojan
40. wouldn't touch it with a ten-foot pole

■ **Exercise 9** Choose five of the ten items below as the basis for five original sentences. Use language that is exact, idiomatic, and fresh.

EXAMPLES
the appearance of her hair
Her hair poked through a broken net like stunted antlers.
                                                —J. F. POWERS
OR
Her dark hair was gathered up in a coil like a crown on her head. —D. H. LAWRENCE

1. the look on his face
2. her response to fear
3. the way she walks
4. the condition of the streets
5. spring in the air
6. the noises of the city
7. the appearance of the room
8. the scene of the accident
9. the final minutes of play
10. the approaching storm

■ **Exercise 10** Read the three paragraphs below in preparation for a class discussion of the authors' choice of words—their use of exact, specific language to communicate their ideas.

¹ I'd expected Oregon to be filled with trees, bearded loggers with friendly smiles, joggers, and hip college types. ² We found, instead, hundreds of miles of desolate ranchland, will-cracking blizzards, hundred-mile spaces between towns of a thousand people, and frozen slush spraying us from passing logging trucks. ——PETER JENKINS, *"A Walk Across America"*

259

[1] Eating artichokes is a somewhat slow and serious business. [2] You must concentrate, focusing on each leaf as you break it off at its fleshy base, dip it in its sauce and draw it carefully to your mouth (being careful not to drip). [3] Between your front teeth it goes, and you scrape off the deliciously blanketed flesh. [4] Languorously you work this combination of flavors and sensations to the back of your mouth, where all the subtleties of the artichoke unfold and mingle with the sharp, rich sauce; and now your taste buds get the full, exciting impact. [5] Down it goes, and you pluck another leaf, sometimes methodically, working around the base of this thistle bud, sometimes with abandon. [6] Yet you can never really "bolt" an artichoke; there is always a measure of pause with each leaf, as it is torn, dipped and tasted.

—MARTHA ROSE SHULMAN, "An Artichoke Memoir"

[1] The biblical story does not present the departure from Egypt as an everyday occurrence, but rather as an event accompanied by violent upheavals of nature. [2] Grave and ominous signs preceded the Exodus: clouds of dust and smoke darkened the sky and colored the water they fell upon with a bloody hue. [3] The dust tore wounds in the skin of man and beast; in the torrid glow vermin and reptiles bred and filled air and earth; wild beasts, plagued by sand and ashes, came from the ravines of the wasteland to the abodes of men. [4] A terrible torrent of hailstones fell, and a wild fire ran upon the ground; a gust of wind brought swarms of locusts, which obscured the light; blasts of cinders blew in wave after wave, day and night, night and day, and the gloom grew to a prolonged night, and blackness extinguished every ray of light. [5] Then came the tenth and most mysterious plague: the Angel of the Lord "passed over the houses of the children of Israel . . . when he smote the Egyptians, and delivered our houses" (Exodus 12:27). [6] The slaves, spared by the angel of destruction, were implored amid groaning and weeping to leave the land the same night. [7] In the ash-gray dawn the multitude moved, leaving behind scorched fields and ruins where a few hours before had been urban and rural habitations.

—IMMANUEL VELIKOVSKY, Ages in Chaos

Wordiness

21

To avoid wordiness, use direct, economical diction. Repeat a word or phrase only when it is needed for emphasis or clarity.

The use of more words than necessary to express meaning is an offense against exact diction: see Section **20**. As you proofread and revise your compositions, delete unneeded words but keep or add exact ones. In this way, you can say more in fewer words.

WORDY FIRST DRAFT

In the early part of the month of August

there was a really mean hurricane with very

high winds that was moving threateningly

toward Port Arthur.

FIRST REVISION

In ~~the~~ early ~~part of the month of~~ August

~~there was~~ a really mean hurricane with very

high winds ~~that~~ was moving threateningly

toward Port Arthur.

SECOND REVISION

In early August a ~~really mean~~ *vicious* hurricane with
93-*mile-an-hour* ~~very high~~ winds was ~~moving threateningly~~ *threatening*
~~toward~~ Port Arthur.

FINISHED COPY

In early August a vicious hurricane with

93—mile—an—hour winds was threatening Port

Arthur.

21a

Make every word count; omit words or phrases that add nothing to the meaning.

(1) Avoid tautology (the use of different words to say the same thing).

WORDY   Commuters going back and forth to work or school formed carpools.

CONCISE   Commuters formed carpools.

WORDY   Each writer has a distinctive style, and he or she uses this in his or her own works.

CONCISE   Each writer has a distinctive style.

Notice below that the useless words in brackets serve only to echo meaning. Avoid such wordiness in your own writing.

yellow [in color]	circular [in shape]
at 9:45 P.M. [that night]	return [back]
[basic] essentials	rich [and wealthy] nations
bitter [-tasting] salad	small [-size] potatoes
but [though]	to apply [or utilize] rules
connect [up together]	[true] facts

Caution: Be sure to avoid double comparisons, the double subject (subject + nominative pronoun referring to the subject), and the double negative.

> [more] easier than, the [most] farthest
> my sister [she] is, the victims [they] are
> could[n't] hardly, did[n't do] nothing [See also *not . . . no,* **19i.**]

(2) Do not use many words when a few will express the idea well. Omit unnecessary words.

WORDY   **In the event that** the grading system is changed, expect complaints **on the part of** the students.

CONCISE   **If** the grading system is changed, expect complaints **from** the students. [Two words take the place of eight.]

WORDY   **As far as sexism is concerned, it seems to me that** a woman can be as guilty of sexism as a man.

CONCISE   A woman can be as guilty of sexism as a man. [Unnecessary words are deleted.]

WORDY   **The reason why** we honor Lincoln **in these various ways** is because he saved the Union.

CONCISE   We honor Lincoln because he saved the Union.

One or two words can replace such expressions as these:

at this point in time	**now**
bring all this to a conclusion	**conclude**
during the same time that	**while**
has a tendency to break	**breaks easily**
has the ability to sing	**can sing**
in a great many instances	**often**
made contact by personal visits	**visited**
on account of the fact that	**because**
situated in the vicinity of	**near**
was of the opinion that	**believed**

Note: One exact word can say as much as many. (See also **20a.**)

spoke in such a low and hard-to-hear voice	**mumbled**
persons who really know their particular field	**experts**

Notice below that the words in brackets are not necessary.

because [of the fact that]	was [more or less] hinting
[really and truly] fearless	by [virtue of] his authority
fans [who were] watching TV	the oil [that exists] in shale

■ **Exercise 1** Revise the following sentences to elimate wordiness.

1. As a usual rule, government officials express concern about public interest, but though it takes a crisis to get them to act.
2. Good health is essential. This is one of the most important things.
3. During the last two innings, many senseless mistakes occurred without any apparent reason for them.
4. When combined together, these ingredients they make a nutritious one-dish meal.
5. The exact date has not been determined and is not known to us.
6. Long lines of starving refugees in need of food were helped by Red Cross volunteer people.
7. Judy delights in giving parties; she really likes to be a hostess.
8. Perhaps maybe the chief cause of or reason for obesity in people who are overweight is lack of exercise.
9. Only beginners, those who are inexperienced, can enter that contest.
10. The tall skyscraper buildings form a dark silhouette against the evening sky.

■ **Exercise 2** Substitute one or two words for each item below.

1. prior to the time that
2. in this day and age
3. did put in an appearance
4. has the capability of working
5. passed away OR met his maker
6. in the not too distant future
7. similar in character to
8. involving a great deal of expense
9. in a more or less serious manner
10. somewhere in the neighborhood of $2500

■ **Exercise 3**   Strike out unnecessary words in the following sentences.

1. It seems to me to be obvious.
2. The reason why I stayed behind was because I had no money.
3. Last weekend, on Saturday afternoon to be exact, I bought a sailboat, which to all intents and purposes is a nice yellow-colored toy that is really a whole lot of fun to play with.
4. Other things being equal, it is my opinion that all of these oil slicks, whether they are massive or not so big, do damage to the environment to a greater or lesser degree.
5. As for the nature of biased newscasts, I can only say that I realize that reporters have to do some editing, though they may not use the finest type of judgment when they are underscoring, as it were, some of the stories and downplaying others.

21b

Eliminate needless words by combining sentences or by simplifying phrases and clauses.

Note differences in emphasis as you study the following examples.

WORDY   He has a special way of telling a story. He makes a big to-do over little details. They sound like they are very important.

CONCISE   When telling a story, he makes little details sound important.

WORDY   A few of the listeners who had become angry called in so that they would have the opportunity of refuting the arguments set forth by Ian.

CONCISE   A few angry listeners called in to refute Ian's arguments.

WORDY   It is within the realm of possibility that what is earned by individual persons, the part that is surplus, will be subject to special taxation as a windfall.

CONCISE   Perhaps an individual's surplus earnings will be subject to a windfall-profits tax.

■ **Exercise 4** Following the pattern of the examples, condense the sentences below.

EXAMPLE
These were theories which were, in essence, concerned with politics.
These were political theories.

1. These are pitfalls that do, of course, pose a real danger.
2. This is an act which, in truth, partakes of the nature of aggression.

EXAMPLE
It was a house built with cheap materials.
It was a cheaply built house.

3. It was a garden planned with a great deal of care.
4. It was a speech delivered with a lot of passion.

EXAMPLE
The stories written by Carson McCullers are different from those composed by Flannery O'Connor.
Carson McCullers' stories are different from Flannery O'Connor's.

5. The dishes prepared by her husband are not as good as those fixed by her father.
6. The ideas shared by the students were different from those promoted by the advertiser.

EXAMPLE
It is unfortunate. A few come to college so that they can avoid work.
Unfortunately, a few come to college to avoid work.

7. It is inevitable. Corporations produce goods so that they can make a profit.
8. It is predictable. Before an election legislators reduce taxation so that they can win the approval of voters.

EXAMPLE
The forces that were against gun control ran an advertisement that covered two pages.
The anti-gun control forces ran a two-page advertisement.

9. A group that is in favor of labor wants vacations that last two months.
10. One editorial against ''nukes'' stressed the need for plants that are state controlled.

■ **Exercise 5** Restructure or combine sentences to reduce the number of words.

1. These hazards are not visible, and they cause accidents, many of which are fatal ones.
2. The United States was being invaded. What I mean by that is a takeover of land. Foreign investors were buying up farms.
3. In spite of the fact that my parents did not approve of it, I was married to Evelyn last June.
4. The fire chief made the recommendation saying that wooden shingles should not be used on homes now being built or in the future.
5. The lawyer that was defending Smith was considered incompetent by many of those who were serving on the jury.

21c

Avoid careless or needless repetition of a word or phrase.

Sometimes a repeated word or phrase, by calling attention to itself rather than to its meaning, can be distracting.

FAULTY This interesting instructor knows how to make an uninteresting subject interesting.

Such repetition is not always easy to avoid or eliminate. But as a rule, you can quickly revise awkward repetition of words by making judicious substitutions or omissions.

REVISED This instructor knows how to make a dull subject interesting.

At times, however, synonyms can be clumsy, needlessly repeating an idea. It may be necessary to rewrite sentences to avoid repetition that weakens your writing.

267

Note: For the effective use of repetition in parallel structures, for emphasis, and as a transitional device, see **26b**, **29e**, and **31c(3)**.

Avoid careless or needless repetition of a word.

CARELESS	We had problems solving those problems.
REVISED	We had a hard time solving those problems.
NEEDLESS	I think that he knows that that girl is not the one for him to marry.
REVISED	I think he knows he should not marry that girl.
NEEDLESS	His uncle is not like her uncle. Her uncle takes more chances than his uncle does.
REVISED	Their uncles are different. Hers takes more chances than his.

Avoid carelessly repeating a root or a word base.

CARELESS	I got the impression that his expression of sympathy was insincere.
REVISED	I felt that his expression of sympathy was insincere.

Do not unintentionally use the same word or root in different senses.

CARELESS	Even at the graveside services, the brothers kept quarreling. It was a grave situation.
BETTER	. . . It was a **serious** situation.

Eliminate careless jingles (like "compared the fares there") and other distracting repetition of sounds: see **19h**.

Use a pronoun instead of needlessly repeating a noun or substituting a clumsy synonym. As long as the reference is clear, several pronouns in succession may refer to the same noun antecedent.

NEEDLESS	The hall outside these offices was empty. The hall had dirty floors, and the walls of this corridor were full of gaudy portraits.

REVISED   The hall outside these offices was empty. It had dirty floors, and its walls were full of gaudy portraits.

Judiciously use elliptical constructions to avoid needless repetition of words. The writers of the sentences below omitted the words in brackets, choosing not to repeat clearly understood phrases.

> Prosperity is the goal for some people, fame [is the goal] for others, and complete independence [is the goal] for still others. . . . —RENÉ DUBOS

> Photography was developed as a means of recording appearances; cinema [was developed] as a vehicle for public entertainment. —EDWARD T. CONE

Sometimes, as an aid to clarity, commas are used to mark omissions that avoid repetition.

> Family life in my parents' home was based upon a cosmic order: Papa was the sun; Mamma, the moon; and we kids, minor satellites. —SAM LEVENSON

■ **Exercise 6**   Revise or rewrite the following sentences to eliminate careless or needless repetition and any clumsy synonyms.

1. The President's recommendation to Congress sounded like an outlandish recommendation.
2. The condition of the floors after I had painted the ceiling floored my wife.
3. Abrupt interruptions like that disrupt my thoughts.
4. A comedy of intrigue (or a comedy of situation) is a comedy that relies on action instead of characterization for its comedy.
5. We had to wait late at Gate 13.
6. *Brunch* is a blend of the words *breakfast* and *lunch*; *fantabulous* is a blend of *fantastic* and *fabulous*.
7. A new addition was added at the side of the house. This addition was used for storage.
8. When debating, a debater should make the best use of time.

9. Leslie likes to go to the mountains to ski, Marcia enjoys going there to fish, and Joseph likes to go to the same type of high country to meditate.
10. Numerous products can be made from tobacco. The nicotine from this plant is used in pesticides. A sugar extracted from tobacco helps control blood pressure.

■ **Exercise 7** Revise the following sentences to eliminate wordiness and careless or needless repetition.

1. The manager returned the application back because of illegible handwriting that could not be read.
2. In this day and time, it is difficult today to find in the field of science a chemist who shows as much promise for the future as Joseph Blake shows.
3. From time to time during one's life, one needs to remember that one who is learning to walk has to put one foot before the other one.
4. A distant hurricane or a seaquake can cause a tidal wave. This wave can form when either occurs.
5. The National Gallery of Art, which is in Washington, D.C., and which houses the Mellon, Kress, and Widener collections, is one of the largest marble structures in the entire world.
6. In my family, schoolwork came first, chores came second, fun and games came next, and discussions came last.
7. The auto industry, not to mention the steel industry, did not relish the thought of Americans importing tens of thousands of foreign cars.
8. The backlash that followed as a result of the Supreme Court ruling was stronger, or more pronounced, than I myself had expected that it would be.
9. When the fans in the stadium shout and yell, the shouting and yelling is deafening, and so the total effect of all this is that it is a contributing factor in decisions to stay home and watch the games on TV.
10. I am of the opinion that one reason why these two newspapers have such power is because so many people are happy to let the reporters and editors tell them what to think and let them form their opinions for them.

Omission of Necessary Words

22

Do not omit a word or phrase necessary to the meaning of the sentence.

In many instances a word or a phrase is optional; a writer may use it or omit it without changing the meaning of the sentence. In the following example, optional words are in brackets:

It seems [that] the security force on [the] campus overreacted.

In other instances a word like *that* or *the* is necessary or desirable for clarity:

I know **that** the security force on **the** other campus overreacted.

If you omit necessary words in your compositions, your mind may be racing ahead of your pen, or your writing may reflect omissions in your spoken English.

The analyst talked about the tax dollar goes. [The writer thought "talked about where" but did not write *where.*]
You better be there on time!   [When speaking, the writer omits *had* before *better.*]

To avoid omitting necessary words, proofread your compositions carefully and study **22a–c.**

22a

Do not omit a necessary article, pronoun, conjunction, or preposition. See also **26b**.

(1) Omitted article or pronoun

INCOMPLETE   Feelings of inferiority are at bottom of person's jealousy.

COMPLETE   Feelings of inferiority are at **the** bottom of **a** person's jealousy.

INCOMPLETE   Beth knows a woman had a lawyer like that.

COMPLETE   Beth knows a woman **who** had a lawyer like that.

To avoid ambiguity, it is often necessary to repeat a pronoun or an article before the second part of a compound.

AMBIGUOUS   A friend and helper stood nearby.   [One person or two?]

CLEAR   A friend and **a** helper stood nearby.   [two persons clearly indicated by repetition of *a*]

ALSO CLEAR   My mother and father were there.   [clearly two persons—repetition of *my* before *father* not necessary]

(2) Omitted conjunction or preposition

CONFUSING   Fran noticed the passenger who was sleeping soundly had dropped his wallet in the aisle. [The reader may be momentarily confused by "noticed the passenger."]

BETTER   Fran noticed **that** the passenger who was sleeping soundly had dropped his wallet in the aisle.

INFORMAL   I had never seen that type movie before.

GENERAL   I had never seen that type **of** movie before.

INCOMPLETE   Such comments neither contribute nor detract from his reputation.

COMPLETE   Such comments neither contribute **to** nor detract from his reputation.
[When two verbs requiring different prepositions are used together, do not omit the first preposition. See also **20b**.]

In sentences such as the following, if you omit the conjunction, use a comma in its place.

> The English used the paints chiefly on churches at first, then later on public buildings and the homes of the wealthy. —E. M. FISHER [Compare "on churches at first *and* then later on public buildings."]

> The fact is, very few people in this society make a habit of thinking in ethical terms. —HARRY STEIN [Compare "The fact is *that* very few people. . . ."]

■ **Exercise 1** Insert needed words below.

1. A revolution was brewing the Panama Canal Zone.
2. Gary reminded Sheila Richard might not approve.
3. What kind course to take is the big question.
4. Winter and spring breaks the campus is dead.
5. The trouble was my good pair shoes got stolen.
6. Boynton will not ask nor listen to any advice.
7. Fires had burned for weeks were still not out.
8. She lent me a dollar then decided to take it back.
9. The book which the professor referred was not in our library.
10. The recipe calls for a variety spices.
11. She saw the boy finally obeyed her.
12. It is always the exception proves the rule.

■ **Exercise 2** Fill in the blanks below with appropriate articles, pronouns, conjunctions, or prepositions.

1. _____ good are not always rewarded; _____ evil often prosper. Life is not _____ morality play.
   —MICHAEL NOVAK
2. The battle left him untouched: it was the peace _____ undid him. —VIRGINIA WOOLF
3. Quarrelling means trying to show _____ the other man is in the wrong. —C. S. LEWIS
4. To me, there are two kinds of liberals: the type _____ fellow _____ would take off his coat in a snowstorm and put it around my shoulders, and the type _____ fellow _____ would caution me to wear a coat against the snow. —JAMES ALAN McPHERSON

22b

Avoid awkward omission of verbs and auxiliaries.

AWKWARD   Preston has never and cannot be wholly honest with himself.

BETTER   Preston has never **been** and cannot be wholly honest with himself.

INCOMPLETE Since I been in college, some of my values have changed.

COMPLETE   Since I **have** been in college, some of my values have changed.

Usage is divided regarding the inclusion or the omission of verbs in such sentences as the following:

The Lions are overwhelming; the event is unavoidable.
—E. B. WHITE   [Plural *are* is used with *Lions,* and singular *is* with *event.*]

The sounds were angry, the manner violent.
—A. E. VAN VOGT   [Plural *were* is used with *sounds,* but singular *was* after *manner* is omitted.]

22c

Do not omit words needed to complete comparisons.

INCOMPLETE Broken bottles around a swimming area are more dangerous than picnic tables.

COMPLETE   Broken bottles around a swimming area are more dangerous than **around** picnic tables.

INCOMPLETE Snow here is as scarce as Miami.
COMPLETE   Snow here is as scarce as **it is in** Miami.

INCOMPLETE The equipment of a soldier is heavier than a sailor.
COMPLETE   The equipment of a soldier is heavier than **that of** a sailor.
            OR A **soldier's** equipment is heavier than a **sailor's.**

CONFUSING	Sometimes a counselor helps an alcoholic less than the rest of the family.
CLEAR	Sometimes a counselor helps an alcoholic less than he or she **does** the rest of the family.
	OR Sometimes a counselor helps an alcoholic less than the rest of the family **does**.
INCOMPLETE	The amateur's performance was as good, possibly even better than, the professional's.
COMPLETE	The amateur's performance was as good **as**, possibly even better than, the professional's.

In a comparison such as the following, the word *other* may indicate a difference in meaning:

O'Brien runs faster than any player on the team. [O'Brien is apparently not on the team. In context, however, this may be an informal sentence meaning that O'Brien is the fastest of the players on the team.]

O'Brien runs faster than any **other** player on the team. [*Other* clearly indicates that O'Brien is on the team.]

■ **Exercise 3** Supply needed words in verb phrases and in comparisons.

1. They been trying to make small cars safe.
2. The consumers better listen to these warnings.
3. Ed's income is less than his wife.
4. Bruce admires Cathy more than Aline.
5. Fiberglass roofs are better.
6. The scenery here is as beautiful as any place.
7. I always have and always will like to read the comics.
8. One argument was as bad, maybe even worse than, the other.
9. The ordinance never has and never will be enforced.
10. The crusty old man irritates his roommate more than the cranky young nurse.

22d

When used as intensifiers in formal writing, *so, such,* and *too* are generally (but not always) followed by a completing phrase or clause.

The grand hotels were **so** grand **that they were known as palaces.** ——HORACE SUTTON

Elizabeth has **such** beautiful hands **that nearly everyone she meets comments on them.**

Many a man is praised for his reserve and so-called shyness when he is simply **too** proud **to risk making a fool of himself.** ——J. B. PRIESTLEY

■ **Exercise 4** Supply needed words in the following sentences.

1. I had my senior year a strange type virus.
2. As far as Boston, I could see the people were proud of their history.
3. The group is opposed and angered by these attempts to amend the Constitution.
4. I wish I been able to play football at university.
5. It's good to talk with a person has a similar problem.
6. His assistant and close friend considered only themselves.
7. The trouble is a good water-purifier costs so much.
8. He entered American Institute for Foreign Trade 1949.
9. Mr. Carter paid me more than Jim.
10. Nick announced the winner of the debate had not yet been voted on.
11. In our state the winter is as mild as Louisiana.
12. The mystery of the stolen jewels reminds me of mysteries like Sherlock Holmes.
13. Here is the hole which the rabbit escaped.
14. If Jack goes into a profession which he is not trained, he will fail.
15. The lawyer had to prove whatever the witness said was false.
16. I been concerned because the tuition is too high.
17. These trainees know they better study.
18. The large stadium was already filled with people and still coming.
19. Nobody interested their problems.
20. Elizabeth saw Nell was not in room.

EFFECTIVE SENTENCES

Unity
and
Logical Thinking

Unity, coherence, emphasis, variety—these are fundamental qualities of effective writing. Unity and coherence in sentences help to make ideas clear. Emphasis makes them forceful. Variety lends interest. But the final test of effective writing is the soundness of its reasoning.

23

Write unified sentences. Base your writing on sound logic.

A study of this section should help you write sentences that are neither cluttered with unrelated ideas or excessive detail, nor marred by mixed or awkward constructions. It should also help you avoid faulty definitions and illogical arguments, two very common mistakes in reasoning.

Unity

A sentence is unified when all its parts contribute to making one clear idea or impression. The parts of an ideal sentence form a perfect whole, so that a clause, a phrase, or even a word cannot be changed without disturbing the clarity of the thought or the focus of the impression.

23a

Bring into a sentence only related thoughts; use two or more sentences for thoughts not closely related.

Unrelated ideas should be developed in separate sentences. If the ideas in a sentence are related, they should be expressed in such a way that the relationship is immediately clear to the reader.

> UNRELATED   Yesterday Ted sprained his ankle, and he could not find his chemistry notes anywhere.
>
> RELATED   Accident-prone all day yesterday, Ted not only sprained his ankle but also lost his chemistry notes. [The relationship of the two ideas is made clear by the addition of the opening phrase.]

■ **Exercise 1**   All the sentences below contain ideas that are apparently unrelated. Adding words when necessary, rewrite each of the sentences to indicate clearly a relationship between ideas. If you cannot establish a close relationship, put the ideas in separate sentences.

1. Although the visiting professor has different and refreshing views, I played badminton on September 20.
2. I hate strong windstorms, and pecans pelted my bedroom roof all night.
3. The fence and barn need repairs, and why are property taxes so high?
4. There are many types of bores at social gatherings, but personally I prefer a quiet evening at home.
5. A telephone lineman who works during heavy storms can prove a hero, and cowards can be found in any walk of life.
6. Jones was advised to hire a tutor in French immediately, but the long hours of work at a service station kept his grades low.

7. Macbeth was not the only man to succumb to ambition, and Professor Stetson, for example, likes to draw parallels between modern men and literary characters.
8. Brad sent his sister a dozen red roses, and she sang on a fifteen-minute program over KTUV.
9. The food in the cafeteria has been the subject of many jokes, and most of the students do not look underfed.
10. Birds migrate to the warmer countries in the fall and in summer get food by eating worms and insects that are pests to the farmer.

23b

Do not allow excessive detail to obscure the central thought of the sentence.

If the detail of an overloaded sentence is important, it should be developed in separate sentences; otherwise it should be omitted.

> EXCESSIVE DETAIL   In 1788, when Andrew Jackson, then a young man of twenty-one years who had been living in the Carolinas, still a virgin country, came into Tennessee, a turbulent place of unknown opportunities, to enforce the law as the new prosecuting attorney, he had the qualifications that would make him equal to the task.

> ADEQUATE DETAIL   In 1788, when Andrew Jackson came into Tennessee as the new prosecuting attorney, he had the necessary qualifications for the task.

As you strive to eliminate excessive detail, remember that length alone does not make a sentence ineffective. Good writers can compose very long sentences, sometimes of paragraph length, without loss of unity. Parallel structure, balance, rhythm, effectively repeated connectives, and careful punctuation can bind a sentence into an emphatic unit, as in the following example:

The rediscovery of fresh air, of home-grown food, of the delights of the apple orchard under a summer sun, of the swimming pool made by damming the creek that flows through the meadow, of fishing for sun perch or catfish from an ancient rowboat, or of an early morning walk down a country lane when the air is cool—all of these things can stir memories of a simpler time and a less troubled world.

—CASKIE STINNETT, "The Wary Traveler"

■ **Exercise 2**   Recast the following sentences to eliminate excessive detail.

1. During the first period last Monday in room 206 of the English building, we freshmen enjoyed discussing the implications of language in various advertisements.

2. The fan that Joan bought for her brother, who frets about any temperature that exceeds seventy and insists that he can't stand the heat, arrived today.

3. When I was only four, living in a house built during the colonial period, little of which remains today, I often walked alone the two miles between my house and the lake.

4. Four cars of various designs and makes piled up on the freeway, which cost the state over $2 million.

5. In a firm voice and in a straight chair, the senator advocated drastic reforms, occasionally taking time out for a sip of water.

6. The dilapidated boat, seaworthy ten years ago but badly in need of repairs now, moved out into the bay.

7. Flames from the gas heater that was given to us three years ago by friends who were moving to Canada licked at the chintz curtains.

8. After finishing breakfast, which consisted of oatmeal, toast, and coffee, Sigrid called the tree surgeon, a cheerful man approximately fifty years old.

9. At last I returned the book that I had used for the report which I made Tuesday to the library.

10. A course in business methods helps undergraduates to get jobs and in addition helps them to find out whether they are fitted for business and thus to avoid postponing the crucial test, as so many do, until it is too late.

23c

Avoid mixed or awkward constructions.

(1) Do not mix metaphors by changing rapidly from one to another. See also 20a(4).

MIXED   Playing with fire can get a person into deep water.
BETTER   Playing with fire can result in burned fingers.

MIXED   Her plans to paint the town red were nipped in the bud.
BETTER   Her plans to paint the town red were thwarted. OR Her plans for a gala evening were nipped in the bud.

(2) Do not mix constructions. See also Section 1.

MIXED   When Howard plays the hypochondriac taxes his wife's patience.   [adverb clause + predicate]
CLEAR   When Howard plays the hypochondriac, **he** taxes his wife's patience.   [adverb clause, main clause]
CLEAR   Howard's playing the hypochondriac taxes his wife's patience.   [subject + predicate]

(3) Avoid awkward or obscure sentences. Complete every construction clearly and sensibly.

OBSCURE   An example of discrimination is a cafe owner, especially after he has refused to serve foreigners. [It is the refusal, not the cafe owner, that is an example of discrimination.]
CLEAR   An example of discrimination is a cafe owner's refusal to serve foreigners.

In defining words, careful writers tell *what* a thing is, not when it is or where it is. See also **23d**.

AWKWARD   A sonnet is when a poem has fourteen lines.
BETTER   A sonnet is a poem of fourteen lines.

AWKWARD   Banishing a man is where he is driven out of his country.
BETTER   Banishing a man is driving him out of his country.

Often a sentence is flawed by a confusion of singular and plural words.

> AWKWARD   Hundreds who attended the convention drove their own car.
>
> BETTER   Hundreds who attended the convention drove their own cars.

■ **Exercise 3** Revise the following sentences to eliminate mixed or awkward constructions.

1. For Don, money does grow on trees, and it also goes down the drain quickly.
2. Because his feet are not the same size explains the difficulty he has finding shoes that fit.
3. Friction is when one surface rubs against another.
4. Several of the applicants brought their résumé with them.
5. One example of a ripoff would be a butcher, because he could weigh his heavy thumb with the steak.
6. Like a bat guided by radar, Mark never skated on thin ice.
7. To be discreet is where a person carefully avoids saying or doing something tactless.
8. Does anyone here know why George resigned or where did he find a better job?
9. Tourists are not permitted to bring their camera indoors.
10. When children need glasses causes them to make mistakes in reading and writing.

Logical Thinking

Be sure that your sentences are well thought out and contain no slips or weaknesses of logic. The following principles of sound thinking may help you avoid the most common errors.

23d

Formulate definitions with care. See also **31b(6)**.

Errors and misunderstanding result when meanings of words and concepts are not clear. The two main types of definition are *formal* and *informal*. Either type can extend to the length of a paragraph, an essay, or even a book.

Formal definition.   In formal writing you may sometimes need to use a technical or unfamiliar term to express your thought precisely. If the exact meaning of such a term is essential to your reader's understanding or interpretation, it may be necessary for you to define it formally. In a formal definition the essential nature of the term to be defined is expressed first by saying what the term *is* and then, implicitly or explicitly, what it is *not*. That is, first the class or category to which the word belongs is identified. Then the term being defined is distinguished from other members of that class or category. The first process is called *classification,* and the second is called *differentiation.*

TERM	An *invertebrate* is
CLASSIFICATION	an animal
DIFFERENTIATION	with no spinal column, ranging in size from minute protozoans to giant squids, and accounting for more than 90 percent of all living animal species.
TERM	A *sonnet* is
CLASSIFICATION	a lyric poem
DIFFERENTIATION	written in a single stanza, consisting of fourteen iambic pentameter lines linked by an intricate rhyme scheme.

As a rule, you can strengthen a definition by sharply restricting the classification. For example, "A sonnet is a lyric poem" is better than "A sonnet is a poem."

Informal definition.   The demands of clarity and precision in writing are frequently satisfied by informal definition, in which synonyms or examples are commonly used.

SYNONYMS

Magendo, or black-market corruption, is flourishing.
—KEN ADELMAN [a lexical definition of a foreign term]

The bicycle, formerly a Christmas-tree item or a Sunday diversion, has become a serious vehicle of transportation in some American cities. —LANCE MORROW [a distinction between former connotative meanings and present denotation]

If you press your forefinger gently against your closed eyelid for a minute or less, you will probably start to see phosphenes: shapes and colors that march and swirl across your darkened field of view. —JEARL WALKER [word substitutions with restrictive details]

EXAMPLES

Many homophones (*be* and *bee, in* and *inn, see* and *sea*) are not common problems for spellers.

For the most part, the "external" arts, such as judo and karate, emphasize the acquisition of physical skills—speed, balance, accuracy, coordination, power. —DON ETHAN MILLER

23e
Base your arguments on sound reasoning.

In compositions an argument is a group of statements that present evidence in support of a thesis. Each argument thus consists of a set of propositions, or premises, offered as justification for the thesis, or conclusion. A valid argument has two characteristics that must always be present: (a) all premises must be true; and (b) the form (or pattern) of the argument must itself be valid. If the premises are true and the form of the argument is valid, the conclusion must be true. Conclusions derived in this way are based on *deductive logic.*

IF	all dogs have four legs, and	[premise]
IF	Bruno is a dog	[premise]
THEN	Bruno must have four legs.	[conclusion]

If a premise is false or only partially true, the conclusion does not necessarily follow. If the form is invalid, then the argument is also faulty.

FALSE PREMISE   All dogs have four ears, and Bruno is a dog; therefore, Bruno has four ears.

INVALID FORM   All cats have four legs, and Bruno has four legs; therefore, Bruno is a cat.

Note: *Inductive logic* goes from specific observations or particular instances to a general conclusion that is probably—but not necessarily—valid. You should carefully state such generalizations (avoiding qualifiers like *all, never, always*) and should support them with sufficient and relevant evidence. See Fallacies of Induction, pages 287–89.

■ **Exercise 4**   Be prepared for a class discussion of the premises and the conclusions in the following items.

1. First, many situations in real life have unhappy endings; therefore, if fiction is to illuminate life, it must present defeat as well as triumph. —LAURENCE PERRINE

2. Creationists say that evolutionary theory, because it seeks not to predict but only to explain what happened already, is not proper science but merely a belief system, which is to say, a religion. And the First Amendment says that no religion shall be fostered over another by the Federal Government; therefore, evolution should only be taught in schools with the caveat that it is theory. —JAKE PAGE

3. Standardized test scores are down, reading test scores are down, and students don't write as well as they used to. So, obviously, we have to go back to the basics.
   This may sound like compelling logic, but in a society that stands on the brink of a communications revolution, I would suggest that equating "the basics" with "the three R's" is a grievous and short-sighted error. —PETER H. WAGSCHAL

23f
Avoid common fallacies or mistakes in reasoning.

FALLACIES OF DEDUCTION (OR INFERENCE)
See also **23e**.

(1) Non sequitur ("It does not follow"): an argument in which the conclusion is not a necessary consequence of the premises.

FAULTY   Billy Joe is honest; therefore, he will get a good job.
BETTER   Billy Joe is honest; this characteristic should help him get a good job.

(2) Self-contradiction: an argument that contains mutually exclusive premises.

FAULTY   The government should control this unmanageable situation.
BETTER   We cannot expect government to control the uncontrollable, but it should try to do something about this situation.

(3) Circular Reasoning, or Begging the Question: a deductive argument in which the conclusion is contained in one of the premises.

FAULTY   I believe that this is an evil because society has always condemned it; society has always condemned it because it is evil.
BETTER   Society has always condemned this as an evil, and I believe society's judgment is correct.

FALLACIES OF INDUCTION

The following fallacies contain patterns of reasoning that misuse evidence or fail to support the general conclusion. See also the note on page 286.

(4) Confusion of Fact and Value Judgment. What can be observed, measured, and tested is a fact. Whether we like the fact or not, whether we believe it should be changed or not, these are value judgments—opinions or personal preferences. Both value judgments and facts are important, but they should not be confused.

FACT AND VALUE CONFUSED Your hair is too long. ["Too" indicates a personal preference, not a fact.]
FACT Your hair is long.
VALUE I don't like your hair long.

(5) Hasty Generalization: a generalization offered on the basis of too little evidence or evidence that is exceptional or biased in some way. *Enough* evidence must be gathered to warrant generalizing, and the evidence must not be exceptional or unusual.

INSUFFICIENT EVIDENCE None of the children in my family drink coffee; therefore, children don't like coffee. [More evidence is needed before this generalization is warranted.]
EXCEPTIONAL OR UNUSUAL EVIDENCE The increasing number of subway riders in Boston, New York, and Washington shows that urban dwellers in this country prefer mass transit to the automobile. [These three cities are unique in that their geographic area favors mass transit. Cities like Los Angeles or Oklahoma City whose geographic area is very large and whose population density is sparse might not favor mass transit.]

(6) Post hoc, ergo propter hoc ("After this, therefore because of this"): the mistake of assuming that because one event followed another, the first must be the cause of the second.

FAULTY Liz got wet and cold in the rain, so now she has a cold. [Many people become cold and wet in the rain and do not catch a cold.]

BETTER   Liz came in contact with and was susceptible to cold
         germs, so now she has a cold.

(7) False Analogy: a weak, far-fetched comparison.

FAULTY   The new mayor is not even the head of his own
         household, so I do not expect him to be a good civic
         leader or to have much influence on the city council.
BETTER   Because he was indecisive during his campaign, I do
         not expect the new mayor to be a good civic leader
         or to have much influence on the city council.

FALLACIES OF IRRELEVANCE

(8) Ignoring the Question, or Rambling: presenting details or facts that are off the point and do not support the thesis.

FAULTY   We should do more to help the poor help themselves. Of course, the Bible says we'll always have the poor with us, even though it does not say we should give them everything we have. [The writer loses sight of the main point: "We should help the poor help themselves.]

(9) Ad hominem ("To the person"): an attempt to disprove an argument by attacking the person who presents it. Do not evade the facts by attacking your opponent's economic, social, philosophical, or ethnic background.

FAULTY   That merchant is allegedly a thief and a liar; his arguments against a sales tax are worthless. [The merchant might steal and lie and yet have excellent views on economic matters such as a sales tax. The evidence is not relevant to the assertion.]

(10) Ad populum ("To the people"): an appeal to popular emotions, prejudices, or beliefs.

289

FAULTY   The majority of Americans today are a generous, compassionate, and freedom-loving people; to reflect the will of the people, immigration laws should not be changed but abolished.

(11) Bandwagon, or Join the Crowd: an argument saying, in effect, "Everyone's doing or saying or thinking this, so you should too."

FAULTY   This novel has been No. 1 on the best-seller list for weeks. You must read it!

(12) Appeal to Authority, or Appeal to Prestige: an argument relying not on facts but on opinions, beliefs, or theories of experts or on testimonials of famous people.

FAULTY   Both the *Washington Post* and the *New York Times* have predicted his reelection, so he will represent us again. [Predictions, even by experts, may or may not be accurate.]

FAULTY   One of the greatest athletes eats this cereal, so it is probably more nutritious than the others.

BETTER   A comparison of nutrition information printed on the boxes indicates that this cereal is probably more nutritious than the others.

FALLACIES OF IMPRECISION

(13) Ambiguity: a statement or argument in which the meaning is unclear; two or more different interpretations are therefore possible.

AMBIGUOUS   "John is a poor mechanic." [This statement could be interpreted as "John is not a competent mechanic" or as "John's financial resources are limited."]

(14) Equivocation: a statement or argument in which an expression or word is used in two different senses.

FAULTY   We Americans have the right to pursue happiness, and we should want to do what is right. So let's make happiness our goal in life.   [The word *right* is used in two different senses.]

FALLACIES OF MISREPRESENTATION

(15) Oversimplification: a statement or argument that leaves out relevant considerations about an issue.

FAULTY   People who pass tests are usually lucky.

BETTER   People who pass tests are usually lucky, although they are prepared to answer most questions well.

FAULTY   World War I was caused by the assassination of Archduke Francis Ferdinand in June, 1914.

BETTER   World War I had many causes, but the immediate precipitating event was the assassination of Archduke Francis Ferdinand in June, 1914.

(16) False Division, or Either-Or: any attempt to eliminate the middle ground by drawing a sharp distinction between parts of a complex whole when the facts show a gradation between the parts.

FAULTY   All living things are either plants or animals.

FAULTY   A nation is either at war or at peace.

■ **Exercise 5**   Prepare for a class discussion of the faulty logic in the sentences below.

1. Everyone goes to Florida in the winter.
2. Breaking a mirror brings seven years of bad luck.
3. Do not elect my opponent to the Senate; his parents were not born in America.
4. Young people today do not obey their parents.
5. Jacqueline will be a good class president because all her classmates like her.
6. The other car was at fault, for the driver was a teenager.
7. All Germans like opera; I have never met a German who did not.

8. Gertrude has a migraine headache because she ate popcorn last night and got that phone call.

9. These razor blades give the smoothest shave; all the baseball players use them.

10. After that oil spill, the fish I caught tasted greasy. The report from the marine lab is wrong. Those fish are contaminated!

11. It is a fact that traveling by air is not safe. Within forty-eight hours eleven persons have been killed in air crashes.

12. If you do not lock your car, someone may steal it. Since someone stole your car, it must not have been locked up.

13. When an automobile accident occurs in the city, the police are never on hand.

14. It is a fact that our nation has become, or is becoming, a police state.

15. Either the train is late or my watch is wrong. Since the train is on time, my watch must be accurate.

16. Poor people cannot afford to go to the doctor, so we can say that poverty causes ill health. But sick people cannot work, so we can also say that ill health causes poverty. Since both ill health and poverty cause each other, if we wipe out one we'll wipe out the other.

17. That night we had our traditional bonfire to hex them, and so they lost the game the next day.

18. Susan is not qualified to talk about honesty in government because only last year she was accused of bribery and extortion.

19. A successful politician must be either a lion or a fox.

20. Frank was not advised of his rights prior to his arrest on charges of drunken driving. It is therefore not right to prosecute him.

Subordination

24

Use subordination to relate ideas concisely and effectively; use coordination only to give ideas equal emphasis.

One of the marks of a mature writing style is the ability to connect and relate ideas effectively, either by coordination or by subordination. *Coordination* means "being of equal structural rank." Coordination gives equal grammatical emphasis to two or more ideas. See also Section **26**.

COORDINATE ELEMENTS
tactless, abrasive language   [coordinate adjectives]
not only **sings** but also **dances**   [verbs]
chicken livers **slowly fried in butter** and **heavily seasoned with garlic**   [participial phrases]
a person **whose last name I do not know** and **whom I have never met.** [coordinate adjective clauses]
If they do get to the Super Bowl, **they will lose the game,** or **they will win it because of lucky breaks.**   [main clauses]
These kindnesses did not go unnoticed. Nor were they unappreciated.   [simple sentences]

Notice in these examples that coordinating conjunctions and correlatives link words, phrases, clauses, and sentences of equal grammatical rank.

Subordination means "being of lower structural rank." It is the use of dependent elements—such as modifiers—that are of less importance grammatically than independent elements. Clauses functioning as nouns, adjectives, or adverbs are called subordinate because they are grammatically secondary to main clauses. Subordinate elements are parts of sentences, not sentences.

SUBORDINATE ELEMENTS

It was **tactless, abrasive** language. [The modifiers are of less importance grammatically than the sentence base: *It was language.*]

Chicken livers **slowly fried in butter and heavily seasoned with garlic** are good with rice. [The compound phrase functions as modifier.]

Gail is a person **whose last name I do not know and whom I have never met**. [The adjective clauses (linked by the coordinating conjunction *and*) are secondary to the main clause: *Gail is a person.*]

In the following sentence, the main clause (*subject* + *compound predicate*) is in boldface. All other elements in the sentence are grammatically subordinate to the main clause.

> Since I was sixteen years old at the time and had been graduated from high school, **I knew a great deal and had opinions** on a variety of subjects that I thought anyone else in the office would consider it a privilege to hear.   —EDWIN NEWMAN

As this example shows, grammatically subordinate structures may contain very important ideas.

Inexperienced writers tend to use too much coordination—too many short simple sentences or stringy compound ones. To express relationships between ideas, do not overwork coordinating connectives like *so* or *and* or conjunctive adverbs like *then* or *however*. Use relative pronouns (*who, which, that*) appropriately as subordinators. Also use subordinating conjunctions to indicate such relationships as cause (*because, since*), concession (*although, though*), time (*after, as, before, since, when, whenever, while, until*), place (*where, wherever*), condition (*if, unless*), and comparison (*as if*). Notice the differences in emphasis in the following sentences:

> **Clem had finished the pre-employment course,** *and* **he was ready for an on-the-job experience.**
> **Clem,** *who* **had finished the pre-employment course, was ready for an on-the-job experience.**
> *Because* **Clem had finished the pre-employment course, he was ready for an on-the-job experience.**

If you cannot distinguish between phrases and clauses and between subordinate and main clauses, study **1d** and **1e**.

24a

Use subordination to combine a related series of short sentences into longer, more effective units.

When combining a series of related sentences, first choose one complete idea for your sentence base; then use subordinate structures (such as modifiers, parenthetical elements, and appositives) to relate the ideas in the other simple sentences to the base.

As you study the following examples of combined sentences, notice that the use of subordinate elements contributes to the concise expression of ideas. See also Section **21**.

CHOPPY	Douglas wrote a quick note. It was to Nora. She is his former employer.
BETTER	Douglas wrote a quick note to Nora, his former employer.
CHOPPY	Two days passed. Then helicopters headed for the mountaintop. The blizzard had stranded several climbers.
BETTER	After two days, helicopters headed for the mountaintop because the blizzard had stranded several climbers.

CHOPPY The limbs were covered with ice. They sparkled in the sunlight. They were beautiful.

BETTER Sparkling in the sunlight, the ice-covered limbs were beautiful.

■ **Exercise 1** Combine the following short sentences into longer sentences by using effective subordination as well as co-ordination. (If you wish, keep one short sentence for emphasis: see **29h**.)

[1] I have just read "The Idea of a University" by John Henry Newman. [2] I am especially interested in his views regarding knowledge. [3] He says that knowledge is its own reward. [4] It is not just a means to an end. [5] Newman says knowledge is a treasure in itself. [6] I had looked upon knowledge only in terms of practical results. [7] One result would be financial security. [8] But that was before I read this essay. [9] Now I accept Newman's definition of knowledge. [10] Such knowledge is worth pursuing for its own sake.

24b

Do not string main clauses together with *and, so,* or *but* when ideas should be subordinated. Use coordination only to give ideas equal emphasis. See also 30c.

AWKWARD I wanted to go to college, so I mowed and trimmed lawns all summer, and that way I could earn enough money to pay my tuition.

BETTER Because I wanted to go to college, I mowed and trimmed lawns all summer to earn enough money for my tuition.

AWKWARD Burns won, and it was a landslide vote, but he had rigged the election.

BETTER Burns, who had rigged the election, won by a landslide vote.

OR

Having rigged the election, Burns won by a landslide vote.

COORDINATION   The offer was tempting, but I did not accept it. [equal grammatical stress on the offer and the refusal]

SUBORDINATION   Although the offer was tempting, I did not accept it. [stress on the refusal]

OR

Although I did not accept it, the offer was tempting. [stress on the offer]

■ **Exercise 2**   To improve sentence unity, revise the following sentences by using effective subordination and, when needed, coordination.

1. First she selected a lancet and sterilized it, and then she gave the patient a local anesthetic and lanced the infected flesh.
2. Yesterday I was taking a shower, so I did not hear the telephone ring, but I got the message in time to go to the party.
3. Two ambulances tore by, and an oncoming bus crowded a truckload of laborers off the road, but nobody got hurt.
4. Jean Henri Dunant was a citizen of Switzerland, and he felt sorry for Austrian soldiers wounded in the Napoleonic Wars; therefore, he started an organization, and it was later named the Red Cross.
5. The administrators stressed career education, and not only did they require back-to-basics courses, but they also kept students informed about job opportunities.

24c

Avoid excessive or overlapping subordination.

AWKWARD   I have never before known a man like Ernie, my friend who is always ready to help anybody who is in trouble that involves finances.

BETTER   I have never before known a man like my friend Ernie, who is always ready to help anybody in financial trouble.

297

AWKWARD   These were the voters who were concerned about
             unemployment that kept rising, who were wor-
             ried about the dollar, which was diminishing in
             value.

BETTER   These were the voters concerned about rising
             unemployment and the diminishing value of the
             dollar.

■ **Exercise 3**   Prepare to contribute to a class discussion of the
subordination and the coordination of ideas in the following paragraph.

¹ Going by canoe is often the best—and sometimes the
only—way to go. ² Some difficult country can't be reached any
other way, and once you arrive, the aches of paddling and sitting
unsupported on a canoe seat seem a small price to pay for being
there. ³ One such place is the Boundary Waters area along the
border of northeastern Minnesota and Ontario. ⁴ The terrain is
rolling and pocked by thousands of glacier lakes. ⁵ Some are no
more than bowls of rock that hold the accumulated clear green
water; others are spring-fed and dark. ⁶ The maze of lakes, islands, and portage trails is inhabited by all sorts of wildlife: bea-
ver, otter, loons, and bear. ⁷ It is a landscape suited to the
canoe and has in fact been canoe country since the time of the
fur-trading voyageurs—hard Frenchmen whose freighters were
up to twenty-five feet long and required eight paddlers.

—GEOFFREY NORMAN, "Rapid Transit"

■ **Exercise 4**   Combine choppy sentences and tighten loose
ones. Use exact conjunctions (see pages 294–95) as you make a
main clause subordinate or convert a sentence into a main
clause.

1. I was walking across the campus. I found a twenty-dollar
   bill.
2. I was musing on the pleasures of loafing, and the idea struck
   me: complete idleness is hard work.
3. Growth stops. Insects eat the plant off. They do their eating
   just below the soil.

4. The little boy slept through it all, and so he was unconscious of our worries and fears.
5. I felt bad. I didn't tell anybody. I didn't want to go to the hospital again.
6. The yearbook had predicted it. Within a year the twins were married. They married twins.
7. The price of peace may be high. The price of war is higher.
8. An intention is not the deed. A blueprint is not a home.
9. The battle is worth fighting, and success is inevitable, or so the optimist believes.
10. Oliver is a bantam boxer, and he likes to throw his weight around, and so he keeps on picking fights.

■ **Exercise 5** Relating your ideas precisely, use each connective below in a sentence. When necessary, consult the dictionary for exact meanings.

as	once	whether
besides	since	where
except for	so	whereas
like	thus	till/until

Coherence: Misplaced Parts, Dangling Modifiers

25

Avoid needless separation of related parts of the sentence. Avoid dangling modifiers.

Since the meaning of most English sentences depends largely on word order, the position of the parts of a sentence is especially important to clear communication.

MISPLACED	The doctor said that there was nothing seriously wrong **with a smile**.
BETTER	**With a smile** the doctor said that there was nothing seriously wrong.
	OR
	The doctor said **with a smile** that there was nothing seriously wrong.
DANGLING	**When discussing creativity**, a person's ability to finish a pun is stressed by John E. Gibson.
BETTER	**When discussing creativity, John E. Gibson** stresses a person's ability to finish a pun.

The parts of a sentence should be placed to convey the precise emphasis or meaning desired. Note how the meaning of the following sentences changes according to the position of the modifiers:

Rex **just** died with his boots on.
Rex died with **just** his boots on.
Just Rex died with his boots on.

The man **who drowned** had tried to help the child.
The man had tried to help the child **who drowned**.

Normally the modifier should be placed as near the word modified as idiomatic English will permit.

Misplaced Parts

25a
Avoid needless separation of related parts of the sentence.

(1) In standard written English, modifiers such as *almost, only, just, even, hardly, nearly,* and *merely* are regularly placed immediately before the words they modify.

In speech such modifiers are often put before the verb.

SPOKEN   The hut only costs $450.   [OR   costs *only* $450]
WRITTEN   The hut costs **only** $450.

SPOKEN   Stacey will not even write us a postcard.
         [OR   write us *even* a postcard]
WRITTEN   Stacey will not write us **even** a postcard.

■ **Exercise 1**   Revise the following sentences, placing the modifiers in correct relation to the words they modify.

1. The bomb of the terrorists only killed one student.
2. Bruce polished his silver dollars almost until they looked like new.
3. The transistor nearly cost fifty dollars.
4. He even works during his vacation.

5. Some contemporary poets hardly show any interest in making their poems intelligible.
6. On Thanksgiving Day the guests almost ate all the turkey.
7. I barely had enough to pay my tuition.

(2) The position of a modifying prepositional phrase should clearly indicate what the phrase modifies.

A prepositional phrase used as an adjective nearly always comes immediately after the word modified. (When used as an adjectival before the noun modified, a prepositional phrase is hyphenated: "on-the-job training." See **18f**.)

MISPLACED   A garish poster attracts the visitor's eye **on the east wall**.

BETTER   A garish poster **on the east wall** attracts the visitor's eye.

Adverb phrases may be placed near the word modified or at the beginning or end of a sentence. Sometimes, however, the usual placement can be awkward or unclear.

MISPLACED   One student said that such singing was not music but a throat ailment **in class**.

BETTER   **In class** one student **said** that such singing was not music but a throat ailment.   OR   One student **said in class** that such singing was not music but a throat ailment.

■ **Exercise 2**   Revise the following sentences to correct undesirable separation of related parts.

1. Newspapers carried the story of the quarterback's fumbling in every part of the country.
2. Lucille bakes date muffins just for her friends with pecans in them.
3. At the picnic Gertrude served sundaes to hungry guests in paper cups.
4. The professor made it clear why plagiarism is wrong on Monday.

(3) Adjective clauses should be placed near the words they modify.

MISPLACED   We bought gasoline in Arkansas at a small country store **which cost $10.25.**

BETTER   At a small country store in Arkansas, we bought gasoline **which cost $10.25.**

(4) Avoid "squinting" constructions—modifiers that may refer to either a preceding or a following word.

SQUINTING   Jogging **often** relaxes her.

BETTER   **Often, jogging** relaxes her.

OR

It relaxes her **to jog often.**

(5) Avoid the awkward separation of the sentence base and the awkward splitting of an infinitive.

AWKWARD   I **had** in spite of my not living in a neighborhood as fine as Jane's **pride.** [awkward separation of a verb from its object]

BETTER   In spite of my not living in a neighborhood as fine as Jane's, I **had pride.**

AWKWARD   Hawkins is the man **to,** whether you are a liberal, conservative, or moderate, **vote for.** [awkward splitting of an infinitive]

BETTER   Whether you are a liberal, conservative, or moderate, Hawkins is the man **to vote for.**

Note: Many times, though, splitting an infinitive is not only natural but also desirable.

For her to **never** complain seems unreal.
I wished to **properly** understand meditating.

■ **Exercise 3**   Revise the following sentences to eliminate squinting modifiers or needless separation of related sentence parts.

1. An official warned the hunter not to carry a rifle in a car that was loaded.
2. Selby said in the evening he would go.
3. Marvin wanted to, even during the 6:15 P.M. sports news, finish our game of checkers.
4. Harriet promised when she was on her way home to stop at the library.
5. The car was advertised in last night's paper which is only two years old and is in excellent condition.

Dangling Modifiers

25b
Avoid dangling modifiers.

Although any misplaced word, phrase, or clause can be said to dangle, the term *dangling* is applied primarily to verbal phrases that do not refer clearly and logically to another word or phrase in the sentence.

To correct a dangling modifier, rearrange the words in the sentence to make the modifier clearly refer to the right word, or add words to make the meaning clear and logical.

(1) Avoid dangling participial phrases.

DANGLING   **Discouraged by low grades**, dropping out made sense.

REVISED   **Because I was discouraged by low grades**, dropping out made sense. OR

Discouraged by low grades, I thought dropping out made sense.

The second revision above follows this pattern:

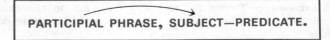

PARTICIPIAL PHRASE, SUBJECT—PREDICATE.

In the following sentence, the participial phrase is placed after the sentence base.

DANGLING   The evening passed very pleasantly, **playing backgammon and swapping jokes**.

REVISED   **They** passed the evening very pleasantly, **playing backgammon and swapping jokes**.

In the revision above, the participial phrase refers to the subject, as the following pattern illustrates:

SUBJECT—PREDICATE, PARTICIPIAL PHRASE.

(2) Avoid dangling phrases containing gerunds or infinitives.

DANGLING   **Instead of watching** *The Late Show,* a novel was read.

REVISED   **Instead of watching** *The Late Show,* **Nancy** read a novel.

DANGLING   **Not able to swim that far**, a lifeguard came to my rescue.

REVISED   **I was not able to swim that far**, so a lifeguard came to my rescue.

     OR **Because I was not able to swim that far**, a lifeguard came to my rescue.

(3) Avoid dangling elliptical adverb clauses.

Elliptical clauses have words that are implied rather than stated.

DANGLING   **When confronted with these facts**, not one word was said.

REVISED   **When confronted with these facts**, **nobody** said a word.

     OR **When they were confronted with these facts**, not one word was said.

DANGLING   **Although only a small boy**, my father expected
me to do a man's work.

REVISED   **Although I was only a small boy**, my father expected me to do a man's work.

Note: Verbal phrases such as the following (often called *sentence modifiers* because they qualify a whole clause or the rest of the sentence) are not classified as dangling modifiers but are considered standard usage.

To judge from reports, all must be going well.
His health is fairly good, **considering his age**.

■ **Exercise 4**   Revise the following sentences to eliminate dangling modifiers. Put a checkmark after any sentence that needs no revision.

1. While wondering about this phenomenon, the sun sank from view.
2. By standing and repeating the pledge, the meeting came to an end.
3. Once made, you must execute the decision promptly.
4. Prepare to make an incision in the abdomen as soon as completely anesthetized.
5. After sitting there awhile, it began to snow, and we went indoors.
6. Darkness having come, we stopped for the night.
7. Having taken his seat, we began to question the witness.
8. Ready to pitch camp, the windstorm hit.
9. The convicts did not yield, thinking they could attract the support of the press.
10. Burned to the ground, the Welches had to build a new house.

■ **Exercise 5** Combine the two sentences in each item below into a single sentence. Use an appropriately placed verbal phrase or elliptical clause as an introductory parenthetical element.

EXAMPLES

We were in a hurry to leave Yellowstone. The dented fender was not noticed.

Being in a hurry to leave Yellowstone, we did not notice the dented fender.

A person may sometimes be confused. At such times he ought to ask questions.

When confused, a person ought to ask questions.

1. The statue has a broken arm and nose. I think it is an interesting antique.
2. James sometimes worried about the world situation. At such times joining the Peace Corps seemed to him a good idea.
3. I read the first three questions on the test. The test covered materials that I had not studied.
4. Larry was only twelve years old. His teachers noticed his inventive abilities.
5. I turned on the flashers and lifted the hood. A passing motorist, I thought, might see my predicament, slow down, and offer me a ride.

Parallelism

26

Use parallel structure as an aid to coherence.

Parallel (grammatically equal) sentence elements regularly appear in lists, series, and compound structures. Connectives like *and, or, but, yet* link and relate balanced sentence elements. (See also Section **24**.) Faulty parallelism disrupts the balance.

AWKWARD   What do the super-rich know about disease, those who are hungry, and poverty?

PARALLEL   What do the super-rich know about **disease, hunger,** and **poverty**?   [nouns in series]

PARALLEL   What do the super-rich know about those who are **sick, hungry, and poor**?   [adjectives in series]

If you cannot readily distinguish between parts of speech and between types of phrases and clauses, study Section **1**.

26a

For parallel structure, balance nouns with nouns, prepositional phrases with prepositional phrases, main clauses with main clauses, and so on.

As you study the parallel words, phrases, clauses, and sentences that follow, notice that repetition can be used to emphasize the balanced structure.

(1) Parallel words and phrases

People begin to feel ‖ **faceless**
      and ‖ **insignificant.**   —S. L. HALLECK

The two most powerful words in the world today are
not ‖ **guns and money,**
but ‖ **wheat and oil.**   —FREDERIC BIRMINGHAM

She had ‖ **no time to be human,**
        ‖ **no time to be happy.**   —SEAN O'FAOLAIN

(2) Parallel clauses

      ‖ **What we say**
and ‖ **what we do**
somehow seem out of joint.   —NORMAN COUSINS

‖ **Top soil, once blown away, can never be returned;**
‖ **virgin prairie, once plowed, can never be reclaimed.**
  —MARILYN COFFEY

(3) Parallel sentences

‖ **When I breathed in, I squeaked.**
‖ **When I breathed out, I rattled.**   —JOHN CARENEN

‖ **The danger of the past was that men became slaves.**
‖ **The danger of the future is that men may become robots.**
  —ERICH FROMM

■ **Exercise 1** Underline the parallel structures. Then write sentences containing parallel (1) words, (2) phrases, (3) clauses, and (4) sentences.

1. In English, there are countless situations, moods, and relationships for which there is no single word.
  —THOMAS H. MIDDLETON
2. Imagine America without baseball, Europe without soccer, England without cricket, the Italians without bocci, China without Ping-Pong, and tennis for no one.
  —BARBARA W. TUCHMAN

3. To say that some truths are simple is not to say they are unimportant. —WILLIAM J. BENNETT

4. Reading through *The Origin* is like eating Cracker Jacks and finding an I O U note at the bottom of the box.
   —JOHN FLUDAS

5. The earth's nearest neighbor has mountains taller than Everest, valleys deeper than the Dead Sea rift, and highlands bigger than Australia. —NEWSWEEK

6. She completed her page, ornamented the foot of it with a rattling row of fancy lines and dots, threw over the release, spun the roller, twitching the foolscap sheets from under it in vicious haste, flung the carbons into the basket, shuffled the copies into order, slapped them vigorously on all four edges to bring them into symmetry, and bounced with them into the inner office. —DOROTHY SAYERS

7. There might be some people in the world who do not need flowers, who cannot be surprised by joy, but I haven't met them. —GLORIA EMERSON

8. Broadly speaking, human beings may be divided into three classes: those who are toiled to death, those who are worried to death, and those who are bored to death.
   —WINSTON CHURCHILL

9. Booms typically attract an oversupply of trained specialists; busts generate an undersupply. —CHRIS WELLES

10. Not for thirty years has political tension reached so dangerous a point as it has attained today. Not in all this time has there been so high a degree of misunderstanding, of suspicion, of bewilderment, and of sheer military fear.
    —GEORGE F. KENNAN

26b

To make the parallel clear, repeat a preposition, an article, the *to* of the infinitive, or the introductory word of a phrase or clause.

> The reward rests not ‖ in the task
> but ‖ in the pay. —JOHN K. GALBRAITH

Life is ‖a mystery
   and ‖an adventure
which he shares with all living things.

—JOSEPH WOOD KRUTCH

It is easier ‖to love humanity as a whole
   than ‖to love one's neighbor.   —ERIC HOFFER

It is the things we think we know—
   ‖because they are so elementary
or ‖because they surround us—
that often present the greatest difficulties when we are actually challenged to explain them. —STEPHEN JAY GOULD

■ **Exercise 2** Insert words needed to bring out the parallel structure in the following sentences.

1. They would lie on the battlefield without medical attention for an hour or day.
2. Two things I intend to do: to try and succeed.
3. I told him politely that I could not go and I had reasons.
4. I finally realized that one can learn much more by studying than worrying.
5. On the safari Eva took photographs of a tiger and elephant.

26c

Correlatives (both . . . and; either . . . or; neither . . . nor; not only . . . but also; whether . . . or) usually connect parallel structures.

AWKWARD   We judge our friends both by what they say and actions.

PARALLEL   We judge our friends
      both ‖ by their words
      and ‖ by their actions.

PARALLEL   We judge our friends
      both ‖ by what they say
      and ‖ by how they act.

AWKWARD   Not only practicing at 6 a.m. during the week, but the team also scrimmages on Sunday afternoons.

PARALLEL   The team
not only ‖ **practices at 6 a.m. during the week**
but also ‖ **scrimmages on Sunday afternoons**.

OR   Not only does the team practice at 6 a.m. during the week, but it also scrimmages on Sunday afternoons.   [The *also* may be omitted.]

AWKWARD   Either they obey the manager or get fired.

PARALLEL   Either ‖ **they obey the manager**
or ‖ **they get fired**.

PARALLEL   They either ‖ **obey the manager**
or ‖ **get fired**.

AWKWARD   Whether drunk or when he was sober, he liked to pick a fight.

PARALLEL   Whether ‖ **drunk**
or ‖ **sober**,
he liked to pick a fight.

26d

Be sure that a *who, whom,* or *which* clause precedes *and who, and whom,* or *and which*.

AWKWARD   Inez Santos is a woman with an open mind and who is seeking office.   [A *who* clause does not precede the *and who.*]

PARALLEL   Inez Santos is a woman ‖ **who has an open mind**
and ‖ **who is seeking office**.

■ **Exercise 3**   Revise the following sentences by using parallel structure to express parallel ideas. Put a checkmark after any sentence that needs no revision.

1. It is a rare disease and which is hard to diagnose.
2. Shirley likes to play tennis and watching basketball.
3. Our personalities are shaped by both heredity and what type of environment we have.
4. Someone has said that Americans cannot enjoy life without a TV set, an automobile, and a summer cottage.
5. My friend told me that the trip would be delayed but to be ready to start on Friday.
6. William is a man with the best intentions and who has the highest principles.
7. A seal watches carefully the way his fellows act and how they obey their trainer.
8. He was quiet and in a serious mood after the talk.
9. The secretary must attend all meetings, call the roll, and keep the minutes.
10. People fall naturally into two classes: the workers and those who like to depend on others.

■ **Exercise 4** First study the parallelism in the sentences below. Then use one of the sentences as a structural model for a sentence of your own.

1. All peoples, past and present, civilized and barbarian, share at least one thing in common: when the need arises, or the humor is upon them, they swear. ——EDWARD C. ECHOLS

2. In the ghetto everybody gets a piece of the action: those who are Jews and those who are Christians; those who are white and those who are black; those who run the numbers and those who operate the churches; those— black and white—who own tenements and those— black and white—who own businesses.

——BAYARD RUSTIN

[Note that semicolons sharply divide the long, compound items in the series and contribute to clarity.]

3. If American English is to be saved, it will, in my view, have to be saved by individuals, or by small guerrilla groups that refuse to accept nonsense, send back unclear and pompous letters with a request for translation, and insist that organizations they are a part of speak plainly. ——EDWIN NEWMAN

Shifts

27

**Avoid needless shifts in grammatical struc-
tures, in tone or style, and in viewpoint.**

Abrupt, unnecessary shifts—for example, from past to present, from singular to plural, from formal diction to slang,
from one perspective to another—tend to obscure a writer's
meaning and thus to cause needless difficulty in reading.

27a

Avoid needless shifts in tense, mood, and voice. See
also Section 7.

> SHIFT During their talk Harvey **complained** about the idi-
> ocy of overkill while his father **discusses** the dangers
> of overlive. [shift from past to present tense]
>
> BETTER During their talk Harvey **complained** about the idi-
> ocy of overkill while his father **discussed** the dangers
> of overlive. [both verbs in the past tense]
>
> SHIFT If I **were** rich and if my father **was** still alive, my life
> would be different. [shift from subjunctive to indic-
> ative mood]
>
> BETTER If I **were** rich and if my father **were** still alive, my life
> would be different. [verbs in the subjunctive
> mood]

SHIFT   The old man finally **had to enter** a nursing home, but it **was** not **liked** by him.   [The voice shifts from active to passive.]

BETTER   The old man finally **had to enter** a nursing home, but he **did** not **like** it.   [Both verbs are active.]

When the literary present is used, as in summarizing plots of novels and plays, care should be taken to avoid slipping from the present tense into the past tense.

Romeo and Juliet fall in love at first sight, marry secretly, and die (NOT *died*) together in the tomb within the same hour.

27b

Avoid needless shifts in person and in number. See also **6b**.

SHIFT   A man has to expect criticism when you succeed. [shift in person]

BETTER   A **man** has to expect criticism when **he** succeeds.
         OR
         You have to expect criticism when **you** succeed.
         OR
         One has to expect criticism when **one**   [OR he OR he or she] succeeds.
         OR
         Successful people have to expect criticism.

SHIFT   Every **student** in favor of the legalization of marijuana **was** asked to sign **their names** on a master ditto sheet.   [shift in number]

BETTER   All **students** in favor of the legalization of marijuana **were** asked to sign **their names** on a master ditto sheet.

■ **Exercise 1**   Correct all needless shifts in tense, mood, voice, person, and number in the following sentences.

1. After his easy victory, Kurt strutted over to me and asks a smart-aleck question.

315

2. Martínez recommended that property taxes be raised and spend wisely for the poor.
3. Marvin added meat to the frozen pizza, and then it was baked fifteen minutes by him.
4. Every bystander was suspect, so they were taken away for questioning.
5. I was told that billions of germs live on one's skin and that you should bathe often.

27c

Avoid needless shifts from indirect to direct discourse. See also 26a.

SHIFT   The Gordons wonder **how the thief got the car keys** and **why didn't he or she steal the tapes?** [shift from indirect to direct discourse—a mixture of indirect and direct questions]

BETTER   The Gordons wonder **how the thief got the car keys** and **why he or she didn't steal the tapes.** [two indirect questions]

OR

The Gordons asked, "**How did the thief get the car keys? Why didn't they steal the tapes?**" [The shift in number from *thief* to *they* is typical of conversational English.]

SHIFT   The secretary said **that he was sick** and **would I please read the minutes.** [shift from indirect to direct discourse]

BETTER   The secretary said **that he was sick** and **asked me to read the minutes.** [indirect discourse]

27d

Avoid needless shifts in tone or style throughout the sentence (as well as throughout the larger elements of the composition).

INAPPROPRIATE   Journalists who contend that the inefficiency of our courts will lead to the total elimination of the jury system are **nuts**.   [a shift from formal to colloquial diction; replace *nuts* with a word like *wrong, uninformed,* or *alarmists.*]

INAPPROPRIATE   After distributing the grass seed evenly over the lawn, rake the ground at least twice and then **gently bedew it with fine spray**.   [The boldfaced expression is too "poetic" in a sentence with a prosaic purpose. Substitute something like *water it lightly.*]

27e

Avoid needless shifts in perspective or viewpoint throughout the sentence (as well as throughout the larger elements of the composition).

FAULTY PERSPECTIVE   The underwater scene was dark and mysterious; the willows lining the shore dipped gracefully into the water.   [The perspective abruptly shifts from beneath the surface of the water to above it.]

BETTER   The underwater scene was dark and mysterious; **above**, the willows lining the shore dipped gracefully into the water.

■ **Exercise 2**   Correct all needless shifts in the following sentences. Put a checkmark after any sentence that needs no revision.

1. A woman stepped forward, grabs the mugger's belt, snatches the purses, and got lost in the crowd.
2. A vacation is enjoyed by all because it refreshes the mind and the body.
3. Aunt Leila spent her summers in Wisconsin but flew to Arizona for the winters.
4. Jim wondered whether Jack had left and did he say when he would return?
5. Every cook has their own recipes for making chili.

6. He told his aunt that there is someone in the room.
7. If she really likes someone, she would make any sacrifice for them.
8. Take your raincoat. They will be needed.
9. The outside of the building looks like a fortress; the comfortable furnishings seem out of place.
10. The darkness of the auditorium, the monotony of the ballet, and the strains of music drifting sleepily from the orchestra aroused in me a great desire to sack out.

■ **Exercise 3** Revise the following paragraph to eliminate all needless shifts.

¹ He was a shrewd businessman, or so it had always seemed to me. ² He has innocent-looking eyes, which are in a baby face, and swaggered when he walks. ³ When questioned about his recent windfall, he up and says, ''I'm lucky enough to have the right contacts.'' ⁴ Not one name was mentioned by him; moreover, his reluctance to discuss his business transactions was evident. ⁵ Take these comments for what they are worth; they may help one in your dealings with this big shot.

Reference
of Pronouns
28

Make a pronoun refer unmistakably to its antecedent. See also 6b.

Each boldfaced pronoun below clearly refers to its italicized antecedent, a single word or a word group:

> *Languages* are not invented; **they** grow with our need for expression. —SUSANNE K. LANGER

> There is no *country* in the world **whose** population is stationary. —KENNETH BOULDING

> Thus, *being busy* is more than merely a national passion; **it** is a national excuse. —NORMAN COUSINS

A pronoun may clearly refer to a whole clause:

> Some people think that *the fall of man had something to do with sex,* but **that**'s a mistake. —C. S. LEWIS [Compare "*To think this* is a mistake."]

As you proofread your compositions, check to see that the meaning of each pronoun is immediately obvious. If there is any chance of confusion, repeat the antecedent, use a synonym for it, or recast your sentence.

Note: For the sake of clarity, you may find it necessary to establish a point of reference for acronyms and abbreviations (although they are not pronouns).

319

UNCLEAR   Some types of MIRVs face special restrictions. [What, a reader may ask, are MIRVs?]

CLEAR   These mainly are the multiwarheads known as **MIRVs**, the acronym for **multiple independently targetable re-entry vehicles**. . . . Some types of **MIRVs** face special restrictions.   —TIME

UNCLEAR   The second promising program is the E.G.S. of the state of Maharashtra. . . . The E.G.S. approach should be extended to all parts of the country. [What is the E.G.S.?]

CLEAR   The second promising program is the **Employment Guarantee Scheme** (**E.G.S.**) of the state of Maharashtra.
. . . The **E.G.S.** approach should be extended to all parts of the country.

—SCIENTIFIC AMERICAN

28a

Avoid an ambiguous reference.

A pronoun, of course, may clearly refer to two or more antecedents: "*Jack* and *Jill* met *their* Waterloo." Ambiguous reference, however, causes the reader to be unsure of the meaning of a pronoun because it could refer to one antecedent or to another.

AMBIGUOUS   Lisa wrote to Jennifer every day when she was in the hospital.

CLEAR   When Lisa was in the hospital, she wrote to Jennifer every day.   OR
When Jennifer was in the hospital, Lisa wrote to her every day.

AMBIGUOUS   After listening to Ray's proposal and to Sam's objections, I liked his ideas better.

CLEAR   I agreed with Sam after listening to his objections to Ray's proposal.

28b

Avoid a remote or an obscure reference.

Do not run the risk of your reader's momentarily losing track of the antecedent of a pronoun because you have placed the pronoun too far from its antecedent. Also avoid an obscure reference to an antecedent in the possessive case.

REMOTE   A freshman found herself the unanimously elected president of a group of enthusiastic reformers, mostly townspeople, **who** was not a joiner of organizations. [*Who* is too far removed from the antecedent *freshman.* See also **25a(3)**.]

BETTER   A **freshman who** was not a joiner of organizations found herself the unanimously elected president of a group of enthusiastic reformers, mostly townspeople.

OBSCURE   When Johnson's club was organized, **he** asked Goldsmith to become a member. [reference to antecedent in the possessive case]

BETTER   When **Johnson** organized his club, **he** asked Goldsmith to become a member.

Note: As a rule, writers avoid using a pronoun like *it, this,* or *he* to refer to the title of a composition or to a word in the title.

Title: Death with Dignity

AWKWARD FIRST SENTENCE   How can this ever be?
BETTER   How can death ever be dignified?

■ **Exercise 1**   Revise each sentence below to eliminate ambiguous, remote, or obscure pronoun reference.

1. The misunderstanding between the Kemps and the Dixons did not end until they invited them over for a swim in their new pool.
2. On the dashboard the various buttons and knobs seldom cause confusion on the part of the driver that are clearly labeled.

3. After Martin's advertising campaign was launched, he had more business than he could handle.
4. The lake covers many acres. Near the shore, water lilies grow in profusion, spreading out their green leaves and sending up white blossoms on slender stems. It is well stocked with fish.
5. Elaine waved to Mrs. Edwards as she was coming down the ramp.

28c

Use broad reference only with discretion.

Pronouns such as *it, this, that, which,* and *such* may refer to a specific word or phrase or to the general idea of a whole clause, sentence, or paragraph:

> SPECIFIC REFERENCE His nose was absolutely covered with warts of different sizes; it looked like a sponge, or some other kind of marine growth. —DAN JACOBSON [*It* refers to *nose.*]

> BROAD REFERENCE This was One World now—and he owned a Volkswagen and a Japanese camera to prove it. —ARNOLD M. AUERBACH [*It* refers to *This was One World now.*]

When used carelessly, however, broad reference can interfere with clear communication. To ensure clarity, inexperienced writers may be advised to make each of their pronouns refer to a specific word.

(1) Avoid reference to the general idea of a preceding clause or sentence unless the meaning is clear.

> VAGUE Although the story referred to James, Henry misapplied it to himself, which is true in real life.
> CLEAR Although the story referred to James, Henry misapplied it to himself. Such mistakes occur in real life.

(2) As a rule, do not refer to a word or an idea not expressed but merely implied.

VAGUE   Eileen said that she would stay in Miami for at least a month. This explains her happiness. [*This* does not refer to a single stated word or idea in the preceding sentence.]

CLEAR   Eileen said that she would stay in Miami for at least a month. This remark suggests that she is happy there.

VAGUE   He wanted his teachers to think he was above average, as he could have been if he had used it to advantage. [*It* has no expressed antecedent.]

CLEAR   He wanted his teachers to think he was above average, as he could have been if he had used his ability to advantage.

(3) Avoid awkward use of the indefinite *you* or *it*.

AWKWARD   When one cannot swim, you fear deep, stormy waters. [See also **27b**.]

BETTER   The person who cannot swim fears deep, stormy waters.

AWKWARD   In the book **it** says that many mushrooms are edible.

BETTER   The book says that many mushrooms are edible.

Note: In some contexts, the use of the impersonal, or indefinite, *you* is both natural and acceptable. Notice in the example below that *you* is equivalent in meaning to "people in general" or "the reader."

The study of dreams has become a significant and respectable scientific exploration, one that can directly benefit **you**.
——PATRICIA GARFIELD

Some writers, however, prefer not to use *you* in a formal context.

28d

Avoid the awkward placement of *it* near another *it* with a different meaning.

AWKWARD   Although it was very hot on the beach, it was a beautiful place. [The first *it* is the indefinite or unspecified *it*. The second *it* refers to beach.]

BETTER   Although it was very hot on the beach, the place was beautiful.

AWKWARD   It would be unwise to buy the new model now, but it is a beautiful machine. [The first *it* is an expletive. The second *it* refers to *model.*]

BETTER   Buying the new model now would be unwise, but it is a beautiful machine.

■ **Exercise 2**   Revise the following sentences as necessary to correct faults in reference. Put a checkmark after any sentence that needs no revision.

1. At the Chinese restaurant, the Meltons had a hard time eating with chopsticks, but that is their favorite food.
2. Apparently the dishwasher was out of order; it leaked all over the kitchen floor.
3. Copiers and other fine modern office machines enable business executives to accomplish more work because their assistants can manage them easily and quickly.
4. In the book it states that Mrs. Garrett can see through her fingertips.
5. Our language is rich in connectives that express fine distinctions of meaning.
6. I did not even buy a season ticket, which was very disloyal to my school.
7. Mary told Ann that she had to read *Shogun.*
8. When building roads the Romans tried to detour around valleys as much as possible for fear that flood waters might cover them and make them useless.
9. The extra fees surprised many freshmen that seemed unreasonably high.
10. In Frank's suitcase he packs only wash-and-wear clothes.

Emphasis

29

Select words and arrange the parts of the sentence to give emphasis to important ideas.

Since ideas vary in importance, expression of them should vary in emphasis. You may emphasize ideas through the use of exact diction (see Section **20**), through economy of language (see Section **21**), and through effective subordination and coordination (see Section **24**). You may also gain emphasis—

a   by placing important words at the beginning or at the end of the sentence;

b   by changing loose sentences into periodic sentences;

c   by arranging ideas in the order of climax;

d   by using the active voice instead of the passive voice;

e   by repeating important words;

f   by putting a word or phrase out of its usual order;

g   by using balanced sentence construction;

h   by abruptly changing sentence length.

29a

Gain emphasis by placing important words at the beginning or end of the sentence—especially at the end.

UNEMPHATIC   Total deafness is worse than total blindness, however, in many ways. [Parenthetical elements in an important position weaken the sentence.]

EMPHATIC   Total deafness, however, is in many ways worse than total blindness.

UNEMPHATIC   There was an underground blast that rocked the whole area. [Unemphatic words begin the sentence.]

EMPHATIC   An underground blast rocked the whole area.

The colon and the dash often precede an emphatic ending.

We have developed something new in politics: the professional amateur. ——MEG GREENFIELD

Most commercial television stations talk about helping their communities, but it is in the main just that—talk.
——JEFF GREENFIELD

Since the semicolon, sometimes called a weak period, is a strong punctuation mark when used between main clauses, words placed before and after a semicolon have an important position. See also **14a**.

A penny saved used to be a penny earned; now, after five years, it is only half a penny. ——ROBERT FRIEDMAN

Note: Introductory transitional expressions do not ordinarily weaken a sentence beginning.

Above all, the spirit of science is the spirit of progress.
——HERMANN J. MULLER

■ **Exercise 1**   Revise the following sentences to make them more emphatic. Change the word order when desirable, and delete unnecessary words and phrases.

1. Music has the power to hypnotize, so they say.
2. In fact, only one person could have written all these articles because of their same political slant, I am convinced.
3. There is one stunt woman who earns five thousand dollars for two hours of work.
4. Lewisville finally decided to enforce the old ordinance; there were nearby towns that revived similar laws and began clean-up campaigns, also.
5. It had never before entered her mind to resent her husband's complacent ignorance or to ignore his unreasonable demands, however.

29b

Gain emphasis by changing loose sentences into periodic sentences.

In a *loose* sentence, the main idea (grammatically a main clause or sentence base) comes first; less important ideas or details (a subordinate clause, parenthetical phrase, an appended element) follow. In a *periodic* sentence, however, the main idea comes last, just before the period.

> LOOSE Hair has always been a statement for men, variously representing strength (Samson), fashionable virtue (King Charles I of England, whose wigs were long-locked and elaborate), bravado (General Custer), and genius (Einstein). —OWEN EDWARDS [The main idea comes first.]

> PERIODIC When you die, when you get a divorce, when you buy a house, when you have an auto accident, not to mention the hundreds of times during your lifetime when you are fleeced in your role as a consumer, a lawyer either must or should be involved. —DAVID HAPGOOD [The main idea comes last.]

Both types of sentences can be effective. The loose sentence is, and should be, the more commonly used. Although the periodic sentence is often the more emphatic, you should take care in your writing not to overuse it to the point of making your style unnatural. Variety is desirable: see Section **30**.

LOOSE   Such sticky labels do not accurately describe any generation—for example, labels like *lost, beat, now, silent, unlucky,* or *found.*

PERIODIC Such sticky labels as *lost, beat, now, silent, unlucky,* or *found* do not accurately describe any generation.

LOOSE   In 1980 Alaska received more federal aid than any other state, if the report indicating the per capita distribution is correct.

PERIODIC If the report indicating the per capita distribution is correct, in 1980 Alaska received more federal aid than any other state.

■ **Exercise 2** Convert the loose sentences to periodic sentences, and the periodic to loose. Notice how your revisions make for varying emphasis.

1. Italy remains cheerful, despite everything.
   —AUBERON WAUGH

2. Even where people want better relations, old habits and reflexes persist.   —HEDRICK SMITH

3. The Milky Way Galaxy is entirely unremarkable, one of billions of other galaxies strewn through the vastness of space.   —CARL SAGAN

4. And then she was sweet and apologetic, as always, as she had been all her life, nervously backing away from the arguments she should have had with my father, turning aside from the talks she should have had with me.
   —JOYCE CAROL OATES

5. As Mays told me, almost with pride, "If I don't know anything about something, or if I don't understand it, I just oppose it."   —BERKELEY RICE

29c

Gain emphasis by arranging ideas in the order of climax.

Notice in the following examples that the ideas are arranged in the order of importance, with the strongest idea last:

> Urban life is unhealthy, morally corrupt, and fundamentally inhuman. —RENÉ DUBOS [adjectives in the series arranged in climactic order]

> They could hear the roar of artillery, the crash of falling timbers, the shrieks of the wounded. [sentence climax reached with *shrieks of the wounded*]

> In the language of screen comedians four of the main grades of laugh are the titter, the yowl, the belly laugh and the boffo. The titter is just a titter. The yowl is a runaway titter. Anyone who has ever had the pleasure knows all about a belly laugh. The boffo is the laugh that kills. —JAMES AGEE [First, words are placed in climactic order, then sentences.]

In a sentence like the following, the order of climax depends on the writer's judgment:

> Summing up for the defense of the small diesel, one can say that it offers excellent fuel consumption, it is long-lasting, it has no ignition system to cause trouble, and its level of pollution is low. —TONY HOGG

Note: Anticlimax—an unexpected shift from the dignified to the trivial or from the serious to the comic—is sometimes used for special effect.

> But I still fear it will all end badly, this Protective Syndrome. I see a future in which the government has stripped us of all worldly goods worth having: clothes hangers, toothpaste, Alka-Seltzer, toasters, pencil sharpeners, and maybe even thumb tacks. —S. L. VARNADO

■ **Exercise 3** Arrange the ideas in the sentences below in what you consider to be the order of climax.

1. Franklin used the ant as a symbol of industry, wisdom, and efficiency.
2. Among the images in the poem are sun-drenched orchards, diamond-eyed children, and golden-flecked birds.
3. He left the city because his health was failing, his taxes were going up, and his pet dog was tired of the leash.
4. Something must be done at once. Unless we act now, the city will be bankrupt in five years. The commission is faced with a deficit.
5. The would-be governor attended a community festival, autographed books for teenagers, promised prosperity to all, and wrote letters to senior citizens.

29d

Gain emphasis by using the active voice instead of the passive voice.

UNEMPHATIC   Little attention is being paid to cheap, nutritious foods by the average shopper.

EMPHATIC   The average shopper is paying little attention to cheap, nutritious foods.

Exception: If the receiver of the action is more important than the doer, the passive voice is more effective.

There in the tin factory, in the first moment of the atomic age, a human being was crushed by books.   —JOHN HERSEY

Freedom can be squashed by the tyrant or suffocated by the bureaucrat.   —WILLIAM F. RICKENBACKER

■ **Exercise 4**   Make each sentence below more emphatic by substituting the active for the passive voice.

1. Pennies are often thrown into the fountain by tourists.
2. Every Saturday morning, television is being watched by easily influenced children.
3. The wastebasket was being filled with illegible photocopies by a student about to run out of coins.
4. When the play was brought to an end, the actors were greeted with a loud burst of applause by the audience.
5. It is greatly feared by the citizens that adequate punishment will not be meted out by the judge.

29e

Gain emphasis by repeating important words.

It is impossible to be simultaneously blasted by a revolution in energy, a revolution in technology, a revolution in family life, a revolution in sexual roles, and a worldwide revolution in communications without also facing—sooner or later—a potentially explosive political revolution.   —ALVIN TOFFLER

COMPARE

It is impossible to be simultaneously blasted by a revolution in energy, in technology, in family life, in sexual roles, and in world communications without also facing—sooner or later—a potentially explosive political insurrection.

■ **Exercise 5**   First make each sentence below more emphatic by substituting repetition for the use of synonyms; then write two sentences of your own using repetition for emphasis.

1. Sometimes we lie to avoid hurting someone's feelings; occasionally we prevaricate to make another person like us.
2. He gripes all the time: he complains about the weather, fusses in heavy traffic, grumbles about high prices, and is critical of his meals.

29f

Gain emphasis by occasionally inverting the word order of a sentence. See also 30b.

> Only recently has this human deficiency been turned into law. —GERALD GRAFF [Compare "This human deficiency has only recently been turned into law."]
>
> Basic to all the Greek achievement was freedom.
> —EDITH HAMILTON [Compare "Freedom was basic to all the Greek achievement."]

Caution: This method of gaining emphasis, if overused, will make the style distinctly artificial. And of course the order of the parts of the sentence should never be such as to cause ambiguity: see **25a**.

29g

Gain emphasis by using balanced sentence construction.

A sentence is balanced when grammatically equal structures—usually main clauses with parallel elements—are used to express contrasted (or similar) ideas: see Section **26**. A balanced sentence emphasizes the contrast (or similarity) between parts of equal length and movement.

> To be French is to be like no one else; to be American is to be like everyone else. —PETER USTINOV
>
> Love is positive; tolerance negative. Love involves passion; tolerance is humdrum and dull. —E. M. FORSTER

■ **Exercise 6**   Write emphatic sentences using balanced construction to show the contrast between the following:

1. summer and winter   3. town and city
2. youth and age   4. hypocrisy and candor

29h

Gain emphasis by abruptly changing sentence length.

In the last two decades there has occurred a series of changes in American life, the extent, durability, and significance of which no one has yet measured. No one can. —IRVING HOWE
[The short sentence, which abruptly follows a much longer one, is emphatic.]

■ **Exercise 7** Write a short, emphatic sentence to follow each long sentence below. Then write another pair of sentences—one long and one short—of your own.

1. According to some minor prophets of doom, the next century will be a push-button era, a computer-controlled and robot-dominated one with life dependent on the movement of a forefinger.

2. In sequined costumes the skaters glide into the huge arena, smile at the applauding spectators, strike a brief pose, and then race into a series of intricate leaps and spins, their feet perfectly balanced on thin wedges of shining steel.

■ **Exercise 8** Prepare for a class discussion of emphasis in the following passages.

1. Opportunity for purposeful activity, opportunity for self-realization, opportunity for work and rest and love and play—this is what men think of as liberty today.
   —CLINTON ROSSITER

2. No one reads anymore—blame television. Families are breaking up—blame television. High culture is being despoiled—blame television. . . . What a splendid all-purpose explanation television has become. —ARISTIDES

3. With the exception of the Civil War period, never before had the sense of hopefulness traditionally associated with the American experience been so damaged. —JOHN LYTELL

■ **Exercise 9**   Revise the following sentences for greater emphasis.

1. I think that experimenting on fetuses should stop, whether they are dead or alive.
2. These retirees fear death, illness, poverty.
3. Fields of wild flowers were all around us.
4. Fools talk about each other; ideas fill the conversations of the wise.
5. At any rate, the gun fired when the fleeing youth tripped over the patrolman's foot.
6. The storm broke in all its fury at the close of a hot day.
7. A fast pass was caught by Milburn, and a thirty-yard gain was made by him before the whistle was blown by the referee.
8. I asked her to marry me, two years ago, in a shop on Tremont Street, late in the fall.
9. The art of the people was crude, but a great deal of originality was shown by some of them.
10. I can identify the guilty person in every Agatha Christie novel by the simple device of choosing the least likely suspect whose alibi is airtight.

Variety

30

Vary the structure and the length of your sentences to make your whole composition pleasing and effective.

Compare the two paragraphs below. Both use good sentences; both use virtually the same diction. It is varied structure and sentence length that make the difference.

NOT VARIED

Yellowstone National Park is traffic congestion to millions of people. It is also crowds and a few hours or days in July. A different kind of Yellowstone, however, begins to appear later. This happens by early September. The nights are growing colder then, and workmen are boarding up lodges and curio shops. [five sentences, four simple and one compound—each beginning with the subject and followed by the verb]

VARIED

To millions of people Yellowstone National Park is traffic congestion, crowds, a few hours or days in July. But by early September, when the nights are growing colder and workmen are boarding up lodges and curio shops, a different kind of Yellowstone begins to appear. —R. STEVEN FULLER [two sentences, one simple and one complex—neither beginning with the subject]

Inexperienced writers tend to rely too heavily—regardless of content or purpose—on a few comfortable, familiar structures. For that reason, Section **30** recommends sentence variety and cautions against monotonous repetition of any one type of sentence.

Note: If you have difficulty distinguishing various types of structures, review the fundamentals of the sentence treated in Section **1**, especially **1d**.

30a

As a rule, avoid a series of short simple sentences. Vary the length. See also **29h**.

Rather than present your ideas in a series of choppy, ineffective sentences, learn how to relate your ideas precisely in a longer sentence. See Section **24**.

CHOPPY   An urban songwriter celebrates the simple values. These are to be found only in small towns. This songwriter probably wouldn't live in one.

EFFECTIVE   The urban songwriter who celebrates the simple values to be found only in small towns probably wouldn't live in one. ——THOMAS GRIFFITH

CHOPPY   Wyoming is a state I cherish. It is one of the truly distinctive areas of the United States. Its university has a proud history.

EFFECTIVE   Wyoming is a state I cherish, one of the truly distinctive areas of the United States, and its university has a proud history. ——JAMES A. MICHENER

CHOPPY   Maybe the video revolution is not materially affecting the mass. It is at least presenting more options. The options are for those on the fringes.

EFFECTIVE   If the video revolution is not materially affecting the mass, it is at least presenting more options for those on the fringes. ——CHRIS WELLES

CHOPPY   Some people simply put coffee in an enamel saucepan. Next, they pour very hot water over it. Then they wait until flavor develops. Finally, they add eggshell or a small amount of cold water. The idea is to get the floating grounds to settle to the bottom.

EFFECTIVE   Some people simply put coffee in an enamel saucepan, pour very hot water over it, wait until flavor develops, and get the floating grounds to settle to the bottom by adding eggshell or a small amount of cold water.

Note: Occasionally, as the example below illustrates, a series of brief, subject-first sentences may be used for special effect:

He stumbled, recovered, picked up his pace. Now he was running. He broke out of the ring. People were throwing things at him. An egg hurtled past his head. A tomato hit someone nearby and splattered onto his suit.   —GERRY NADEL
[The short sentences suggest staccato action.]

■ **Exercise 1**   Study the structure of the sentences below, giving special attention to the variety of sentence lengths.

As she picked her way toward the garden chairs beside the front porch, she poured out a customary torrent of complaint. Her eyesight was failing. She found herself swatting raisins on the kitchen table, thinking they were flies, and bringing her stick down on spiders that turned out to be scurrying tufts of lint. Her hearing was going, and she suffered from head noises. She imagined she heard drums beating.

—PETER DE VRIES

■ **Exercise 2**   Convert each of the following series of short simple sentences to one long sentence in which ideas are carefully related.

1. There were thirty seconds of play left. Harrison intercepted the pass and raced downfield. He dropped the ball at the five-yard line.

2. Her speech had an interesting thesis. Salespersons should solve the existing problems of their customers. They should also point out new problems in order to solve them.

3. Bennett's Comet appeared in 1969. It disappeared again in 1970. It will not be visible again for thousands of years.

4. Ellen Dolan did not buy a second car. She bought a Piper. It is a cub plane. It flies at almost a hundred miles an hour.

5. J. Allen Boone is the author of *Kinship with All Life.* In his book Boone describes his ability to communicate with animals. He converses mentally with a dog. He orders ants to leave his home. They obey his orders. He even tames an ordinary housefly.

30b

Avoid a long series of sentences beginning with the subject. Vary the beginning.

Most writers begin about half their sentences with the subject—far more than the number of sentences begun in any other one way. But overuse of the subject-first beginning results in monotonous writing.

(1) Begin with an adverb or an adverb clause.

> **Suddenly** a hissing and clattering came from the heights around us.   —DOUGLAS LEE   [adverb]

> **Even though baseball is essentially the same**, the strategy of play then and now is different.   —JAMES T. FARRELL   [adverb clause]

(2) Begin with a prepositional phrase or a participial phrase.

> **For chain stores**, price information can be stored in a central computer serving an entire city.   —IRENE MALBIN   [prepositional phrase]

Disturbed by the discord of American life in recent decades, Manchester took flight for the Pacific Islands.
            —JAMES SLOAN ALLEN [participial phrase]

(3) Begin with a sentence connective—a coordinating conjunction, a conjunctive adverb, or a transitional expression.

Notice below how each sentence connective relates the ideas in each set of sentences. See also **31c(4)**.

It's slow. **But** it's democracy, and it works.
—DAVID S. BOYER [The coordinating conjunction *but* makes a contrast. Compare "slow but efficient."]

We cut him off. We denounce. **And**, whenever possible, we diagnose. —WALTER REICH [Compare the less emphatic "We cut him off, denounce, and diagnose."]

Engine speed also affected the heater's output. **Nonetheless**, the system did manage to keep us warm enough throughout a New England winter. —CONSUMER REPORTS [conjunctive adverb]

The nuclei of atoms become radioactive when they absorb neutrons. **That is**, they decay by giving off some kind of radiation. —ROBERT HOFSTADTER [transitional expression]

(4) Begin with an appositive or with an absolute.

A city of ancient origins, Varna lies on the Black Sea coast. —COLIN RENFREW [appositive referring to the subject]

True, we have occasional debates, but they do not tell us much. —TERRY SANFORD [single-word absolute]

His eyebrows raised high in resignation, he began to examine his hand. —LIONEL TRILLING [absolute phrase]

Note: An occasional declarative sentence with inverted word order can contribute to sentence variety. See also **29f**.

At the feet of the tallest and plushiest offices lie the crummiest slums. —E. B. WHITE [Compare "The crummiest slums lie at the feet of the tallest and plushiest offices."]

■ **Exercise 3**   Prepare for a class discussion of the types of sentence beginnings in the following paragraph.

¹ No longer do we Americans want to destroy wantonly, but our new-found sources of power—to take the burden of work from our shoulders, to warm us, and cool us, and give us light, to transport us quickly, and to make the things we use and wear and eat—these power sources spew pollution in our country, so that the rivers and streams are becoming poisonous and lifeless.   ² The birds die for lack of food; a noxious cloud hangs over our cities that burns our lungs and reddens our eyes.   ³ Our ability to conserve has not grown with our power to create, but this slow and sullen poisoning is no longer ignored or justified. ⁴Almost daily, the pressure of outrage among Americans grows.   ⁵ We are no longer content to destroy our beloved country.   ⁶ We are slow to learn; but we learn.   ⁷ When a superhighway was proposed in California which would trample the redwood trees in its path, an outcry arose all over the land, so strident and fierce that the plan was put aside.   ⁸ And we no longer believe that a man, by owning a piece of America, is free to outrage it.

—JOHN STEINBECK, *America and Americans*

■ **Exercise 4**   Each of the sentences below begins with the subject. Recast each sentence twice to vary the beginning.

EXAMPLE
Two businessmen dropped by the dean's office and requested reasons for the inefficiency of the school's graduates.
a. *Dropping by the dean's office, two businessmen requested reasons for the inefficiency of the school's graduates.*
b. *In the dean's office, two businessmen requested reasons for the inefficiency of the school's graduates.*

1. We still need a better understanding between the members of our sororities and fraternities.
2. Reporters interviewed the newly appointed ambassador and asked him some tricky questions about world affairs.
3. Hundreds of students will line up in order to register in a floating university, the *Queen Victoria.*
4. Jesse enjoyed the course in science-fiction literature most of all.
5. The green fireballs traveled at great speed and fascinated sky watchers throughout the Southwest.

30c

Avoid loose, stringy compound sentences. See also 24b.

To revise an ineffective compound sentence, try one of the following methods.

(1) Convert a compound sentence into a complex sentence.

COMPOUND	The Mississippi River is one of the longest rivers in the world, and in the springtime it often overflows its banks, and the lives of many people are endangered.
COMPLEX	The Mississippi River, which is one of the longest rivers in the world, often overflows its banks in the springtime, endangering the lives of many people.

(2) Use a compound predicate in a simple sentence.

COMPOUND	He put on his coat, and next he picked up his hat and umbrella, and then he hurried from the house.
SIMPLE	He put on his coat, picked up his hat and umbrella, and hurried from the house.

(3) Use a modifier or an appositive in a simple sentence.

COMPOUND   The town was north of the Red River, and a tornado struck it, and it was practically demolished.

SIMPLE   The town, located north of the Red River, was struck by a tornado and practically demolished.

COMPOUND   She was the mayor of the town, and she was an amiable person, and she invited the four students into her office.

SIMPLE   The mayor of the town, an amiable person, invited the four students into her office.

(4) Use phrases in a simple sentence.

COMPOUND   The streets were icy, and we could not drive the car.

SIMPLE   Because of the icy streets, we could not drive the car.

COMPOUND   He arrived in Fresno at 1:30 A.M., and then he made the toll-free call.

SIMPLE   After arriving in Fresno at 1:30 A.M., he made the toll-free call.

■ **Exercise 5** Using the methods illustrated in **30c**, revise the loose, stringy compound sentences below.

1. The small car hugs the road, and it is easy to drive in traffic, but it is not comfortable.
2. The Johnsons grew tired of city smog and noise pollution, so they moved to the country, but there they had no fire department or police protection.
3. Americans at first traded their products, and then they began to use money and bank checks, and now they use the all-inclusive plastic credit card.
4. Harvey kept criticizing middle-class values, and he mentioned such things as marriage and two-car garages, but he did not define upper-class or lower-class values.

30d

Vary the conventional subject–verb sequence by occasionally separating subject and verb with words or phrases.

SUBJECT–VERB **The auditorium is** across from the park, and **it is** a gift of the alumni. [compound sentence]

VARIED **The auditorium**, across from the park, **is** a gift of the alumni. [simple sentence]

SUBJECT–VERB **The crowd sympathized** with the visitors and **applauded** every good play.

VARIED **The crowd**, sympathizing with the visitors, **applauded** every good play.

SUBJECT–VERB **Her ability to listen is** an acquired skill that attracts many friends.

VARIED **Her ability to listen**, an acquired skill, **attracts** many friends.

■ **Exercise 6** Using the methods illustrated in **30d**, vary the conventional subject-verb sequence.

1. Roger is like his mother, and he is an excellent conversationalist.
2. Rhode Island is east of Connecticut, and it has a forty-mile coastline.
3. My grandparents valued strong family ties and encouraged us young ones "to always keep in touch."
4. Margaret was racing back to the dormitory to avoid getting wet, and she fell broadside into a big puddle of water.
5. Wizzard Wells was a popular resort once, but it is a ghost town now.

30e

Occasionally, instead of the usual declarative sentence, use a question, an exclamation, or a command.

343

How can anybody assert that "growth" is a good thing? If my children grow, it is a very good thing; if I should suddenly start growing, it would be a disaster. —E. F. SCHUMACHER [Here a rhetorical question is followed by the usual declarative statement.]

Their eyes appear covered. One shudders for them. At the same time, what courage! —ALEXANDER ELIOT [The exclamation concludes a discussion of a Japanese print, Hakuin Ekaku's *Two Blind Men Crossing a Log Bridge.*]

All sentences in the following paragraph are declarative except for the third one, an imperative.

For our hypothetical family, the estimated annual saving with solar would be roughly $69 at today's prices. That's not a very dramatic yield. Note, however, that our calculations do not take into account any increases in the cost of conventional energy. Obviously, a change in the price of conventional energy would make a substantial difference in the saving. —CONSUMER REPORTS

■ **Exercise 7** Prepare for a class discussion of sentence variety in the following paragraph.

[1] Some people collect stamps or coins or antique cars. [2] I collect practically useless scraps of information without really wanting to. [3] Things that most people don't bother to remember accumulate in my mind like unused wire hangers in a coat closet. [4] For instance, hardly anybody except me remembers the names of the four models of the Edsel (Pacer, Ranger, Corsair and Citation), or the name of the only New York newspaper that supported Harry Truman in 1948 (the now-defunct New York *Star*). [5] Do you know there's enough concrete in Boulder Dam to build a six-lane highway from Seattle to Miami? [6] I do. [7] I also know the origin of the word *hitchhike* (two people traveling with one horse), and that the Japanese word for first lieutenant (*chūi*) is the same as the Swahili word for leopard. [8] Just don't ask me why. —WILLIAM ATTWOOD, "The Birth of the Bikini"

LARGER ELEMENTS

The Paragraph

31

Write paragraphs that are coherent, adequately developed, and unified.

The paragraph is the essential unit of thought in writing. Although it may consist of a single sentence, it is usually a group of sentences that develop one main point or controlling idea. The form of a paragraph is distinctive: the first line is indented, about one inch in handwriting and five spaces in typewritten copy.

Certain conventions or rules govern the construction of a paragraph. The reader expects a paragraph to be *coherent* (with its organization following a definite plan), *developed* (with its sentences adequately explaining or qualifying the main point), and *unified* (with all its sentences relevant to the main point). In general, most paragraphs are between 100 and 250 words long and usually consist of five to ten sentences.

Paragraph 1 observes the three conventions of coherence, development, and unity. Each of its sentences supports the controlling idea of the paragraph (called the *topic sentence*)—the fact that people have certain "curious experiences" when they fall asleep.

1   A number of curious experiences occur at the onset of sleep. A person just about to go to sleep may experience an electric shock, a flash of light, or a crash of thunder—but the most common sensation is that of floating or falling, which is why "falling alseep" is a scientifically valid description. A nearly universal occurrence at the beginning of sleep (although not everyone recalls it) is a sudden, uncoordinated jerk of the head, the limbs, or even the entire body. Most people tend to think of going to sleep as a slow slippage into oblivion, but the onset of sleep is not gradual at all. It happens in an instant. One moment the individual is awake, the next moment not.   —PETER FARB, *Humankind*

31a

Construct coherent paragraphs.

To construct a coherent paragraph you must have a controlling idea, usually expressed in the form of a question or statement, and a plan or pattern for organizing the supporting material.

(1) Construct a clear topic sentence and restrict it carefully.

The paragraph consists of a topic sentence (the controlling idea) and sentences that elaborate or qualify the topic sentence, much as modifiers do in a sentence. The first step in constructing a coherent paragraph is to formulate a clear, restricted topic sentence that tells the reader what the paragraph will be about.

One method of constructing a topic sentence is to put the controlling idea into the form of a question. If you wanted to write about draft registration, for example, you might ask a question like the following, which could be the topic sentence of your paragraph: Should draft registration be universal?

A second method of constructing a topic sentence is to think of your controlling idea as if it were a problem and to state the problem as clearly as possible. For example, if you wanted to write about the physics of light, you might state the idea in a topic sentence like the following:

> A problem in discussing the physics of light is that two different theories account for certain aspects of light but neither theory accounts for all the aspects of light.

A third method of constructing a topic sentence is to start with a general statement and then to restate it in a more particular way in a second sentence. These two sentences may then be combined into an introductory clause (general) and a main clause (more particular). If you wanted to write about communication, for example, you might arrive at a topic sentence as follows:

1. Many members of the animal kingdom communicate. [general statement]
   But humans communicate in the most sophisticated way. [particular statement]
2. While many members of the animal kingdom communicate, humans communicate in the most sophisticated way.   [topic sentence]

This method of presenting a topic sentence has the advantage of orienting the reader in a general way and then directing the reader to the particular aspect of the general statement the writer intends to discuss.

Because paragraphs are short, the more precise or restricted the topic sentence, the better. The more general the topic sentence, the more difficulty you will have in constructing a coherent paragraph. Thus the question "What is love?" is not as good a topic sentence as "What is love among teenagers?" Although almost any statement or question can be made into a topic sentence, to be an effective topic sentence it must be precise enough to control every sentence in the paragraph.

In paragraph 2 the topic sentence begins with reasons why the author would like to know more about the yeti (the Abominable Snowman), but it concludes with the statement that the author would be saddened if the yeti were to be discovered. This topic sentence, in turn, controls all the remaining sentences. They explain why the author would be sad.

2   Even though I am intrigued with the yeti, both for its scientific importance and for what it says about our own interests and biases, I would be deeply saddened to have it discovered. If it were to be found and captured, studied and confined, we might well slay our nightmares. But the mystery and imagination it evokes would also be slain. If the yeti is an old form that we have driven into the mountains, now we would be driving it into the zoos. We would gain another possession, another ragged exhibit in the concrete world or the zoological park, another Latin name to enter on our scientific ledgers. But what about the wild creature that now roams free of man in the forests of the Himalayas? Every time man asserts his mastery over nature, he gains something in knowledge, but loses something in spirit.
                                              —EDWARD W. CRONIN, "The Yeti"

■ **Exercise 1**   Construct carefully restricted topic sentences from the following list of ideas. The more specific your topic sentences, the better.

1. Campus parking
2. Censoring television programs
3. The price of college textbooks
4. Competition for graduate school admissions
5. Reduced federal spending for student aid
6. Technical education

(2) Place the topic sentence where the reader can find it.

The topic sentence is usually the first or second sentence in the paragraph. Stated immediately, it thus provides the reader with the key idea that shapes the paragraph. At times, when the controlling idea is stated early in the paragraph, it may also be restated at the end, to point up its importance. In paragraph 3 compare "the intolerable has become normal" with the final "Ugliness is accepted, no longer even noticed."

3   In the towns and cities of Ulster, the intolerable has become normal. The civic environment is scarred. In Belfast and Derry, it is hard to find a shop with windows; shopkeepers have had so many broken that they are content to leave the boards up. Burned-out houses and shops are left as abandoned hulks. The army has run out its barbed wire, concrete and corrugated iron in dozens of checkpoints, barricades and gun emplacements. Ugliness is accepted, no longer even noticed.

—PAUL HARRISON, "The Dark Age of Ulster"

Occasionally, as in paragraph 4, the topic sentence is the last sentence, especially when the writer progresses from particulars or from a specific example to a generalization.

4   Imagine waking up and glancing at your clock, which reads 8:55 a.m. This information means nothing, until you apply your perception to it. If it's a weekday, you're due at work at 9 a.m., and being punctual is important, 8:55 becomes a negative stressor. If it's Saturday, your perception of 8:55 may result in a feeling of luxurious anticipation of a lazy day. The information in both cases was the same. Your perception of it determined your response.

—JENNIFER BOLCH, "How to Manage Stress"

Note: In many paragraphs the controlling idea is not expressly stated in a topic sentence, but in a unified paragraph it is implied distinctly. The implied idea of paragraph 5 ("These are steps in the embalming process") can be clearly understood in the context of Jessica Mitford's description. (The quotations are from an embalming textbook.)

5   About three to six gallons of a dyed and perfumed solution of formaldehyde, glycerin, borax, phenol, alcohol and water is soon circulating through Mr. Jones, whose mouth has been sewn together with a "needle directed upward between the upper lip and gum and brought out through the left nostril," with the corners raised slightly "for a more pleasant expression." If he should be bucktoothed, his teeth are cleaned with Bon Ami and coated with colorless nail polish. His eyes, meanwhile, are closed with flesh-tinted eye caps and eye cement.

—JESSICA MITFORD, *The American Way of Death*

■ **Exercise 2**   Identify the topic sentences in paragraphs 6–8. If the topic sentence is implied, construct one.

6   Certainly the [U.S.] political problems, difficult and delicate though they may be, are not insoluble. Some, like the control or the liquidation of monopolies which stand in the way of individual initiative, have a long history in this country. Others, like the struggle to liberate individuals from the degrading fear of unemployment or old age or sickness, are less familiar—at least in the United States. Still others, like the overriding question of the relation between individual freedom and the intervention of the state, have a meaning for our generation which they did not have for generations before. But only a man who did not wish to find an answer to questions such as these would argue that no answer can be found.

—ARCHIBALD MacLEISH, "The Conquest of America"

7   When we watch a person walk away from us, his image shrinks in size. But since we know for a fact that he is not shrinking, we make an unconscious correcting and "see" him as retaining his full stature. Past experience tells us what his true stature is with respect to our own. Any sane and dependable expectation of the future requires that he have the same true stature when we next encounter him. Our perception is thus a prediction; it embraces the past and the future as well as the present.

—WARREN J. WITTREICH, "Visual Perception & Personality"

8   A TV set stood close to a wall in the small living room crowded with an assortment of chairs and tables. An aquarium crowded the mantelpiece of a fake fireplace. A lighted bulb inside the tank showed many colored fish swimming about in a haze of fish food. Some of it lay scattered on the edge of the shelf. The carpet underneath was sodden black. Old magazines and tabloids lay just about everywhere.
—BIENVENIDO SANTOS, "Immigration Blues"

(3) Organize paragraphs according to a definite pattern.

Most paragraphs are organized according to one of these three patterns: question-answer; problem-solution; topic-restriction-illustration.

a. Question-answer pattern

In this pattern the topic sentence asks a question and the supporting sentences answer it, as in paragraph 9.

9   Why did the Civil Rights movement arise? There are several possible reasons. Although the Supreme Court had ruled in 1954 that segregated schools were inherently unequal, the United States made little progress toward integration in the next few years. Therefore, American blacks began to believe that their equality could come only through their own actions. Another reason may be that the late 1950's and 1960's provided the right climate for direct social action. Finally, it is possible that the social and economic condition of the blacks had become sufficiently good by the late fifties to enable them to act on their own.
—STUDENT

b. Problem-solution pattern

In this pattern the topic sentence states a problem, and the supporting sentences offer a solution, as in paragraph 10.

10   The trouble with the clans and tribes many of us were
born into is not that they consist of meddlesome ogres but
that they are too far away. [*problem*] In emergencies we
rush across continents and if need be oceans to their sides,
as they do to ours. Maybe we even make a habit of seeing
them, once or twice a year, for the sheer pleasure of it. But
blood ties seldom dictate our addresses. Our blood kin are
often too remote to ease us from our Tuesdays to our Wed-
nesdays. [*restatement of the problem*] For this we must rely
on our families of friends. If our relatives are not, do not
wish to be, or for whatever reasons cannot be our friends,
then by some complex alchemy we must try to transform
our friends into our relatives. If blood and roots don't do the
job, then we must look to water and branches, and sort
ourselves into new constellations, new families.

——JANE HOWARD, "All Happy Clans Are Alike"

c. Topic-restriction-illustration pattern

In this pattern, the writer announces the topic, then restricts
or qualifies it in the same sentence or in the next sentence.
Then the writer illustrates the restriction in the remaining
sentences of the paragraph. In paragraph 11 the general
topic "the fascination of lost worlds" begins the paragraph.
The next sentence restates the general topic. The third sentence restricts the topic to "the scholar," and two illustrations
are given, Jefferson and the unnamed South American traveler.

11   The fascination of lost worlds has long preoccupied
humanity. It is inevitable that transitory man, student of the
galaxies and computer of light-years, should entertain nostalgic yearnings for some island outside of time, some Ava-
lon untouched by human loss. Even the scholar has not been
averse to searching for the living past on islands or preci-
pice-guarded plateaus. Jefferson repeated the story of a
trapper who had heard of the mammoth roaring in the Vir-

ginia woods; in 1823 a South American traveler imaginatively viewed through his spyglass mastodons grazing in remote Andean valleys.

—LOREN EISELEY, *The Immense Journey*

These patterns can be varied to suit your intention. The question-answer pattern, for example, can be rearranged as answer-question. Topic-restriction-illustration can be varied in a number of ways. The topic may be such that restriction is unnecessary and can be omitted. Or illustration can be first in the paragraph with the topic saved for last.

■ **Exercise 3** In paragraphs 12–15, identify the pattern of each paragraph as question-answer, problem-solution, or topic-restriction-illustration. Remember that the patterns can be rearranged.

12   What's wrong with the student-union bookshop? Everything. It's interested in selling sweatshirts and college mugs rather than good books. Its staff often is incompetent and uncivil. The manager may not be intelligent enough even to order a sufficient number of copies of required textbooks for the beginning of a term. As for more lively books—why, there are masses of paperbacks, perhaps, that could be procured at any drugstore; there are a few shelves or racks of volumes labeled "Gift Books," usually lavishly illustrated and inordinately costly, intended as presents to fond parents; but there are virtually no *book* books, of the sort that students might like to buy.

—RUSSELL KIRK, "From the Academy: Campus Bookshops"

13   What a day that 11th of November [1918] was! It was not quite three o'clock in the morning when the State Department gave out to the dozing newspaper men the news that the Armistice had really been signed. Four days before, a false report of the end of hostilities had thrown the whole United States into a delirium of joy. People had poured out of offices and shops and paraded the streets singing and shouting, ringing bells, blowing tin horns, smashing one another's hats, cheering soldiers in uniform, draping themselves in American flags, gathering in closely packed crowds before the newspaper bulletin boards, making a wild and hilarious holiday; in New York, Fifth Avenue had been closed to traffic and packed solid with surging men and women, while down from the windows of the city fluttered 155 tons of ticker tape and torn paper. It did not seem possible that such an outburst could be repeated. But it was. ——FREDERICK LEWIS ALLEN, *Only Yesterday*

14 I started this diary as a personal document after coming into teaching from a Wall Street brokerage firm. I felt that I wanted to become a part of a larger human experience and in some small way to make a contribution to that experience. I was soon to discover that under the then present and still going strong bureaucracy, doing that was almost impossible unless one was willing to become a part of that bureaucracy. I chose not to and in short order found myself, along with a few other young teachers, alienated, our hands tied, unable to offer suggestions or bring about change. After grappling with the decision to remain or get out I decided to record this diary, hoping it would help calm my frustrations.

——JIM HASKINS, *Diary of a Harlem Schoolteacher*

15 Our most important environmental problem, certainly the most urgent, is the burning of fossil fuels, which has significantly increased the carbon dioxide in the atmosphere. It is important to get rid of it because as the CO_2 concentration goes up, it acts as a sort of greenhouse. If we increase the CO_2 in the atmosphere at the rate it's been going, atmospheric warming has been predicted to be as much as a degree and a half or so over the next ten to fifteen years. This will have major consequences for the climate, and could start to melt the icecaps.

——DEREK SPENCER, "Is the World Getting Warmer?"

31b
Construct well-developed paragraphs.

Once you have decided on a pattern for your paragraph (question-answer, problem-solution, topic-restriction-illustration), you must then consider how to develop the answer, the solution, or the illustrations. The method of paragraph development that you choose depends upon your purpose. Do you want to tell a story? Use a chronological order. Do you want to say how something is done? Explain a step-by-step process.

(1) Narration

Narrative paragraphs present a series of events that begin at a particular time and are organized chronologically. Narrative writing longer than a paragraph often uses a flashback (a jump back in time), but in a paragraph the reader expects that the material will be arranged in time order.

In paragraph 16, Charles Schulz's narrative begins with second grade and proceeds chronologically through high school. Often the topic sentence in a narrative paragraph is a kind of frame that pulls the various series of incidents of the paragraph together. Schulz begins his paragraph with a topic sentence that serves as such a frame. The paragraph follows the pattern of topic-restriction-illustration.

16   My scholastic career got off to a good start when I was very young. I received a special diploma in the second grade for being the outstanding boy student, and in the third and fifth grades I was moved ahead so suddenly that I was the smallest kid in the class. Somehow, I survived the early years of grade school, but when I entered junior high school, I failed everything in sight. High school proved not much better. There was no doubt that I was absolutely the worst physics student in the history of St. Paul Central High School. It was not until I became a senior that I earned any respectable grades at all. I have often felt that some semblance of maturity began to arrive at last. I saved that final report card because it was the only one that seemed to justify those long years of agony.

——CHARLES M. SCHULZ, *Peanuts Jubilee*

(2) Process

Process paragraphs explain how something is done or made. For this reason, they often have a temporal element that makes a step-by-step chronological arrangement both possible and natural, as in paragraph 17.

17   The best of all scientific tricks with an egg is the well-known one in which air pressure forces a peeled hard-boiled egg into a glass milk bottle and then forces it out again undamaged. The mouth of the bottle must be only slightly smaller than the egg, and so you must be careful not to use too large an egg or too small a bottle. It is impossible to push the egg into the bottle. To get the egg through the mouth you must heat the air in the bottle. That is best done by standing the bottle in boiling water for a few minutes. Put the egg upright on the mouth and take the bottle off the stove. As the air in the bottle cools it contracts, creating a partial vacuum that draws the peeled egg inside. To get the egg out again invert the bottle so that the egg falls into the neck. Place the opening of the bottle against your mouth and blow vigorously. This will compress the air in the bottle. When you stop blowing, the air expands, pushing the egg through the neck of the bottle and into your waiting hands.   ——MARTIN GARDNER, "Mathematical Games"

(3) Description

Description requires a sequential arrangement of details that move in a consistent way: from near to far, from general to particular, from right to left, from top to bottom, and so forth. As the description moves in one of these ways, it provides a framework for individual details. Thus, the reader has an orderly scheme to use as he or she visualizes what you are describing.

In paragraph 18, using a near-to-far movement, Thomas Merton describes the monastery that was to become his home.

18   I looked at the rolling country, and at the pale ribbon of road in front of us, stretching out as grey as lead in the light of the moon. Then suddenly I saw a steeple that shone like silver in the moonlight, growing into sight from behind a rounded knoll. The tires sang on the empty road, and, breathless, I looked at the monastery that was revealed before me as we came over the rise. At the end of an avenue of trees was a big rectangular block of buildings, all dark, with a church crowned by a tower and a steeple and a cross: and the steeple was as bright as platinum and the whole place was as quiet as midnight and lost in the all-absorbing silence and solitude of the fields. Behind the monastery was a dark curtain of woods, and over to the west was a wooded valley, and beyond that a rampart of wooded hills, a barrier and a defense against the world.

—THOMAS MERTON, *The Seven Storey Mountain*

(4) Classification

Classification paragraphs divide a group or class of things into parts that will explain the group or class for the reader. In paragraph 19, the class is "book owners." Adler divides book owners into three types, not according to how many books they own, but according to how thoroughly they read their books.

19   There are three kinds of book owners. The first has all the standard sets and best-sellers—unread, untouched. (This deluded individual owns woodpulp and ink, not books.) The second has a great many books—a few of them read through, most of them dipped into, but all of them as clean and shiny as the day they were bought. (This person would probably like to make books his own, but is restrained by

a false respect for their physical appearance.) The third has a few books or many—every one of them dog-eared and dilapidated, shaken and loosened by continual use, marked and scribbled in from front to back. (This man owns books.)
—MORTIMER J. ADLER, "How To Mark A Book"

Once you have decided on the parts of the class you are dividing, you must decide what order you want to describe them in and maintain that order throughout. Depending on the purpose of the classification, the system of ordering might be from first to last, from largest to smallest, or from least important to most important.

(5) Analysis

Analysis is similar to classification in that the subject of the analysis is divided into parts. However, the purpose of the analysis is to suggest that the parts are related as causes or effects of the thing analyzed. In paragraph 20 the authors analyze the causes of a volcanic eruption.

20   Volcanic eruptions are the final stage of a process that begins with the melting of rock in a planet's interior, the "source region." The most usual source of the heat that leads to melting is energy released by the decay of radioactive elements. The material in the source region is generally only partially molten, being made up of magma, or liquid rock, and unmelted crystals. The lighter liquid gradually rises above the denser crystals through the action of gravity and collects in magma chambers. The segregation process that drives the liquid upward can take anywhere from hundreds of years to hundreds of millions, depending primarily on the force of gravity, which varies with depth and the planet's size, on the nature of the crystals in the source region, on the amount of liquid produced by the heat available and on the viscosity of the liquid.
—HARRY Y. McSWEEN, JR., and EDWARD M. STOLPER,
"Basaltic Meteorites"

(6) Definition   See also **23d.**

Paragraphs of definition attempt to explain who a person is
or what a place or thing is. Definitions can be formal or
informal depending on your purpose. A *formal* definition is
used in academic writing to explain as precisely as possible
what a thing is by putting it in its class (in biology, its *genus*)
and then by distinguishing it from other members of that
genus. Paragraph 21 illustrates formal definition.

21   The purple martin (*Progne subis*) is locally common
where proper multicelled nesting boxes or gourds are provided. No other North American swallow is dark all over.
Females, young, and first-year males are light-bellied and
could be confused with smaller swallows. Watch for purple
iridescence on head and top of wings. Note the broad wings
and more soaring flight of martins. In late summer flocks of
thousands roost together in shade trees of some cities. Song
and calls are a distinctive, low-pitched, liquid, rolling
twitter.   —*A Guide to Field Identification: Birds of North America*

Paragraph 22 illustrates an *informal* definition, which is
designed to explain a term or idea for the general reader,
often by providing examples or synonyms.

22   Biofeedback, Dr. Green said, means getting immediate,
ongoing information about one's own biological processes or
conditions—such as heart behavior, temperature, brain-
wave activity, blood pressure or muscle tension—and using
the information to change and control voluntarily the specific process or response being monitored.
—THOMAS W. PEW JR.,
"Biofeedback seeks new medical uses for concept of yoga"

A less common type of definition, but one that you may
need to use from time to time, is a form of *historical* definition. In this type of definition you explain the meaning of a
thing at a particular time in history. Paragraph 23 defines
English in a historical setting.

23   English, in its original form, is Anglo-Saxon, a Low German dialect of the western sub-branch of the Germanic branch of Indo-European. Perhaps 25 per cent of our words (at least 50 per cent, however, of our words of most frequent occurrence) go back to Anglo-Saxon or to Middle English (when the dictionary describes a word as being of Middle English origin, it means that it cannot be traced all the way back to Anglo-Saxon, but also that there is no evidence that it was borrowed from any other source; this means that it is more likely to be of native, or Anglo-Saxon, origin than of any other). ——MARIO PEI, *The Families of Words*

(7) Comparison/Contrast

A comparison points out the similarities of two things; a contrast points out the differences. The important thing to remember is to compare or contrast the thing with something else the reader knows better. For example, to tell the reader how large England is, you might say that it is about the size of Virginia. You can then contrast the two in terms of climate, population density, and so forth. Paragraph 24 is an example of contrast—the differences between two kinds of terror.

24   Most of us enjoy the gooseflesh and the tingle along the spine produced by the successful ghost story. There is something agreeable in letting our blood be chilled by bats in the moonlight, guttering candles, creaking doors, eerie shadows, piercing screams, inexplicable bloodstains, and weird noises. But the terror aroused by tricks and external "machinery" is a far cry from the terror evoked by some terrifying treatment of the human situation. The horror we experience in watching the Werewolf or Dracula or Frankenstein is far less significant than that we get from watching the bloody ambition of Macbeth or the jealousy of Othello. In the first, terror is the end-product; in the second, it is the natural accompaniment of a powerful revelation of life. In the first, we are always aware of a basic unreality; in the second, reality is terrifying. ——LAURENCE PERRINE, *Literature: Structure, Sound, and Sense,* 3rd edition

The comparison in paragraph 25 is between language and games.

25   The language game shares certain characteristics with all other true games. First of all, it has a minimum of two players (the private, incomprehensible speech of a schizophrenic is no more a true game than is solitaire). Second, a person within speaking distance of any stranger can be forced by social pressure to commit himself to play, in the same way that a bystander in the vicinity of any other kind of game may be asked to play or to look on. Third, something must be at stake and both players must strive to win it—whether the reward be a tangible gain like convincing an employer of the need for a raise or an intangible one like the satisfaction of besting someone in an argument. Fourth, a player of any game has a particular style that distinguishes him as well as the ability to shift styles depending upon where the game is played and who the other players are. In the case of the language game, the style might be a preference for certain expressions or a folksy way of speaking, and the style shift might be the bringing into play of different verbal strategies when speaking in the home, at the office, on the street, or in a place of worship.

—PETER FARB, *Word Play*

(8) Example

A paragraph developed by example is very common. In this type of paragraph you make a statement and then supply one or more examples to illustrate it. Paragraph 26 illustrates this technique.

26   In the past decade, however, "facts" have blossomed into a fad. The sales of *Guinness Book of World Records* rival those of the Bible. The popularity of *The People's Almanac, Fascinating Facts, Isaac Asimov's Book of Facts, Easy Answers to Hard Questions, Dictionary of Misinformation, Encyclopedia of Ignorance,* as well as of television shows such as *Real People,* testifies to the public's growing appetite for mental snacks.   —CARLL TUCKER, "In the Matter of Facts"

■ **Exercise 4**   Identify the pattern and the method of development in paragraphs 27–29.

27   Without doubt the most famous of all megalithic monuments is Stonehenge, on the Wiltshire plain of southern Britain. Visited by thousands yearly, it is second only to the Tower of London as a tourist attraction. It has a larger literature than any other archaeological site in the world, including the pyramids of Egypt and the great statues of Easter Island, as well as mythical sites such as Atlantis. The number of books on Stonehenge and on other megalithic monuments that have poured from the presses in the past decade or so is a measure of the continued interest in these antiquities.   —GLYN DANIEL, "Megalithic Monuments"

28   Watching a millipede crawl slowly, softly over decaying humus is like watching a symphony in movement. Children marvel that this thousand-legged worm can coordinate so many legs without getting them all tangled up. Of course, millipedes do not have a thousand legs, nor are they worms. Careful observation reveals that each body block, or segment, has two pairs of legs, in contrast with the one pair per body block in centipedes. Though they have more legs than centipedes, they move much more slowly, feeding mainly on decaying plant tissues.
      —CECIL E. JOHNSON, "The Wild World of Compost"

29   The electronic revolution in data processing, which dominated the '70s, is anything but over. A decade ago, for instance, sixteen "bits," or pieces of information, could be packed on one chip of silicon inside a computer. Within five years, the capacity of a single chip will be 256,000 bits and rising, with no increase in price. This means that ever-smaller computers can deal with ever-larger amounts of data. Portable minicomputers may well become almost as commonplace in ten years as handheld calculators are now.   —NEWSWEEK

31c

Construct unified paragraphs.

(1) Make each sentence contribute to the main idea.

A paragraph has unity when every sentence is relevant to the main or controlling idea. Any sentence that violates this unity should be deleted. Paragraph 30 is unified because every sentence contributes to the main idea—the high profits of the popular-music industry.

30   Popular music in America now outgrosses the combined revenue of movies, theater, opera, ballet, and sport. The recording industry produces 1,000 new songs each week, the sole purpose being for a few to become hits and make money. It is a staggeringly competitive business, for the profits are staggeringly high: in 1979, sales of LP and single records totaled $2.5 billion. With sales of taped cartridges of record albums added to this figure, total revenues approach $3.25 billion.   —ROBERT RICHMAN, "Trash Theory"

To check the unity of your paragraph, you may find it helpful to write down its plan, so that any irrelevant sentences will be apparent. The preceding paragraph reveals this plan:

Topic:
   Popular music outgrosses other entertainments.

Illustration:
   number of songs produced, size of record sales

Caution: Do not make rambling statements that are only vaguely related to your topic. As you write a paragraph, hold to the main idea. For example, if the controlling idea of your paragraph is "My roommate Bill Jones cannot keep a secret," irrelevant sentences about Bill's sense of humor or about secrecy in general will disrupt the unity. Every sentence should pertain to Bill's inability to keep a secret.

■ **Exercise 5**   Revise the following student paragraph to improve unity. Be prepared to give reasons for your revisions.

31   The expression "environmental problems" encompasses a wide range. Since the beginning of time, human beings have struggled against elements in their environment. They have always attempted to protect themselves against such natural disasters as fire and flood. As time went on, and the human population grew, abuse of land, overcrowding of cities, famine, and the extinction of various animal species became environmental problems. Human beings progressed, gaining more control over their environment and creating more problems in it. They were less dependent on environmental conditions for their lives: if it was dark, they could snap on a light, and if it was cold, they could turn up the furnace. People became very mobile, able to hop into a car and drive practically anywhere. Life was made easier by new products. But all of this "progress" had negative effects on the environment. It became increasingly more difficult to find efficient methods of disposing of waste, and air and water pollution resulted. Land, energy, and food became more scarce. Progress began as we defended ourselves against what often seemed a hostile environment, but somewhere along the way we not only gained control over—but also began to destroy—our environment.

TRANSITIONS BETWEEN SENTENCES

Sentences linked by transitional devices such as pronouns, repeated key words, transitional expressions, or parallel structure help create a unified paragraph.

(2) Link sentences by your use of pronouns.

In paragraph 32 Carin Rubenstein links her sentences by
using the pronouns *their* and *they*. Although these same two
pronouns are used repeatedly, their referent, "easy victims,"
is always clear.

32   Several movements characterized easy victims: their
strides were either very long or very short; they moved awk-
wardly, raising their left legs with their left arms (instead of
alternating them); on each step, they tended to lift their
whole foot up and then place it down (less muggable sorts
took steps in which their feet rocked from heel to toe). Overall, the people rated most muggable walked as if they were
in conflict with themselves; they seemed to make each
move in the most difficult way possible.

—CARIN RUBENSTEIN,
"Body Language That Speaks to Muggers"

(3) Link sentences by repeating key words or ideas.

In paragraph 33, the repetition of the key word "no" links
the sentences. (The repetition also serves to provide emphasis: see **29e**.)

33   If you ask the American people what they detest most,
it will probably be the word *"no."* We have been brain-
washed into thinking that if we wrap our lips around that
nasty little word, we will immediately turn into kill-joys,
grouches, nags, villains, tightwads, ogres, prudes or fanatics.
I would like to say yes to *no* once again. *No* is a good word,
especially if you can be brave and swashbuckling and reasonably sane about using it. I know people who say *no* just
because. I want my kids and their kids to have something
left to say *no* about. *No* is, after all, a part of life.

—SUZANNE JORDAN, "The Joy of Abstinence"
(italics added)

Notice in paragraph 34 how repetition of key words binds
together the sentences.

34

Social change takes many forms in modern society, and people are affected by it in several different ways. *change* For example, in the past, a man's prestige as well as much of his life satisfaction lay in his occupation and in his work. However, signs indicate that the traditional basis *satisfaction* for satisfaction is changing. Now, the source often lies outside of "work." The satisfaction formerly obtained in an occupation is being pursued in clubs, sports, and many kinds of projects. This change in attitude toward work stems not only from the character of job duties, but also from shorter work hours and higher incomes.

occupation, work, job

—THERON ALEXANDER, "The Individual and Social Change"

(4) Link sentences by using transitional expressions.

Below is a list of various transitional expressions:

1. *Addition:* moreover, further, furthermore, besides, and, and then, likewise, also, nor, too, again, in addition, equally important, next, first, second, third, in the first place, in the second place, finally, last.
2. *Comparison:* similarly, likewise, in like manner.

3. *Contrast:* but, yet, and yet, however, still, nevertheless, on the other hand, on the contrary, even so, notwithstanding, for all that, in contrast to this, at the same time, although this may be true, otherwise, nonetheless. (Note: Addition, comparison, and contrast are used for items of equal importance.)

4. *Place:* here, beyond, nearby, opposite to, adjacent to, on the opposite side.

5. *Purpose:* to this end, for this purpose, with this object.

6. *Result:* hence, therefore, accordingly, consequently, thus, thereupon, as a result, then.

7. *Summary, repetition, exemplification, intensification:* to sum up, in brief, on the whole, in sum, in short, as I have said, in other words, that is, to be sure, as has been noted, for example, for instance, in fact, indeed, to tell the truth, in any event.

8. *Time:* meanwhile, at length, soon, after a few days, in the meantime, afterward, later, now, in the past.

Notice the various ways that transitional expressions connect and relate ideas in the sentences of paragraphs 9 and 25.

(5) Link sentences by means of parallel structure.

Parallelism is the repetition of the sentence pattern or of other grammatical structures. See also Section **26**.

In paragraph 35 notice the parallelism in the second and third sentences, which develop the topic stated in the first sentence. The repeated pattern is *adverb clause, main clause.* This parallelism serves as a unifying force. See also **26a(3)**.

35   You must give up believing that all the riches of life will come from reaching the goals of your idealized self. If your ideal self is evidently not going to be attainable and you refuse to adjust down, you will go the route of chronic depression. On the other hand, if you recognize that you will never be president of the big-city bank, you can get on with becoming branch manager in your favorite community and maybe find your greatest pleasure in becoming a Little League coach or starting a choir. —GAIL SHEEHY, *Passages*

In the series of paragraphs below, paragraph 36 states and explains the controlling idea, and 37–39 repeat parallel structures in the question-answer pattern that serves as a unifying force. For effective variety, the final emphatic one-sentence paragraph breaks the parallel pattern.

36   Somehow this nation has become caught in what I call the mire of "technofix": the belief, reinforced in us by the highest corporate and political forces, that all our current crises can be solved, or at least significantly eased, by the application of modern high technology. In the words of former Atomic Energy Commission chairman Glenn Seaborg: "We must pursue the idea that it is more science, better science, more wisely applied that is going to free us from [our] predicaments."

37   Energy crisis? Try synfuels. Never mind that they will require billions—eventually trillions—of dollars transferred out of the public coffers into the energy companies' pockets, or that nobody has yet fully explored, much less solved, the problems of environmental damage, pollution, hazardous-waste disposal and occupational dangers their production will create. Never mind—it's technofix.

38   Food for the hungry world? Try the "Green Revolution." Never mind that such farming is far more energy- and chemical-intensive than any other method known, and therefore generally too expensive for the poor countries that are supposed to benefit from it, or that its principle of monoculture over crop diversity places whole regions, even whole countries, at the risk of a single breed of disease or pest. Never mind—it's scientific.

39   Diseases? Try wonder drugs. Never mind that few of the thousands of drugs introduced every year have ever been fully tested for long-range effects, or that they are vastly overprescribed and overused, or that nearly half of them prove to be totally ineffective in treating the ailments they are administered for and half of the rest produce unintended side effects. Never mind—it's progress.

40 And progress, God help us all, may be our most important product.   —KIRKPATRICK SALE, "The 'Miracle' of Technofix"

■ **Exercise 6** Prepare for a class discussion of the specific linking devices (pronouns, transitional words, repetition, parallelism) used in paragraph 41.

41 Electronic music is a new departure from orthodox, or generally accepted, music in that it is electrically originated or modified sound. This sound is the output of electric pianos, organs, synthesizers, saxophones, guitars, flutes, violins, trumpets, and many other instruments. It is the product of composers who use tape recorders and tape manipulation to distort, for better or worse, conventional sounds. Also, it is the sounds we hear in concerts and on records that use amplification to boost or alter the volume of instruments.   —MERRILL C. LEHRER, "The Electronic Music Revolution"

■ **Exercise 7** Revise the sentences in paragraph 42, the work of a student, so that the thought flows smoothly from one sentence to the next.

42 When we hear the word "environment," one of the first words that comes to mind is the weather. We cannot control our climate; however we have created an artificial environment which can be either hot or cool to suit our needs. But no one can make a substitute for the sun. We depend on the sun for both heat and ultraviolet radiation, which forms the Vitamin D in man's body. The sun is the catalyst which continues our never-ending food chain, and now we have changed the sun's light to a form of heating called solar energy. Without the sun, we could not survive.

31d

Provide clear transitions between paragraphs.

Transitions from one paragraph to the next are just as necessary as those between sentences within the paragraph because the reader needs to be reminded of the direction of the writer's thought.

For example, read paragraph 43, which sets forth a claim made by those who promote transcendental meditation(TM). Then observe the two types of transitional devices used in the first sentences of subsequent paragraphs that refute this claim.

43

As the saying goes, "You can prove anything with statistics." TM promoters claim that the higher the meditation rate, the lower the crime rate, and specifically that in cities where one percent of the population practice TM, the crime rate is lower than in other cities.

transitional expressions

First, a correlation does not necessarily indicate a cause and effect relationship. . . .

Second, in large samples it is easy to get correlations. . . .

Third, the one percent may not represent a cross section of each city's populace. . . .

repetition of words / ideas

—RANDAL MONTGOMERY, "TM and Science: Friends or Foes?"

The closely related words in each group below are often placed at or near the beginnings of sentences to link ideas in separate paragraphs (as illustrated in paragraph 43) or within a paragraph (as in paragraph 25).

1. First. . . . Second. . . . Third. . . .
2. First. . . . Then. . . . Next. . . . Finally. . . .
3. Then. . . . Now. . . . Soon. . . . Later. . . .
4. One. . . . Another. . . . Still another. . . .
5. Some. . . . Others. . . . Still others. . . .
6. A few. . . . Many. . . . More. . . . Most. . . .
7. Just as significant. . . . more important. . . . most important of all. . . .

Sometimes a transitional paragraph (usually short, often consisting of only one sentence) serves as a bridge between two paragraphs. Notice below that the first noun phrase in the transitional paragraph 45 echoes the preceding key idea and that the second noun phrase points to a fact to be explained next.

44   Indeed, instead of seeing evolution as a smooth process, many of today's life scientists and archaeologists are studying the "theory of catastrophes" to explain "gaps" and "jumps" in the multiple branches of the evolutionary record. Others are studying small changes that may have been amplified through feedback into sudden structural transformations. Heated controversies divide the scientific community over every one of these issues.

45   But all such controversies are dwarfed by a single history-changing fact.

46   One day in 1953 at Cambridge in England a young biologist, James Watson, was sitting in the Eagle pub when his colleague, Francis Crick, ran excitedly in and announced to "everyone within hearing distance that we had found the secret of life." They had. Watson and Crick had unraveled the structure of DNA.

—ALVIN TOFFLER, *The Third Wave*

31e

Construct effective opening, concluding, and transitional paragraphs.

(1) Opening paragraphs

An opening paragraph, the one that begins an essay, functions as the writer's game plan. It must guide both writer and reader through the rest of the essay. The topic sentence of the opening paragraph is usually the thesis statement that will control all the remaining paragraphs of the essay. (See Section **32**.) The other sentences in the opening paragraph, the ones that support the topic sentence, are often used later in the essay, usually reworded, as the topic sentences of separate paragraphs.

The second function of the opening paragraph is to interest the reader. Often a writer will begin with a specific example or illustration, a quotation, an interesting statistic—whatever the writer believes will encourage the reader to read further. In magazines and newspapers, the first paragraph is often called "the hooker" because it acts like a baited hook. In academic writing, the first paragraph can be less enticing, but the writer still needs to attract the reader's attention and to focus the problem under discussion.

Paragraph 47, from a student essay, is an example of a beginning paragraph that attracts the reader's attention.

47   The faded yellow 5 × 8-inch card, taped at the head of the plain pine coffin, read: "Ronnie A. Ward, 51960573, died from wounds received during an armed conflict with the enemy, September 14, 1967, Republic of Viet Nam." Ronnie had now given all of himself.

(2) Concluding paragraphs

A concluding paragraph, the one that ends an essay, is the writer's final opportunity to restate the main idea of the essay. Often the concluding paragraph repeats in other words what was stated in the opening paragraph. In a short essay, the concluding paragraph may be no more than a sentence, but the longer the essay or the more complex its ideas, the more developed the concluding paragraph will need to be. The topic sentence of a concluding paragraph is usually a restatement of the main idea of the essay, and its supporting sentences are often reworded versions of the topic sentences of earlier paragraphs.

Checklist for Paragraph Revision

Coherence

1. Is the topic sentence effectively placed?
2. Is the topic sentence carefully restricted?
3. Is the paragraph pattern appropriate?

Development

4. Is the method of development appropriate?
5. Is the paragraph adequately developed?

Unity

6. Does each sentence support the main idea in the topic sentence?
7. Are the sentences smoothly linked?

Special types of paragraphs

8. If an opening paragraph, does it indicate the subject of the essay? Is it designed to interest the reader?
9. If a concluding paragraph, does it sum up the major ideas of the essay? Does it provide a convincing ending?
10. If a transitional paragraph, does it link what has gone before with what is to come?

---

(3) Transitional paragraphs

Paragraphs sometimes serve as transitions from one idea to another. As you saw in paragraph 45, transitional paragraphs may be as short as one sentence that sums up what went before (usually in a subordinate clause) and shows where the thought will now lead (usually in the main clause). Such a paragraph is usually short because the writer intends it to be merely a signpost.

■ **Exercise 8**   Revise the following student paragraph.

48   My friend Michelle often lends her textbooks, her class notes, and even her clothes. Borrowers seldom return them. Of course, some people are luckier than Michelle. The other day, when two "hungry" boys asked my roommate for spare dimes, he quickly reached for his billfold, but they beat him to it and ran off. Again, a motorist ran out of gasoline: and when my sister Alicia stopped to help him, she parked too near the mainstream of traffic. Her brand new Honda got sideswiped.

■ **Exercise 9**   The following student essay appears without paragraphs. Indicate where the essay might be divided into paragraphs.

Ronnie A. Ward

    The faded yellow 5 × 8-inch card, taped at the head of the plain pine coffin, read: "Ronnie A. Ward, 51960573, died from wounds received during an armed conflict with the enemy, September 14, 1967, Republic of Viet Nam." Ronnie had now given all of himself. Ronnie A. Ward, born July 10, 1949, Wichita, Kansas, was the first of four children. Most people considered Ronnie as being short for a boy. At eighteen he was only 5'5" tall and weighed 110 pounds, but what he lacked in height, Ronnie made up for with his warm smile, soft voice, and patience and understanding. He had brown eyes and short brown hair that complemented his fair skin. The first time I met Ronnie was in 1957, in grade school. Even then Ronnie was different from most kids his age. Ronnie would be playing with the kids in the neighborhood, and his mother would call him home to help with the house work or to watch his sisters and brothers. Ronnie never complained about having to help at home. He was twelve when his father died of Hodgkin's disease. Without being told or asked, Ronnie assumed the task of "man of the house." He helped by taking care of the house and by watching the younger kids in the evening, while his mother worked. When Ronnie was sixteen, he quit school and took on a full-time job because his mother's health was poor, and she could no longer work. Ronnie enjoyed school and was active in sports and dramatics, but gave these up knowing the family needed his help. He thought first about the family's needs before his own. On payday, Ronnie always managed to bring home some small gift for his sister and brothers to make their life a little more enjoyable. When Ronnie turned eighteen, he decided to enlist in the Army, hoping to make more money in the service to send home for the family. I saw Ronnie two days before I left home myself to join the Army. The next time I saw Ronnie was August 1967, Quang Tri, South Viet Nam. Ronnie had been attached to the unit I was in. It was good to have a long-time friend in the same outfit. We talked often of the good times we had together during our early years in Wichita. Ronnie hadn't changed, still quiet-spoken, friendly, and considerate to all. With a smile on his face he was usually doing something for someone else, without asking or wanting anything in return. That was Ronnie's way for as long as I had known him. September 14, 1967, started out like any other day. Our unit had been on many "sweep and destroy" missions in the past. When word was given that today's mission was to advance on a village in Quang Tri Province, suspected of being a Viet Cong stronghold, everything seemed superficially routine. On the outskirts of the village our unit stopped its advance to wait for nightfall. As Ronnie and I lay in the hot and humid stench of rot and decay in the woven wall-like underbrush of the jungle, we talked of home. Ronnie said he was going to send his mother some extra money this month, because his sister needed braces. He was worried that his sister's good looks would be spoiled if she did not get braces. At dusk our unit entered the village and started a hut-to-hut search for the Viet Cong. Ronnie entered one hut in which we heard a baby crying. He saw the half-naked baby lying in a homemade cradle, picked it up, and headed for the door, unaware that the cradle was a booby trap. I saw Ronnie standing in the doorway of the hut holding the baby in his arms when the booby trap exploded. Ronnie was blown out of the hut with the baby still in his arms and held tight to his chest. His left arm was blown off at the shoulder from the explosion. Blood was pouring across his face as I ran to him. He looked up at me with a half-frightened and sad look on his face. He didn't ask "Am I going to die?" Ronnie didn't complain about the pain either; instead he asked in a shallow soft voice, "Is the baby all right? Is the baby alive?" I picked up the still crying baby and held it out for Ronnie to see. Ronnie didn't say anything. He just smiled, reached for the baby, then died. All his life, Ronnie gave what he could of himself to others; and, in the end, he gave more than most. Ronnie gave his life.   —NICHOLAS J. WEBER

■ **Exercise 10** Prepare for a class discussion of the strengths and weaknesses of the following professional and student paragraphs.

49   Can hailstorms be suppressed? Attempts to modify them have been made throughout history. The Romans shot arrows toward the storm. In medieval Europe, church bells were rung—a practice that tended to increase the casualty rate because lightning often struck the unprotected belfrey, electrocuting the bell ringer. With advancing technology, the hail cannon, a device that fired a ring of smoke and gas instead of a solid missile, became popular. The sound of the discharge was supposed to break up the hailstones. It at least provided some psychological comfort. Cannons were later replaced by rockets, which exploded aloft with a resounding bang. None of these remedies had any obvious success.   —JOHN HALLETT, "When Hail Breaks Loose"

50   Among the things I find hardest to do is to let a ringing telephone go unanswered. Suppose, for example, I have a good reason for not answering it. The first two rings I can easily endure, and then I start counting the rings. After I hit six, I wonder why it keeps ringing. Could it be that Dad has had another heart attack? When I finally do lift the receiver, no one is there. For the rest of the day or until it rings again and I answer it on the first ring, I have no peace of mind.   —STUDENT

51   Whatever their calling, most people spend most of their time doing chores. A chore may be defined as a somewhat disagreeable or boring task that must be done in order to accomplish one's real objective. The detective has his legwork and endless checking of details. The athlete and the musician practice what they already know. The politician makes his appearances; the lawyer prepares his briefs. Most human achievements conceal a vast, hidden background of chores, a world of routine humdrum that no one really likes but that everyone recognizes as necessary.   —STUDENT

52   A soap opera deals with the plights and problems brought about in the lives of its permanent principal characters by the advent and interference of one group of individuals after another. Thus, a soap opera is an endless sequence of narratives whose only cohesive element is the eternal presence of its bedeviled and beleaguered principal characters. A narrative, or story sequence, may run from eight weeks to several months. The ending of one plot is always hooked up with the beginning of the next, but the connection is unimportant and soon forgotten. Almost all the villains in the small-town daytime serials are émigrés from the cities—gangsters, white-collar criminals, designing women, unnatural mothers, cold wives, and selfish, ruthless, and just plain cussed rich men. They always come up against a shrewdness that outwits them or destroys them, or a kindness that wins them over to the good way of life.
                    —E. B. WHITE, "Soapland"

The Whole Composition

32

Arrange and express your ideas effectively.

An essay (also called a theme or paper) is a short nonfiction composition, the content and organization of which are guided by a single controlling idea, the *thesis*. Just as a topic sentence directs the development of a paragraph, the thesis, or controlling statement, limits and sums up the point of the essay. And just as a paragraph is a series of sentences developing one topic, an essay is a series of paragraphs arranged to elaborate and support the thesis. Both an essay and a paragraph contain similar parts: a controlling sentence, supporting explanation and details, logical transitions, and a conclusion. Both consist of a beginning, a middle, and an end; both are unified and coherent.

An essay has a *purpose*. Depending on what that purpose is, the writer will choose one of the four basic kinds of writing:

Narration. The purpose of a narrative essay is to tell a story—to relate a sequence of events in chronological order. Usually the writer's further purpose is to make a stated or implied point about the significance of the events.

Description. In a descriptive essay, the purpose is to evoke a mood or create a dominant impression about a person, place, or object. Using concrete, vivid images that appeal to the reader's senses, the writer tries to make the reader see, hear, or feel what the writer saw, heard, or felt.

Exposition. Here the purpose is to inform, clarify, define, explain, or analyze. Most college writing—themes, research papers, essay examinations, lab reports—is expository, that is, students are asked to explain or clarify their ideas. Essays that explain the causes of stress, that classify types of students, that contrast solar heating and wood-burning stoves, that define the word *romantic,* or that analyze the effects of television on family meals—all are examples of exposition.

Argumentation. An argumentative essay attempts to convince, bring about an event, or move the reader to action. In an orderly way the writer analyzes a problem, offers a solution, acknowledges opposing solutions, and restates the one given in the essay. The appeal to the reader may be strictly logical or it may involve the reader's emotions.

Essays have many purposes, such as to entertain, inspire, or persuade, so the writer usually combines several kinds of writing, with one of them predominant. For example, an essay persuading legislators to require helmets for all motorcycle riders might include a description of a car-motorcycle collision, the story of how the accident happened, and an explanation of how helmets are designed to absorb the shock of impact.

An essay is designed for a particular *audience.* Both its content and its diction must be appropriate to the background, needs, and interests of that audience. If the topic is the pros and cons of buying a condominium in California, the audience does not want to read about the difficulties of moving from Omaha to Los Angeles, either along with or in place of the topic. If the writer is a specialist, and the audience shares the writer's expertise, the essay can have a more sophisticated thesis and use more specialized language than an essay on the same subject written for a general audience that knows little or nothing about the subject.

Writing an essay is a *process*—a series of steps in which writers expand and organize their ideas according to their central purpose and their audience. First, they choose and limit their subject **(32a)**. Then, after they have collected ideas about their subject **(32b)**, they arrange the main ideas into a pattern **(32c)**. Their next step is to shape the sentence that controls the entire essay—the thesis statement **(32d)**—a step in which choosing and evaluating their audience **(32e)** is a crucial factor. Finally, they prepare a rough or working outline **(32f)** as an aid in writing the various drafts of the essay **(32 g–i)**. As writers move through each of these steps, they may need to repeat one or more of them. For example, they may need to collect more ideas. Or they may write their essay only to discover that it does not develop the ideas announced in the thesis. They may thus have to revise their thesis, their paragraphs, or both; they may even have to choose another thesis.

No matter how much repetition of the steps is necessary, the goal is a clear statement of the thesis, developed with coherent and unified supporting information. Beginning writers sometimes think that experienced writers produce a single draft of flawless prose—that they start with the title and proceed from the introduction through the conclusion without ever stopping to rearrange the order of ideas, to eliminate wordiness, or to revise diction. The fact is that experienced writers follow the same steps described above—selecting, writing, and revising again and again—until the essay is a unified, coherent, and well-developed statement of ideas.

■ **Exercise 1** Prepare for a discussion of the following essay by deciding which of the four kinds of writing predominates and which kinds, if any, are secondary.

Some Preservation Definitions

1   Preserved. This is the word a lot of people use to describe what they have done to a building or area of a certain age. They "preserved" the colonial village, although only half of it was around before the Revolution (and the second half not until yesterday). They "preserved" the home of the town founder, even though they first had to go out and buy the bricks and the mortar and the framing and the windows and the roof. They "preserved" the old factory by gutting the interior and making three floors where only one had existed, the better to put in more boutiques. They "preserved" the bank by sandblasting its façade. They "preserved" the old house, after moving it, by stripping the Victorian additions and ordering out for colonial-style replacements. And they "preserved" the neighborhood by demanding that the new building down the street be Federal-style and not that avant-garde thing, even if it would have been the right size and its materials would have fit right in with all the others on the block.

2   Demolition is not just a wrecking ball swinging against brick and mortar. Any building or structure or site that is not being cared for properly is being demolished. Demolition can be inaction; in fact, it often is, destroying buildings and their environments by neglect. Demolition can also take place when people think they are preserving. Out of slavish devotion to what they believe or have been told the past is, they strip real structures and put on deceptive masks, or tear down the really old and construct new "old" buildings, actions that stem from misconceptions of what preservation is and can be.

3   At one time, everyone who thought about it had a fairly sure idea of what constituted historic preservation: it was an effort to save buildings that were considered important for one reason or another in the development of the country. But because preservation now covers a broad spectrum of activities, what "preserving" means is not as simple any more. In its dictionary sense, preservation means saving something pretty much the way it is. This often takes much work to accomplish. On the most basic level, it means keeping things in good condition by maintaining them. According to general priorities supported by the National Trust for Historic Preser-

vation and other preservationists: "It is better to preserve than repair, better to repair than restore, better to restore than reconstruct." In other words, the less done to good structures the better, and if it is done in time, more extensive work will not be necessary.

4 By the time most preservationists enter the picture, a structure has usually passed the point of needing only the status quo—preservation in its literal meaning. Because the world is not static, buildings too must adapt to change, especially if they are to continue their prime function of use. Thus, preservation means not stasis but an effort to ward off detrimental changes—to maintain the qualities and contributions that made a structure or area a candidate for protection in the first place.

5 Maintenance of existing buildings is a vital means of preservation. Old farms can be maintained by being farmed, old business structures by being rented, and old houses by being lived in. Preservation by maintenance is taking place in areas like East Baltimore, where householders scrub the marble steps of their row houses, proud of a trademark that is both useful and beautiful and that gives residents a sense of identity. Preservation is taking place in towns where county courthouses and city halls are maintained in use either as courthouses or for other services because they are recognized as unique symbols of civic success and continuity. Some department store and business owners are proud of their landmarks and take steps to assure their preservation because the condition they are in serves as a visible statement of the continuing success of the owners' enterprises. Preservation is also happening where civic organizations keep the park bandstand painted and in use or where they persuade their government to exercise control over the kinds of commercial signs used in a downtown area.

6 Although some may not even know the term, all of the people involved in these activities may properly be called preservationists. They value their property, the structures and sites they have collectively inherited, and appreciate them as factors that create the quality of life in their environment. The stabilization and the maintenance of older buildings without undue change is a holding action against the tooth of time. —TONY P. WRENN and ELIZABETH D. MULLOY

32a

Choose a subject that interests you and limit it properly.

(1) Choosing a subject.

Whether you have been assigned a subject for an essay or must choose one, you should ask yourself what you know about it, for writers write best about what they know best. While every writer brings a unique set of experiences to the writing task, not all of those experiences will generate a good essay. Although writers often discover what they know as they write, they are also able to gauge the extent of their knowledge as they list possible subjects.

These following questions will suggest some areas to explore as you discover what subjects you are interested in and know most about:

1. If you weren't writing an essay, what would you rather be doing? Why?
2. What things are you good at?
3. What subjects are you least interested in writing about?
4. If you could solve any one problem, what would it be? Why? How would you solve it?
5. Which of the following areas do you enjoy talking or reading about?

sports	ecology	famous people
hobbies	space exploration	marriage
politics	money	drama
religion	parenting	psychology
television	careers	philosophy
advertising	movies	energy
food	music	travel

The answers to some of these questions may suggest subjects. One student, Shawn Redfield, answered as follows:

I'd rather be—sleeping, stripping that old rocking chair, drawing political cartoons, washing and waxing the car

I'm good at—finding bargains, listening to other people's problems, coaching soccer, cutting firewood

> I like talking about—my favorite country-western bands, my
> job in the antique shop, my plans to run for Congress

Ideas that occur in more than one answer are usually a logical starting point. In addition to Shawn's obvious interest in
politics, the answers above suggest an essay on antiques
(stripping a rocking chair, finding bargains, working in an
antique shop). But what about antiques? One subject can
produce many possible topics. *Antiques* names a general category, and to write one essay that treats every aspect of it is
impossible—not even a whole book is sufficient for a thorough discussion.

(2) Limiting the subject.

How can an essay subject—in this case, antiques—be limited
or narrowed? One way is to reduce the general category
(subject) to increasingly restricted ones (topics). The more
restricted the category, the more specific the idea. Shawn
Redfield came up with three possible topics by limiting the
general category of antiques in three different ways:

1. *Antiques*

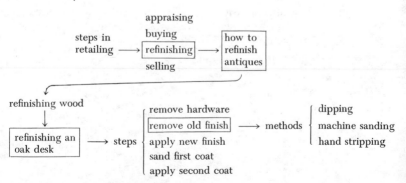

Limited topic: the factors that determine whether a refinisher
uses dipping, sanding, or hand stripping to remove the finish
from an old desk.

2. *Antiques*

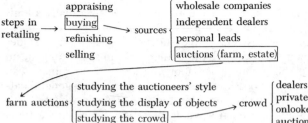

Limited topic: the motivation of bidders at farm auctions—why are they bidding? Who is most likely to drive the bidding beyond the appraised price? Why?

3. *Antiques*   (Note how the two false starts below lead Shawn to his third topic.)

(a) American vs. European $\begin{cases} \text{expense} \\ \text{availability} \\ \text{condition} \end{cases}$

all American and European antiques? (no—too many to cover, and I don't know anything about European antiques)

(b) American antiques

	home	business	
		professional	*trades*
17th century	furniture	surveyors' instruments	firemen's badges
18th century	decorations	pharmacists' mortars	carpenters' planes
19th century	utensils	and pestles	blacksmiths' bellow
		dentists' cabinets	

all types for all three centuries?
(no—too many categories)

(c) American 19th-century antiques

manufactured		*handmade* (**primitives**)		
china		⎧ butter molds		⎧ wooden rakes
glassware	kitchen	⎪ bowls	farm	⎪ plows
	utensils	⎨ spatulas	tools	⎨ wagon seats
		⎩ measuring cups		⎩ horseshoes

Limited topic: the reasons for collecting American primitives

Another way to narrow the subject is to consider the four kinds of writing. Narration, description, exposition, argumentation—each of these is more appropriate to certain subjects than to others, and each suggests limits for an essay. When these four kinds are applied to the subject of antiques, the following topics might result:

1. *Narration:* a story relating how cleaning out an attic created an instant collection; a story about an elderly woman's preference for the objects of her youth rather than for modern things
2. *Description:* a description of an antique shop crammed with hundreds of items; a description of the apparent restraint of bidders at a formal auction
3. *Exposition:* an explanation of how to distinguish fakes and reproductions from genuine antique furniture; an explanation of the training programs for people who want to become auctioneers
4. *Argumentation:* an argument against buying antiques as a means of financial investment; an argument for developing a bidding strategy to use at auctions

■ **Exercise 2**   Draw up a list of six subjects that interest you and about which you know something. Ask questions to produce two properly limited topics for one of the subjects. Apply the four kinds of writing to produce two limited topics for another subject.

32b

Collect ideas about your topic.

From his three possible topics about antiques, Shawn Red-field has decided to explore the reasons people collect primi-tives—antique handmade objects. To generate ideas for the explanations and supporting details he needs, he may use one or all of the following methods.

(1) List-making.

Like grocery lists and lists of things to do, lists of ideas to include in an essay help you accomplish a task. Just as you jot down grocery items as they occur to you—not according to the order of the aisles at the store—you list ideas without regard to their order in the essay. And just as you delete some foods and add others during the walk through the store, you will delete some ideas and add others as you work out a plan of organization. The important thing, however, is to have ideas to organize. Write down every idea that occurs to you; save their organization for later.

Here is Shawn Redfield's list for his primitives topic:

> antiques that are handmade or handcrafted = primitives
> sometimes made at home, sometimes not
> not very smoothly finished
> practical furniture—beds, dressers, dry sinks, pie safes, rock-ing chairs, chests, cupboards
> household things—butter molds, bowls
> functional
> also handcrafted metal things (usually not homemade)
> blacksmiths—candlesticks, flatirons, pots, skillets, tools, horseshoes, nails, axles
> tinsmiths—pie-safe panels, candlesticks—?
> pewtersmiths—such a word?—candlesticks, spoons, picture frames, mugs, plates, pitchers, ladles, teaspoons, por-ridge bowls
> brasssmiths(?)—pots, kettles, keys, teakettles, ladles, candle-sticks, bells

copper—teakettles, pitchers, wash boilers
craftsmanship of unique pieces not all that polished
antique—defined how?
primitive—defined how?
estate or farm auctions—a good place to look
prices cheaper than really fine furniture, but prices on both
    keep going up
they remind me of stories Grandpa told me about using them
what did they use to mow grass—were there lawns?
go with furniture today; can still be used today
some are used for decoration, others are put to work—old
    dough bowl now a centerpiece, flatirons = bookends,
    etc.
inexpensive—lots of them around
they're popular
they'll increase in value

(2) Asking who, what, why, where, when, and how.

To be sure they have covered all aspects of a story, reporters ask the six questions above. The same questions can help you explore your topic. Here are some of the ideas Shawn came up with, asking himself the journalist's questions:

Who?   Who collects handcrafted antiques? Who appraises primitives?

What?   What items appeal most to me? What's the difference between a primitive and a collectible?

Why?   Why is collecting primitives popular? Why are there more pieces of primitive furniture than fine furniture around?

Where?   Where can the novice collector find out about the different kinds of primitives? Where in the United States are primitives most likely to be found?

When?   When is the best time, if there is one, to buy primitives? When did the interest in primitives start?

How?   How is *primitive* defined? How can a collection of farm implements be displayed? How does a person begin collecting? How do I re-cane a chair or clean up a pair of candlesticks?

(3) Asking questions based on paragraph-developing methods (see Section 31).

The same strategies that are used to expand a paragraph may suggest some ways to approach a topic. For example:

Narration—How do I respond to something I've just added to my collection? What do I remember about starting my collection?

Process—How was a rocking chair made? How were fields plowed? How is market value determined?

Description—How can the antique shop I work in be described? What is the chief impression conveyed by a kitchen decorated with primitives?

Classification—What types of people attend auctions? What types of primitives can I use in my home?

Analysis—What are the parts of the collecting process? What was the function of some of the farm tools?

Definition—What does *primitive* mean? What does *antique* mean?

Comparison and contrast—What's the difference between a cupboard and a hutch? How do Shaker furniture and Pennsylvania Dutch furniture differ in style?

Example—What objects represent the typical farmhouse of the mid-1800's? What objects were made at home? What objects were made by craftsmen?

Cause and effect—What causes people to collect primitives? What effect has the popularity of primitives had on buying them? How can the popularity of collecting primitives be interpreted? What effects did daily use have on primitives?

■ **Exercise 3**   From the narrowed topics you produced in Exercise 2, select the two you know most about. Use list-making, the journalist's questions, and methods of development to collect ideas for both.

32c

Arrange your ideas into a general pattern.

To make sense out of all the information you gather, you will need to identify your main ideas. Once those are clear, you can match details, facts, examples, definitions, and explanations with the corresponding main points. Set aside anything unrelated, no matter how proud or fond of it you may be. The object is to sift through the abundance of ideas you have collected, distinguishing the main ones first, and then the supporting ones.

Shawn Redfield has decided that he will try to explain why collecting primitives appeals as a hobby. On his list of ideas are these eight reasons:

1. craftsmanship of unique pieces not all that polished
2. prices cheaper than fine furniture
3. reminders of Grandpa's things and stories
4. go with furniture today
5. some are used decoratively, others put to work
6. inexpensive—lots of them around
7. they're popular
8. they'll increase in value

Essentially these boil down to three main reasons:

1. moderate expense (reasons 2, 6, 8)
2. the contrast of tradition and novelty (reasons 1, 3)
3. scope for individual taste—lots to choose from (reasons 4, 5, 6)

Notice that reason 7 is redundant and has been omitted, and that reason 8 is only indirectly related to expense. Working through the list and adding details suggested by the key words, Shawn now begins to supply information for each reason.

1. inexpensive
        prices of primitives vs. prices of antiques
        produced in quantity, common in every household

mahogany desk ($5,000) vs. teakettle ($50), butter
  bowl ($30), tin candlestick ($15)
  2. craftsmanship of pieces offers contrast of tradition and
     novelty
          homemade, not smoothly finished vs. polished, skilled
              finish of modern things
          durable
          reminders of Grandpa's stories
  3. suit individual tastes
          lots to choose from, relatively little duplication—can-
              dlesticks of pewter, brass, iron, tin
          appropriate for either decorative or functional use
          decorative—butter mold, spoon set
          functional then, functional now
          functional—flatirons as bookends, chests as coffee
              tables, quilts as tablecloths

Shawn will continue to add supporting ideas as he writes,
but only if they develop the points he is making. Whether an
idea was in his original list or suggested by the process of
writing, he will have to discard it if it does not belong with
the three main ideas.

■ **Exercise 4**   For each of the following topics, identify the unrelated material.

1. arranging for house care during a two-week vacation—stopping the mail; vacuuming and dusting; locking the doors;
   mowing the lawn.
2. definition of *friend*—distinction between a friend and a
   neighbor; anecdote of someone who smuggled bacon and
   doughnuts through your bedroom window so you could feed
   unexpected visitors; titles of three essays on friendship.
3. story showing the value of budgeting money—definition of
   money; having to pass up a stereo system at 40 percent off;
   peace of mind from knowing the rent is paid.

■ **Exercise 5**   For one of the topics for which you have collected information, arrange your ideas into a general pattern.

32d
Shape a thesis statement.

The thesis statement is a single declarative sentence that announces the writer's attitude toward the subject and suggests the essay's overall pattern of organization. It is the single most important sentence in the entire essay. If it is lucid and precise, the essay usually is too. Although a thesis statement may be implied or delayed until the closing paragraph, as a rule it is stated as the final sentence of the introduction. If the introduction is a single paragraph, then the thesis concludes it; if the introduction is two or more paragraphs long, the thesis ends the final introductory paragraph. Placing a sentence after the thesis may weaken its emphasis, and opening the essay with the thesis seldom prepares the reader for either the topic or the writer's approach.

Like a road map showing a driver's route on interstate highways, a thesis statement directs the movement of ideas through an essay. An effective thesis statement is incisive, offering specific guidelines to the essay's content and organization. It limits the scope of the topic so that the thesis is appropriate for the length of the paper. An effective thesis statement does not state the obvious. Nor does it use vague, abstract terms (such as *really, things, great, nice, very*), weak verbs (*to be, to have, to seem*), or the passive voice (as in "Primitives have been called the poor person's antiques"), which weaken the force of the thesis.

Compare the following thesis statements:

1. It's really interesting to collect things.
2. There are three reasons to collect primitives.
3. Weekends are spent bidding against other collectors when you collect primitives.
4. Bidding successfully for a sugar scoop indicates that the collector of primitives knows both the value of the prize and the limits of the competition.

5. Stripping a painted table by using ammonia and steel wool is easy, but it exposes the wood to a harsh chemical; using a power sander saves time, but it requires an even, light touch to avoid gouging the wood.

The first thesis statement gives no indication of either the topic or the approach; it is an all-purpose, say-nothing sentence that could lead to any number of different essays—which is exactly why it is useless. A thesis should suit only the essay it governs. Thesis statement 2 is weak for the same reason. It could fit several different essays with entirely different sets of reasons. Including the three reasons in the thesis would provide a more definite focus.

Thesis statement 3 provides only a general subject and no idea of the essay's organization. The reader might well ask: Who is meant by *you*? Are the other collectors also collectors of primitives? Under what conditions are they bidding against each other? Why is the competition limited to weekends?

Just as a general subject is narrowed, a general thesis statement can also be revised to make it more specific. Thesis statement 4 is appropriate for an essay on human behavior, while thesis statement 5 is appropriate for an essay on the advantages and disadvantages of two methods of stripping furniture.

Shawn Redfield produced the following thesis statements for his essay, and rightly decided that the fifth was the best of them all:

1. Primitives are inexpensive and adaptable. [weak verb, inexact topic, imprecise adjectives]
2. Inexpensive primitives are a combination of the traditional and the personal. [unclear whether all primitives are inexpensive or only inexpensive ones combine the two features]
3. Collecting primitives offers an inexpensive way to express individuality. [unclear what a ''way to express individuality'' means]

4. There are three reasons for the popularity of collecting primitives. [reasons not specified]
5. Collecting primitives will grow in popularity because primitives are relatively inexpensive, blend well with current trends in home decorating, and adapt to individual tastes. [contains an assertion and offers supporting reasons; clearest of the five]

Once you have created a clear and precise thesis statement, you have done the most difficult part of the job, for the thesis now determines what you will discuss when, and you have simply to fulfill your announced commitment to ideas and structure.

■ **Exercise 6**   Improve each of the following thesis statements.

1. Baseball and softball are different but fun.
2. My summer job taught me I could do anything as well as a man could.
3. Photography is an interesting hobby for anyone who doesn't know anything about it.
4. Many factors must be considered when deciding to become a pharmacist.
5. It's the car to buy for high gas mileage and low maintenance costs.
6. For a fun vacation that tests your ingenuity, try wilderness camping.

■ **Exercise 7**   Create a thesis statement for your topic.

32e
Choose and evaluate your audience.

Your audience deserves your respect. Whether generalists or specialists on the topic, your readers are entitled to a clear thesis statement, coherent explanations, logical transitions, and exact diction. The more precisely you define your audience, the more you can show your respect for their intelligence and curiosity. Writers who know their audience can develop examples or draw comparisons from their shared experiences. And such writers also know which terms, if any, must be defined and how fully. Further, if they know their audience is indifferent or hostile toward the subject, they will consider that too.

In short, establishing the audience for your essay helps to determine your tone and attitude. Only after you have evaluated your audience should you decide to be witty or ironic, reverent or impudent, for an inappropriate tone will offend your readers and reduce their willingness to consider your ideas.

Use the following guidelines for evaluating your audience:

1. What does the audience already know about the topic?
2. What is the attitude of the audience toward the topic?
3. Is the audience interested in the topic? Why? Why not?
4. For what purpose is the audience likely to read about the topic?
5. What kind of information will the audience accept as convincing support?

You can assume that most of the writing you do in college is for a *general* audience—educated and intellectually curious adults with a variety of political, ethnic, religious, and social backgrounds. Such an audience is potentially interested in any subject, so it does not need to have its interest aroused. It does expect, however, that the writer will present the subject in nontechnical language and will define or illustrate any specialized terms. For example, a general audience interested in the subatomic particles known as quarks wants a thorough but nontechnical explanation of how they function, but it does *not* want to read an academic research report to find out. (On the other hand, a group of physicists debating the evidence for quarks would expect a thorough and highly technical argument from a colleague writing an essay for a professional journal.)

Any topic can be shaped for any audience—general or specialized—depending on the knowledge of the writer and the background of the audience. But it is not possible to write for both kinds of audience at once, since their needs and expectations are entirely different. Here, for example, are two thesis statements on the topic of opening moves in chess:

GENERAL

Having mastered the moves of the pieces, the novice chess player needs to learn several standard openings, such as Ruy Lopez, Sicilian Defense, and Queen's Gambit. [appropriate for a chess beginner, who needs to have each of these strategies described]

SPECIALIZED

Although some modern chess theorists argue that if White opens P-K4, White's game is lost, this opening provides more flexibility than P-Q3. [appropriate for a reader who knows chess notation, who understands what the two moves involve, and who is interested in a controversial defense of P-K4]

■ **Exercise 8** Prepare to discuss how to shape each of the following topics for the audiences specified.

1. rock music: college students, country-western fans, composers
2. your school: state taxpayers, high school seniors, alumni
3. off-campus housing: city commissioners, school administrators, students, property owners
4. potatoes: home gardeners, commercial growers, nutritionists
5. changing attitudes toward marriage and the family: general audience, religious groups, sociologists

■ **Exercise 9** Read Wilfrid Sheed's essay "A Thought a Day Isn't Enough." Be prepared to discuss his attitude toward his subject and his audience (college seniors).

397

A Thought a Day Isn't Enough

1   When I was, say, twenty I thought I was a pretty bright and interesting fellow, although I was much too polite to show it. And I wondered why people of, say, forty were not twice as bright and interesting and so on up the line. A few, very few, of them were. Most of them seemed to get a little bit duller every year. They had fewer and fewer things to talk about—who are you going to vote for; how about those Yankees, etc. Their minds actually seemed to have shrunk and they preferred the company of people in the same boat, fellow dentists or morticians, who would never bring up anything new. This meant that there was either some dreadful biological law at work whereby old age sets in on the very day you leave campus or else there was a massive national act of laziness, of just giving up, performed every year at this time. Only later when I tried it myself did I come to realize how difficult it is to remain alive when nobody's watching and making you. Because we have this quaint custom of getting all our education over with early in life, we find ourselves fussed over excessively for sixteen years and then just like that abandoned and left for dead. This process is known as graduation, and welcome to it.

2   Of course, only in extreme cases do graduates become dull immediately. I've seen some of them do it on the way out of the final examinations but usually the first little gray hairs of the mind don't begin to show for ten years or so. At first, new jobs, marriages, relocations, etc., are stimulating enough. You don't need books or new ideas for a while. So you learn to live without them and you learn all too well. The world of work actually encourages this narrowness if you let it. Outside interests only slow you down in the rat race anyway. So the professional world becomes a kind of Franz Kafka mansion where the rooms get spiritually smaller and grayer the further up the stairs you go, and this is known as promotion.

3   You start out in a large bright space with lots of friends and lots of windows to look out of, but the windows are removed one by one so you can concentrate better on your work until you reach top management where you live, to judge from the conversation, in almost total darkness. Since this is the exact opposite of the way it looks, because the offices actually seem

to get bigger, many people sometimes go right to the top without knowing what's happening to them. I have met some quite prominent businessmen who had less to say for themselves than New York taxi drivers. Perhaps that's too high a standard but these people hadn't read anything or heard of anybody outside their own tiny world in years and years. Even their politics were simple-minded. They would be ashamed to know so little about football. I don't read novels they say—clank, there's a window gone. I never get to the movies, theater, opera.

4 As my father used to say about people who don't read poetry—neither does a cow. I should add that I'm not just talking about business businessmen but about doctors, lawyers, the works. In every case, they claim that the pressure of work is walling them in. Yet in every field you're likely to find that the very best people do miraculously make time for books and the arts and it's the second-raters who don't. So time isn't the real problem. The problem is character. Character, once upon a time, referred exclusively to work. It can also be applied to play. It requires will power to stay playful, to keep your mind open. It takes character to stay alive. And it is not only between nine and five that people age. There are plenty of unemployed bores who work at it around the clock. Whenever you find yourself repeating the same thoughts in exactly the same words, you're jogging along with Father Time and gaining. Listen in on any barroom or even executive lunch and you will find people eagerly looking for ways to say the things they said a million times before. If you pull something new on them, they will look stunned and then drag it back somehow to their old turf. "As I always say" is their motto, and did you ever find yourself using this phrase yourself? You are in the club. And the next generation will be thinking, how did he get to be so dull?

5 The fact is that staying intellectually alive is very hard work. They made you do it in school, so you did it. But now that nobody's making you do it, you'll probably stop. Nobody marches you into the bookstore anymore, so you stop attending as with church. After all, what do books know anyway? You'll learn from life itself. But your particular life would fill no more than one slim volume in a library, and all around it there would be oceans of life in the other books. A book is just

a stranger talking brilliantly; he's probably better company than you'll meet in a saloon. After all, he's usually sober and giving you the best hours of his day and he's forcing you to look at things in a new way and face new experience. It's no use saying, "As I was saying," to a book; incidentally, the fact that I happen to be in the book business myself has nothing to do with all this, nor the fact that I'm counting on this generation to keep me in cigars and caviar. You can read other people's books if you insist. I'm sure equally impassioned cases can be made for music and painting, and there's no need to quarrel.

6   An educated European assumes, often to my own embarrassment, that a college man will at least know the names of the world's leading composers, painters, architects and what they've been up to lately. So, since a patriotic note is also appropriate to these occasions, I call on you simply as Americans to stop being the Mortimer Snerds of the Western world, the Fred Flintstones, and to pick up your hem of the Western tradition. It is not too late to recover from your rotten educations, not the one you got here in this excellent place, but from the tube and lesser schools. Simply read a book. If not today, well at least by the end of next year. And if you repeat the dose often enough, you will have done more to stay young than all the jogging and rolling put together. And not just stay young. You will have pulled that one-in-a-million trick— growing up. And you will be twice as good twenty years from now as you think you are today.

—WILFRID SHEED

32f

Develop a working plan or rough outline.

You will find it easier to shape an essay from all the elements discussed thus far—subject, narrowed topic, thesis, audience, tone, attitude—by preparing a rough outline that shows the pattern in which you will develop your ideas as well as the sequence in which you will arrange them. (To develop a topic or sentence outline see **33d**.)

(1) Choosing a sequence for your ideas.

One of the patterns in **31a(3)**—question-answer, problem-solution, or topic-restriction-illustration—will give you a structure for your ideas. But you must also consider the sequence of ideas and paragraphs in the essay. If you choose the problem-solution pattern, for example, you must also consider in what order to present the elements of the problem and then the steps in the solution.

Your choice of sequence depends on the subject and purpose of your essay. In a description, for example, *spatial* order is useful to create an exact and orderly picture that enables the audience to recreate the scene: details move from left to right, from foreground to background, from top to bottom, and from inside to outside.

Exposition often uses *chronological* order, which presents events or details in a time sequence—from first to last, from past to present, and so forth. A chronological sequence would be appropriate in explaining how to make sourdough bread or in recounting the events that caused the Civil Rights movement.

The sequence of *climax* or *emphasis* moves from least important to most important. Just as the most emphatic point in a sentence occurs before the period, so the most emphatic point in an essay occurs before the conclusion. Thus, for example, a writer may choose to list the effects of a sunburn from the least dangerous to the most dangerous. Sometimes, however, when one item is of such immediate importance that it cannot be delayed, the order must be revised.

Finally, a writer may order ideas from general to specific or specific to general. An essay on the effects of the Mount St. Helens eruptions might proceed from specific, immediately recognized effects, such as volcanic ash in the streets, to general ones, such as long-term changes in weather patterns. Or an essay comparing two methods of decision-making might move from a discussion of general aims and appropriate situations for their use to the specific steps in each method.

(2) Preparing the rough outline.

In addition to listing the sequence of ideas, a rough outline should show the thesis, the audience, the purpose, and the general pattern.

Read "Do Animals Really Play?" by Eugene J. Walter, Jr., and then compare it with the rough outline that follows the essay.

Do Animals Really Play?

1   Do animals really "play"? Yes, and sometimes it's nothing more than fun and games, as when a monkey swings from a vine and tosses a stick, or when polar bears amuse themselves with stones, which they sometimes balance on their heads. Often, though, the seemingly frivolous antics we interpret as "play" are serious.

2   Play can be viewed as a pleasurable way of developing survival skills. The next time you're at a zoo, watch how the lion cubs frolic. One will crouch low against the ground, stalk slowly toward its littermate and then pounce on the surprised "victim." That usually touches off a knockabout wrestling match, with the cubs cuffing each other harmlessly. Such roughhouse sessions occur frequently among most carnivores such as wolves, tigers, cheetahs, raccoons, and coyotes. As they play, these young develop the abilities they need to become efficient predators.

3   Among monkeys and apes, playing helps lay the foundation for social order—a requirement for the survival of primate communities. Through play-fighting, a young monkey learns—in a harmless way—where it stands among its peers. The individuals that are most often victorious in the "matches" of infancy are most likely to assume a dominant role when they mature. Others that are lower on the social ladder learn their places early in life. This reduces more violent clashes among the monkeys as adults.

4   Many hoofed mammals engage in play, too. In herds of Mongolian wild horses, the breeding stallion will play-fight with his offspring, thereby helping the youngsters develop the agility they will need when confronted by predators or other stallions.

5   It appears that even whales play. A calf will perform all sorts of acrobatic gyrations on and around its mother, sliding over her tail, standing on its head or slapping its tail or flipper against the water's surface. It's possible that such play helps cement the bond between mother and offspring.

6   And what of birds—do they play? Some ornithologists are convinced that a few of the brainier ones do. The subject needs further inquiry. At this point, it's the mammals who appear to dominate the animal playground.

—EUGENE J. WALTER, JR.

Rough outline for "Do Animals Really Play?"

Thesis: The seemingly frivolous antics of animals' "play" prepare the young for adult life.
Audience: general (no specialized knowledge of animal behavior required)
Purpose: to explain why animals play by classifying types of play
Pattern: question-answer

1. Play develops survival skills.
        carnivores (lion cubs, wolves, tigers, cheetahs, raccoons, coyotes)
2. Play lays the foundation for social order.
        primates (monkeys)
3. Play develops agility.
        hoofed mammals (Mongolian wild horses)
4. Play develops mother-offspring bond
        marine mammals (whales)
5. Basis for choosing examples—mammals

Before Walters could write his essay, he took the following steps: he chose a subject (animal behavior), narrowed it (animal "play"), collected ideas (types of play and animals that engage in each type), chose a pattern (question-answer), and chose a sequence of ideas (general to specific—from a species-wide focus on survival skills to a narrow focus on the mother-offspring bond). Finally, he decided to shape his thesis for a general audience. Notice too that point 5 of the outline calls attention to the principle for choosing examples, which becomes an idea for the conclusion.

Here is Shawn Redfield's rough outline for his essay:

Rough outline for primitives essay

Thesis: Collecting primitives will grow in popularity because they are relatively inexpensive, they blend well with current home-decorating trends, and they adapt to individual tastes.

Audience: young couples beginning to decorate a home

Purpose: to explain the appeal of primitives to young homemakers

Pattern: question-answer—What explains the growing popularity of primitives?

1. primitives = common antiques of rural homes; hand-crafted if not homemade
   - furniture—chairs, tables, cupboards, dressers, chests
   - kitchen tools—spatulas, butter paddles, spoons, dough bowls, measuring cups, candlesticks, etc.
   - farm tools—rakes, plows, scythes, axes
2. comparison of readily available primitives vs. hard-to-find antiques
   - any of the above vs. paintings
   - teakettles vs. secretary desks
3. home decoration trends today
   - chrome and glass—contrasts in texture, style
   - eclectic—primitives go with most things
   - oak and calico—the appeal of tradition
4. primitives as collected by one person
   - a unique collection possible because so many items available
     - kinds of candlesticks
   - original use or invented use
     - quilt, flatiron, crock

■ **Exercise 10**   Write a rough outline for your essay. (You may find that typing it rather than handwriting it helps you to see the essay's emerging structure.)

32g
Write and revise the first draft.

In this first draft Shawn Redfield concentrates on explaining each of the three parts of his thesis statement. He has kept his main ideas in mind by including the thesis and by under-lining his topic sentences, and he has adhered to his outline. However, he has made no attempt to write an introduction or a conclusion nor has he supplied transitions from para-graph to paragraph. Read through the first draft and then look at Shawn's comments to himself.

FIRST DRAFT

Thesis statement: (Collecting primitives) will ~awk~
grow in popularity because (they) are relatively
inexpensive, they blend well with current home-
decorating trends, and they adapt to individual
tastes.

weak verb
Primitives (are) relatively inexpensive.
Compared to collecting art or fine furniture,
collecting primitives is very inexpensive. The
current *clarify* economic crunch makes this feature more
important now than ever. Primitives are the
common handcrafted or homemade utensils of the
rural home. *They* they were high priced when they   *can I prove?*
were new and are not expensive now. These   *Does it belong?*
objects were produced in quantity, which makes
collecting them a hobby suitable to a large

405

number of participants. Candlesticks, a
skillet, a butter paddle, or a chest—compared
to a silver tea service or a <u>mahogony</u> buffet
these things are <u>show #</u>
these things are <u>inexpensive</u> but satisfying to
collect.

check sp.

show #

2   <u>Primitives (blend) well</u> with <u>current</u> <u>home-</u>
<u>decorating trends.</u> Whether decorators choose
sleek chrome and glass contemporary or cozy
oak-and-calico decors, primitives add the
contrast of tradition and the novelty of
another lifestyle. The growing nostalgia
(infatuation) is well served by primitives. A
1929 Sears and Roebuck catalog among magazines
of the day provides a nostalgic link with days
gone by. There is a certain air of security
which surrounds the tools of people's ancestors.
There is security in a child's toy made of cast
iron, a barrel with walls of three-inch oak, or
hatracks made of brass, security which is
missing in today's disposable, plastic world.
Besides security, primitives provide an
interesting contrast in decor. The contrast
between an iron dutch oven that came to this
country in a wagon and a microwave oven flown in
from Japan can add character to a kitchen. A
coal scuttle as a magazine holder can supply the
same character of contrast to an electrically

right word?

right word?

Why?

heated living room. Home-decorating trends
reflect people's needs. Tradition and novelty
are two needs that will continue to be filled by
the preservation of articles of past life.

3   <u>Primitives adapt to individual tastes</u>.
~~Its~~ It's a hobby that allows for "mass individu-
ality~~.~~" Because of the way these objects were
produced, today a~~l~~ a lot of people could collect
the same thing, say candlesticks, yet no two
collections would be the same. ~~You~~ One person might
collect only brass candlesticks while ~~somebody~~ a second
~~else~~ collected only pewter, and ~~somebody else~~ a third
collected candlesticks of any metal. How do
primitives adapt to ~~your~~ individual tastes?
They serve a function in today's home, often a
function quite different from the original one.
An old crock may become a planter or a magazine
holder; it may even serve its original purpose.
A patchwork quilt may become a cushion, a chair
cover, a wall hanging, or a tablecloth. A flat-
iron may become a door stop, a bookend, or a
paperweight.   *Summary needed*

The first draft of Shawn Redfield's essay is a preliminary
sketch of the essay under construction. Each paragraph has a
topic sentence and the order of the paragraphs follows that
announced in the thesis statement, but the answers to the
questions implied by the topic sentences are general and the
supporting examples few.

In revising this draft, Shawn needs to analyze every word—beginning with the thesis—for clarity, coherence, and adequate support. Shawn's notes to himself and your own analysis might suggest the following revisions:

OVERALL	1. creating an introduction and a conclusion
	2. rewording the thesis to avoid the awkwardness of *collecting primitives—they*
	3. revising topic sentences so that they are not mechanical restatements of sections of the thesis
PARAGRAPH 1	4. choosing a strong verb for the topic sentence
	5. defining *primitives* before beginning a discussion of their appeal
	6. replacing general categories that illustrate the definition with specific examples
	7. providing market values to prove the relative expense
	8. omitting *satisfying* if the idea isn't proven in the paragraph
PARAGRAPH 2	9. clarifying the topic sentence by deciding whether objects blend with trends or with other objects
	10. considering whether the discussions of tradition and novelty are ordered in the paragraph according to emphasis
PARAGRAPH 3	11. deciding whether primitives adapt to one's tastes or reflect them and then, if necessary, revising the topic sentence
	12. clarifying the relationship between the making of objects and their availability
	13. adding a summary sentence

■ **Exercise 11** Reread the first draft of Shawn Redfield's essay, marking everything that is unclear to you or that you think needs revision. Compare your questions and comments with those of your classmates.

■ **Exercise 12** Write the first draft of your essay.

32h
Write and revise the second draft.

Shawn Redfield's notes for changes to be made in the first draft create guidelines for the writing of the second draft. Using the rough outline (but not being rigidly committed to it), the first draft, his comments on that draft, and new ideas that occur as he writes, he creates a second version, which begins to look like a conventional essay.

SECOND DRAFT

add title

1

weak

Cut—takes too long to get to thesis

prepare reader for this

There exists an ever-growing concern about people's leisure time. Since Clarence Darrow opened the way for labor unions, the work week has declined steadily. What will people do with all this extra time? Photography, gardening, and collecting are pastimes that have recently grown in interest. Collecting what? Anything and everything, from the expensive to the inexpensive, from the useful to the useless— rare coins, Edsels, duck decoys, mechanical banks, and Beatles albums. Yet the would-be collector with little money to spend need not feel left out, for collecting primitives is an inexpensive way to decorate an apartment or house. Primitives are the common handcrafted or homemade antique utensils of the rural home; they were high priced when they were new *but they* are not very expensive now. Because primitives are relatively inexpensive, adapt to individual

tastes, and blend with current decorating

schemes, collecting primitives will continue to

increase in popularity. *Do I prove this? No, I'm explaining the advantages of collecting.*

2   Compared to collecting art or fine *still weak?*

in terms of both time and money furniture, collecting primitives is very

inexpensive. Because they were produced in *awk.*

quantity, they are now more common—-and less

expensive—-than one-of-a-kind items or objects

of limited use. A fifteen dollar vase or a *effec. example*

potato digger does not require floating a loan,

awk. use of it but it can make a unique addition to a

collector's home. Cleaning up an old horse

collar is not a major project, but it may result

in a handsome frame for a mirror. Refinishing

an oak keg won't necessitate canceling the

bowling league membership, but it can provide a

one-of-a-kind end table. Collecting primitives

is not a hobby of kings, but it can be one for

anyone with an average income. *What's average?*

3   Collecting primitives not only suits modest

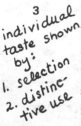 *individual taste shown by: 1. selection 2. distinctive use* budgets but also individual tastes. In fact, it

allows for "mass individuality." While today

twenty international corporations may

manufacture the same item, in 1890 perhaps as

many as one hundred small but independent

companies made the same object, each company

crafting a distinctive design. Thus, today hundreds of people may collect teakettles, for example, yet a high degree of duplication would be unlikely. [¶] While collectors are gathering [New ¶?] objects which say something about their likes and dislikes and their knowledge of antiques and history, they are also choosing objects which may serve a function in today's home, though often not the original function. An old crock may become a planter or a magazine holder; a patchwork quilt, a chair cover, a wall hanging or a tablecloth; a flatiron, a door stop or a bookend. A collection of primitives is in some ways a definition of the person who has assembled them; they are chosen and used according to the tastes of their owner.

4   Whether the collector prefers a sleek chrome-and-glass or a cozy oak-and-calico decor, primitives add the contrast of tradition and the novelty of another lifestyle. The cover of a 1929 Sears and Roebuck catalog among magazines of the day, for instance, provides a nostalgic [unclear] link with days gone by. The contrast between an iron dutch oven that crossed the plains ~~came to this country~~ in a wagon and a microwave oven flown in from Japan adds character to a kitchen. A coal scuttle used as a magazine holder supplies the same

overuse of contrast

character of <u>contrast</u> to an electrically heated living room. The preservation of these articles from the past continues to fill the need for <u>contrast</u> as it also reassures the need for tradition. There is security in a child's toy of cast iron, a barrel with walls of three-inch oak, or a hat rack made of brass--security which is missing in today's disposable, plastic world.

good idea

At once <u>removed from the present and a part of it,</u> primitives satisfy decorating needs and, in a large sense, family needs. → *clarify*

5

not proven

To sum up, collecting primitives is a thriving, inexpensive pastime which allows collectors to be at once individuals with unique tastes and a part of the cultural tradition from which their objects come. Whether the objects are from the best of times or worst, collectors

fix ambig-uous reference

delight in ⟨their⟩ history. Even as they dust and arrange, sort and catalog, they are making room for more.

After setting this second draft aside for a day or two, Shawn Redfield once again analyzes his work, checking matters of content, organization, sentence structure, paragraph unity, and diction. At this point, he is still more interested in revising (that is, rethinking the scope and shape of his ideas and how they relate to the thesis) than in proofreading (that is, looking for errors in spelling, grammar, punctuation, and mechanics).

When you revise your own work, use the checklist on pages 414–15, which will help you to evaluate all of the ideas in your essay.

■ **Exercise 13** Compare the first and second drafts of Shawn Redfield's essay to see whether the revisions have answered your questions. Are there any points that the writer made a note to revise but did not? Which questions on the checklist still need Shawn's attention?

■ **Exercise 14** Write the second draft of your essay and then answer all the questions on the revision checklist.

After using the revision checklist, Shawn makes three major decisions:

1. to begin the introduction with collecting instead of with increased leisure time
2. to revise the thesis so that it clearly defines the three points covered in the essay
3. to divide the paragraph on individual tastes and to reserve the topic sentence until the second part

He will also select a title and correct errors in spelling, punctuation, grammar, and mechanics. The result is the final draft on pages 416–19.

Reviser's Checklist

Overall considerations

1. Is every idea in the thesis stated clearly and given appropriate emphasis?

2. Does the thesis statement indicate the structure of the essay?

3. Does the sequence of paragraphs follow the order established in the thesis?

4. Do any terms require definition? If so, where should the definition(s) be introduced?

5. Do the body paragraphs prove the assertion of the thesis?

6. Are the ideas in the introduction logically related to the thesis?

7. Does the introduction attract the audience and prepare for the thesis?

8. Is there sufficient information to develop specific ideas?

9. Do the details, examples, and illustrations adequately support the ideas?

10. Is the conclusion complete without being abrupt?

11. Are all statements logically sound?

12. Is the tone consistent and appropriate for the audience?

13. Is the diction appropriate for both the content and the thesis?

Paragraphs

14. Is every paragraph controlled by a topic sentence, either stated or implied?
15. Does each paragraph explain and support its main idea? Are transitions within the paragraph clear and smooth?
16. Does each paragraph have a beginning, a middle, and an end?
17. Are the transitions between paragraphs adequate?

Sentences

18. Are the sentences varied in length? type? means of emphasis?
19. Are any words overused?
20. Are ideas within sentences given proper emphasis?
21. Are sentences grammatically correct?

Punctuation, Spelling, Mechanics

22. Are capitalization and abbreviations used correctly?
23. Have words at the ends of lines been divided correctly?
24. Are all words spelled correctly?
25. Are marks of punctuation used correctly and effectively?

32i
Prepare the final draft.

Now that Shawn Redfield has revised and proofread the second draft of his essay, he is ready to prepare a final copy. He is careful to extend the same conscientious effort that went into the writing process to the neatness and accuracy of his manuscript, for he thinks his ideas are significant, and he wants to convey that view by the appearance of his essay.

FINAL DRAFT

Primitives for the Present

1   What are at least one third of Americans doing with part of their leisure time? They are collecting anything and everything, from the expensive to the inexpensive, from the useful to the useless—typewriters, jukeboxes, fishing tackle, fruit-crate labels, Edsels. Collecting some things, like jukeboxes or Edsels, is both expensive and time-consuming. Yet the would-be collector with limited money or time need not feel left out, for collecting primitives is an inexpensive and practical way to decorate a home. Primitives are the common antique utensils associated with nineteenth-century rural life; handcrafted or homemade rather than manufactured, primitives may be wooden, pottery, or leather. But kitchen tools and farm implements—butter bowls, skillets, candlesticks, wooden

rakes, and scythes—most often come to mind. While they are relatively inexpensive, primitives reflect the tastes of the collector and complement modern lifestyles.

2   Compared to collecting fine furniture, collecting primitives costs little in either money or time. Like pieces of furniture, primitives were common to every household; yet they are still common—and thus less expensive than pieces of elaborate furniture. For example, a mahogany desk with inlaid panel doors may cost as much as five thousand dollars; while an iron teakettle with a porcelain finish may cost fifty. An afternoon spent cleaning great-grandmother's spoon set does not necessitate rescheduling the family vacation, but it does produce a grouping for the kitchen wall. Cleaning up an old horse collar is not a major project, but the result is a handsome mirror frame. Refinishing an oak keg won't mean cancelling the bowling league membership, but it does produce a rugged end table. Thus, collecting primitives is an economical pastime for anyone with limited money and time.

3   Collecting primitives suits not only modest budgets but also individual tastes. In fact, it allows for mass individuality. Unlike international corporations today, the small, independent companies of yesterday relied on the skills of their craftsmen. Because many companies made the same utensil, each company using a distinctive design (not to mention the work of self-employed

craftsmen), today duplication among collections is relatively rare. Collections of candlesticks, for example, may contain only a few of the same most common ones. One person might collect only brass candlesticks while another collects only pewter and a third collects candlesticks of all kinds.

4   At the same time that collectors are gathering pieces which suit their taste, they are also choosing items they can use in a distinctive way, though the use is sometimes not the original one. For instance, an old crock becomes a planter or a magazine holder (it may even be used to make pickles or sauerkraut); a patchwork quilt may become a chair cover or a wall hanging; a flat-iron, a door stop or a bookend. Thus, a collection of primitives defines the person who has assembled them; they are chosen and used according to the tastes of their owner.

5   Whether collectors prefer the sleekness of chrome and glass or the coziness of oak and calico, primitives add the novelty of another lifestyle. An iron dutch oven that was brought to the frontier in a wagon contrasts with a microwave flown in from Japan. A coal scuttle used as a magazine holder emphasizes the same contrast in an electrically heated living room. As preserving these articles from past life fills a need for variety, it also fills a need for continuity and tradition. There is security in a child's toy of cast

iron, a barrel with walls of three-inch oak, or hatracks made of brass--security which is missing in
today's disposable, plastic world. At once removed from
the present but a part of it, primitives satisfy
decorating and personnel needs.

6   To sum up, collecting primitives allows collectors
to be at once individuals with unique tastes and a part
of the cultural tradition from which their objects came.
Whether the primitives come from the best of times or
the worst, collectors delight in the history of these
objects and in the contrast they provide with the modern
world. Even as collectors dust and arrange, sort and
catalog, they are making room for more.

■ **Exercise 15** Revise the final draft of Shawn Redfield's
essay for emphasis and sentence variety. Notice, for example,
that every sentence except the first is declarative, and that all but
a few are either simple or complex. Try also to vary sentence
lengths. What other changes would you suggest? Finally, proofread for any errors in spelling, punctuation, grammar, and mechanics.

■ **Exercise 16** Prepare the final draft of your essay.

The Research Paper
33

Learn how to prepare a research paper.

A research paper (also called a library paper or term paper) is like a short expository composition (see Section **32**) in that it is an organized series of paragraphs developing a controlling idea or thesis. A research paper differs from a short composition in that it involves the use of library sources from which facts, quotations, and the opinions of others are drawn to explain, support, or authenticate ideas in the paper. These sources are identified in the text by parenthetical citations that refer the reader to an alphabetical list of all sources cited. This list of works cited concludes the paper.

The rules in this section describe the usual steps in the preparation of a research paper:

1. Selecting and limiting the subject
2. Preparing a preliminary bibliography
3. Developing the outline
4. Taking notes
5. Writing and documenting the paper

Each of these steps is illustrated in the preparation of a sample research paper, which is then given in full at the end of the section.

33a

Choose a subject that is suitable for a research paper and then limit it appropriately. See also 32a.

Not all subjects are suitable for a paper that relies on source materials found in the library. For example, you would probably find it difficult to document adequately a paper on your favorite childhood fantasies or on your opinions of an event so recent that little or nothing has yet been written on it.

Select a subject that you want to learn more about through reading. You might begin by selecting a general topic like literature, music, organic farming, cults, the media, or electronics.

Then start reading about your subject and decide what facets of it you could develop in a research paper. How much you limit your subject depends on the assigned length of the paper and on the availability and the adequacy of relevant books, newspapers, magazines, and so on. Below are examples of possible ways a general subject may be limited:

GENERAL   literature → fiction → futuristic novels

LIMITED   three futuristic novels: Orwell's *1984*, Huxley's *Brave New World*, Wells' *War of the Worlds*

MORE LIMITED   Big Brother (in *1984*) and Mustapha Mond (in *Brave New World*) as world controllers

EVEN MORE LIMITED   Big Brother's propaganda in the totalitarian world of *1984*

Note: You should be aware of the differences between a city or public library and a university or college library. A public library, which is designed for general use, contains mostly popular books and magazines. A university library is designed for research. It contains specialized journals, indexes, and critical works not found in a public library. For research papers, a university or college library is an indispensable tool.

■ **Exercise 1** Select a subject that would be suitable for a library paper. Then check the availability of materials. (If you cannot find enough books, periodicals, and so on, try another subject). As you skim through the information, perhaps beginning with an encyclopedia, single out facets of the subject that you would like to investigate further. Finally, limit the subject so that you can develop it in a paper of the assigned length.

33b

Making good use of the materials in the library, prepare a preliminary bibliography. Learn an acceptable form for bibliographical entries.

A preliminary bibliography contains information (titles, authors, dates, and so on) about the materials (books, magazines, newspapers, videotapes, audiodiscs, and so on) that you are likely to use as sources. Use the main catalog, indexes to periodicals, and reference books (as explained on the following pages) to make a preliminary bibliography by writing down the most promising titles you can find. Copy each title on a separate card (generally 3 × 5 inches) in an acceptable form: see page 432. You should keep these cards in alphabetical order until you complete your paper, adding useful titles as you find them and discarding those that prove useless. The final bibliography, to be typed at the end of your paper, will most often include only the works that help in the actual writing—usually only those cited in the text of your paper.

A computer-aided search generally saves time in preparing a preliminary bibliography. Check to see whether your library has a terminal, or "on-line" system, connected with data bases.

(1) Learn to use library catalogs.

When first established, libraries in America used a book catalog as the main index to library holdings, updating it with supplements. As the number of holdings grew larger, librarians began using a file of 3×5-inch cards for catalog purposes. In 1902, the Library of Congress started selling printed cards to libraries, and in time the card catalog replaced the book catalog.

SAMPLE CATALOG CARDS

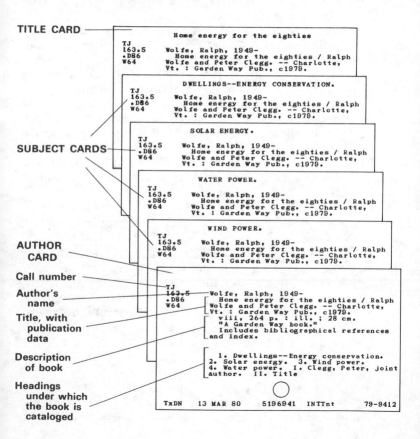

TITLE CARD

SUBJECT CARDS

AUTHOR CARD

Call number

Author's name

Title, with publication data

Description of book

Headings under which the book is cataloged

The card catalog

Still an active file in many libraries, the card catalog is the index to the whole library. It lists all books and all bound magazines, whether they are housed in the stacks, on the open shelves of the reference room, or in any other part of the building. In many libraries one general card catalog lists all books owned by the college or university and shows whether the book is in the general library or in a special collection in another building.

Usually the card catalog consists of cards arranged alphabetically in drawers. These may be "author" cards, "title" cards, or "subject" cards, for in most libraries each book is listed alphabetically in at least three places, once according to its author, again according to its title, and again according to its subject or subjects. These cards are identical except that the title card and the subject card have extra headings. As book collections in libraries mushroomed, the card catalog became costly and cumbersome. Since 1960, many libraries have turned to the microfilm or microfiche catalog, which photographically reproduces basically the same information found on the familiar cards.

The microfilm or microfiche catalog

When using a microfilm catalog housed in cartridges or cassettes, you need a microfilm viewer to read the record of library holdings. Since formats vary, you also need to find out if one alphabet covers all entries or if there are separate sections for author, title, and subject. Basically the microfiche catalog is the microfilm entry or record arranged in rows on small (usually 4 × 6 inches) sheets. As a rule, the microfiche catalog indexes authors, titles, and subjects separately.

A newer development in micrographics is the COM or Computer Output Microfilm catalog. Microimages on film are exact records of output from a computer. Formatted in different ways, the COM catalog is flexible and easy to use, although the user does need a microfilm or microfiche reader.

The computer catalog

Today, more and more college and university libraries are computerizing their library catalogs. To query the computer, students use typewriter-like terminals (located in the library and usually elsewhere on campus). By pressing a few lettered keys, users have instant access to information about an author, a title, a subject, an editor, and so on. The computer also indicates whether the library owns a particular work. Printouts provide copies of the information given on the video screen.

SAMPLE PRINTOUT

```
INT - FOR OTHER HOLDINGS, ENTER dh DEPRESS DISPLAY RECD SEND
  OCLC: 5196941      Rec stat: c Entrd: 790703      Used: 800523
Type: a Bib lvl: m Govt pub:    Lang: eng Source:    Illus: a
Repr:    Enc lvl:    Conf pub: 0 Ctry:  vtu Dat tp: s M/F/B: 10
Indx: 1 Mod rec:    Festschr: 0 Cont: b
Desc: i Int lvl:    Dates: 1979,
  1 010      79-9412
  2 040      DLC c DLC d OCL
  3 020      0882661582 : c $10.95
  4 050 0    TJ163.5.D86 b W64
  5 082      696
  6 049      INTT
  7 100 10   Wolfe, Ralph, d 1949-
  8 245 10   Home energy for the eighties / c Ralph Wolfe and Peter Clegg.
  9 260 0    Charlotte, Vt. : b Garden Way Pub., c c1979.
 10 300      viii, 264 p. : b ill. ; c 28 cm.
 11 500      "A Garden Way book."
 12 504      Includes bibliographical references and index.
 13 650 0    Dwellings x Energy conservation.
 14 650 0    Solar energy.
 15 650 0    Wind power.
 16 650 0    Water-power.
```

Note: After using the main catalog, you may wish to refer to the *Cumulative Book Index, Books in Print,* and *Paperbound Books in Print* to find titles that are closely related to your subject. Or you may wish to read what others have written about a book, perhaps one your library does not have, in the *Book Review Digest* or in a periodical referred to by a book such as *Book Review Index.*

(2) Use indexes to periodicals.

When preparing your bibliography, remember that the periodical indexes do for articles what the main catalog does for books in the library. You will probably find the *Readers' Guide to Periodical Literature* (an index to over one hundred periodicals) the most useful of these indexes. The front matter of each issue of the *Readers' Guide* provides an explanation of a sample entry as well as a key to abbreviations.

SUBJECT ENTRY
(May 10, 1980 issue)

Nineteen hundred and eighty-four
   Fighting 1984. M. Maddocks. Current 221:14–18 Mr/Ap '80
   Was Orwell right? D. Ingram. il World Press R 27:37–8 Mr '80

This issue contains an entry for George Orwell's *1984:* an illustrated article entitled "Was Orwell Right?" by D. Ingram—published in Vol. 27 of the *World Press Review* on pages 37–38 of the March 1980 issue.

PERSONAL NAME ENTRY
(March 1982–February 1983 issue)

Orwell, George
   Guest editorial [excerpt from The road to Wigan Pier] Natl
      Rev 34:212 Mr 5 '82
                        about
   Dear George Orwell: a personal letter. J. Wain. Am Sch
      52:21–37 Wint '82/'83
   Enigmas of power [excerpt from 1984 revisited] I. Howe. por
      New Repub 188 Sp Issue:27–32 Ja 3 '83

This entry for Orwell lists first an article by Orwell and then two articles about him. The article written by Orwell is excerpted from his 1937 novel *The Road to Wigan Pier*. The excerpt appears as a guest editorial in the March 5, 1982 issue of *National Review*. The volume number of this issue is 34; the page number of the excerpt is 212.

Indexes to Periodicals

General

Poole's Index. 1802–1907. (subject index only)
Nineteenth Century Readers' Guide. 1890–99. (author, subject)
Readers' Guide. 1900–. (author, title, subject)
New York Times Index. 1913–. (a useful guide for finding the dates of important events, which can then be looked up in the *Times*, often available on microfilm, or in other newspapers)

Special

Applied Science and Technology Index. 1958–. Formerly *Industrial Arts Index*. 1913–57.
Art Index. 1929–.
Biography Index. 1946–.
Biological and Agricultural Index. 1964–. Formerly *Agricultural Index*. 1916–64.
Business Periodicals Index. 1958–.
Current Index to Journals in Education. 1969–.
Education Index. 1929–.
Engineering Index. 1884–.
Humanities Index. 1974–. Formerly *Social Sciences and Humanities Index*. 1965–73. *International Index*. 1907–65.
Index to Legal Periodicals. 1908–.
Music Index. 1949–.
Public Affairs Information Service (Bulletin). 1915–.
Social Sciences Index. 1974–. Formerly *Social Sciences and Humanities Index*. 1965–73. *International Index*. 1907–65.
United States Government Publications (Monthly Catalogue). 1895–.
See also the various abstracts, such as *Chemical Abstracts*, 1907–; *Abstracts of English Studies*, 1958–; *Abstracts of Popular Culture*, 1976–.

(3) Use reference books.

Learn the general location of the chief classes of reference books in order that you may turn to them without loss of time. For a detailed list of such books, with a short description of each, consult *Guide to Reference Books* by Eugene P. Sheehy (formerly by Constance M. Winchell) and *American Reference Books Annual (ARBA)*, edited by Janet H. Littlefield. Since many reference books, especially some of the encyclopedias, are kept up to date by frequent revisions, you should remember to cite the latest copyright date of the edition you are using. A few of the more important reference books are listed on the following pages (with abbreviated bibliographical information).

Reference Books

General dictionaries (unabridged)

A Dictionary of American English on Historical Principles. 4 vols. 1938–44.

Century Dictionary and Cyclopedia. 12 vols. 1911. 3 vols. 1927–33.

New Standard Dictionary of the English Language. 1947, 1952, 1966.

The Oxford English Dictionary. 13 vols. 1933. Originally issued as *A New English Dictionary on Historical Principles.* 10 vols. and Supplement. 1888–1933. (Supplements)

The Random House Dictionary of the English Language. 1967.

Webster's Third New International Dictionary. 1961. (Supplement, 6000 words, 1976)

Special dictionaries

Cowie, A. P., and R. Mackin. *Oxford Dictionary of Current Idiomatic English.* Vol. I–. 1975–.

Fowler, H. W. *Dictionary of Modern English Usage.* 2nd ed. Rev. Sir Ernest Gowers. 1965.

Hayakawa, S. I., and the Funk & Wagnalls dictionary staff. *Modern Guide to Synonyms and Related Words.* 1968.

Mawson, C. O. S. *Dictionary of Foreign Terms.* 2nd ed. Rev. Charles Berlitz. 1975.

Morris, William, and Mary Morris. *Harper Dictionary of Contemporary Usage.* 1975.

Onions, C. T. *Oxford Dictionary of English Etymology.* 1967.

Partridge, Eric. *Dictionary of Catch Phrases.* 1979.

—————. *Dictionary of Slang and Unconventional English.* 7th ed. 1970.

Roget's International Thesaurus. 4th ed. 1977.

Webster's Collegiate Thesaurus. 1976.

Wentworth, Harold, and Stuart B. Flexner. *Dictionary of American Slang.* 2nd ed. 1975.

General encyclopedias

Academic American Encyclopedia. 21 vols.

Chambers's Encyclopaedia. 15 vols.

Collier's Encyclopedia. 24 vols.

Encyclopedia Americana. 30 vols.

Encyclopaedia Britannica. 30 vols.

Special encyclopedias

Adams, James T. *Dictionary of American History.* Rev. ed. 8 vols. 1976.

Cambridge Encyclopaedia of Astronomy. Ed. Simon Mitton. 1977.

Dictionary of the History of Ideas. Ed. Philip P. Wierner et al. 5 vols. 1973.

Encyclopedia of American Foreign Policy. Ed. Alexander De-Conde. 3 vols. 1978.

Encyclopedia of Computers and Data Processing. Vol. I–. 1978–.

Encyclopedia of Philosophy. Ed. Paul Edwards et al. 4 vols. 1973.

Encyclopedia of Psychology. 2nd ed. Ed. Hans Jurgen Eysenck et al. 1979.

Encyclopedia of World Art. 15 vols. 1959–68.

Focal Encyclopedia of Photography. Rev. ed. 1969.

Grzimek's Animal Life Encyclopedia. 13 vols. 1972–75.

International Encyclopedia of Higher Education. Ed. Asa K. Knowles. 10 vols. 1977.

International Encyclopedia of the Social Sciences. Ed. D. E. Sills. 17 vols. 1968. Supplements.

Klein, Barry, and D. Icolari. *Reference Encyclopedia of the American Indian.* 3rd ed. 1978.

Kurian, George Thomas. *Encyclopedia of the Third World.* 2 vols. 1978.

Langer, William L. *An Encyclopedia of World History.* 5th ed. 1972.

McGraw-Hill Encyclopedia of Science & Technology. 15 vols. 4th ed. 1977. Yearbooks.

Munn, Glenn G. *Encyclopedia of Banking and Finance.* 7th rev. ed. Ed. Ferdinand L. Garcia. 1973.

The New Grove Dictionary of Music and Musicians. Ed. Stanley Sadie. 20 vols. 1980.

Stierlin, Henri. *Encyclopedia of World Architecture.* 2 vols. 2nd ed. 1979.

Thompson, Oscar. *International Cyclopedia of Music and Musicians.* 10th ed. Rev. ed. [Ed. Bruce Bohle]. 1975.

Atlases

Commercial Atlas and Marketing Guide (Rand McNally). 1981.

Cosmopolitan World Atlas (Rand McNally). Rev. ed. 1978.

Hammond Medallion World Atlas. 1977.

National Geographic Atlas of the World. 4th ed. 1975.

Oxford Economic Atlas of the World. 4th ed. 1972.

The Times (London) Atlas of the World: Comprehensive Edition. 5th ed. 1975.

U.S. Department of the Interior Geological Survey. *The National Atlas of the United States of America.* 1970.

Yearbooks—current events

Americana Annual. 1923–.

Annual Register. 1758–.

Britannica Book of the Year. 1938–.

Facts on File. 1940–.

Information Please Almanac. 1947–.

Reader's Digest Almanac and Yearbook. 1966–.

Statesman's Year-Book. 1864–.

Statistical Abstract of the United States. 1878–.

World Almanac and Book of Facts. 1868–.

Biography

Contemporary Authors. 1962–.
Current Biography. 1940–.
Dictionary of American Biography. 16 vols. and index. 1927–80.
  Supplements.
Dictionary of National Biography (British). 22 vols. 1882–1953.
  Supplements.
Dictionary of Scientific Biography. 16 vols. 1970–80.
International Who's Who (London). 1935–.
McGraw-Hill Encyclopedia of World Biography. 12 vols. 1973.
Webster's Biographical Dictionary. 1976.
Who's Who in America. 1899–. [See also *Marquis Who's Who Publications: Index to All Books* (revised annually).]

Literature

Bartlett's Familiar Quotations. 15th ed. 1980.
Benét, William Rose. *The Reader's Encyclopedia.* 2nd ed. 1965.
Cambridge History of American Literature. 3 vols. in 1. 1943.
Cambridge History of English Literature. 15 vols. 1907–33.
Essay and General Literature Index. 1900–.
Evans, Bergen. *Dictionary of Quotations.* 1968.
Fiction Catalog. 9th ed. 1976. Supplements.
Fleischman, W. B. *Encyclopedia of World Literature in the 20th Century.* 4 vols. 1967–75.
Granger's Index to Poetry. 6th ed. 1973.
Hart, James D. *Oxford Companion to American Literature.* 4th ed. 1965.
Harvey, Sir Paul. *Oxford Companion to Classical Literature.* 2nd ed. 1937.
——————. *Oxford Companion to English Literature.* 4th ed. 1967.
Holman, C. Hugh. *Handbook to Literature.* 4th ed. 1980.
New Cambridge Bibliography of English Literature. 4 vols. 1973. Index, 1977.
Oxford Dictionary of Quotations. 3rd ed. 1979.
Play Index (Wilson). 1949–.
Seymour-Smith, Martin. *Funk and Wagnalls Guide to Modern World Literature.* 1975.

Short Story Index (Wilson). 1953. Supplements.

Smith, Horatio. *Columbia Dictionary of Modern European Literature.* 1947.

Spiller, Robert E., et al. *Literary History of the United States.* 4th ed. 2 vols. 1974.

(4) Use a standard bibliographical form.

Put each item of your bibliography on a separate card (preferably 3 × 5 inches) so that you can readily drop or add a card and can arrange the list alphabetically without recopying it. Follow exactly and consistently the bibliographical form you are instructed to use. By following that style from the start of your research, you can save yourself valuable time when, later, you must compile a formal list of works cited to appear at the end of your paper. The form illustrated by the samples on pages 433–40 follows the new guidelines of the Modern Language Association (MLA).

Bibliographical entries often consist of only three units, which are separated by periods:

```
Toffler, Alvin.  The Third Wave.  New York: Morrow,

     1980.
```

1. *Name of the author.* Give the last name first. Your final list of works cited will be arranged alphabetically by authors' last names.

2. *Title of the book.* Underline (italicize) the title, and capitalize it in accordance with **9c**. Always include the book's subtitle.

3. *Publication data.* Include the place of publication, the publisher, and the latest copyright date as shown on the copyright page. You may give a shortened form of the publisher's name as long as it is clear.

Some entries, however, require more than three units and must be given special treatment. As you study the following MLA-style bibliographical entries, which cover most of the special problems you are likely to encounter, observe both the punctuation and the arrangement of information. See also pages 441–43 for a list of abbreviations that are permissible in bibliographies, notes, and tables. Note that the MLA style favors Arabic numbers throughout and that such abbreviations as *vol.* and *sec.* are not capitalized.

Sample Bibliographical Entries

Books

One author

```
Bird, Caroline.  The Two-Paycheck Marriage: How Women
    at Work Are Changing Life in America.  New York:
    Rawson, 1979.
```

Notice that the subtitle is always included in bibliographical entries and that the underlining of the complete title is continuous.

```
Michener, James A.  Sports in America.  New York:
    Random, 1976.
```

The publisher's name (in this instance, Random House) is shortened as much as possible while remaining clearly identifiable.

Two authors

```
Cutlip, Scott M., and Allen H. Center.  Effective
    Public Relations.  5th ed.  Englewood Cliffs:
    Prentice, 1978.
```

Three authors

Aiken, Michael, Lewis A. Ferman, and Harold L.

     Sheppard. <u>Economic Failure, Alienation, and</u>

     <u>Extremism</u>. Ann Arbor: U of Michigan P, 1968.

More than three authors

Bailyn, Bernard, et al. <u>The Great Republic: A</u>

     <u>History of the American People</u>. Lexington:

     Heath, 1977.

Corporate author

American Red Cross. <u>Standard First Aid and Personal</u>

     <u>Safety</u>. 2nd ed. Garden City: Doubleday, 1979.

Edition after the first

Grout, Donald Jay. <u>A History of Western Music</u>. 3rd

     ed. New York: Norton, 1980.

See also sample bibliographical entries directly above and below.

Editors

Barnet, Sylvan, Morton Berman, and William Burto,

     eds. <u>An Introduction to Literature</u>. 7th ed.

     Boston: Little, 1981.

Story or article from an anthology

Bond, Nelson. "The Voice from the Curious Cube."

     <u>100 Great Science Fiction Short Stories</u>. Ed.

     Isaac Asimov, Martin Harry Greenberg, and Joseph

     D. Olander. New York: Doubleday, 1978. 172–75.

434

Translation

Laborit, Henri. <u>Decoding the Human Message</u>. Trans.

Stephen Bodington and Alison Wilson. New York:

St. Martin's, 1977.

Reprint

Sheehy, Gail. <u>Passages: Predictable Crises of Adult</u>

<u>Life</u>. 1976. New York: Bantam, 1977.

The original hard-cover edition was published a year earlier than this paperback version.

Zimmern, Alfred. <u>America and Europe and Other</u>

<u>Essays</u>. 1920. Freeport: Books for

Libraries, 1969.

A work in more than one volume

Odell, George C. D. <u>Annals of the New York Stage</u>.

15 vols. New York: Columbia UP, 1927–49.

The multivolume work was published over a period of years.

Sandburg, Carl. <u>Abraham Lincoln: The War Years</u>.

4 vols. New York: Harcourt, 1939.

The work consists of four volumes published in the same year.

A work in a series

Bebout, John E., and Ronald J. Grele. <u>Where Cities</u>

<u>Meet: The Urbanization of New Jersey</u>. New

Jersey Historical Series 22. Princeton: Van

Nostrand, 1964.

The volume number is given in Arabic numerals and without the abbreviation *vol.*

Gillin, John Lewis, et al. <u>Social Problems</u>. 3rd ed.

    Century Social Science Series. New York:

    Appleton, 1943.

Green, Otis Howard. <u>The Literary Mind of Medieval</u>

    <u>and Renaissance Spain</u>. Introd. John E. Keller.

    Studies in Romance Langs. 1. Lexington: UP of

    Kentucky, 1970.

Notice that a separate author wrote the introduction.

Magazines and newspapers

Unsigned article

"Fertilizing Trees and Shrubs." <u>Southern Living</u>

    Feb. 1980: 170–71.

As a rule, the names of months except May, June, and July are abbreviated.

Daily newspaper

"Study Labels Alcohol Fuel as Threat to Food Supply."

    <u>Dallas Times Herald</u> 16 Mar. 1980, sec. A: 14.

When not part of the newspaper's name, the city's name should be given in brackets after the title. Column numbers are not used.

Weekly magazine or newspaper

Clark, Matt, Sharon Begley, and Mary Hager. "The

    Miracles of Spliced Genes." <u>Newsweek</u> 17 Mar.

    1980: 62–71.

Munro, Julie W. "A New Elitism in China?" <u>Chronicle</u>

    <u>of Higher Education</u> 28 Nov. 1977: 3–4.

Notice that no period is used with the question mark (or with an exclamation point) after a title.

Monthly magazine
Frohlich, Cliff. "The Physics of Somersaulting and

  Twisting." <u>Scientific American</u> Mar. 1980:

  154-64.

Journal—continuous pagination
Wurmser, Leon. "Drug Abuse: Nemesis of Psychiatry."

  <u>American Scholar</u> 41 (1972): 393-407.

The pages of the journal issues are numbered continuously throughout each year.

Journal—separate pagination
Graham, Loren R. "Concerns about Science and

  Attempts to Regulate Inquiry." <u>Daedalus</u> 107

  (1978): 1-21.

The pages of each issue of the journal are numbered separately. An issue number follows a volume number, separated by a period: *NEA Journal* 55.3 (1966): 35.

Editorial
"Elections in Rhodesia." Editorial. <u>San Francisco

  Chronicle</u> 5 Mar. 1980: 64.

Book review
Wolfe, Alan. "Turning Economics to Dust." Rev. of

  <u>Free to Choose: A Personal Statement</u>, by Milton

  and Rose Friedman. <u>Saturday Review</u> 2 Feb.

  1980: 35-36.

437

Note: Sometimes a magazine article is printed on pages that are separated by other articles; for example, the first part appears on pages 137–39, the last on pages 188–203. In such a case, give only the first page number followed by a "plus" sign: 137+.

Encyclopedias and almanacs

Signed with name or initials

Allen, Frederick G. "Leyden Jar." <u>Encyclopedia

Americana</u>. 1977 ed.

Full publication information is not required for a familiar reference work.

R[asmussen], J[ohn] O., [Jr.] "Radioactivity."

<u>Encyclopaedia Britannica: Macropaedia</u>. 1974 ed.

Brackets enclose the added parts of the name. A list of contributors is ordinarily supplied in the index volume or in the front matter of an encyclopedia.

Unsigned

"Language: New Words." <u>Reader's Digest Almanac

and Yearbook</u>. 1980 ed.

In this almanac main sections (like "Language") are arranged alphabetically in the text.

"Portsmouth, Treaty of." <u>Columbia Encyclopedia</u>.

1975 ed.

The title indicates that the article is listed under *P.*

"Pulitzer Prizes in Journalism, Letters, and Music."

<u>World Almanac and Book of Facts</u>. 1979 ed.

409–14.

Notice that page numbers are supplied for ease of reference, though the front matter of this almanac does list topics alphabetically.

Pamphlets and bulletins

Safety Data Sheet—Kitchen Machines.   Pamphlet 690.

    Chicago: Natl. Restaurant Assn., 1970.

Titles of pamphlets are italicized (underlined).

United States.   Bureau of Labor Statistics.   Tomorrow's

    Manpower Needs.   Washington: GPO, 1973.

Notice the sequence for a government publication: government, agency, title—each followed by a period and two spaces. The publisher in this example is the Government Printing Office.

Unpublished dissertation

Woodall, Guy Ramon.   "Robert Walsh, Jr., as an Editor

    and Literary Critic: 1797–1836."   Diss. U of

    Tennessee, 1966.

Micropublications

Document a book or periodical photographically reproduced in miniature form as though the work were in its original form. Rarely is it necessary to refer to a microform as such in a list of works cited.

Nonprint sources

Motion picture

The Empire Strikes Back.   Twentieth—Century Fox,

    1980.

Television or radio program

"Paul's Case." <u>The American Short Story</u>. PBS.

WNET, New York. 11 Feb. 1980.

White, Jim. <u>At Your Service</u>. KMOX, St. Louis. 13

Mar. 1981.

Stage play

<u>Morning's at Seven</u>. Lyceum Theatre, New York. 16

Apr. 1980.

Recording

Newhart, Bob. "Merchandising the Wright Brothers."

<u>The Button-Down Mind of Bob Newhart</u>. Warner

Bros., WS 137, 1960.

Lecture

Dumas, Annette. "Shirley Jackson's "The Lottery.'"

Fine Arts Lecture Series. Mount St.

Clare College, Clinton. 15 Feb. 1981.

Interview

Young, Mary W. Personal interview. 22 Oct. 1981.

For samples of citations of other nonprint sources—such as games, globes, filmstrips, microscope slides, and transparencies—consult Eugene B. Fleischer's *A Style Manual for Citing Microform and Nonprint Media* (Chicago: American Library Association, 1978).

Note: Although the final form may not be required for preliminary-bibliography cards, it is a helpful practice to use from the beginning a complete form that is appropriate for the final bibliography. (You may wish to add a call number to help you relocate a book in the library.)

BIBLIOGRAPHY CARDS

Kanfer, Stefan. "Orwell 25 Years Later: Future Imperfect." _Time_ 24 March 1975: 77-78.

Meyers, Jeffrey. _A Reader's Guide to George Orwell_. Totowa: Littlefield, 1977.

PR
6029
.R8
Z737
1977

COMMON ABBREVIATIONS

Below is a list of abbreviations commonly used in bibliographies, tables, or notes (but not the text) of research papers.

abr.	abridged, abridgment
Acad.	Academy
anon.	anonymous
app.	appendix
Apr.	April
Assn.	Association
Aug.	August

441

biog.	biography, biographer, biographical
bk., bks.	book, books
bull.	bulletin
c.	*circa,* "about" (for example, "c. 1966")
cf.	compare
ch., chs.	chapter, chapters
col., cols.	column, columns
Coll.	College
comp.	compiled by, compiler
Cong. Rec.	*Congressional Record*
cont.	contents; continued
DAB	*Dictionary of American Biography*
Dec.	December
dept.	department
dir.	directed by, director
diss.	dissertation
div.	division
DNB	*Dictionary of National Biography*
ed., eds.	edition(s) OR editor(s)
enl.	enlarged (as in "rev. and enl. ed.")
et al.	*et alii,* "and others"
Feb.	February
fig.	figure
fwd.	foreword, foreword by
gen. ed.	general editor
govt.	government
GPO	Government Printing Office
HR	House of Representatives
illus.	illustrated by, illustrator, illustration
inc.	incorporated, including
Inst.	Institute, Institution
intl.	international
introd.	[author of] introduction, introduced by
Jan.	January
jour.	journal
mag.	magazine
Mar.	March
ms., mss.	manuscript, manuscripts
n, nn	note, notes (used immediately after page number: 6n3)

natl.	national
n.d.	no date [of publication]
no., nos.	number [of issue], numbers
Nov.	November
n.p.	no place [of publication], no publisher
n. pag.	no pagination
Oct.	October
P	Press (used in documentation; see "UP")
p., pp.	page, pages (omitted before page numbers unless reference would be unclear)
pref.	preface, preface by
pseud.	pseudonym
pt., pts.	part, parts
rept.	reported by, report
rev.	revision, revised, revised by OR review, reviewed by
rpt.	reprinted, reprint
sec., secs.	section, sections
Sept.	September
ser.	series
Soc.	Society
supp.	supplement
trans.	translated by, translator, translation
U	University (used in documentation; see "UP")
UP	University Press (used in documentation: Wesleyan UP)
vol., vols.	volume, volumes (omitted before volume numbers unless reference would be unclear)

Standard two-letter postal abbreviations for states (such as *CA* for California, *KY* for Kentucky) and standard abbreviations for countries (*Gt. Brit.* for Great Britain, *Mex.* for Mexico).

Spell out *and* rather than use &, even when the ampersand appears in the title: *U.S. News and World Report.*

■ **Exercise 2** Select a subject (the one you chose for Exercise 1 on page 422 or a different one) and prepare a preliminary bibliography. (Often you will find helpful bibliographies in the books that you consult, especially in encyclopedias and other reference works.)

Varying Styles of Documentation

Each department of a college or university ordinarily suggests a particular style for bibliographies and citations. As previously stated, the style of the Modern Language Association is used for the bibliographical and citation models on pages 433–40 and 459–66 and in the sample research paper (pages 472–512), and you may use that style unless your instructor specifies a different one. Instructors in the sciences, business, economics, and so forth, may recommend a documentation form in one of the style books listed below, which are available in most university and public libraries. If you are asked to use one of these manuals, study it carefully, and make sure your bibliography and notes correspond exactly to the examples it provides. Following the list are some examples of documentation in the style of the American Psychological Association (APA), a style commonly used in the social and behavioral sciences.

Style books and manuals

American Institute of Physics. Publications Board. *Style Manual for Guidance in the Preparation of Papers.* 3rd ed. New York: American Inst. of Physics, 1978.

American Chemical Society. *Handbook for Authors of Papers in American Chemical Society Publications.* Washington: American Chemical Soc., 1980.

American Mathematical Society. *A Manual for Authors of Mathematical Papers.* 7th ed. Providence: American Mathematical Soc., 1980.

American Psychological Association. *Publication Manual of the American Psychological Association.* 3rd ed. Washington: American Psychological Assn., 1983.

Associated Press. *The Associated Press Stylebook.* Dayton: Lorenz, 1980.

Council of Biology Editors. Style Manual Committee. *CBE Style Manual: A Guide for Authors, Editors, and Publishers in the Biological Sciences.* 5th ed. Bethesda: Council of Biology Editors, 1983.

Harvard Law Review. *A Uniform System of Citation.* 12th ed. Cambridge: Harvard Law Review Assn., 1976.

Turabian, Kate L. *A Manual for Writers of Term Papers, Theses, and Dissertations.* 4th ed. Chicago: U of Chicago P, 1973.

United States. Government Printing Office. *Style Manual.* Rev. ed. Washington: GPO, 1973.

References in APA style

In APA style, the alphabetical list of works cited is called "References." The reference entries below follow the style of the 1983 edition of the APA *Publication Manual.* Carefully observe all details of indentation, spacing, punctuation, and mechanics.

Book—one author

Liptz, A. (1979). <u>Prisons as social structures</u>. Los

   Angeles: Scholarly Press.

Book—two authors

Klein, D. F. & Wender, P. H. (1981). <u>Mind, mood,

   and medicine: A guide to the new biological

   psychiatry</u>. New York: Farrar, Straus & Giroux.

Journal—one author

Pinker, S. (1980). Mental imagery and the third

   dimension. <u>Journal of Experimental Psychology:

   General</u>, <u>109</u>, 354–71.

Journal—multiple authors

Johnson, M. K., Raye, C. L., Hasher, L., & Chromiak,

   W. (1979). Are there developmental differences

   in reality monitoring? Journal of Experimental

   Child Psychology, 27, 120, 128.

33c

Make a preliminary outline and develop it as you take notes on readings and as you write your research paper. See also 32f.

After completing a preliminary bibliography and a minimum of general reading on your subject (an encyclopedia article and parts of one or two other works may suffice), make a preliminary outline that will give direction to your investigation. The outline will enable you to discard irrelevant material from your bibliography and to begin spotting valuable passages on which you will want to take notes. If you attempt to take notes without first knowing what you are looking for, your efforts will lead only to frustration.

Be careful, however, not to adhere too rigidly to your preliminary outline. For although the outline will direct your reading, your reading will almost certainly suggest ways in which the outline may be improved. No outline should be regarded as complete until the research paper has been finished. As you take notes, you will probably revise your original outline frequently, adding subheadings to it, changing subheadings to major headings, perhaps dropping some headings entirely.

You may wish to compare the form and the content of the following preliminary outline with that of the final outline on pages 475 and 477.

Preliminary Outline

Big Brother and His Propaganda Machine

<u>Thesis</u>: Used just for the sake of power, BB's
propaganda is a particularly dangerous type.

George Orwell as propagandist and <u>1984</u> as propaganda

1. BB's totalitarian government related to
   propaganda:
   Its impact on Oceanians
   Their Leader—propagandist myth
   Pyramidal power structure
   Political machinery—the ministries
2. BB's use of propaganda to get uniformity
   Totally controls media
   History falsified
3. Newspeak—related to propaganda
   Why
   How
4. Main teachings of BB's propaganda:
   Love BB and hate his enemies.
   All else falls into place—no need to fear!

33d

Learn how to prepare a final outline.

Once you have developed and revised your preliminary outline as part of the process of organizing information, you are ready to select one of the conventional outline forms with standard notation so that your final outline shows the relationship of your main ideas and supporting information to the thesis.

First decide whether to use a topic outline, a sentence outline, or a paragraph outline. A topic outline presents information in parallel phrases or single words (see pages 473 and 475). A sentence outline presents the same ideas in complete grammatically parallel declarative statements (see pages 469–470). And a paragraph outline presents ideas in paragraph form.

PARAGRAPH OUTLINE

Big Brother's Propaganda

<u>Thesis</u>: Big Brother disseminates the most dangerous kind of propaganda.

<u>Introduction</u>: In <u>Nineteen Eighty-Four</u>, Orwell (a propagandist) satirizes totalitarian propaganda as he presents his vision of life—in reverse.

   I. The Oceanians are propaganda targets. They act like a stupid herd, and they revere a mythical leader. They even accept the hierarchy in a "classless" society.

II. Big Brother's bureaucracy serves as a propaganda machine. Its housing is a symbol, and its parts are interrelated.

III. Big Brother has complete control of the media. He supplies all materials, and he propagates the Party's ideal.

IV. The State falsifies history to control the past and make it fit the present. Winston's use of the memory hole and the clerks' rectifying old propaganda are evidence of this efficient, systematic, frightening attack on the past.

V. Totalitarian propaganda manipulates thought and emotion. Just as the State uses Newspeak to prevent thought, it also controls love and hate by teaching love for Big Brother and hate for his enemies.

Conclusion: Much of Big Brother's propaganda is outdated, but Nineteen Eighty-Four is still widely read as a warning.

Formal outlines use a system of notation that divides ideas and ranks them according to their level of importance. In the humanities, this system consists of Roman numerals, capital letters, Arabic numerals, and lower-case letters. Thus, for instance, ideas numbered with Roman numerals are of equal rank; they are also more important than ideas lettered A and B. The equality and relative importance of ideas are also shown by indention. Major ideas are flush with the left margin with each succeeding level indented as shown below:

Thesis:
I. Major idea
   A. Supporting idea
      1. Example or illustration for supporting idea
      2. Example or illustration for supporting idea
         a. Detail for example or illustration
         b. Detail for example or illustration
   B. Supporting idea
II. Major idea

Notice that:

1. The thesis statement is not marked with a Roman numeral because it is the single most important idea in the essay; it therefore has no equal.

2. The closer to the left margin an idea is, the more important it is.

3. At least two parts are required for the division of ideas at every level used.

4. Ideas at each level are cast in grammatically parallel structures, but it is not necessary to have parallel structure between levels. (See Section **26**.)

As you can see, the form of an outline—the system of notation, the pattern of indention, and the parallel structure within ranks—emphasizes the order of and relationships among ideas.

As mentioned earlier, the system of numbers and letters discussed above is used for papers in the humanities. In the social and behavioral sciences, physical sciences, business, and engineering, a system of Arabic numerals alone is preferred:

1. Major idea
    1.1 Supporting idea
    1.2 Supporting idea
        1.2.1 Example or illustration for supporting idea
        1.2.2 Example or illustration for supporting idea
            1.2.2.1 Detail for example or illustration
            1.2.2.2 Detail for example or illustration

As you can see, both systems of notation emphasize the order of ideas and the relationships among them. Both are designed to provide a blueprint for the paper, and both serve as a table of contents for the reader.

33e

Take notes on readings (after evaluating the sources).

As you take notes on your readings, learn how to find and evaluate useful passages with a minimum of time and effort. Seldom will a whole book, or even a whole article, be of use as subject matter for any given research paper. To get what is needed for your paper, you will find that you must turn to many books and articles, rejecting most of them altogether and using from others only a section here and there. You cannot take the time to read each book completely. Use the table of contents and the index of a book, and learn to skim the pages rapidly until you find the passages you need.

One important consideration always is the reliability of the source. Do others speak of the writer as an authority? As you read, do you find evidence that the author is competent, well-informed, not prejudiced in any way? Is the work recent enough to provide up-to-date information? Is the edition the latest one available? Use your best judgment to determine the most dependable sources for your paper. You may find in the *Book Review Digest* convenient summaries of critical opinion on a book in your bibliography.

One of the best ways to take notes is on cards of uniform size, preferably 4 × 6 inches. (A smaller card may be used for the bibliography.) Each card must show the source of the note, including the exact page from which it is drawn. (When information is taken from more than one page, be sure to indicate in your notes exactly where one page ends and another begins.) It is a good idea to put a single note on one card (or ideas from a single source on a set of cards) with a heading keyed to a word or phrase in the outline. You can then easily arrange your note cards as you make changes in organization.

BIBLIOGRAPHY CARD WITH SOURCE

Voorhees, Richard J. *The Paradox of George Orwell*. Humanities Series. Lafayette: Purdue U Studies, 1961.

SOURCE (from page 87)

From the middle thirties until his death Orwell was a propagandist harping on the significance of totalitarianism because he knew that thousands upon thousands of people in democratic countries were only remotely aware of it, and still more thousands thought that there was a lot to be said for it in one form or another. *Nineteen Eighty-Four* is his fiercest piece of propaganda.

NOTE CARD

Orwell as propagandist (introduction)
(Voorhees 87)

Orwell a propagandist from mid 1930s on —
Kept "harping on" totalitarianism.

Why? He knew many people didn't know about
its evils.

"_Nineteen Eighty-Four_ is his fiercest piece of
propaganda."

For other examples of note cards, see pages 484, 486, 498.

Another way to take notes is to use regular notebook paper, perhaps adding photocopies of short excerpts from materials you think you may quote directly. On a photocopy you may mark quotable material and jot down your own ideas as you study the source.

PHOTOCOPIED SOURCE WITH NOTES

from Vol. IV - Orwell's Essays

Politics and the English Language (137) ✓

covering up all the details. The great enemy of clear language is
insincerity. When there is a gap between one's real and one's declared   NEWSPEAK
aims, one turns as it were instinctively to long words and exhausted
idioms, like a cuttlefish squirting out ink. <u>In our age there is no such</u>
<u>thing as "keeping out of politics". All issues are political issues, and</u>
<u>politics itself is a mass of lies, evasions, folly, hatred and schizo-</u> ← 1984
<u>phrenia.</u> When the general atmosphere is bad, language must suffer. ✓
I should expect to find—this is a guess which I have not sufficient
knowledge to verify—that the German, Russian and Italian languages
have all deteriorated in the last ten or fifteen years, as a result of
dictatorship. → *like Big Brother's*
[But] <u>if thought corrupts language, language can also corrupt</u>   debatable
thought. A bad usage can spread by tradition and imitation, even } BUT
among people who should and do know better. The debased lan-   quotable
guage that I have been discussing is in some ways very convenient.

Direct quotations

Any quotations that you use in your paper should be convincing and important ones. They should be made an integral part of your text. (For examples of ways this can be
done, see pages 479, 487.) When you discover a quotable
passage in your reading, you should take it down verba-
tim—that is, copy every word, every capital letter, and
every mark of punctuation exactly as in the original. Be sure
to enclose the quoted passage in quotation marks. When you
are quoting, quote accurately. When you are not quoting,
use your own sentence structure and phraseology, not a
slightly altered version of your source. Any conscious quotation (except well-known or proverbial passages) of the words

of another should be placed inside quotation marks (or indented if over four lines in length), and exact sources should
be cited.

In <u>Nineteen Eighty–Four</u>, Orwell defines <u>doublethink</u>

as "the power of holding two contradictory beliefs in

one's mind simultaneously, and accepting both of

them" (215).

[Quotation marks enclose copied words, and internal documentation indicates the source.]

For other examples of the use and the documentation of
direct quotations, see the sample research paper on pages
472–511.

As you write your research paper, keep a few guidelines in
mind when you are quoting the exact words of another. Pay
close attention to form, punctuation, and spacing: see **16a**.
Use periods appropriately to indicate ellipsis: see **17i**. But do
not use ellipsis periods before quotations that are only parts
of sentences. To avoid these periods at the beginning of a
quotation (especially one that begins a paragraph), use a
word like *that* or an introductory word group before the
quotation. You may use a period to end a quotation that is a
grammatically complete sentence, even though the source
may have a semicolon or another mark of punctuation.

Paraphrase

A paraphrase is a restatement of the source in about the
same number of words. As you compare the source on the
next page with the paraphrase that follows, notice differences in sentence structure and word choice.

SOURCE (from *Propaganda* by Jacques Ellul)

> The aim of modern propaganda is no longer to modify ideas, but to provoke action. It is no longer to change adherence to a doctrine, but to make the individual cling irrationally to a process of action.

PARAPHRASE

Jacques Ellul states that modern propaganda does not try any longer to change a person's ideas or loyalties to certain principles; instead, it seeks to make individuals irrationally follow a given procedure (25).

For further examples of the use and documentation of paraphrases in a research paper, see pages 500–01.

Précis

A précis is a concise summary (shorter than the source). When you make a paraphrase or write a précis, avoid copying not only the actual words but also the writer's style or sentence structure. If you cannot do this, much of the material may be worth quoting directly.

SOURCE (from *Nineteen Eighty-Four* by George Orwell)

> . . . the subtlest practitioners of *doublethink* are those who invented *doublethink* and know that it is a vast system of mental cheating. In our society, those who have the best knowledge of what is happening are also those who are furthest from seeing the world as it is. In general, the greater the understanding, the greater the delusion: the more intelligent, the less sane.

PRÉCIS

As Orwell observed in <u>Nineteen Eighty—Four</u>, it is the
inventors of doublethink who are best at using their
brand of "mental cheating." In modern times, he
contends, even the best—informed do not see
realities; generally speaking, "the greater the
understanding, the greater the delusion: the more
intelligent, the less sane" (216).

■ **Exercise 3** Carefully read paragraphs 1 (page 347) and 20
(page 359) in Section 31. First write a paraphrase of one of these
paragraphs. Then write a précis of the same paragraph. Unless
you are quoting directly, avoid using the sentence patterns of the
source. To convey the ideas in the source exactly, choose your
words carefully.

PLAGIARISM

You must acknowledge all material quoted, paraphrased, or
summarized from any work. If you fail to cite a source,
whether deliberately or accidentally, you are guilty of plagiarism—of presenting as your own work the words or ideas
of another. As the most recent edition of the *MLA Handbook*
(New York: Modern Language Assn., 1984) states:

> The most blatant form of plagiarism is to repeat as your
> own someone else's sentences, more or less verbatim. . . .
> Other forms of plagiarism include repeating someone else's
> particularly apt phrase without appropriate acknowledg-

ment, paraphrasing another person's argument as your own, and presenting another's line of thinking as though it were your own. (sec. 1.6)

After you have done a good deal of reading about a given subject, you will be able to distinguish between common knowledge in that field—facts, dates, and figures—and the distinctive ideas or interpretations of specific writers. When you use the ideas or information that these writers provide, be sure to cite the exact source of the material used.

NOT In *Nineteen Eighty-Four*, doublethink is defined as the power of holding two contradictory beliefs in one's mind simultaneously, and accepting both of them. [undocumented copying]

BUT In *Nineteen Eighty-Four*, Orwell defines doublethink as "the power of holding two contradictory beliefs in one's mind simultaneously, and accepting both of them" (215). [Quotation marks enclose copied words, and the page number in parentheses cites the source.]

NOT In fact, *Nineteen Eighty-Four* is Orwell's most ferocious propaganda. [an undocumented idea from the work of another writer]

BUT In fact, *Nineteen Eighty-Four* has been called Orwell's most ferocious propaganda (Voorhees 87).
OR
In fact, Richard J. Voorhees states: "*Nineteen Eighty-Four* is his [Orwell's] fiercest piece of propaganda" (87).

If you are in doubt about whether you need to cite a source, the best policy is to cite it.

33f
**Using the outline, the bibliography cards, and the
notes, write a properly documented research paper.**

After you have made your outline as complete as possible
and have taken notes on major headings and subheadings of
the outline, you are ready to begin writing. Arrange your
notes in the order of the outline, and then use them as the
basis of your paper. Naturally you will need to expand some
parts and to cut others, and you will need to provide transitional sentences—sometimes even transitional paragraphs.
Write the material in the best way you can—in your own
style, in your own words.

(1) Citations

Since the material in your research paper comes largely
from the work of others, you will need to give proper credit
by citing your sources. Traditionally, such citations took the
form of notes numbered consecutively throughout the paper
and placed either at the bottoms of the appropriate pages
(footnotes) or all together at the end of the paper (endnotes).
Beginning in 1984, however, the practice recommended by
the Modern Language Association is to place citations of
sources directly in the text, in parentheses. Numbered notes
are now used only for supplementary or explanatory comments (as in note 1 on page 487). Parenthetical citations refer the reader to a list of works cited at the end of the paper.

The basic elements of the citation are the author's last
name, a shortened but easily understood form of the title
(with, if necessary, the volume number), and the page number of the material used from the source. However, only
enough information to guide the reader to the appropriate
source is necessary. In other words, the author's name and
the title of the source can be omitted from the parenthetical
citation if they are clearly identified outside the parentheses

in the text of the paper. Further, if only one work by a given author is listed in "Works Cited," the work's title can be omitted from the parenthetical citation. As you study the following examples, observe that common sense rather than hard and fast rules determines the information that must be included in a parenthetical citation.

A work by one author

The following examples from the research paper on pages 473–511 provide sufficient information to refer readers to the appropriate pages of the works listed alphabetically in the list of works cited at the end of the paper.

> <u>Nineteen Eighty–Four</u> has been called George
> Orwell's most ferocious propaganda (Voorhees 87).
> Orwell was quick to admit that he was a propagandist.
> In fact, in 1940, during a BBC radio broadcast, he
> said that "every artist is a propagandist in the
> sense that he is trying, directly or indirectly, to
> impose a vision of life that seems to him desirable"
> (<u>Essays</u> 2: 41).

In the first citation, the author is not identified in the text and his name therefore appears within parentheses. Because only one work by Voorhees is included in the list of works cited, there is no need to use the title in the parentheses. However, the reference to a specific passage and not to the Voorhees work as a whole requires citing the page number.

In the second citation, Orwell has been identified in the text of the paper as the source of the quotation and need not be named in the citation. However, since Orwell is the author of three works appearing in the list of works cited, the title (shortened) is necessary. Further, because this work comprises four volumes, the volume number must be given as well as the specific page of the quotation.

Both citations supply only the information the reader needs to identify the source, but suppose the opening sentence were worded differently, as in the following example. Notice the information that must change for the citations to be complete.

> <u>Nineteen Eighty-Four</u>—unquestionably a work of art—supports the argument that "every artist is a propagandist in the sense that he is trying, directly or indirectly, to impose a vision of life that to him seems desirable" (Orwell, <u>Essays</u> 2: 41). The critic Richard Voorhees has called the novel Orwell's most ferocious propaganda (87), suggesting that Orwell believed in the forceful if indirect imposition of his own values.

Observe that although the same sources as before are cited, Orwell must now be identified as the author of the direct quotation, and Voorhees, now named in the actual text of the second sentence, needs no further mention in the citation.

Suppose that the text of the first sentence of this example had been written differently and provided additional information about the source, as in the following version.

> In the second volume of his <u>Collected Essays</u>, Orwell suggests that "every artist is a propagandist in the sense that he is trying, directly or

indirectly, to impose a vision of life that to him

seems desirable" (41).

Because author, title, and volume are clear from the context, the citation is simply a page number.

A work by two authors

By cleverly manipulating carefully selected facts,

propagandists today either ignore or downplay any

evidence that might effectively refute their one—

sided arguments—the old card—stacking trick (Cantril

and Hart).

Both authors are included in the parenthetical citation. Note, incidentally, that this citation of an encyclopedia article does not require a page reference, since encyclopedias are arranged alphabetically and a reader would have no trouble locating the source.

A work by three authors

If you are citing a source by three authors, supply the names of all three.

During the 1960s, economic failure was widely blamed

for social alienation and political extremism (Aiken,

Ferman, and Sheppard).

The absence of a page number in this citation indicates that the reference is to an entire work rather than to a specific passage (see page 434 for the corresponding bibliographic entry).

More than three authors

If you are citing a source by more than three authors, supply the name of the first author and follow the name with *et al.*, the Latin abbreviation for "and others."

These arguments have occasionally been challenged by

leading historians (Bailyn et al.).

Works by different authors with the same last name

Occasionally your list of works cited will contain sources by two authors with the same last name—for example, Joan Johnson and Jerome Johnson (imaginary sources included here only for illustration). In such cases, whenever mention of an author's name is required, you must use the first name as well as the last.

At least one critic has observed that Orwell became

less bitter as he grew older (Joan Johnson 14–16).

The critic Joan Johnson has suggested that "with

age, Orwell became increasingly optimistic" (14–16).

However, others have disagreed strongly (Jerome

Johnson 286, 291).

Notice also in these examples the treatment of references to more than one page: 14-16 identifies continuous pages; 286, 291 indicates that the reference is to two separate pages.

Poetry, drama, and the Bible

When you refer to poetry, drama, and the Bible, you must often give numbers of lines, acts, and scenes, or of chapters and verses, rather than page numbers. This practice enables a reader to consult an edition other than the one you are using. Nonetheless, your list of works cited should still identify your edition.

Act, scene, and line numbers (all Arabic) are separated by periods with no space before or after them. Biblical chapters and verses are treated similarly. In both cases, the progression is from larger to smaller units.

The following example illustrates a typical citation of lines of poetry.

```
Emily Dickinson concludes "I'm Nobody! Who Are You?"

with a characteristically bittersweet stanza:

     How dreary to be somebody!

     How public, like a frog

     To tell your name the livelong June

     To an admiring bog!   (5-8)
```

The following citation shows that Hamlet's "To be, or not to be" soliloquy appears in Act 3, Scene 1, lines 56-89 of *Hamlet*.

```
In Hamlet Shakespeare presents the most famous

soliloquy in the history of the theater: "To be, or

not to be . . ." (3.1.56-89).
```

The following reference to the Bible indicates that the account of creation in Genesis extends from chapter 1, verse 1, through chapter 2, verse 22.

```
The Old Testament creation story (Gen. 1.1-2.22),

told with remarkable economy, culminates in the

arrival of Eve.
```

Notice that names of books of the Bible are neither under-lined (italicized) nor enclosed in quotation marks and that abbreviation is desirable.

Punctuation and mechanics

Notice finally that in all the foregoing citations, punctuation is minimal. Commas are used to separate authors' names and titles (Orwell, *Essays*) and to indicate interruptions in a sequence of pages or lines (44, 47). Hyphens are used to indicate continuous sequences of pages (44–47) and lines (1–4). Colons separate volume and page numbers (*Essays* 2: 41). A space follows the colon. Periods separate acts, scenes, and lines in drama (3.1.56–89) and chapters and verses in the Bible (Gen. 1.1).

Citations should, wherever possible, appear just before punctuation in the text of the paper.

Joan Johnson has suggested that Orwell became less

bitter as he grew older (14–16), but Jerome Johnson

takes issue with this suggestion and argues that the

author's pessimism expanded from "personal complaint

to global despair" (286).

Joan Johnson's citation falls just before a comma, Jerome Johnson's just before a period. However, in the following sentence the citations cannot precede punctuation.

Joan Johnson (14–16) and Jerome Johnson (286, 291)

disagree over Orwell's gradually brightening

outlook.

In quotations set off from the text (see section **16a**), citations follow the final punctuation.

As Ralph A. Ranald has observed,

> Orwell's <u>1984</u> is about religion reversed,
> and above all, language reversed: not simply
> corrupt, but reversed. . . . [Orwell
> converts] all the positives of Western
> civilization into their negatives. (544–45)

Citations in APA style

In APA style (as in MLA style) parenthetical citations are used. The basic elements of APA citations are the author's last name, the year of publication, and the page number if the reference is to a specific passage in the source. If the author's name is mentioned in the text of the paper, the date alone or the date and the page number are given within the parentheses. In the following examples, note the details of punctuation and the treatment of the page number.

Short quotation

> One writer has stated, "Prisons can be divided
> into specific social groups organized by type of
> crime" (Liptz, 1979, p. 235), an observation with
> which many criminologists agree.

Long quotation (*four lines or more*)

> Liptz (1979) has stated the following:

> Prisons can be divided into specific social
> groups organized by types of crime. Social

```
structures reflecting theft, arson, white-collar

crime, and so on, were discovered within the

prison walls.  (p. 235)
```

Paraphrase

```
    Liptz (1979) discovered that the social groups

established by prisoners within a prison are

organized according to the type of crime.  For

example, thieves tend to congregate and so do

arsonists. (p. 235)
```

Notice that an APA citation never uses the title. The reader can easily find the title, however, by checking the references to find the entry with the same author and date.

(2) Final list of works cited or references

When you are ready to make your final revision, you will know which works from your preliminary bibliography you cite in your paper. Now eliminate the bibliography cards for the works that you do not cite, and arrange the remaining cards in alphabetical order by authors' last names. You are now ready to prepare the list of "Works Cited" or "References" that will conclude your paper. As you make your final revision, you will be checking your citations against this list to ensure that they are complete and correct.

The list of works cited or references is arranged alphabetically by author and is double-spaced throughout. In MLA style, the first line of each entry is flush with the left margin; subsequent lines are indented five spaces. If you use more than one work by the same author, list the works alphabetically by title. Give the author's name with the first title, but substitute three hyphens for the name in subsequent entries.

MLA style

Thomas, Lewis.   <u>The Lives of a Cell: Notes of</u>

     <u>a Biology Watcher</u>.   New York: Viking, 1975.

———.   <u>The Medusa and the Snail: More Notes of</u>

     <u>a Biology Watcher</u>.   New York: Viking, 1979

APA style

If you use more than one work by the same author,
list the works in order of publication date, earliest
first. Repeat the author's name for each entry. The
first line of each entry is flush with the left margin,
and subsequent lines are indented three spaces.

Thomas, L. (1974).   <u>The lives of a cell: Notes of a</u>

     <u>biology watcher</u>.   New York: Viking.

Thomas, L. (1979).   <u>The medusa and the snail: More</u>

     <u>notes of a biology watcher</u>. New York: Viking.

(3) Final outline

The content of your outline should have been developing
steadily throughout your note-taking and writing of the
paper, and you should now be ready to prepare a final copy.
Before you do, however, correlate the ideas in your outline
with those in your text, and make any needed revisions. Also
check the form of your outline: see **33d**, pages 448–51. As
you study the sample research paper on pages 473–511, notice that the arrangement of paragraphs accords with that of
the divisions of the sentence outline below.

OUTLINE

Title: Big Brother's Propaganda

¶1   Introduction: In <u>Nineteen Eighty-Four</u>, Orwell
(a propagandist) satirizes
totalitarian propaganda as he
presents his vision of life—in
reverse.

2   Thesis: Big Brother disseminates the
most dangerous kind of
propaganda.

    I. The Oceanians are propaganda targets.

3   A. They act like a stupid herd.

4   B. They revere a mythical leader.

5   C. They accept the hierarchy in a
"classless" society.

    II. Big Brother's bureaucracy serves as a
propaganda machine.

6   A. Its very housing is a symbol.

7   B. Its parts are interrelated.

    III. Big Brother has complete control of the
media.

8   A. He supplies all materials.

9   B. He propagates the Party's ideal.

		IV.	The State falsifies history.
10–11		A.	The purpose is to control the past and make it fit the present.
		B.	The method is efficient.
12			1. Winston uses the memory hole.
13			2. Clerks "rectify" old propaganda.
14		C.	The systematic attack on the past is frightening.
	V.		Totalitarian propaganda manipulates thought and emotion.
15		A.	The state uses Newspeak to prevent thought.
16		B.	Love and hate are state-controlled.
17			1. One must love Big Brother.
18			2. One must hate his enemies.
19–20	Conclusion:		Much of Big Brother's propaganda is outdated, but Nineteen Eighty-Four is still widely read as a warning.

The outline serves primarily as a guide to writing an organized and carefully developed composition; but it can also serve, when submitted in its final state along with the finished paper, as a kind of table of contents.

(4) Final revision and proofreading

After writing and carefully documenting the first draft of your paper, make needed revisions. To make your writing as clear and effective as possible, you will probably need to rewrite some sentences, and strike out or add others. Use the Reviser's Checklist on page 414. (You may wish to review pages 405–15 of Section **32**.) Refer to **8b** as you put your paper in final form. Even when writing final copy, you will probably continue to make changes in phraseology and to correct occasional errors in spelling, mechanics, or grammar. Type or write legibly. Proofread your final revision before handing it in, using the Proofreader's Checklist on page 102.

Students are often asked to submit, along with the completed paper, both the final and the preliminary outlines; the notes, on cards; and the rough draft of the documented paper.

Sample Research Paper

On the following pages is a completed sample research paper. For purposes of comparison, the pages facing those of the paper contain not only selected passages from the sources but also note cards used in preparing the paper. Comments on content and form are also provided. Notice, as you read the paper, how Tracy Monahan credits other authors.

■ **Exercise 4** Prepare for a class discussion of the strengths and the weaknesses of the following research paper. Give special attention to content and form, organization, and documentation.

COMMENTS

This research paper consists of five parts:

1. *Title page.* The title page usually gives the title of the paper, the author, the name of the course and its section number, the instructor's name, and the date. (See also **8b**.)

2. *Final outline.* The final outline serves as a table of contents. If the outline occupies only one page, it is not numbered. In outlines occupying more than one page, all pages after the first are numbered with small Roman numerals in the upper right-hand corner of the page. Notice that a topic outline is used here. If your instructor specifies a sentence outline, see the sample one on pages 469–70.

3. *Text of the paper.* The title is repeated on the first page of the text, which is not numbered. All pages after the first are numbered with Arabic numerals in the upper right-hand corner of the page. Notice that no period follows the page numbers.

4. *Note.* The notes begin on a new page, following the text and preceding the list of works cited. The page is numbered consecutively with the text pages.

5. *Works cited.* The list of works cited begins on a new page, which is numbered consecutively with the text and notes pages.

BIG BROTHER'S PROPAGANDA

by

Tracy Monahan

English 131, Section 3

Mr. Richards

March 12, 1982

OUTLINE

<u>Thesis</u>: Big Brother disseminates the most dangerous
         kind of propaganda.

<u>Introduction</u>: In <u>Nineteen Eighty-Four</u>, Orwell (a
         propagandist) satirizes totalitarian propaganda
         as he presents his vision of life—in reverse.

I. The propagandized Oceanians

   A. Their loss of individuality
   B. Their reverence for Big Brother
   C. Their use of doublethink

II. The bureaucratic propaganda machine

   A. Its housing—symbolic
   B. Its parts—interrelated

III. The media in a totalitarian world

   A. All materials supplied
   B. The Party's ideal propagated

IV. The falsification of history

    A. Purpose of changes

    B. Methods of "rectification"

        1. Use of memory hole

        2. Use of clerical teams

    C. Effect on Winston

V. The manipulation of thought and emotion

    A. Preventing thought—Newspeak

    B. Rousing the emotions

        1. Love for Big Brother

        2. Hatred of his enemies

Conclusion: Much of Big Brother's propaganda is outdated, but Nineteen Eighty-Four is still widely read as a warning.

COMMENTS

1. Paragraph 1 is the introduction.

2. The Voorhees and Colmer citations credit the sources of ideas; the *Essays* citation credits the source of the quoted passage. See the list of works cited on pages 509 and 511.

3. Observe the way direct quotations are made an integral part of the text. The first one is introduced by *that,* the second by an introductory clause followed by a comma. In accordance with MLA style, the second quotation, because more than four lines long, is set off by a ten-space indention and double-spaced. The first line is indented an additional three spaces if, as here, it marks the beginning of a paragraph in the source. For student papers, some instructors prefer that set-off quotations be single-spaced with a double space before and after (see **16a**).

4. On the title page of the hard-cover edition of Orwell's novel is *Nineteen Eighty-Four*. On the title page of the Signet paperback edition is *1984*, the form used by Ralph Ranald and copied exactly by Tracy Monahan.

SOURCE

For Orwell quotation:

> ORWELL: "I have always maintained that every artist is a propagandist. I don't mean a political propagandist. If he has any honesty or talent at all he cannot be that. Most political propaganda is a matter of telling lies, not only about the facts but about your own feelings. But every artist is a propagandist in the sense that he is trying, directly or indirectly, to impose a vision of life that seems to him desirable. I think that we are broadly agreed about the vision of life that proletarian literature is trying to impose."

BIG BROTHER'S PROPAGANDA

1   Nineteen Eighty—Four has been called George
Orwell's most ferocious propaganda (Voorhees 87).
Orwell was quick to admit that he was a propagandist.
In fact, in 1940, during a BBC radio discussion, he
said that "every artist is a propagandist in the
sense that he is trying, directly or indirectly, to
impose a vision of life that seems to him desirable"
(Essays 2: 41). But Orwell hated political
propaganda which deliberately falsifies reality,
especially the hypocritical kind used solely for the
purpose of keeping totalitarian regimes in power.
During the 1930s and 1940s he was repelled by the
propaganda machines of dictators like Hitler and
Stalin (Colmer 183). It is this variety of
propaganda that Orwell satirizes in Nineteen Eighty—
Four, a novel that presents his vision of life—in
reverse. As Ralph A. Ranald has observed,

            Orwell's 1984 is about religion
         reversed, law and government reversed, and

COMMENTS

1. Paragraph 2 states the thesis, or central idea. Paragraph 3 begins the discussion of point I of the outline: The propagandized Oceanians.

2. In the indented quotation (over four lines in length), the interpolation in brackets supplies a subject and verb to complete the shortened sentence. See also **17g**. Notice that the citation follows the final punctuation of a quotation set off from the text.

3. Notice that the punctuation before the first ellipsis mark is retained to insure clarity. See also **17i**.

SOURCE

For Ranald quotation:

> Orwell's *1984* is about religion reversed, law and government reversed, and above all, language reversed: not simply corrupted, but reversed. In the mad world of *1984*, the mad world which Orwell sought by his writing to lead men to *avoid*—for he was a political activist not interested in simple prediction—in this world, which I call Orwell's "antiuniverse," because of his conversion of all the positives of Western civilization into their negatives, all the channels of communication are systematically being closed down, restricted to just the minimums necessary for the technical functioning of society.

2

above all, language reversed: not simply
corrupted, but reversed. In the world of
1984, the mad world which Orwell sought by
his writing to lead men to <u>avoid</u>—for he
was a political activist not interested in
simple prediction—in this world, which I
call Orwell's "antiuniverse," . . .
[Orwell converts] all the positives of
Western civilization into their negatives.
(544–45)

And in Orwell's crazy world, it is Big Brother's
political propaganda that helps to sustain and
perpetuate this reversal of values.

2   To control society, to sustain the awesome
power of the State, Big Brother uses what Oliver
Thompson calls the most dangerous kind of
propaganda: a "steady drip, drip" of toxic,
power-oriented ideas not recognized as propaganda.
These ideas pollute the environment and saturate
all art forms. Such propaganda deadens the awareness of its targets (132).

3   Big Brother is always watching, and his
hypnotic eyes have cast a spell over the
inhabitants of Oceania. Thoroughly propagandized,

COMMENTS

1. Paragraphs 4 and 5 continue point I of the outline.
2. As you read the source (below) for the last sentence of paragraph 4, observe how Tracy Monahan has combined paraphrase and direct quotation.

SOURCE

Nineteen Eighty-Four (209)

Given this background, one could infer, if one did not know it already, the general structure of Oceanic society. At the apex of the pyramid comes Big Brother. Big Brother is infallible and all-powerful. Every success, every achievement, every victory, every scientific discovery, all knowledge, all wisdom, all happiness, all virtue, are held to issue directly from his leadership and inspiration. Nobody has ever seen Big Brother. He is a face on the hoardings, a voice on the telescreen. We may be reasonably sure that he will never die, and there is already considerable uncertainty as to when he was born. Big Brother is the guise in which the Party chooses to exhibit itself to the world. His function is to act as a focusing point for love, fear, and reverence, emotions which are more easily felt toward an individual than toward an organization.

3

they act like a stupid herd. They mechanically
respond to every command, no matter how illogical
it is. If any person dares to act or even think
like an independent human being, Big Brother
resorts to liquidation or re—education. Such an
individual either becomes an "unperson," one who
has never existed, or a reprogramed android, one
who again loves and serves the State.

4   Ironically enough, the Oceanians have never
seen Big Brother—just big pictures of him. In
fact, Big Brother does not exist. He is the
mythical Leader so often created by propagandists.
His image is projected by the Inner Party to
maintain its ruling powers. Propaganda depicts Big
Brother as a deity. He is omnipresent, omniscient,
and omnipotent in the world of Nineteen Eighty-Four:
"Every suooess, every achievement, every victory,
every scientific discovery, all knowledge, all
wisdom, all happiness, all virtue, are held to issue
directly from his leadership and inspiration" (209).

5   Oceanians are programed in the art of
doublethink, which the novel defines as "the power of
holding two contradictory beliefs in one's mind

COMMENT

Paragraph 6 begins point II of the outline: The bureaucratic propaganda machine.

BIBLIOGRAPHY CARD FOR THOMSON

Thomson, Oliver. *Mass Persuasion in History*. New York: Crane, 1977.

NOTE CARD USED FOR PARAGRAPH 6

Big Brother's pyramidal power structure (Thomson 41)

T. thinks <u>architecture</u> is an important propagandist medium that people don't pay much attention to.

A building can be "graphic communication." Can inspire awe and power—with long-term impact.

". . . the pyramids projected the massive dominance of the Pharaohs."

4

simultaneously, and accepting both of them" (215).
The Oceanians, not aware of their loss of human
rights, firmly believe that everybody is equal in
their society, but they serve their king and accept
the State's rigid hierarchy. The pyramidal power
structure is the natural order of things in their
classless society. Naturally, Big Brother sits on
top of the pyramid; he represents the Inner Party,
less than 2 percent of society. Just below him or
them is the Outer Party, the bureaucratic toadies,
about 13 percent. At the base of the pyramid are the
proles—"the dumb masses" (209)—about 85 percent.

6   Big Brother's bureaucracy consists of four
ministries. These ministries are housed in huge
white buildings, enormous pyramidal structures
dominating London, the capital of Airstrip One, a
province of Oceania. These towers contrast sharply
with the run-down stores and shabby houses of the
rest of the city. The very architecture of Big
Brother's government buildings is an important
propagandistic symbol because it is a "graphic
communication" of awesomeness. Like the great
Egyptian pyramids, they project a political image
of massive, lasting power (Thomson 41).

COMMENTS

1. The discussion of point II continues. Paragraph 8 turns to point III: The media in a totalitarian world.

2. In paragraphs 7 and 8, Tracy Monahan uses superscript numbers to refer readers to endnotes that supply additional information.

3. In paragraph 8, the use of such phrases as "According to Richard S. Lambert," "knows *this*," and "Jacques Ellul writes" helps make direct quotations fit smoothly into the text.

NOTE CARD

Notice below that Tracy Monahan's own ideas are placed in brackets.

Propaganda machine

Thomson, 7 TYPES OF PROPAGANDA listed. [Five seem closely related to Big Brother's machine.]

11 political — rhetoric, subtle images
   economic — promotes confidence in economy

12 war/military — concerned with morale. Uses war films, military music, etc.
   ideological — "spread of complete idea systems"

12-13 escapist — media entertainment distracts, gets "social acquiescence"

   [Relate this to the proles?]

---

7   All four ministries are active, interrelated parts of Big Brother's massive propaganda machine. For example, they work together when grinding out materials for Hate Week. Each cog, however, has its particular job to do. The Ministry of Plenty (Miniplenty), specializes in economic propaganda; the Ministry of Peace (Minipax) in the military type. The Ministry of Love (Miniluv) reinforces or intensifies ideologic propaganda.[1] Perhaps the biggest, most responsible cog in the machine, however, is the Ministry of Truth (Minitrue). Minitrue—with its slogans WAR IS PEACE, FREEDOM IS SLAVERY, IGNORANCE IS STRENGTH—not only produces political images and rhetoric in accordance with Big Brother's input but also coordinates and edits the propagandistic output of Miniplenty and Minipax. The huge machine never stops its propagandizing, and its perpetual, continuous noise has a mesmerizing effect on the whole society.

8   According to Richard S. Lambert, the internal propaganda of a totalitarian government "seeks to impose complete uniformity of thought, as well as of action, upon its citizens" (138).[2] All-wise Big Brother knows this. "Where film production, the

COMMENTS

As a rule, a comma or a colon precedes an introduced quotation. Examples from the paper:

¶1   As Ralph A. Ranald has observed,

¶4   He is . . . omnipotent:

In paragraph 8, however, are two illustrations of a different way to make a quotation an integral part of the text. Notice that the first indented quotation provides an object for the preposition *with;* the second, an object for the verb *supplies*.

Read the source, and notice the way Tracy Monahan combines paraphrase with quotation.

SOURCE

Nineteen Eighty-Four (43–44)

And the Records Department, after all, was itself only a single branch of the Ministry of Truth, whose primary job was not to reconstruct the past but to supply the citizens of Oceania with newspapers, films, textbooks, telescreen programs, plays, novels—with every conceivable kind of information, instruction, or entertainment, from a statue to a slogan, from a lyric poem to a biological treatise and from a child's spelling book to a Newspeak dictionary. And the Ministry had not only to supply the multifarious needs of the Party, but also to repeat the whole operation at a lower level for the benefit of the proletariat. There was a whole chain of separate departments dealing with proletarian literature, music, drama, and entertainment generally. Here were produced rubbishy newspapers containing almost nothing except sport, crime, and astrology, sensational five-cent novelettes, films oozing with sex, and sentimental songs which were composed entirely by mechanical means on a special kind of kaleidoscope known as a versificator.

6

press, and radio transmission are not centrally controlled," Jacques Ellul writes, "no propaganda is possible" (102). Big Brother knows this too. In fact, he harnesses every channel of communication, holding tight reins on the Party specialists who run the Ministry of Truth. Minitrue provides Oceanic society with all its

> newspapers, films, textbooks, telescreen
> programs, plays, novels—with every
> conceivable kind of information,
> instruction, or entertainment, from a
> statue to a slogan, from a lyric poem to a
> biological treatise, and from a child's
> spelling book to a Newspeak dictionary.
> (<u>Nineteen Eighty-Four</u> 43–44)

Those outside the Party—the proles—have such limited intelligence that Big Brother has to adapt his communication to their level. For their benefit, Minitrue supplies

> rubbishy newspapers containing almost
> nothing except sport, crime, and astrology,
> sensational five-cent novelettes, films
> oozing with sex, and sentimental songs

COMMENTS

1. Observe Tracy Monahan's use of repetition as a transitional device in paragraph 9. The introduction to the long quotation ends with "the Party's ideal," and the quotation begins with "The ideal set up by the Party."

2. Paragraph 9 discusses point III(B) of the outline: Big Brother's use of the media to propagate the Party's ideal.

7

> which were composed entirely by mechanical
> means on a special kind of kaleidoscope
> known as a versificator. (44)

This kind of escapist material, along with the
state lottery and numerous pubs, not only
contributes to the contentment of the proles but
also keeps their minds busy with things other than
the impact of power politics on their lives.

9   Big Brother uses the media for mass hypnosis.
He disseminates misinformation (largely lies but a
number of selected, twisted truths) that goes un-
recognized as propaganda. His propaganda preaches
only one gospel: the Party's ideal.

> The ideal set up by the Party was something
> huge, terrible, and glittering—a world of
> steel and concrete, of monstrous machines
> and terrifying weapons—a nation of
> warriors and fanatics, marching forward in
> perfect unity, all thinking the same
> thoughts and shouting the same slogans,
> perpetually working, fighting, triumphing,
> persecuting—three hundred million people
> all with the same face. (74)

COMMENTS

1. Paragraphs 10–14 develop point IV of the outline: The falsification of history. Observe the unified flow of Tracy Monahan's ideas as you read these paragraphs, paying special attention to the selection and arrangement of the three quotations, the first and third from Orwell, the second from Zwerdling.

2. Reread paragraphs 10–14 and carefully observe interrelations, a few of which are connected by arrows on page 494.

8

With the exception of a few characters like the
lovers Winston and Julia, the doublethinkers of
Oceania parrot the media's message; and, putting no
gods before Big Brother, they—as one body—live
their religion.

10   Orwell considered "the disappearance of objective history and the willingness of individuals to
work toward its elimination" as the "most frightening propagandistic achievement of the twentieth
century" (Zwerdling 52). In <u>Nineteen Eighty-Four</u>,
the work of the Records Department in Minitrue is the
control of history. A Party slogan declares: "Who
controls the past controls the future: who controls
the present controls the past" (35). Always
tampering with records, Big Brother distorts, re-
creates, or destroys the past. As Zwerdling has
noted:

                No matter how intolerable the present is,
                the sense of alternative possibilities that
                objective history inevitably presents can
                still liberate the imagination and perhaps
                lead to significant change. But once the

<u>IV</u>.   <u>The falsification of history</u>

¶10   a reference to propagandistic achievement

Orwell: Two things are frightening:

     (1)   the disappearance of history
     (2)   the willingness of people
           to eliminate history

Zwerdling: A "rectified" past makes escape
from present impossible.

11   a transitional paragraph echoing Zwerdling
and referring to "rectification" as routine
in the Records Department

12   One example of "rectification":

     Winston makes history disappear—a
     routine part of his job.

13   Another example:

     Many individuals work to eliminate
     history—a constant chore.

14   a reference to totalitarian propaganda

Winston thinks that wiping out the past is
"more terrifying than torture and death."

Even Winston's thought may remind the reader
of what Zwerdling said. Why <u>this</u> analogy?
Does Winston sense, like Zwerdling, that no
escape is possible except torture and death?

9

       past is perpetually "rectified" to
conform to the present, this escape is no
longer possible. (53)

11   Thousands working in the Records Department
look upon such "rectification" as daily routine.
This department falsifies the past to make it fit
changes in present government policies.

12   False promises must be changed to suit present
conditions. A clerk at the Speakwrite machine,
Winston Smith "rectifies" materials sent to him
through a pneumatic tube. Proficient in Newspeak
(the official language), he reads a message: "times
14. 2. 84 miniplenty malquoted chocolate rectify"
(39). Winston dials on the telescreen for the
copy of the _Times_ (February 14, 1984) that carries
Miniplenty's promise not to reduce the chocolate
ration in 1984. He changes the optimistic promise
to a pessimistic prediction: rationing may be necessary in April. He returns the altered version
for filing and destroys the original by putting it
into the memory hole, a kind of incinerator for
irrelevant history, outdated information about va-
porized persons, and other trash.

COMMENT

"As might be expected" at the beginning of paragraph 15 provides the transition from point IV to point V. Paragraph 15 covers point V(A): Newspeak as a thought preventive.

10

13   It is the state's policy to be in a constant
state of war either with Eurasia or with Eastasia.
Yet the Party insists that the present enemy has
always been the enemy. When roles are reversed,
the former enemy has never been an enemy but always
an ally. Record clerks work frantically to make
expedient changes in mountains of references to
Eurasia and Eastasia. Minipax's military propaganda must constantly be "rectified" to protect the
vital interest of the State: maintenance of power.

14   Eventually, Winston's experiences teach him to
recognize totalitarian propaganda for what it is.
Very disturbed by the systematic attack on the
past, he thinks: "If the Party could thrust its
hand into the past and say of this or that event,
it never happened––that, surely, was more terrifying than torture and death" (35).

15   As might be expected, Big Brother manipulates
language to suit his purpose. His aim is to destroy words––the material for expressing ideas––and
to eventually wipe out completely the necessity for
thought. The words in Newspeak are formed in various ways: for example, by compounding (thought-

COMMENTS

1. Four paragraphs (15–18) develop point V of the outline: The manipulation of thought and emotion.

2. Of these, three (16–18) develop parts of the second sub-heading: Rousing the emotions.

NOTE CARDS

Newspeak   ②

Steinhoff   166: "Newspeak is the principal intellectual means by which doublethink is transformed into a conditioned reflex."

Newspeak—doublethink   ③

Zwerdling   54: from a discussion of schizophrenic thinking in 1984: "an occupational disease of propagandists that is called 'reality control' or 'doublethink.'"

Newspeak   ①

In 1984—   51 AND the appendix— aim, nature, etc.

Newspeak words—compounding, adding prefixes and suffixes

    bellyfeel, prolefeed, Minitrue, Pornosec, facecrime, sexcrime, crimestop, thoughtcrime— ungood, doubleplusgood, goodwise, gooder — duckspeaking

a duckspeaker, a fast talker in love with own voice, keeps quacking on and on.

11

crime, duckspeak, prolefeed, Minipax) and by
adding prefixes or suffixes (ungood, thinkful).
Doubleplusgood gets rid of superlatives like best
or finest and synonyms like superb or excellent.
According to William Steinhoff, Newspeak is "the
principal intellectual means by which doublethink
is transformed into a conditioned reflex" (166).
Doublethink is Big Brother's "reality control" (indeed "the occupational disease of propagandists")
(Zwerdling 54). Working in the Research Department as
a compiler of the Newspeak dictionary, a clerk re-
marks that, unlike Oldspeak, the new language has a
vocabulary that grows smaller, not larger. He says,
"We're destroying words—scores of them, hundreds of
them every day. . . . It's a beautiful thing, the
destruction of words" (Nineteen Eighty-Four 51-52).

16   Big Brother's propaganda not only straight-
jackets thought but also manipulates emotions.
Doublethinking Oceanians know that unqualified hatred of the State's enemies is a social necessity
in their kingdom of love—love for Big Brother.
Though living in a police state and (except for

COMMENT

Note the acknowledgment of sources of ideas that are expressed in paraphrases (rather than in the exact words of the author).

SOURCES

Below are two statements by Irving Howe that are paraphrased in paragraphs 17 and 18. Note the differences between the paraphrases and the originals.

> Oceania seeks to blot out spontaneous affection because it assumes, for good reason, that whatever is uncalculated is subversive.   —IRVING HOWE

> For the faithful [in Oceania], sexual energy is transformed into political hysteria.   —IRVING HOWE

12

proles) under constant surveillance by Thought Police and Junior Spies, <u>loyal</u> citizens have nothing
to fear, for they love their Leader and hate his
enemies.

17   Those who love their leader, however, must
have no room in their hearts for anyone else. When
affection for others rises spontaneously, that love
is considered subversive, something to be eliminated
(Howe 48). Though necessary for child-bearing, the
sex act must be state-controlled. Winston's affair
with Julia is a capital offense; the State must
purify his heart in Miniluv's torture chambers.

18   Big Brother wisely turns the sex drive into
political hysteria (Howe 49). The fanatical
Oceanians stand ready to strike terror into the
hearts of any enemies. To stimulate hatred, Big
Brother not only sets up a mythical Adversary but
also uses such propaganda techniques as exciting
rituals, stirring military music, barbaric rhythms,
noisy rallies, slogan-chanting mobs, rabble-rousing
war films, staged hangings. The Two Minute Hate and
Hate Week intensify the mood. Like many another

COMMENTS

1. The main discussion ends with paragraph 18. The conclusion begins with paragraph 19.

2. Reread the first paragraph of the paper. Notice there the words and ideas that are repeated in paragraph 19. References to the title of Orwell's novel and to the nature of totalitarian propaganda are two examples of repetition. Linking the ideas in the introduction and those in the conclusion contributes to the unity of the paper.

SOURCE

For first sentence of paragraph 20 (a book review):

> Orwell was never very clear about what sort of political system might work, nor was he particularly sophisticated about the peculiarities of *any* political organization. But he knew what he didn't like, and he knew why; the two short novels that emerged from this metamorphosis—*Animal Farm* and *1984*—are probably the most widely read literary/political polemics ever written in English.   —ATLANTIC MONTHLY

13

propagandist, Big Brother knows the unifying value
of hate.

19   In <u>Nineteen Eighty-Four</u>, Orwell uses artistic
exaggeration to help make his warning clear.[3]
The reader can easily recognize Big Brother's propaganda for what it is—an obvious mixture of absurd
lies and gross distortions of truth. Today's propaganda, however, is not always so easily recognized,
for it tells the truth—convincing parts of it. By
cleverly manipulating carefully selected facts,
propagandists today either ignore or downplay any
evidence that might effectively refute their one-
sided arguments—the old card-stacking trick (Cantril
and Hart). Modern propaganda has various names, such
as government "publicity," political "advertising,"
or even official "communication packages." Such
propaganda, like Big Brother's, often eulogizes the
Leaders, hiding their mistakes and magnifying their
successes (Lang 43).

20   It has been said that Orwell's <u>Animal Farm</u> and
<u>Nineteen Eighty-Four</u> "are probably the most widely
read literary/political polemics ever written in

14

English" (<u>Transformation</u> 126). Of the two novels,
perhaps <u>Nineteen Eighty-Four</u> is more likely to be
remembered. It is a kind of nightmare that haunts
the memory because its world looks much like our own.
Readers of this novel ask questions like these: Was
1984 in 1948? Is 1984 almost here? Will it come
soon? Maybe in 1994? Fortunately, the nightmare has
not yet become reality.

> For it can be said that, so long as we can
> talk about <u>1984</u> and discuss whether it has
> come or not, then certainly it has not
> come: the one thing certain is that when
> 1984 is actually here and we are living in
> the kind of world that Orwell described as
> a warning, we shall be unconscious of it,
> and the very title of his book, which has
> become a monitory symbol for us, will have
> ceased to have any of its present meaning.
> (Small 21)

COMMENT

Three endnotes provide supplementary information that is not directly related to the thesis but that might be of interest to readers. (See page 459).

15

NOTES

[1] For a description of seven types of propaganda, see Thomson (11-13).

[2] Lambert also points out that the totalitarian state is more concerned with internal propaganda than with external: "But great as have been the external propagandist efforts of the dictator-ruled countries, they are half-hearted and indirect as compared with their internal organization" (138).

[3] Orwell also warns us about "veiled censorship" in a free press. See "The Freedom of the Press."

COMMENTS

1. All (and only) works cited as sources in the paper should be included in the list of works cited.

2. Alphabetization: Initial articles (*A, An, The*) are ignored in alphabetizing. For example, Orwell's *The Collected Essays* precedes *Nineteen Eighty-Four* (*C* before *N*).

3. Punctuation: Observe the use and placement of periods and commas, especially in relation to parentheses and quotation marks. A colon separates titles from subtitles.

4. For Cantril and Hart, an encyclopedia article, page numbers are not required.

5. For Colmer, Tracy Monahan copies the title exactly as it is given on the title page of Colmer's book. For the usual treatment of titles within titles, see the Howe entry.

16

WORKS CITED

Cantril, Hadley, and Clyde W. Hart. "Propaganda."
World Book Encyclopedia. 1975 ed.

Colmer, John. Coleridge to Catch-22: Images of
Society. New York: St. Martin's, 1978.

Ellul, Jacques. Propaganda: the Formation of Men's
Attitudes. Trans. Konrad Kellen and Jean
Lerner. New York: Knopf, 1965.

Howe, Irving. "1984: History as Nightmare."
Twentieth Century Interpretations of 1984: A
Collection of Critical Essays. Ed. Samuel
Hynes. Englewood Cliffs: Prentice, 1971.

Lambert, Richard S. Propaganda. Discussion Books
13. London: Nelson, 1938.

Lang, John S. "The Great American Bureaucratic
Propaganda Machine." U.S. News and World Report
27 Aug. 1979: 43-47.

Orwell, George. The Collected Essays, Journalism
and Letters of George Orwell. Ed. Sonia
Orwell and Ian Angus. 4 vols. New York:
Harcourt, 1968.

COMMENTS

1. Annotation: If you are asked to submit an annotated bibliography, supply a brief description of each entry, as in
   this example:

   Spoehr, Luther. Rev. of <u>A People's History of the</u>

   <u>United States</u>, by Howard Zinn. <u>Saturday Review</u>

   2 Feb. 1980: 37.

   Considered a radical historian, Zinn describes a

   kind of pyramidal power structure (the powerful

   elite, their servile "guards," and the oppressed

   underclass) and advocates "decentralized social-

   ism that will run society 'from the bottom up.'"

2. Note that the anonymous, untitled review of Stansky and
   Abrahams' book *The Transformation* (cited in paragraph
   20 of Tracy Monahan's paper) is alphabetized by the title
   of the work reviewed: *Transformation*. (The designation
   Rev. of and the article *The* are ignored for alphabetizing.)

18

———. "The Freedom of the Press." <u>New York
Times Magazine</u> 8 Oct. 1972: 12.

———. <u>Nineteen Eighty-Four</u>. New York:
Harcourt, 1949.

Ranald, Ralph A. "George Orwell and the Mad World:
The Anti-Universe of <u>1984</u>." <u>South Atlantic
Quarterly</u> 66 (1967): 544–53.

Small, Christopher. <u>The Road to Miniluv: George
Orwell, the State, and God</u>. Pittsburgh: U
of Pittsburgh P, 1975.

Steinhoff, William. <u>George Orwell and the Origins of
1984</u>. Ann Arbor: U of Michigan P, 1975.

Thomson, Oliver. <u>Mass Persuasion in History: An
Historical Analysis of the Development of
Propaganda Techniques</u>. New York: Crane, 1977.

Rev. of <u>The Transformation</u>, by Peter Stansky and
William Abrahams. <u>Atlantic Monthly</u> Apr. 1980:
126–27.

Voorhees, Richard J. <u>The Paradox of George Orwell</u>.
Humanities Series. Lafayette: Purdue U Studies,
1961.

Zwerdling, Alex. <u>Orwell and the Left</u>. New Haven:
Yale UP, 1974.

Note: Some instructors prefer to receive handwritten rather than typewritten papers. Below is a sample page from a handwritten research paper.

9

"Where film production, the press, and radio transmission are not centrally controlled," writes Jacques Ellul, "no propaganda is possible" (102). Knowing this, Big Brother holds tight reins on the Party specialists who run the Ministry of Truth. Minitrue provides Oceania with all its

> newspapers, films, textbooks, telescreen programs, plays, novels — with every conceivable kind of information, instruction, or entertainment, from a statue to a slogan, from a lyric poem to a biological treatise, and from a child's spelling book to a Newspeak dictionary. (_Nineteen Eighty-Four_ 43-44)

Those outside the Party have such limited intelligence that Big Brother has to adapt his communication to their level. For their benefit, Minitrue supplies "rubbishy newspapers" (44).

Business Writing

34

Write effective business letters and resumés.

Business letters are usually typed on only one side of white, unlined, $8\frac{1}{2} \times 11$ inch paper. Standard business envelopes measure about $3\frac{1}{2} \times 6\frac{1}{2}$ inches or 4×10 inches. (Letterhead stationery and envelopes vary in both size and color.)

34a
Business Letters

A business letter has six parts: (1) the heading, (2) the inside address, (3) the salutation, (4) the body of the letter, (5) the closing, which consists of the complimentary close and the signature (handwritten and then typed), and (6) any added notations.

BUSINESS LETTER FORMATS

If you work for a company, you should check to see if it has a policy about the format for business letters. Many do. Most companies use one of three styles: full block, modified block, or indented. In full block, the most formal style, all parts of the letter, including the first lines of paragraphs, are flush with the left margin. The model letter on page 517 is in full-block style. In modified-block style, shown in the letter on page 519, the heading and the complimentary close are moved to the right. The indented format (pages 521 and 523) also moves the heading and the closing to the right and uses paragraph indention. This format is the least formal, the most like a personal letter. By and large, businesses or officials use the modified block, whereas individuals use the indented format.

(1) The heading of the letter gives the full address of the writer and the date of the letter.

If letterhead stationery is used, the date is typed beneath it in the center of the page. If plain stationery is used, the address of the writer followed by the date is put at the top of the page, flush with the right-hand margin, as in the letters on pages 521 and 523. Notice that the heading is blocked and has no end punctuation.

(2) The inside address gives the name and full address of the addressee.

Four to six lines usually separate the heading from the inside address, depending on how much space is needed to center the body of the letter on the page.

(3) The salutation greets the addressee appropriately.

The salutation is written flush with the left margin, two spaces below the inside address, and is followed by a colon. The salutation should be consistent with the tone of the letter, the first line of the inside address, and the complimentary close.

When the surname of the addressee is known, it is used in

the salutation of a business letter, as in the following examples.

Dear Dr. Davis: Dear Mayor Rodriguez:
Dear Mrs. Greissman: Dear Ms. Joseph:

Note: Use *Miss* or *Mrs.* if the woman you are addressing has indicated a preference. Otherwise, use *Ms.*, which is always appropriate and which is preferred by many businesswomen, whatever their marital status.

In letters to organizations, or to persons whose name and sex are unknown, such salutations as the following are customary:

Dear Sir or Madam: Dear L. L. Bean:
Dear Subscription Manager: Dear Registrar:

If you do not know the name of the addressee, but you do know the sex, use either *Dear Sir* or *Dear Madam*.

For the appropriate forms of salutations and addresses in letters to government officials, military personnel, and so on, check an etiquette book or the front or back of your college dictionary.

(4) The body of the letter should follow the principles of good writing.

Typewritten letters are usually single-spaced, with double spacing between paragraphs. All paragraphs should begin flush with the left margin (in full block or modified block) or should be indented five to ten spaces (in indented format). The subject matter should be organized so that the reader can grasp immediately what is wanted, and the style should be clear and direct. Do not use stilted or abbreviated phrasing:

NOT "The aforementioned letter"   BUT "Your letter"
NOT "Please send me it ASAP"   BUT "Please send it
                                       to me as soon
                                       as possible."

(5) The closing ends the letter.

In full-block style, the closing is typed flush with the left-hand margin. In modified block and indented style, it is typed to the right of the letter, in alignment with the heading. The parts of the closing are as follows:

The complimentary close: This conventional ending is typed three lines below the last paragraph of the body of the letter. Among the endings commonly used in business letters are the following:

FORMAL	LESS FORMAL
Very truly yours,	Sincerely,
Sincerely yours,	Cordially,

The typed name: The name (as it will be written) is typed four lines below the closing.

Title of sender: This line, following the typed name, indicates the sender's position, if he or she is acting in an official capacity.

> Manager, Employee Relations
> Chairperson, Search Committee

Signature: The letter is signed between the complimentary close and the typed name.

(6) Notations supply additional information.

Notations are typed below the closing, flush with the left margin. They indicate, among other things, whether anything is enclosed with or attached to the letter (*enc., att.*); to whom copies of the letter have been sent (*cc: AAW, PTN*); and the initials of the sender and the typist (*DM/cll*).

MODEL BUSINESS LETTER

MIRACLE MILE COMMUNITY LEAGUE

1992 South Cochran Avenue   Los Angeles, CA 90036

February 1, 1982

Dr. Nathan T. Swift
Community Health Center
1101 Figueroa Street
Los Angeles, CA 90027 } **INSIDE ADDRESS**

Dear Dr. Swift: **SALUTATION**

We have completed our evaluation of the nutrition
education program being conducted by your organization. While the results are encouraging,
some aspects of the program might be modified.
Awareness training for the staff, a few schedule
changes, and greater involvement of the parents
could significantly improve the results of the
program.

We have prepared a study outlining the problems as
we see them and our recommendations for improving
the program. Angel Chavez, our Vice President for
Management Development, has agreed to work with you,
if you would like his assistance.

We look forward to hearing from you soon.

BODY

Sincerely,   **Complimentary close**

Dorothy Muir   **Signature**   } **CLOSING**

Dorothy Muir   **Typed name**
Chairman, Advisory Committee   **Title**

DM/ewl   **NOTATION**

TYPES OF BUSINESS LETTERS

(1) Thank-you letter

Thank-you letters are written often in private life, but they are also used in business. If a representative of a company has been helpful or done more than you expected, a thank-you letter or note is an appropriate way of showing appreciation. A gift, recommendation, award, or prize should also be acknowledged with a letter of thanks.

Usually, thank-you letters are in the informal indented style. It is not necessary to include an inside address, and a comma replaces the colon after the salutation. There are some who think thank-you letters should be handwritten, but typewritten ones are equally correct.

THANK-YOU LETTER

107 Kentin Drive
Mobile, AL   21304
December 12, 1981

Dear Dean Rutledge,

 Thank you very much for recommending me for The Honor Society of Phi Kappa Phi. I was chosen as one of the members and attended the installation ceremony last Tuesday evening. I told my parents about your recommendation, and they are as pleased as I am.

Sincerely,

John Trevant

John Trevant

(2) Claim and adjustment letter

One of the most common business letters is the letter of claim and adjustment, which should include the following information.

Your claim: Describe exactly what is wrong. The more specific your description, the easier and quicker it will be to correct the situation. If an airline has lost your suitcase, for example, describe it fully and also include the flight number, date, and your destination. If an appliance is faulty, include the model and serial numbers in addition to the brand name and style.

Your request: Often a company will do exactly what you suggest, as long as it is possible. Again, the more specific your request—and the more reasonable and courteous your tone—the better your chance of getting what you want.

**CLAIM AND
ADJUSTMENT LETTER**

742 Rock Street
Chicago, IL   60646
February 11, 1982

Mr. Norman Huckley
Huckley Electronics, Inc.
235 Central Avenue
Chicago, IL   60637

Dear Mr. Huckley:

A week ago today I bought a 19" Supersonic color television set from you, model number 0300-B, serial number 0137-8112-77. All week the set has worked perfectly, but when I turned it on today, nothing happened. The trouble is not with the electrical outlet, which I checked by plugging in another appliance.

I would like you to examine the set here in my apartment, and either repair it free of charge or replace it with another 19" Supersonic. My telephone number is 689-4140, and you can call me any day from noon to 5:00 p.m.

Sincerely,

Thomas McNally

Thomas McNally

(3) Order letter

In an order letter, supply the following information as exactly as possible:

Description: Indicate the name of the product, the model or stock number if you know it, the page of the catalog from which you are ordering, the quantity of each item, and the price.

Destination: State whether you want the order shipped to the inside address at the top of your letter or to another address.

Any special circumstances: State such things as whether you need the order by a particular date, whether you want it sent a particular way (air freight, for example), or whether you will not pay more than a certain price.

Payment information: Include payment or indicate how you plan to pay for the merchandise.

ORDER LETTER

736 Minette Avenue
Cary, NC 27511
February 5, 1982

Trailblazers, Inc.
4200 West Washington Boulevard
Tacoma, WA 90876

Dear Trailblazers:

I wish to order the following merchandise from your
Fall 1981 catalog:

1 Western camp shirt, #007, p. 5, size 10, blue,
  $18.95
2 Ragg sweaters, #095, p. 7, size 36, tan and navy,
  $19.95 each
1 Greenleaf sleeping bag, #432, p. 34, $43.00
1 Trailblazers dome tent, #212, p. 46, $112.00

Please ship this merchandise by surface carrier to my
address as shown at the top of this letter.

I have enclosed a check for $230.00, which includes
the $16.15 parcel post and handling charges specified in
your ordering instructions.

Sincerely,

Susan Walters

Susan Walters

enc.

(4) Application letter

The purpose of an application letter is to convince the reader that he or she should examine your resumé. In it you should indicate the job you want and, briefly, your qualifications. In the last paragraph you should indicate when you are available for an interview. A letter of application is usually accompanied by a resumé (page 527), which gives more information about you than your letter can. Neither your letter nor your resumé should be longer than one typed page.

BUSINESS ENVELOPES

The address that appears on the envelope is identical to the inside address. The return address regularly gives the full name and address of the writer. With the zip code, special postal abbreviations not followed by periods may be used for names of states.

MODEL ADDRESSED ENVELOPE

```
Diane Bellows
1830 Lexington Avenue
Louisville, KY  40227


              Mr. Aaron Navik
              Personnel Manager
              Echo Electronics
              627 East 3rd Street
              Louisville, KY  40223
```

APPLICATION LETTER

1830 Lexington Avenue
Louisville, KY 40227
June 8, 1981

Mr. Aaron Navik
Personnel Manager
Echo Electronics
627 East 3rd Street
Louisville, KY 40223

Dear Mr. Navik:

Please consider me for the position of Assistant
Director of Employee Benefits in the Personnel Division
of Echo Electronics. I was an administrative intern
with Echo last summer and, now that I have graduated
from the University of Louisville, I would like to join
your company.

As you can see from the attached resumé, my major
was Business Administration with special emphasis in
personnel management. Whenever possible, I have looked
for jobs and campus activities that would give me
experience in dealing with people. As an assistant in
the Admissions Office, I dealt with students, parents,
alumni, and faculty. The position required both a
knowledge of university regulations and sympathy for
other people.

As an intern with Echo, I learned about the
management of a company at first hand and gained a
firmer grasp of the contribution personnel management
makes to the overall objectives of the company.
Participants in the intern program were required to
write a paper analyzing the company where we were
placed. If you are interested, I will be happy to send
you a copy of my paper.

I would very much like to put my interests and my
training to work for Echo Electronics, and I am
available for an interview at your convenience.

Sincerely,

Diane Bellows

Diane Bellows

enc.

34b
The Resumé

A resumé is a list of a person's qualifications for a job and is enclosed with a letter of application. It is made up of four categories of information:

(1) Personal data: name, mailing address, telephone number
(2) Educational background
(3) Work experience
(4) Location of credentials file, which includes letters of recommendation

Like the letter of application, the resumé is a form of persuasion designed to emphasize your qualifications for a job and to get you an interview. Since there is usually more than one applicant for every job, your resumé should make the most of your qualifications. After reading all the letters and resumés received, a potential employer usually decides to interview only the three or four strongest candidates.

Writing a resumé requires the same planning and attention to detail that writing a paper does. First, make a list of the jobs you have had, the activities and clubs you have been part of, and the offices you have held. Amplify these items by adding dates, job titles and responsibilities, and a brief statement about what you learned from each of them. Arrange these items with the most recent first: March 1981–present, September 1979–February 1981. Remember that activities that do not appear to be relevant to the job you want may be explained to show that you learned important things from them. The resumés on pages 526–27 illustrate the points in the list on the opposite page.

You may find it helpful to consult one of the following books for further information on application letters, resumés, and interviews:

Juvenal L. Angel. *The Complete Resume Book and Job-Getter's Guide.* New York: Pocket Books, 1980.

Richard N. Bolles. *What Color Is Your Parachute? A Practical Manual for Job-Hunters and Career Changers.* 5th edition. Berkeley: Ten Speed Press, 1979.

John J. Komar. *The Interview Game: Winning Strategies for the Job Seeker.* New York: Follett, 1979.

Michael H. Smith. *The Resumé Writer's Handbook.* 2nd edition. New York: Barnes and Noble, 1980.

RESUMÉ DO'S AND DON'TS

DON'T	DO
1. Don't include personal material—age, marital status, photograph, etc.—that is not relevant to the job.	1. Do include your address and telephone number.
2. Don't mention specific courses unless they are directly relevant to the job.	2. Do mention your degree and the *areas* in which you received special training.
3. Don't include career goals. You may wish to change them or raise them.	3. Do *think* about your career goals so that you can discuss them during the interview.
4. Don't include salary unless you will not accept less.	4. Do *think* about the salary you will accept so that you can discuss it during the interview.
5. Don't mention jobs and activities unless you can make them relevant to the job.	5. Do explain briefly how each job and activity included pertains to the job you want.
6. Don't use a cluttered, sprawling format. It looks inefficient and unprofessional.	6. Do use a clear, crisp format. It shows the reader you are efficient and professional.

RESUMÉ 1 — DON'T

Diane Bellows	Marital status: Single
1830 Lexington Avenue	Health: Excellent
Louisville, KY 40227	Date of birth: 3/29/57

Education:

    University of Louisville, B.A., 1981
      Major: Business Administration—Personnel
      Management.
         Courses: Labor Relations, Personnel
         Management, etc.
      Minor: Economics.
         Courses: Money and Banking, Production
         Analysis, etc.

Career goal: To be personnel manager for a large
company.

Salary desired: $1500/mo.

Experience:

    Volunteer worker for Arthur Schneider's School
    Board campaign, Summer, 1979.

    Academic Committee for Alpha Phi Sorority, 1979–81.

    Advertising Manager for University Yearbook, 1980.

    Student Worker in Admissions Office, 1979–81.

    Intern, Echo Electronics, Louisville, KY, 1980.

Activities:

    Active in Alpha Phi Sorority, 1979–81.

    Member of Heights Christian Church.

    Coach, Girls' Softball League.

    Cheerleader, Southeast High School.

References: Placement Office
             University of Louisville
             Louisville, KY   40222

PHOTOGRAPH

RESUMÉ 2 — DO

Diane Bellows
1830 Lexington Avenue
Louisville, KY   40227
(502) 689-3137

EDUCATION   University of Louisville, B.A., 1981

Major: Business Administration with
emphasis in personnel management
Minor: Economics with emphasis in
corporate finance

EXPERIENCE

College   Orientation Leader, University Admissions
Office, 1979-81. Met with prospective
students and their parents; conducted tours
of campus; answered questions; wrote reports
for each orientation meeting.

Academic Committee, Alpha Phi Sorority,
1979-81. Organized study halls and tutoring
services for disadvantaged students.

Advertising Manager, University Yearbook,
1980. Responsible for securing advertising
that made the Yearbook self-supporting;
wrote monthly progress report.

Summers   Intern, Echo Electronics, June, 1980.
Spent two weeks learning about pension plans,
health care benefits, employee associations,
and work regulations as they affect employee
relations and personnel management.

Volunteer Worker, Arthur Schneider's
School Board reelection campaign, 1979.
Wrote press releases, campaign brochures,
direct mailers; researched information on
teacher competence.

REFERENCES   Placement Office
University of Louisville
Louisville, KY   40222
(502) 744-3219

527

■ **Exercise**

1. Prepare a resumé and then write a letter of application for a position you are competent to fill.
2. Write to the principal of the high school you graduated from, thanking her for recommending you for a summer job.
3. Call the attention of your representative in city government to repairs that are needed in your neighborhood playground.
4. Write to a national record company complaining about the technical quality of the record you ordered from them.
5. Order a particular ten-speed bicycle part from a bicycle warehouse.

Glossary of Grammatical Terms

This glossary presents brief explanations of frequently used grammatical terms. Consult the index for references to further discussion of most of the terms and for a number of terms not listed.

absolute　A parenthetical word or phrase that qualifies the rest of the sentence and is not related to it by a connective. An absolute does not modify a specific word or phrase in the sentence.

>**True**, Rome was not built in a day.
>**Considering the risks**, giving up cigarettes is sensible.

The term *absolute phrase* is often used for the type of absolute illustrated below.

>**The hostages free at last**, Americans rejoiced.
>COMPARE　The hostages *were* free at last. Americans rejoiced.

>**The expressway jammed with rush-hour traffic**, we were delayed two hours.
>COMPARE　The expressway **was** jammed with rush-hour traffic, **so** we were delayed two hours.

>I do not get much studying done in my dormitory room—**students running up and down the hall and yelling at one another and TV sets and stereos outblaring my FM music**.
>COMPARE　I do not get much studying done in my dormitory room **because** students **run** up and down the hall and **yell** at one another and TV sets and stereos **outblare** my FM music.

See **2a**. See also **parenthetical element, phrase**, and **participle**.

abstract noun   See **noun.**

acronym   A word made up of the first letter or two of a series of words.

>scuba   [self-contained underwater breathing apparatus]
>radar   [radio detecting and ranging]
>NASA   [National Aeronautics Space Administration]

active voice   See **voice.**

adjectival   Any word or word group functioning as an adjective: "*happy* people," "those *living on a fixed income.*" The term is especially useful when it refers to a modifier without degrees of comparison.

>**this** one, **subscription** TV, **its** value, **an OPEC** decision
>people **on the street**, **Nancy's end-of-term** jitters
>one **who has a good sense of humor**, films **I like best**

See also **comparison.**

adjective   A part of speech regularly used to modify (describe or limit) a noun or a pronoun. Descriptive adjectives, unlike limiting adjectives, can usually be compared. See **comparison** and **adjectival.**

>**blue** sky, **newer** car, **best** joke, **beautiful** art [descriptive]
>**a** boy, **that** one, **its** nest, **both** men—**Whose** idea? [limiting]

Proper adjectives are capitalized. See **9a(3).**

>**Christlike** figure   **Irish** humor   **Victorian** styles

Predicate adjectives function as complements of linking verbs (such as *feel, look, smell, sound, taste,* and forms of *be*). See **linking verb.**

>The milk tasted **sour.**   They may be **lucky.**   How **tall** is he?

See Section **4.**

adjective clause   An adjectival containing a subject and verb. See also **adjectival** and **clause.**

We usually like the people **who like us**.

adverb A part of speech regularly used to modify (describe or limit) a verb, an adjective, or another adverb.

> **slowly** ate, **too** tall, entered **very quietly** [*Slowly* modifies the verb *ate; too* the adjective *tall; very* the adverb *quietly; quietly* the verb *entered.*]

An adverb may also modify a verbal, or a whole phrase, clause, or sentence.

> **Naturally**, the villain succeeds at first by **completely** outwitting the hero. [*Naturally* modifies the rest of the sentence, and *completely* modifies the gerund *outwitting.*]

See Section **4**. See also **intensifier**.

adverb clause An adverbial containing a subject and a verb. See also **adverbial** and **clause**.

> **Although George Mason is not famous**, his ideas were used in our Bill of Rights.
> Cartoonists make at least eighteen drawings **so that Woody Woodpecker can laugh victoriously**.

adverbial A word (an adverb, but especially a noun, a conjunction, or an interjection), phrase, or clause functioning as an adverb.

> **Wow**, I forgot to ask; **however**, I'll see him **Friday**.
> **When the hail started**, we ran **into the library**.

adverbial conjunction See **conjunctive adverb**.

agreement The correspondence in form of one word with another to indicate number, person, or gender.

NUMBER	the boy asks, boys ask	this type, these types
PERSON	I am, you are, he is	I was, you were, he was
GENDER	the man himself, the woman herself, the book itself	

See Section **6**.

antecedent A word or word group that a pronoun refers to.

> Before **Ron** left, **he** paid the **man** and **woman who** delivered
> the firewood.   [*Ron* is the antecedent of the personal pro-
> noun *he; man* and *woman* are the antecedents of the rela-
> tive pronoun *who.*]

See **6b** and Section **28**.

appositive A noun or noun substitute set beside another noun or
noun substitute and identifying or explaining it.

> Davis, our **guide**, did not see the grizzly.   [Compare "Davis
> was our guide." See also page 11.]
> A tasty **preservative**, salt is nutritious.   [*Preservative* is in
> apposition with *salt.*]

See also **12d(2)**.

article *The, a,* or *an,* used adjectivally before nouns (**the** *cups,*
a *cup,* **an** *apple*). *The* is a definite article. *A* and *an* are indefinite
articles: see **19i** and **indefinite**.

attributive A noun used as an adjective (***examination*** *questions*)
or an adjective placed beside the word it modifies (***difficult*** *ques-*
tions OR *questions,* ***difficult but clear***). See **adjectival**; contrast
predicate adjective.

auxiliary verb A verb (like *be, have, do*) used with a main verb
in a verb phrase. An auxiliary regularly indicates tense but may
also indicate voice, mood, person, number.

> **are** eating   **will be** eating   **was** eaten
> **has** eaten   **Do** eat with us.   **have been** eaten

Modal auxiliaries (such as *will, would, shall, should, may, might,*
must, can, could) do not take such inflectional endings as *-s, -ing,*
or *-en.*
See also **1a** and Section **7**.

case The form or position of a word that shows its use or relationship to other words in a sentence. The three cases in English
are the *subjective* (or nominative), the *possessive* (or genitive), and

the *objective*. Pronouns and nouns have case: see Section **5** and **15a**.

clause   A group of related words that contains both a subject and a predicate and that functions as a part of a sentence. A clause is either *main* (independent) or *subordinate* (dependent).

SENTENCES
Only a few stars came out.   The moon was bright.
I know Herb.   He will run for office.

MAIN CLAUSES
Only a few stars came out, for **the moon was bright**.
I know Herb; he will run for office.
[sentences connected by using the coordinating conjunction *for* and by using a semicolon and lower case for *he*]

SUBORDINATE CLAUSES
Only a few stars came out **because the moon was bright**.
   [adverb clause]
I know Herb, **who will run for office**.   [adjective clause]
I know **that Herb will run for office**.   [noun clause—direct object]
[sentences converted to subordinate clauses by using the subordinating conjunctions *because* and *that* and the relative pronoun *who,* a subordinator]

Elliptical clauses have omitted elements that are clearly understood: see **elliptical construction**.

clipped form   A shortened word like [tele]*phone, ad*[vertisement], or [in]*flu*[enza]. Dictionaries include no usage labels for many clipped forms; they label many others *informal* or *slang*.

collective noun   See **noun**.

comma splice   Misuse of a comma between main clauses not connected by a coordinating conjunction. See Section **3**.

common noun   See **noun**.

comparative   See **comparison**.

comparison The inflection or modification of an adjective or adverb to indicate degrees in quality, quantity, or manner. There are three degrees: positive, comparative, and superlative.

POSITIVE	COMPARATIVE	SUPERLATIVE
good, well	better	best
high	higher	highest
quickly	more quickly	most quickly
active	less active	least active

See **4c**.

complement A word or words used to complete the sense of a verb. Although the term may refer to a direct or an indirect object, it usually refers to a subject complement, an object complement, or the complement of a verbal like *to be*.

The lasagna tasted **delicious**. [subject complement]
We made the ferret our **mascot**. [object complement]
To be a good **leader**, one must learn how to follow.
[complement of the infinitive *to be*]

complete predicate See **predicate**.

complete subject See **subject**.

complex sentence See **sentence**.

compound A word or word group with two or more parts that function as a unit.

COMPOUND NOUNS dropout, hunger strike, sister-in-law
COMPOUND SUBJECT **Republicans**, **Democrats**, and **Independents** are working together.
COMPOUND PREDICATE Kate **has tried** but **has not succeeded**.

See also **sentence**.

compound-complex sentence See **sentence**.

compound predicate See **compound**.

compound sentence See **sentence**.

compound subject See **compound**.

534

concrete noun See **noun**.

conjugation A set or table of the inflected forms of a verb that indicate tense, person, number, voice, and mood.

PRINCIPAL PARTS

see   saw   seen

Active voice   *Passive voice*

INDICATIVE MOOD

PRESENT TENSE

I / you / we / they *see*   I *am seen*
he / she / it *sees*   he / she / it *is seen*
                                   you / we / they *are seen*

PAST TENSE

I / he / you / we / they *saw*   I / he *was seen*
                                   you / we / they *were seen*

FUTURE TENSE

I / he / you / we / they *will*   I / he / you / we / they *will*
  (OR *shall*) *see*   (OR *shall*) *be seen*

PRESENT PERFECT TENSE

I / you / we / they *have seen*   I / you / we / they *have been*
he *has seen*   *seen*
                                   he *has been seen*

PAST PERFECT TENSE

I / he / you / we / they *had*   I / he / you / we / they *had*
  seen   *been seen*

FUTURE PERFECT TENSE

I / he / you / we / they *will*   I / he / you / we / they *will*
  (OR *shall*) *have seen*   (OR *shall*) *have been seen*

Active voice	*Passive voice*

SUBJUNCTIVE MOOD

PRESENT TENSE

that he / I / you / we / they *see*	that he / I / you / we / they *be seen*

PAST TENSE

that he / I / you / we / they *saw*	that he / I / you / we / they *were seen*

PRESENT PERFECT TENSE

that he / I / you / we / they *have seen*	that he / I / you / we / they *have been seen*

PAST PERFECT TENSE

(same as the indicative)

IMPERATIVE MOOD

PRESENT TENSE

see	*be seen*

See pages 80–81 for a synopsis of the progressive forms.

conjunction   A part of speech used to connect and relate words, phrases, clauses, or sentences. There are two kinds of conjunctions: coordinating and subordinating.

Coordinating conjunctions connect words and word groups of equal grammatical rank: *and, but, or, nor, for, so,* and *yet.*

Dick **and** Mario will go into politics **or** social work.
Not only did the temperature fall below zero, **but** the wind was blowing.

See also Section **26** and **correlatives**.

Subordinating conjunctions mark a dependent clause and connect it with a main clause: *after, although, as, as if, because, before, if, since, unless, until, when, while,* and so forth.

> **When** Frank does not wish to hear, he acts **as if** he were deaf.

conjunctive adverb   An adverbial connective, such as *consequently, then, nonetheless.* See the list on page 45.

> Inflation and recession affect the purchasing power of the dollar; **moreover**, they have an impact on the consumer's buying habits.

connective   A word or phrase that links and relates words, phrases, clauses, or sentences, such as *and, although, otherwise, finally, on the contrary, which, not only . . . but also.* Conjunctions, conjunctive adverbs, transitional expressions, relative pronouns, and correlatives function as connectives. See also **31c(4)**.

construction   A grammatical unit (such as a sentence, clause, or phrase) or the arrangement of related words in a grammatical unit.

contact clause   One clause, usually subordinate, attached to another clause without the use of a connective. A contact clause that functions as an adjective is restrictive.

> Luke did not have a friend **he could fully trust**.   [*whom* or *that* omitted after *friend*]
> The trivia **I am interested in** can be found in newspaper fillers.   [*which* or *that* omitted after *trivia*]

See also **restrictive**.

coordinating conjunction   See **conjunction**.

correlatives   Connectives used in pairs: *both . . . and; either . . . or; neither . . . nor; not only . . . but also; whether . . . or.* See also **26c** and **coordinating conjunctions**.

count noun   See **noun**.

dangling modifier   A word or word group that does not modify (or modify clearly) another word or word group in the sentence. An absolute expression is not a dangling modifier.

DANGLING   **Racing to class**, that open manhole went unnoticed. [*Racing* modifies nothing in the sentence. The reader expects *racing* to modify the subject—which is *manhole*.]

REVISED   **Racing** to class, **I** did not notice that open manhole. [*Racing* clearly modifies the subject *I*.]

See also **25b.**

declension   A set or table of inflected forms of nouns or pronouns. As the following table shows, nouns are inflected only in the possessive case. The personal pronouns and the relative/interrogative pronoun *who* are inflected in all three cases.

NOUN

	Subjective	*Possessive*	*Objective*
SINGULAR	day	day's	day
PLURAL	days	days'	days

PRONOUNS

	Subjective	*Possessive*	*Objective*
		Singular	
FIRST PERSON	I	my, mine	me
SECOND PERSON	you	your, yours	you
THIRD PERSON	he, she, it	his, her, hers, its	him, her, it
		Plural	
FIRST PERSON	we	our, ours	us
SECOND PERSON	you	your, yours	you
THIRD PERSON	they	their, theirs	them
	Subjective	*Possessive*	*Objective*
		Singular and Plural	
	who	whose	whom

demonstrative pronoun   One of the four pronouns that point out: *this, that, these, those.* These words often function in sentences as adjectives.

> **This** brand is as good as **that**.

dependent clause   A subordinate clause: see **clause**.

descriptive adjective   See **adjective**.

determiner   A word (such as *a, an, the, my, their,* or *our*) which signals the approach of a noun.

diagraming   A graphic means of showing relationships within the sentence. Various forms are used; any form is serviceable if it helps to show how the sentence works. Illustrations of three kinds of diagrams follow:

The dark clouds on the horizon had appeared suddenly.

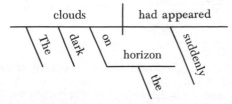

The key to the diagram:

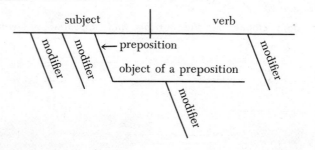

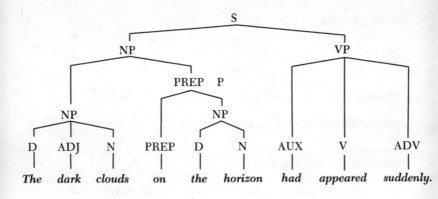

The key to the abbreviations:

ADJ	Adjective	PREP	Preposition
ADV	Adverb	PREP P	Prepositional Phrase
AUX	Auxiliary	S	Sentence
D	Determiner	V	Verb
N	Noun	VP	Verb Phrase
NP	Noun Phrase		

A key to the diagram below (which shows the layers of structure) is not provided. Terminology is left to the analyst's choice. (For example, one analyst might write *complete subject* on the line connecting *on the horizon* with *The dark clouds*, but another might prefer *noun phrase*.)

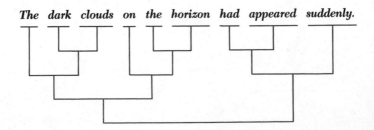

direct address   A parenthetical word or phrase naming or denoting the person(s) spoken to.

> Falstaff enters and exclaims, "Well said, **Hal**!"
> Don't forget, **backseat passengers**, to use those seatbelts.

direct object   See **object**.

direct quotation   The exact spoken or written words of others.

> DIRECT QUOTATION   John asked, "Why haven't you joined the group, Martha?"
> INDIRECT QUOTATION   John asked Martha why she had not joined the group.

See also **16a**.

double negative   A nonstandard construction containing two negatives and having a negative meaning, such as *I didn't have no change with me*. See **not . . . no**, page 239.

elliptical construction   A construction in which words are omitted but clearly understood.

> The curtains are newer than the carpet [is].
> Whenever [it is] possible, get a full night's sleep.
> His hair is black; his face [is] deeply tanned.

expletive   The word *there* or *it* used as a structural filler and not adding to the meaning of the sentence.

> **There** were only a few ballet tickets left.   [Compare "Only a few ballet tickets were left."]
> **It** is obvious that they do not like us.   [Compare "That they do not like us is obvious."]

finite verb   The principal verb of a sentence or a clause. A finite verb can serve as the only verb of a sentence. Verb forms classified as gerunds, infinitives, and participles (verbals) are nonfinite verbs.

> One prisoner **escaped**.   Clyde **will read** the book.

See also **nonfinite verb**.

form change   See **inflection**.

fragment   See **sentence fragment**.

function words   Words (such as prepositions, conjunctions, auxiliaries, and articles) that indicate the functions of other words
(*vocabulary words*) in a sentence and the grammatical relationships between them. See also **vocabulary words**.

fused sentence   Two sentences run together without any punctuation or a coordinating conjunction. See Section **3**.

gerund   A verbal (nonfinite verb) that ends in -*ing* and functions
as a noun. Gerunds may take objects, complements, or modifiers.

> He escaped by *swimming* **rapidly**.   [The gerund *swimming*
> is the object of the preposition *by* and is modified by the
> adverb *rapidly.*]
> *Borrowing* **money** is a mistake.   [The gerund phrase—the
> gerund *borrowing* and its object, *money*—serves as the
> subject of the sentence.]

A possessive noun or pronoun before a gerund may be classified
either as an adjectival (modifying the noun element of the verbal)
or as the subject of the gerund.

> **His borrowing** money is a mistake.   [Compare "*his* action"
> and "*He borrowed* the money."]

See also **nonfinite verb**.

idiom   An expression in good use that is characteristic of or peculiar to a language. Perfectly acceptable idioms may seem illogical
if taken literally or may violate established rules of grammar.

> He **gave himself away** by smiling.
> I have known him for **many a year**.

imperative   See **mood**.

indefinite   An article (*a, an*), a pronoun (*anybody, everyone,* and
so on) or an adjective (*any* book, a *few* friends, *several* replies, and
so on) that does not specify distinct limits.

independent clause A main clause: see **clause**.

indicative See **mood**.

indirect object See **object**.

indirect quotation See **direct quotation**.

infinitive A verbal (nonfinite verb) used chiefly as a noun, less frequently as an adjective or an adverb. The infinitive is usually made up of the word *to* plus the present form of a verb (called the *stem* of the infinitive), but the *to* may be omitted after such verbs as *let, make,* and *dare*. Infinitives may have subjects, objects, complements, or modifiers.

> Hal wanted *to open* **the present**. [*Present* is the object of the infinitive *to open;* the whole infinitive phrase is the object of the verb *wanted.*]
> The work *to be done* overwhelms me. [The infinitive is used adjectivally to modify the noun *work.*]
> *To tell* **the truth**, our team almost lost. [The infinitive phrase is used adverbially to modify the rest of the sentence.]

See also **nonfinite verb**.

inflection A change in the form of a word to show a specific meaning or grammatical relationship to some other word or group of words.

> VERBS drink, drinks, drank, drunk; grasp, grasps, grasped
> PRONOUNS **I**, **my** life, a gift for **me**
> NOUNS dog, dogs; dog's, dogs'
> ADJECTIVES a **good** one, a **better** one, the **best** one
> ADVERBS carefully, **more** carefully, **most** carefully

See also **conjugation, declension,** and **comparison**.

intensifier (intensive) A modifier used for emphasis. Such adverbs as "*very* boring," "*certainly* did," and "*so* pleased" are intensifiers. See also **qualifier**.

intensive pronoun   A *-self* pronoun used to emphasize another word in the sentence.

> The president **himself** answered my letter.   [The pronoun *himself* refers to and emphasizes *president*.]

interjection   A part of speech used for simple exclamations: *Oh! Ouch! Whew!* When used in sentences, mild interjections are set off by commas.

intransitive   See **verb**.

interrogative pronoun   A pronoun (*which, what, who, whom, whose*) used to ask a question. An interrogative pronoun may function as a noun or as an adjective.

> **What** happened?   **Which** did he choose?   **Whose** car is it?

inversion   A change in the usual word order of a sentence.

> Up go the referee's hands.
> In the middle of the lake is a small island.

irregular verb   A verb that does not form its past tense and past participle in the standard way—that is, by the addition of *-d* or *-ed* to the stem of the infinitive (as with the regular verbs *hope, hoped; look, looked*). The principal parts of five common types of irregular verbs are given below.

> swim, swam, swum   [vowels changed]
> beat, beat, beaten   [*-en* added]
> feel, felt, felt   [vowel shortened, *ee* changed to *e*]
> send, sent, sent   [*-d* changed to *-t*]
> set, set, set   [no change]

lexical words   See **vocabulary words**.

linking verb   A verb which relates the subject to the subject complement. Words commonly used as linking verbs are *become, seem, appear, feel, look, taste, smell, sound,* and the forms of the verb *be*.

> She **is** a pharmacist.   The panels **feel** rough.

main clause   An independent clause: see **clause**.

mass noun   See **noun**.

misplaced modifier   An adjectival or adverbial in an awkward position—usually, far away from what it modifies. Sometimes a misplaced modifier confuses the reader because it could qualify either of two words.

MISPLACED	I heard how to make catsup flow out of the bottle **on the radio**.
REVISED	I heard **on the radio** how to make catsup flow out of the bottle.
MISPLACED	To do one's best **sometimes** is not enough.
REVISED	To do one's best is **sometimes** not enough.
	OR It is not enough to do one's best **sometimes**.

See also **25a**.

modal auxiliary   See **auxiliary verb**.

modifier   An adjective or adverb (adjectival or adverbial), which describes, limits, or qualifies another word or word group: see Section **4**.

mood (mode)   The way a speaker or writer regards an assertion—that is, as a declarative statement or a question (*indicative* mood), as a command or request (*imperative*), or as a supposition, hypothesis, recommendation, or condition contrary to fact (*subjunctive*). Verb forms indicate mood.

INDICATIVE	Joe **was** a winner. **Does** he drop by?
IMPERATIVE	**Be** a winner. **Do** drop by!
SUBJUNCTIVE	Joe talked as though he **were** a loser.
	I recommend that he **do** this soon.

See Section **7**.

nominal   A word (such as a pronoun or gerund), phrase, or clause used as a noun.

Repairing that machine was not easy.
He contends **that selfless love is power**.

nominative   See **case**.

nonfinite verb   A verbal functioning as a noun, an adjective, or an adverb. A nonfinite verb cannot stand as the only verb in a sentence.

> NONFINITE VERBS IN PHRASES
> **to take** a vacation together
> shoppers **milling** around
> by just **remaining** silent

> NONFINITE VERBS IN SENTENCES
> My family wanted **to take** a vacation together.
> Shoppers **milling** around did not buy much.
> Some people win arguments by just **remaining** silent.

See also **verbal** and **finite verb**.

nonrestrictive   Nonessential to the meaning of a sentence. A phrase or clause is nonrestrictive (parenthetical) when it is not necessary to the meaning of the main clause and may be omitted: see **12d**.

> The old horse, **slow but confident**, plodded on.   [phrase]
> The airplane, **now being manufactured in large numbers**, is of immense commercial value.   [phrase]
> The airplane, **which is now being manufactured in large numbers**, is of immense commercial value.   [clause]

See also **restrictive**.

noun   A part of speech that names a person, place, thing, idea, animal, quality, or action: *Mary, America, apples, justice, goose, strength, departure*. A noun usually changes form to indicate the plural and the possessive case, as in *man, men; man's, men's.*

Types of nouns

COMMON	a **man**, the **cities**, some **trout** [general classes]
PROPER	**Mr. Ford**, in **Boston**, the **Forum** [capitalized, specific names]
COLLECTIVE	a **flock**, the **jury**, my **family** [groups]
CONCRETE	an **egg**, the **bus**, his **ear**, two **trees** [tangibles]
ABSTRACT	**honor, jealousy, pity, hatred** [ideas, qualities]

COUNT   one **dime**, ten **dollars**, a **job**, many **times**
[singular or plural—often preceded by
adjectivals telling how many]

MASS   much **money**, more **work**, less **time** [singular in
meaning—often preceded by adjectivals telling
how much]

Functions of nouns

SUBJECT OF FINITE VERB   **Dogs** barked.

OBJECT OF FINITE VERB OR OF PREPOSITION   He gave **Jane** the
key to the **house**.

SUBJECT COMPLEMENT (PREDICATE NOUN)   She is a **nurse**.

OBJECT COMPLEMENT   They named him **Jonathan**.

SUBJECT OF NONFINITE VERB   I want **Ed** to be here.

OBJECT OF NONFINITE VERB   I prefer to drive a **truck**.

APPOSITIVE   Moses, a **prophet**, saw the promised land.

ADVERBIAL   **Yesterday** they went **home**.

ADJECTIVAL   The **mountain** laurel is the **state** flower of Connecticut and Pennsylvania.

DIRECT ADDRESS   What do you think, **Angela**?

KEY WORD OF ABSOLUTE PHRASE   The **food** being cold, no one
really enjoyed the meal.

noun clause   A subordinate clause used as a noun.

> **Whoever comes** will be welcome.   [subject]
> I hope **that he will recover**.   [direct object]
> I will give **whoever comes first** the best seat.   [indirect object]
> Spend it for **whatever seems best**.   [object of a preposition]
> This is **what you need**.   [subject complement]
> I loved it, **whatever it was**.   [appositive]
> **Whoever you are**, show yourself!   [direct address]

See also **nominal** and **clause**.

noun phrase   See **phrase**.

number   The inflectional form of a noun, a pronoun, a demonstrative adjective, or a verb that indicates number, either singular (one) or plural (more than one). See Section **6** and **18e**.

object   A noun or noun substitute governed by a transitive active verb, by a nonfinite verb, or by a preposition.

A *direct object*, or the *object of a finite verb*, is any noun or noun substitute that answers the question *What?* or *Whom?* after a transitive active verb. A direct object frequently receives, or is in some way affected by, the action of the verb.

> William raked **leaves**.   **What** did he say?
> The Andersons do not know **where we live**.

As a rule, a direct object may be converted into a subject with a passive verb: see **voice**.

An *object of a nonfinite verb* is any noun or its equivalent that follows and completes the meaning of a participle, a gerund, or an infinitive.

> Washing a **car** takes time.   He likes to wear a **tie**.
> Following the **truck**, a bus rounded the bend.

An *indirect object* is any noun or noun substitute that states *to whom* or *for whom* (or *to what* or *for what*) something is done. An indirect object ordinarily precedes a direct object.

> He bought **her** a watch.
> I gave the **floor** a second coat of varnish.

It is usually possible to substitute a prepositional phrase beginning with *to* or *for* for the indirect object.

> He bought a watch for her.

An *object of a preposition* is any noun or noun substitute which a preposition relates to another word or word group.

> Cedars grow tall in these **hills**.   [*Hills* is the object of *in.*]
> **What** am I responsible for?   [*What* is the object of *for.*]

object complement   See **complement**.

objective   See **case**.

parenthetical element   Nonessential matter (such as an aside or interpolation) that is set off by commas, dashes, or parentheses to mark pauses and intonation. A word, phrase, clause, or sentence may be parenthetical.

> **Granted**, over eighty million people, **according to that estimate**, did watch one episode.
>
> **In fact**, the parachute ride—**believe it or not**—is as safe as the ferris wheel.

See also **12d**, **17e**, and **17f**.

participle   A verb form that may function as part of a verb phrase (was *laughing*, had *finished*), as an adjective (the *laughing* children, the *finished* product), or as a nonfinite verb (The children, *laughing* loudly, left).

The present participle ends in *-ing* (the form also used for verbal nouns: see **gerund**. The past participle of regular verbs ends in *-d* or *-ed*; for a list of past participles of irregular verbs, see pages 83–84.

Functioning as nonfinite verbs in *participial phrases*, participles may take objects, complements, modifiers:

> The prisoner *carrying* the heaviest load toppled forward. [The participle *carrying* takes the object *load;* the whole participial phrase modifies *prisoner.*]
>
> The telephone operator, very *confused* by my request, suggested that I place the call later. [The participle *confused* is modified by the adverb *very* and by the prepositional phrase *by my request;* the participial phrase modifies *telephone operator.*]

See also **nonfinite verb**.

particle with verb   A phrasal unit consisting of a verb plus one or two uninflected words like *after, in, up, off,* or *out* and having the force of a single-word verb.

> We **ran out on** them.   [Compare "We deserted them."]
> He **cut** me **off** without a cent.   [Compare "He disinherited me."]

parts of speech   The eight classes into which most grammarians group words according to their form changes and their position, meaning, and use in the sentence: *verbs, nouns, pronouns, adjectives, adverbs, prepositions, conjunctions,* and *interjections.* Each of these is discussed separately in this glossary. See also **1c.**

passive voice See **voice.**

person Changes in the form of pronouns and verbs denoting or indicating whether one is speaking (*I am*—first person), spoken to (*you are*—second person), or spoken about (*it is*—third person). In the present tense, a verb changes its form to agree grammatically with a third-person singular subject (*a bird eats, everybody does*). See **6a** and **27b.**

personal pronoun Any one of a group of pronouns—*I, you, he, she, it* and their inflected forms—referring to the one (or ones) speaking, spoken to, or spoken about. See **declension.**

phrase A group of related words without both a subject and a (finite) verb.

NOUN PHRASE **A young stranger** stepped forward.
VERB PHRASE All day long they **had been worrying**.
PREPOSITIONAL PHRASES **By seven o'clock**, the lines stretched **from the box office to the corner**.
GERUND PHRASE **Building a sun deck** can be fun.
INFINITIVE PHRASE Do you want **to use your time that way**?
PARTICIPIAL PHRASE My friends **traveling in Italy** felt the earthquake.
APPOSITIVE PHRASE I introduced her to Bob, **my roommate**.
ABSOLUTE PHRASE **The game over**, we shook hands.

positive See **comparison.**

possessive See **case.**

predicate A basic grammatical division of a sentence. A predicate is the part of the sentence comprising what is said about the subject. The *complete predicate* consists of the main verb along with its auxiliaries (the *simple predicate*) and any complements and modifiers.

We *used* a patriotic theme for our homecoming parade that year. [*Used* is the simple predicate. *Used* and all the words that follow it make up the complete predicate.]

Had the team **already** *been preparing* themselves psychologically? [The simple predicate is the verb phrase *had been preparing.*]

predicate adjective An adjective functioning as a subject complement; see **complement** and **linking verb**.

predicate noun A noun functioning as a subject complement: see **complement** and **linking verb**.

prefix An added syllable or group of syllables attached to the beginning of a base or root (or another prefix). A prefix changes the meaning or creates a new word: *meditated, premeditated, unpremeditated.* See **18c**. See also **suffix**.

preposition A part of speech (a function word) that links and relates a vocabulary word to some other word in the sentence. See pages 17–18 for a list of words commonly used as prepositions.

These paintings hung **in** the hall. [The preposition *in* connects and relates *hall* (the object of the preposition *in*) to the verb *hung.*]

prepositional phrase See **phrase**.

principal parts The forms of any verb from which the various tenses are derived: the present infinitive (*take, laugh*), the past (*took, laughed*), and the past participle (*taken, laughed*).

See also Section **7**.

progressive verb A verb phrase consisting of a present participle (ending in *-ing*) used with a form of *be* and denoting continuous action.

I **have been playing** tennis all afternoon.

See also pages 80–81.

pronoun   One of the eight parts of speech. Pronouns take the position of nouns and function as nouns do.

NOUNS	The old **house** was sold to Fred's aunt.
PRONOUNS	**It** was sold to **his** aunt.
	OR
	That was sold to **her**.

Types of pronouns

PERSONAL	**She** and **I** will see **him** in St. Paul.
INTERROGATIVE	**Who** are they? **What** is right?
	Which car is better?
RELATIVE	Leslie is the one **who** likes to bowl.
	A dog **that** barks may bite.
DEMONSTRATIVE	**This** is better than **that**.
INDEFINITE	**Each** of you should help **someone**.
RECIPROCAL	Help **each other**. They like **one another**.
REFLEXIVE	Carl blames **himself**.
	Did you injure **yourself**?
INTENSIVE	We need a vacation **ourselves**.
	I **myself** saw the crash.

See Sections **5**, **6**, and **28**.

See also the separate entry for each type of pronoun: **personal pronoun, interrogative pronoun,** and so on.

proper adjective   A capitalized adjective (*a Scottish tune*) derived from a proper noun (*Scotland*).

See also **adjective**.

proper noun   See **noun**.

qualifier   Any modifier, descriptive or limiting. Frequently, however, the term refers only to those modifiers that restrict or intensify the meaning of other words.

Many thieves lie. **Almost** all of them do.   [Compare "Thieves lie."]
Sometimes children are **too** selfish to share.

See also **intensifier**.

quotation See **direct quotation**.

reciprocal pronoun A compound pronoun expressing an inter-changeable or mutual action or relationship: *each other* or *one another*.

> They compete with **each other**.
> We respect **one another**.

reflexive pronoun A *-self* pronoun used as an object or a com-plement and referring to the individual or individuals named by the subject.

> They denied **themselves** nothing.   I am not **myself** today.

regular verb A verb that forms its past tense and past participle by adding *-d* or *-ed* to the stem of the infinitive: *love, loved; laugh, laughed*.

relative pronoun One of a small group of noun substitutes (*who, whom, whose, that, which, what, whoever, whomever, whichever, whatever*) used to introduce subordinate clauses.

> He has a son *who* **is a genius**. [adjective clause introduced by the relative pronoun *who*]
> *Whoever* **wins the prize** must have talent. [noun clause in-troduced by the relative pronoun *whoever*]

restrictive Essential to sentence meaning. A phrase or clause is restrictive when it is necessary to the meaning of the main clause and cannot be omitted: see **12d**.

> Every drug **condemned by doctors** should be taken off the market. [restrictive phrase]
> Every drug **that doctors condemn** should be taken off the market. [restrictive clause]

See also **nonrestrictive**.

sentence An independent unit of expression. A simple sentence follows the pattern **SUBJECT—PREDICATE**. Sentences are often classified according to structure as *simple, compound, complex,* or *compound-complex.*

> SIMPLE   We won.   [subject—predicate]
>
> COMPOUND   They outplayed us, but we won.   [two main clauses]
>
> COMPLEX   Although we did win, they outplayed us. [subordinate clause, main clause]
>
> COMPOUND-COMPLEX   I know that they outplayed us, but we did win.   [two main clauses—the first of which contains a subordinate clause]

Sentences are also classified according to their purpose.

> | | | |
> |---|---|---|
> | DECLARATIVE | We will fly to Portland. | [statement] |
> | IMPERATIVE | Fly to Portland. | [command] |
> | INTERROGATIVE | Shall we fly to Portland? | [question] |
> | EXCLAMATORY | Would we like to fly to Portland! | [exclamation] |

See Section **1**.

sentence fragment   A nonsentence written as though it were a sentence. The term generally refers to a grammatically incomplete declarative sentence. See Section **2**.

sentence modifier   A word or word group that modifies the rest of the sentence.

> **Yes**, the bus arrived late.
> **Fortunately**, no one was hurt.
> The best professional teams win important games, **as a rule**.

subject   A basic grammatical division of a sentence. The subject is a noun or noun substitute about which something is asserted or asked in the predicate. It usually precedes the predicate. (Imperative sentences have subjects that are not stated but are implied.) The *complete subject* consists of the *simple subject* and the words associated with it.

The dog locked in the hot car needed air. [*Dog* is the simple
subject. *The dog locked in the hot car* is the complete
subject.]

See also **1a**.

subject complement   See **complement**.

subjective   See **case**.

subjunctive   See **mood**.

subordinating conjunction   See **conjunction**.

subordinate clause   A dependent clause: see **clause**.

subordinator   A word that marks a dependent, or subordinate,
clause: see page 25.

suffix   An added sound, syllable, or group of syllables attached to
the end of a base or root (or another suffix). Suffixes change meanings, create new words, and indicate grammatical functions.

the plays	play**er**	play**er's**	play**ing**
play**ed**	play**ful**	play**fully**	play**fulness**

See also **inflection** and **18c**.

superlative   See **comparison**.

syntax   Sentence structure. The grammatical arrangement of
words, phrases, and clauses.

tense   The form of the verb which indicates its relation to time.
Inflection (*eat, eats, eating, ate, eaten*) and the use of auxiliaries
(*will* eat, *have* eaten, *had* eaten, *will have* eaten, and so on) show
the tense of a verb. See **conjugation** and Section **7**.

transitive   See **verb**.

verb A part of speech denoting action, occurrence, or existence (state of being). Inflections indicate tense (and sometimes person and number) and mood of a verb: see **inflection, mood, voice,** and Section **7.**

A *transitive verb* is a verb that requires an object to complete its meaning. Transitive verbs can usually be changed from the active to the passive voice: see **object** and **voice.**

> Sid **hung** a wreath on his door.   [direct object: *wreath*]

An *intransitive verb* is a verb (such as *go* or *sit*) that does not have an object to complete its meaning. Linking verbs, which take subject complements, are intransitive.

> She **has been waiting** patiently for hours.
> I **was** sick last Christmas.

The same verb may be transitive in one sentence and intransitive in another.

> TRANSITIVE   Dee **reads** novels.   [direct object: *novels*]
> INTRANSITIVE   Dee **reads** well.

verb phrase See **phrase.**

verbal A nonfinite verb used as a noun, an adjective, or an adverb. Infinitives, participles, and gerunds are verbals. Verbals (like finite verbs) may take objects, complements, modifiers, and sometimes subjects.

> Mr. Nelson went *to see* his daughter.   [*To see,* an infinitive, functions as an adverb modifying the verb *went.* The object of the infinitive is *daughter.*]
>
> Cars *parked* in the loading zone will be towed away. [*Parked,* a participle, modifies cars.]
>
> *Studying* dialects in our area was fun.   [*Studying,* a gerund, heads the phrase that is the subject of the verb *was.*]

See also **nonfinite verb** and **gerund, infinitive, participle.**

vocabulary (lexical) words Nouns, verbs, and most modifiers—those words found in vocabulary-building lists. See also **function words.**

voice The form of a transitive verb that indicates whether or not the subject performs the action denoted by the verb. A verb with a direct object is in the *active voice.* When the direct object is converted into a subject, the verb is in the *passive voice.* A passive verb is always a verb phrase consisting of a form of the verb *be* (or sometimes *get*) followed by a past participle.

> ACTIVE Priscilla **chose** John.   [The subject (*Priscilla*) acts.]
> PASSIVE John **was chosen** by Priscilla.   [The subject (John) does not act.]

Speakers and writers often omit the *by*-phrase after a passive verb, especially when the performer of the action is not known or is not the focus of attention.

> Those flowers **were picked** yesterday.
> The guilty ones **should be punished** severely.
> We just heard that a new secretary **was hired**.

See also **29d**.

word order The arrangement of words in sentences. Because of lost inflections, modern English depends heavily on word order to convey meaning.

> Nancy gave Henry $14,000.
> Henry gave Nancy $14,000.
>
> Tony had built a barbecue pit.
> Tony had a barbecue pit built.

Index

Numbers in **boldface** refer to rules; other numbers refer to pages. A colon is used after each boldface number to indicate that the following pages refer to the rule or the part of the rule concerned. The **boldface** rule is given in detail—**9a(4)** or **20a(3)**, for example—in order to pinpoint a needed correction, but a less detailed reference **(9** or **9a)** will usually be sufficient for the student.

A

a

before common nouns, **9f:** 113
before consonant sound, **19i:** 225
See also *article*.

abbreviations, **11:** 120–23
acronyms formed from, 110
as shown in dictionary, 108
capitalization of, **9a(4):** 110
common, 441–43
distinguished from clipped forms, 123
division of, **8d(7):** 100
Mr., Mrs., Dr., etc., **11a:** 120–21
Ms, Miss, Mrs., in business letters, 515
names of courses, **11d:** 122
names of organizations, 122
names of states, months, days of week, etc., **11b:** 121
point of reference for, **28:** 319–20
periods after, **17a(2):** 174–75
Street, Company, etc., **11c:** 121–22
titles and degrees, with proper names, **11a:** 121, 122
U.S., as adjectival, 122

volume, chapter, page, **11d:** 122
with dates or figures, 122
absolute, defined, 529
absolute meaning, comparison of modifier with, **4c:** 54
absolute phrase
defined, 529
introductory, comma after, **12b:** 133
misused as sentence, **2a:** 35
parenthetical, commas with, **12d(3):** 143
use of, for variety, **30b(4):** 339
abstract and concrete words, **20a(3):** 250–53
abstract noun, defined, 546
accept, except, **19i:** 233
accidentally, **19i:** 225
acronyms
capitalization of, **9a(4):** 110
defined, 530
division of, **8d(7):** 100
periods not used with, 123
point of reference for, **28:** 319
active voice
defined, 79, 557

Index

567

Index

as preposition, case with, **5a**: 59

for example, as transitional phrase, **3b**: 45

foreign spellings, retention of, 200

foreign words, italicized, **10b**: 116–17

form of argument, **23e**: 285–86

formal definition, **23d**: 283–85; **31b(6)**: 360

formal English, **19b**: 219–20

former, **19i**: 234

fractions
hyphen with, **18f(2)**: 208
use of figures for, **11**: 125

fragment, sentence, **2**: 32–39
appositive as, **2c**: 37–38
defined, 32, 554
in dialogue, **9e**: 112
part of predicate as, **2c**: 37–38
phrase as, **2a**: 35
recognition of, 32–34
revision of, 34

fun, **19i**: 234

function words, 14, 542

further, farther, **19i**: 233

furthermore, as conjunctive adverb, **3b**: 45

fused sentence, **3**: 40–49
defined, 542
revision of, 41

future and future perfect tenses, 79, 88–89

G

gender, 68, 74

general vs. specialized audience, 395–97

general English, defined, 224

general and specific words, **20a(3)**: 250–53

generalizations
hasty, **23f(5)**: 288
in inductive argument, **23e**: 286

genitive case, 532
See also *possessive case.*

geographical names
capitalization of, **9a(1)**: 109
commas with, **12d(2)**: 141

use of apostrophe with, 161

gerund
defined, 542
in dangling phrase, **25b(2)**; 305
in noun phrase, 22
possessive before, **5d**: 64

get, **19i**: 234

girls, boys, **19i**: 234

Glossary of Grammatical Terms, 529–57

Glossary of Usage, 224–45

good, for *well*, **4a**: 51; **19i**: 234

Grammatical Terms, Glossary of, 529–57

great, **19i**: 234

guy(s), **19i**: 234

H

hackneyed phrases, **20c**: 257–59

had better, better, **19i**: 229

had of, had have, **19i**: 234

had ought, hadn't ought, **19i**: 234

half, agreement of verb with, **6a**: 71

handwritten paper
legibility of, **8c(1)**: 98
manuscript form for, **8a-b**: 96–98
revision of, **8e**: 101–05
sample page from, 512

hang, **19i**: 234

hanged, hung, **19i**: 234

hardly
position of, **25a(1)**: 301
with negative, **19i**: 235

hasty generalization, **23f(5)**: 288

have, of, **19i**: 239

heading of business letter, **34a(1)**: 514

hence, as conjunctive adverb, **3b**: 45

here, after *this*, **19i**: 244

himself, not *hisself*, **5**: 57; **19i**: 235

historical definition, **31b(6)**: 360–61

historical present, **7**: 87

hooked on, **19i**: 235

hopefully, **19i**: 235

how come, **19i**: 235

however, as conjunctive adverb, **3b**: 45

Index

Index

Index

Index

4
5
C 6
D 7
E 8
F 9
G 0
H 1
I 2
J 3